JOHN HOLLANDER

Never Again Would Birds' Song Be the Same

ESSAYS ON EARLY MODERN
AND MODERN POETRY
IN HONOR OF JOHN HOLLANDER

Edited by

JENNIFER LEWIN

BEINECKE LIBRARY   YALE UNIVERSITY
2002

Library of Congress Cataloging-in-Publication Data

Never again would birds' song be the same : essays on early modern
and modern poetry in honor of John Hollander / edited by Jennifer
Lewin.
    p. cm.
Includes bibliographical references and index.
  ISBN 0-8457-3143-2
  1. English literature—History and criticism. 2. Hollander, John
—Criticism and interpretation. I. Lewin, Jennifer. II. Hollander, John.
PR14 .N47 2002
821.009—dc21

2002011925

Contents

I

Introduction

The general rubric of this volume is not just John Hollander and his work but, in a sense, the field he creates. To say that that field, as represented here, stretches across the history of Western art, music, philosophy, and literature from Homer and Plato to Hawthorne and Bishop would be to offer one version of the story, but it still would not say much *about* that story. His work at every turn insistently challenges one's ability—and, more importantly, one's *desire*—to impose limitations on its scope, by asking questions of itself and of its audience that we may not have thought to ask but that fold out, as if addicted to their own fierce energy, into an interpretive space where answers are convenient resting places but never enduring solutions.

All of the essayists in this collection wrote dissertations with John Hollander, as did Stephen Cushman whose poem "In Translation" appears in the third section. Their work here shares with Hollander's a strong commitment to the idea that attention to poetry's tropes and schemes is inseparable from the historical knowledge that informs all persuasive readings of literary texts. Using this approach, in the volume's first essay John Watkins looks at how early modern poets from Tasso to Milton refashioned the figures and properties of Circe and Venus arguing for aesthetic and political implications of the long tradition of the "goddess with the human voice." In Homer and Virgil, the liminal status of their speech and divinity sets the stage for confrontations and distinctions between central characters in the later epic poems, calling for a reconsideration of the meaning of "pagan echoes." By the time we get to Milton's *Comus* "male fraud sets off female integrity," leading to the gendered republican politics that inform his treatment of Satan, Eve, and the Son. Concentrating on Spenser, Jeff Dolven looks at literary interpretation from the opposite end, so to speak, provocatively asking "how do you know when to stop reading *The Faerie Queene*?" Like Lee Edelman's essay in the second section, he looks at the limitations of allegorical reading, and when and how we know that the poem has entered the realm of the ordinary, or where allegory has literally become exhausted by itself in the figure of Arthur, for example. Matthew Greenfield's "Satire and Epyllion: Hermaphroditic Forms" looks at how "the hybrid body of the hermaphrodite becomes an emblem of these uncomfortably intimate encounters between genres" in Elizabethan verse satire. The work of John Marston, George Gascoigne, and John Weever rely on figures from Ovid in order to describe and contribute to an ongoing war of the genres that reveals "an intimate antagonism" between erotic narrative and satire, each projecting an image of the other as threatening to seduce the unwary reader.

Hannibal Hamlin emphasizes Shakespeare's juxtaposition of human and divine forces in the allusive visual cues that compare Coriolanus to both Roman and biblical gods. Shakespeare scholars are more likely to track biblical allusions than to attempt to explain their presence in *Coriolanus*, but considered in depth together, "these allusions to divinity, both explicit and implicit, provide a supplementary context for Shakespeare's explanation of the conflict between aristocratic and republican political values in terms of a conflict between antithetical models of godhood." The wrathfulness of the god of the Old Testament and Jesus Christ finally yields in the fifth act to a version of leadership modeled on Christ's humility and humanness, and his very recognition of mortality is what finally may cause Coriolanus' destruction. The last two essays in this section share a concern to situate literary texts within early modern Christian notions of temporality: Hamlin notes that the anachronism of allusions to the Bible would have been overlooked by Shakespeare's audience, and John Rogers begins his essay "The Timing of Redemption" by noticing the "always already" character of the Protestant concepts of sin and redemption. Rogers shows how lyric poets such as Donne and Herbert manifest "a profound and sophisticated appreciation of the ironic timing of sin and atonement," and as in Watkins's essay, it is Milton who becomes the culminating example of how perplexing, and pressured, the search becomes for an adequate response to the tradition.

Section two of the collection contains essays on topics ranging from Tennyson to textual criticism. The study of poetry moves into the nineteenth century with Cornelia Pearsall's "Tennyson and the Rapture of 'Tithonus'" that shows how a fascination with the mythological figure and his genealogy allows the poet powerfully to investigate a fascination with beauty defined as both "the complex experience of rapture" and active, deliberate reasoning and choice. Pearsall persuasively suggests that the dramatic monologue's speaker is more in control of his emotions and identification with Aurora than we initially might believe. Staying in the same century but turning to another popular literary genre, my essay looks at quotation and misquotation of songs in novels, and the kinds of generic confrontations that are staged when characters perform or recall words and contexts that enrich not only our understanding of the social world of the novel, but the social relationships between texts that shape literary history. In "Reason is also Choice: Reflection, Freedom, and the Euthyphro Problem" John Burt looks at social life from a different angle, finding suggestively poetic solutions to the problem of morality and freedom that Milton inherited from Plato and Aristotle, and that distinguishes American thought from the writings of Jefferson and Madison to contemporary debates about liberalism and political community.

Like Burt, David Greetham's "Contamination and / of 'Resistance'" also redraws the boundaries of what constitutes another kind of interdisciplinary polemic, arguing simultaneously with and against de Man and Derrida for the "'conflation,' indeed even the 'contamination' of textual theory and literary hermeneutics," two fields whose strong links are sometimes easy to forget. The last two essays bring the collection into the twentieth century and beyond with their close analyses of Wallace Stevens and Elizabeth Bishop, on both of whom Hollander recently republished essays in *The Work of Poetry* (1997). Joan Richardson's "'Music is thinking, then, sound': An Aesthetic Exercise," plays with "Peter Quince at the Clavier," Stevens's exercise around the reciprocal theme, to argue that music, in its compositional process and in its reception by the well-tempered listener, offers the perfect analogue for thinking as it is coming to be understood in evolutionary terms. In "Aesthetic Value and Literary Language: Bishop and de Man," Lee Edelman follows Greetham in crossing and collapsing another border, this time the space inhabited by poet and philosopher in "Santarém," and "The Epistemology of Metaphor," in order to reaffirm how, despite hesitations about allegorization, "the aesthetic always finds a way to load each rift with ore."

The third section investigates the work of John Hollander.

An unplanned connection between the essays within the section is the recently reissued (1999) *Reflections on Espionage*, which almost every essay refers to. By discussing influences that appear in the first two sections, such as Spenser, Milton, Emerson, Bishop, Harold Bloom, and especially Stevens, the essays here unify the volume itself. The title poem of *Spectral Emanations* is the subject of David Mikics's essay, in which he explores Hollander's construal of a unique poetic identity that combines aspects of Jewish and American mythmaking. Mikics separates that identity into its constituent parts of Judaic traditions and American tropes even as he subtly acknowledges their surfacing in the fiction of Hawthorne, one of Hollander's sources, as well as their overlapping concerns with the acquisition of capital, knowledge, and the problem of belatedness. Kenneth Gross also meditates on what work is in "John Hollander's Game of Patience." He emphasizes the refraction of poetic vocation and its boundaries in the creation of characters like Cupcake (whom Gross calls "one of Hollander's subtlest and most moving figures of poetic vocation, of its complex patience"), Image, Grusha, and Steampump in *Reflections on Espionage*. Even as "the work" of writing allows Hollander to notice the mutually informing kinds of code making and breaking that spy games share with language games, the poem contains dark moments of intense self-questioning and expressions of fears of failure that one does not find in other poems.

David Bromwich looks at earlier poems, especially the "element of portrait-painting" in poems like "Helicon" whose version of the college friendship between Hollander and Allen Ginsberg is defined both by content and form, and "Early Birds," which Bromwich thinks of as a later companion piece of sorts; in poems like these, he concludes: "we feel we are on the scene as a gifted contemporary performs the work of listening that is another name for self-knowledge and for sanity." Comfortably moving between Hollander's poetry and his prose, Steven Meyer reports on his teaching four of Hollander's essays in a course on electronic poetry, which provide his students with a series of practical models for how to think about more traditional forms of poetry before moving on to e-poetry. Using a diaristic structure modeled on *Reflections on Espionage* (conveniently, his course occurs during spring semester), he discovers that the essays provide a suitable context for exploring "links between writing and computing, and by extension poetry and computing." Computing resonates with both technology and Hollander's language of tales, telling, and counting with which Aidan Wasley's essay, described below, is concerned. In her personal essay Elise B. Jorgens recognizes the indispensability of John Hollander's pedagogical example. Jorgens explores her career in academia, describing occasions on which she was able to incorporate music into her teaching of literature, using it especially to open up the nuances of Renaissance poetry to students for whom this was a new experience altogether. She shows how her interdisciplinary approach to teaching more generally expanded the range of students' interest in reading literature.

In the last essay in the collection, Aidan Wasley uncovers the deep interest in "telling" that informs and illuminates not only several of John Hollander's book and poem titles, such as *Tales Told of the Fathers*, but so much more — Hollander's pedagogy, his irony, all his writings, and indeed what we mean when we attempt to define the world that his being in the world has made. "Telling" is his version of a living command akin to that given to Yeats by Auden, called upon him to "teach the free man how to praise": containing multitudes of meanings in any one instance, it can encompass activities like counting, instructing, bequeathing, controling, disclosing, and keeping secret. It is at the heart of Hollander's work; it also captures what is at once liberating and daunting about the transmission of knowledge, liberating because it leaves one free to create the truth for oneself and to be free from dependence on received wisdom, and daunting because it recognizes indebtedness to that wisdom, the fear of not measuring up. Surely one fear haunting the contemporary poet is Auden's "poetry makes nothing happen." Hollander delivers what I consider to be his deepest response to this provocative statement in lines (quoted by both David Mikics and Kenneth Gross) that refer to a lit candle in a pitcher: "Like a star reflected / In a cup of water, / It will light up no path: // Neither will it go out." As the various essays in this collection implicitly show, Hollander's own work provides examples that light up no single path. One keeps going, then, perhaps because of a playful faith in the world that work creates: "In future, then, / Something would never be the same again" ("Making Nothing Happen").

2

For

Joining the celebration at last—a little later than I

Ought perhaps, but here we are—what fresh twitchings

Hoist the mantle now, John, and by whose leave, in naughty

Nature's cow-patted pastures or Art's humming would-bes,

Have you lined up the day's false dawn, the evening's afterglow?

O, the light you've made of those shadows of a certainty

Long since set in place by the custom of the country,

Long since ransacked and restored, written up and over.

Answers provoke the questioner. Silence nourishes soul.

Nothing changes but, by and by, our wishes, and your poems

Dear friend, bring to bear down the years on our restlessness

Emanations, powers, ideas orbiting the pull of a feeling—a regret

Really, for a world that has so much to offer and withdraw.

J. D. McCLATCHY

3

He Dares Say

DAVID BROMWICH

Anyone who has known John long enough has had the experience of receiving strong encouragement of the best kind—he sees what you are up to and gives you heart for going on—but encouragement that is likely also to contain an element of discontent with things-in-general. "Take it," he will urge about some possibly unearned windfall. "If you don't, it will go to someone who deserves it less." A sort of compliment peculiar to John, drained of smarm by a gleeful moroseness. His favorite metaphor of *minding the shop*, that is, doing well and responsibly the work you were put in the world to do, is part of a larger mundane habit of thought about how teachers and critics ought to take themselves. This comes out almost as a physical gesture, in his plain readiness for exhortation, an open-handed way with advice (meekly offered when unsought, otherwise given with relish) that seems to have flourished in a different air from what an American childhood can have absorbed in the late twentieth century. Not that full-scale holding forth is always put into play: the time-savers "Absolutely not" and "Goody!" are as commonplace with him as "I'm not sure" and "OK" are for the ordinary person. In reaction to some dishing of expectations by an academic aristocrat, you may hear him say, you may even see him think, the old word "unconscionable." It had become usual over the past few years for the younger scholars John dealt with, precisely because they were conscientious, to lament to him the fate that puts them under the control of fashions that grow more constrictive with each generation. A new professional turn-of-the-screw keeps being added, and all the while they are asked to perform service jobs like the teaching of writing, with which the educational methods of our time offer no assistance whatever. Eventually, John came up with a response, an inspired and a wholly characteristic one. "You went into this line of work to have the time to think for yourself. Probably you will get what you wanted. Meanwhile be glad that you have the chance to be as much of a hero as an honest cop."

Never easy to take, this solidity and assurance; but always possible to parry—"You're clueless"—a form of resistance (when supported by evidence) that John has always shown respect for. He shoulders his way into a discussion because that is the only way, for him; clears out the obstructions so that he seems to stand on a patch of his own, and then is apt to show fascination, dissent, complicity, or sometimes (a terrible sign, to be avoided) chagrin on your behalf. Somewhere in back of all these attitudes and effects is the promise of laughter. There is the definitive wicked chortle. There is the childlike rasping "Ooh," in the presence of suspicious yet delightful doings, close to the sound of Billy Gilbert as Joe Pettibone in *His Girl Friday* being offered a bribe that he has no intention of taking without first being scandalized by. As well as other shadings: a cry of "*Yes*" that rushes toward hilarity and stops just short; a skitter of treble approval uncorked to applaud a stroke of wit. In the tenor of this conduct is a gruff assumption of prerogative, surprisingly agreeable to most of those who encounter it. I said a few months ago to a mutual friend that New Haven seemed full of academic gentry, and, making reference to John's estate (which somebody called The Hacienda), added that John perhaps was a duke. This feeble trial balloon was greeted by a proper admonishment. "A duke? When I first knew John, he seemed more like a king than anyone I ever met."

Nobody else so queerly combines traits of the sociable and the secretive. At any given time, John is up to more than you can realize. But he long ago perfected an array of methods for letting the rest of us in on the secret, from time to time, or at least an idea of the secret—the phrase "one might adduce," for example, brought in at the start of a description of some path for research he intends to indicate but not to pursue. Another and a more confiding manner captures far more of him, a gesture entirely impulsive, frankly exhibited and at the same time private. I mean the giggle at an observed coincidence or at the timely understatement of some gross fact, scored for the loudest possible *sotto voce* and followed by the words "I daresay!" A phrase that has an interesting history. You daresay, at first, because it takes some real daring to say so. Later the expression draws in its wake the room-temperature vibes of sickly wit or undernourished irony, which can cover the range from "Well, it would, wouldn't it?" to "No surprise in that." At present, when used at all, the phrase is liable to signify nothing but a low conversational putter with ignition ready to die, one more optionally supercilious way of registering "Yes?" with even less commitment than "Indeed." By contrast, the "I daresay" of John takes us all the way back to the great age between senses 1 and 2, puts us again in the drawing room with Miss Bingley, Mr Darcy, and Miss Eliza Bennet, even as it recalls to listener and speaker alike how much nerve power the mere daring now presupposes.

"We have bread and circuses. And there isn't even any bread." A comment by John on the state of the culture, I forget at what moment—the threat by the new congress of the Contract with America in 1995 to shut down government? Or did it come at the beginning of a scandal on the order of Senator Packwood's diaries? John likes to keep up, mainly with gossip of people who are good or events that are ruinous, as distinct from ordinary personalities. Nobody will regret the path he took in the latter half of his career, where the poems have been so largely elegiac, but when he went that way American poetry lost a natural born satirist, one who would have made interesting company for Irving Feldman. Yet his gift of rapid characterization is also, though incidentally, novelistic. John said of my older son and his habit of getting in a post-ultimate shot in every argument, a last recorded refusal to knuckle under no matter how staggering the defeat: "So he's like the MGM lion with that extra *ra-ah-ahr* after you think it's over." These characterizations are far from casual, and not unimportant to their maker. John called up once to mention a colleague's "uptight laid-back style." How many other one-liners, by how many authors, are indebted to this vein of his talk? Saul Steinberg said about Ronald Reagan "He sang us lullabies"—reported to me by John, but it is just his sort of thought, and one would not be surprised to learn that it was invented in his company. On the other side of the satire lies John's devotion to the style of the generation before his own, a true democratic luster he is sometimes tempted to think has been extinguished forever. I owe to him my first acquaintance with the Rodgers and Hart songbook and much of the Gershwin: he would play the songs on the piano, while Lizzie sang and I—*whistled* improvisations, feeling very illegitimate and very happy.

There is always also a silent accompaniment, in John, a voice behind the voice, an almost impersonal mischief and detachment that sees, from without, the long scrimmage of articulation and stands aside a little. If you listen carefully, you can hear this other voice muttering. It knows the interest, as urgent and pointless as curiosity, with which we learn the names of things. It knows the comedy and pathos of coming to cherish arbitrary feelings about those names—and woe to the man or woman who has not cared enough to pronounce them correctly! I am touched most when I think of this reserve in John's poems, which makes them finally coherent with the person who wrote them, enthusiastic or baffled as he must often have been at what was coming from him. The work adds up to a comment on his belief that science is not an enemy of wonder, any more than learning is an enemy of vision or criticism an enemy of poetry. You discover in the poems, what you perceive as well in the person, a wakeful curiosity about the imaginable purposes of human petition, prayer, aberration, and energy. In the jacket photograph for the first edition of *Reflections on Espionage*, he stands with folded arms, looking tough, knowing what he knows, but the mirror image shows a different aspect, oddly softened by a touch of doubt. Both pictures are true. To have known John is to recognize that there was hardly ever a time when he did not resemble both.

4

"A Goddess Among the Gods":
Virgil, Milton, and the Woman
of Immortal Voice

JOHN WATKINS

When Homer first described Circe as a "dread goddess" who
spoke with a human voice, he established a *topos* through
which later writers defined their relationship to earlier epics.
Virgil's Venus, Spenser's Belphoebe, and Milton's yet unfallen
Eve bewilder their interlocutors by violating boundaries between
human and divine, intimate and inaccessible, familiar and unfath-
omable. In an analogous way, epic poetry bewilders its audience by transforming everyday vernacular into a medium for
reviving voices and conventions of a culturally alien past. Figured as a numinous woman whose beauty overpowers everyone
who beholds her, that past can serve as a guide, an inspiration,
a distraction, or an impediment to the poet's didactic and aesthetic aims.

Circe's mortal-sounding voice suggested to post-Homeric
writers multiple ways of imagining poetic history. It also suggested divergent ways of interpreting the poet's relationship to
extrapoetic authority, whether imagined in religious, secular,
imperial, absolutist, or proto-nationalist terms. The same
figure that encouraged writers like Virgil, Tasso, Spenser, and
Milton to re-envision humanity's subservience to the divine
invited them to ponder new ways of conceiving the individual's
relationship to the *imperium*. The goddess's Homeric linea-
ments remained intact, but the political valence of her epipha-
nies shifted with the rise and fall of empires, dynasties, and
commonwealths. Her appearances provide a particularly rich
chapter in the large story of poetry's relationship to society. As
a goddess speaking with a human voice, or in her complementary guise as a mortal woman speaking with a divine voice, she
offered an image of poetry as a liminal force whose engagement
with the political present, however immediate and intense,

never lost an imagined affinity with earlier moments of aesthetic expression.

Although the goddess with the human voice figured prominently in almost every Renaissance vernacular epic, she played a particularly crucial role in the poetry of John Milton. For several decades, scholars have emphasized Milton's engagement in the fray of seventeenth-century English politics over his humanist inheritance. Critics have not ignored his humanism, but they have treated it primarily as one of many influences on a career primarily shaped by politics.[1] I do not want to minimize either the significance of this critical project, or my own indebtedness to it. But I do want to note its limitations. As the imperative to historicize yields throughout our profession to an imperative to globalize, our synchronic, historically precise readings of Milton restrict him to an unduly nationalistic curriculum. Milton, the poet who aspired to a place in a pan-European, and arguably global cultural tradition, threatens to become the most provincial of all English poets in his championship of English liberties.

In this essay, I hope to resist that provincialization by re-situating Milton in a diachronic, European context. Because his dialogue with continental influences unfolded as instances of discrete textual imitation, my own project may first appear unsettlingly formalist, particularly in contrast to the reading practices that have dominated much historicist work. By stressing the persistence of Milton's classicism, even in passages where one might expect it to be most compromised by the synchronic imperatives of politics or theology, I want to suggest that, far from subverting his commitment to the European poetic legacy, Milton's politics depended on it. Instead of insisting that politics and theology shaped Milton's response to his poetic models, I will argue that pre-Christian poetry shaped his views of church and state. Homer was never far from his thoughts, even when pondering the mysteries of the Christian incarnation as a model for godly behavior in a fallen world.

While my argument ends with *Paradise Regained*, it begins with Circe's first appearance in the *Odyssey*:

1 For a particularly fine discussion of Milton's classicism and its relationship to politics, see David Norbrook, *Writing the English Republic: Poetry, Rhetoric, and Politics, 1627–1660* (Cambridge: Cambridge University Press, 1999), pp. 433–90.

Αἰαίην δ' ἐς νῆσον ἀφίκομεθ'· ἔνθα δ' ἔναιε
Κίρκη ἐυπλόκαμος, δεινὴ θεὸς αὐδήεσσα
(And we came to the isle of Aeaea, where dwelt
fair-tressed Circe, a dread goddess of human speech)[2]

The phrase δεινὴ θεὸς αὐδήεσσα, "dread goddess of human speech," may sound like yet another formulaic epithet, a stock phrase that has no figurative relationship with the narrative in which it occurs. But in contrast to other Homeric epithets, the word αὐδήεσσα occurs only nine times in extant Greek texts, and only three times outside the *Odyssey*.[3] Each time it underscores an uncanny crossing of the boundary between human and non-human experience. In Book Nineteen of the *Iliad*, for example, Homer uses it to describe Achilles' horse Xanthus when Hera inspires it with human speech to prophesy its master's doom (αὐδήεντα δ' ἔθηκε θεὰ λευκώλενος Ἥρη [19.407]). Pausanias records an epitaph for the Delphic sibyl that uses the same word to characterize the woman who once uttered the prophecies of Phoebus:

ἅδ' ἐγὼ ἁ Φοίβοιο σαφηγορὶς εἰμι Σίβυλλα
τῷδ' ὑπὸ λαϊνέῳ σάματι κευθομένα,
παρθένος αὐδάεσσα τὸ πρίν, νῦν δ' αἰὲν ἄναυδος,
μοίρᾳ ὑπὸ στιβαρᾷ τάνδε λαχοῦσα πέδαν.[4]

Here I am, the plain-speaking Sibyl of Phoebus,
Hidden beneath this stone tomb.
A maiden once gifted with [human] voice, but now for
   ever voiceless,
By hard fate doomed to this fetter.

The Sibyl mourns the loss of her human voice (αὐδάεσσα), but the epitaph's peculiar poignancy depends on the fact that death

---

2 *The Odyssey with an English Translation by A. T. Murray* (Cambridge: Harvard University Press, 1919), 10.135–36. All references are to this addition.

3 The word λευκώλενος as in λευκώλενος Ἥρη ("white-armed Hera"), for example, occurs 54 times. I am indebted for these statistics to the "Word-Study" information on the Perseus Web site, www.perseus.tufts.edu.

4 Pausanias, *Description of Greece with an English Translation by W. H. S. Jones, Litt.D. and H. A. Ormerod, M.A.*, 4 vols (Cambridge: Harvard University Press, 1918), 10.12.6.

has also deprived her of the divine voice that once spoke through her. She is now doubly "voiceless" (ἄναυδος), a word that echoes and negates the prior description of her as "human-voiced." The verbal play between αὐδάεσσα and ἄναυδος foregrounds the paradox central to many epitaphs as the imagined voice of the voiceless deceased. But the consciousness that this particular speaker once spoke with the voice of an immortal compounds the pathos of her silence. Phoebus may have used her as his instrument, but he did not bequeath his power over death.

In both the *Iliad* and the Sibyllic epitaph, the gods' power to violate the integrity of the human voice—either by giving human-sounding speech to an animal or by transforming a plain-speaking virgin into a mouthpiece for divine enigmas—epitomizes their detachment from mortal experience. Here as in much of the Greek canon, their sublimity is simultaneously wondrous and appalling. The attributes that distinguish them from mortals cast them both as powerful benefactors and as enemies. Above all, their immunity to death encourages a pervasive indifference in their relationships with every human being except the rare objects of their focused passions, the Achilles or the Odysseus whose commerce with the gods sets him apart from other mortals.

In the *Odyssey*, nothing sums up the human characters' desire to escape the gods' power more poignantly than their longing to hear another human voice. When Odysseus washes ashore on the Phaeacian coast and hears the nymph-like cries of Nausicaa and her companions, he wonders whether he is safely among "men of human speech" (ἦ νύ που ἀνθρώπων εἰμὶ σχεδὸν αὐδηέντων [6.125]). When he and his men, traumatized by the inhuman feasting of the Cyclops and the Laestrigonians, first land on Circe's island, Odysseus climbs a crag in the hope of *hearing* as well as seeing signs of human industry (10.148). His men hear Circe singing her quasi-mortal song at her loom before they ever see her. The more human her voice sounds, the more she seems to fulfill their dream of hearing the comforting sound of human industry.

But as comforting as her song may first sound to Odysseus' battle-wearied men, the "dread goddess of human speech" epitomizes the ambivalence built into their relationship to the divine. The moment they hear her singing, one of them comments on the doubleness of her nature in words that have echoed throughout later poetic history:

Friends, within someone goes to and fro before a great web, singing sweetly, so that the floor echoes; some goddess it is, or some woman

Ὦ φίλοι, ἔνδον γάρ τις ἐποιχομένη μέγαν ἱστὸν καλὸν ἀοιδιάει, δάπεδον δ' ἅπαν ἀμφιμέμυκεν, ἢ θεὸς ἠὲ γυνή.   (10.226–28)

As sweet as her song might be, it invites antithetical readings. The question of whether she is a goddess or a woman intersects the question of whether her human sounding voice is an illusion to ensnare her listeners or a foreshadowing of her later benevolence. As the episode unfolds, Circe seduces the Greek scouts with her siren-like singing only to deprive them of their humanity. Turned into animals with human minds, their metamorphosis mirrors in a grotesque fashion her own blending of human and divine attributes.

But the episode does not end with the Greeks' transformation, and its eventual denouement complicates the impression of Circe's nature and of her attitude toward human beings. Once Odysseus challenges her to reverse her spells and transform his men back into human beings, she becomes their protectress. The Greeks then spend a full year on her island, where she never harms them again and bestows on them a hospitality that compensates for horrors they first experienced. When the reluctant men finally leave her island, Homer uses again the same epithet, Κίρκη ἐυπλόκαμος, δεινὴ θεὸς αὐδήεσσα, describing how she sends them on their way with a favorable wind. The human-sounding voice that once lured them into danger now confirms the possibility of divine sympathy for imperiled humanity.

The ambiguous cadences of Circe's voice resounded in later poetic representations of mortals' relationship to the divine. In a passage that had a particularly profound impact on later European writers, Virgil transformed her encounter with Odysseus and his men into Aeneas' meeting with his disguised mother Venus on the road to Carthage.[5] The passage retains

5 I am indebted throughout this section to several previous discussions of Virgil's relationship to Homer. See especially G. N. Knauer, *Die Aeneis und Homer*, "Hypomnemata" 7 (Göttingen: Vandenhoeck & Ruprecht, 1964); Mihoko Suzuki, *Metamorphoses of Helen: Authority, Difference, and the Epic* (Ithaca: Cornell University Press, 1989); W. R. Johnson, *Darkness Visible: A Study of Virgil's* Aeneid (Berkeley: Univer-

many elements of its Hellenic source. Like their Ithacan predecessors, the Trojans land on the North African coast after
enduring trials imposed on them by the gods. Just as Odysseus
killed a stag on Aeaea and feasted his men on its carcass, Aeneas
kills seven stags for his exhausted and famished Trojans. Like
Odysseus' men, he too sets out to see if the country is inhabited by human beings only to find himself in the presence of a
goddess. His conversation with Venus recalls the Homeric concern with her voice and her confusion of human and divine
attributes:

o how might I call you, virgin? For neither is your visage mortal,
nor does your voice sound human; O surely a goddess!

*o quam te memorem, virgo? namque haud tibi vultus mortalis, nec vox
hominem sonat; o, dea certe.* (1.327–38)[6]

Virgil does not merely reenact his Odyssean subtext. He revises
it in ways that signal a more general departure from Homer's
representation of the gods. In contrast to Circe's human-sounding
voice, that of Venus is unmistakably divine. Along with the
radiance of her face, it foils her effort to convince Aeneas that
she is just another Tyrean girl. When Odysseus' men heard
Circe singing, they wondered whether she was a goddess or a
woman. When Aeneas hears Venus, he only wonders whether
she is "the sister of Phoebus or one of her nymphs" (*an Phoebi
soror? an Nympharum sanguinis una?* 1.329). He never thinks
that she is human. These reversals of Homeric precedent have
several striking effects. Whereas Circe's human-sounding voice
kept open the possibility of her eventual intimacy with the Ith-
acans, Venus' insistently divine voice precludes it. As Aeneas'
mother and the Trojans' patroness, Venus is never, like Circe,
overtly malignant. But she retains an aloofness that leaves
Aeneas frustrated when she suddenly disappears at the end of
their conversation: "Why do you too, cruel one, deceive your

---

sity of California Press, 1976); Gordon Williams, *Technique and Ideas in
the* Aeneid (New Haven: Yale University Press, 1983), pp. 82–119;
David Quint, *Epic and Empire: Politics and Generic Form from Virgil to
Milton* (Princeton: Princeton University Press, 1993), pp. 50–96.
6 *P. Vergili Maronis Opera*, ed. R. A. B. Mynors (Oxford: Clarendon
Press, 1969). All references are to this edition; translation mine.

son so many times with false imaginations?" (*quid natum totiens, crudelis tu quoque, falsis / ludis imaginibus?* 1.407–08). Like all members of the Virgilian pantheon, even the most benevolent, Venus never stoops to the familiarity with human beings that characterizes Odysseus' interactions with goddesses like Athena, Circe, and Calypso.

Classicists continue to debate whether the ludic behavior of Virgil's gods reflects his critique of an *imperium* whose tastes and images he helped to forge.[7] One can imagine how Aeneas' resentment of Venus' mortal disguises might obliquely express Virgil's own resentment of his emperor's affectations of divinity. But this passage's reception history makes one thing clear.[8] For later readers, the Venerean interplay of mortal and divine attributes created a hermeneutic anxiety that some tried to resolve by dismissing one set of qualities as a sham and privileging the other as real. Commentators like Petrarch and Jodocus Badius Ascensius glossed the episode as an allegory about the dangers of lust, a deadly sin disguised as the most voluptuous of pleasures. Misreading Virgil along Homeric lines, Badius focused specifically on the seductiveness of Venus' voice. According to him, the episode shows how lust "misleads the imprudent not only by its appearance but even by its speeches."[9] Another exegetical tradition downplayed Venus' deceptions and focused instead on the episode as a testimony to humanity's receptiveness to divine illumination. In an influential treatment of the episode, Cristoforo Landino identified Virgil's goddess as the *Venus coelestis*, who leads men from sensuality to heavenly contemplation. He distinguished her from the *Venus naturalis*, the generative Venus who stirred sexual desires. Humanist editors typically invited readers to weigh the merits of these competing inter-

---

7 For further discussion, see Johnson; Quint; Michael C. J. Putnam, *The Poetry of the Aeneid* (Cambridge: Harvard University Press, 1965); Philip Hardie, *Virgil's Aeneid: Cosmos and Imperium* (Oxford: Oxford University Press, 1986).

8 For more extensive discussion of the passage's reception history, see Anthony di Matteo, "Spenser's Venus-Virgo: The Poetics and Interpretive History of a Dissembling Figure," *Spenser Studies* 10 (1989): 37–70.

9 Badius, *P. Virgili Maronis* Aeneida *Commentarium*, in Giunta's edition of Virgil's *Opera* (Venice, 1544), 176, verso.

pretations by including them in the glosses annotating their editions of Virgil's poem.

When poets like Ariosto, Tasso, and Spenser began to build vernacular epic traditions on classical models, they drew on both interpretations of the elusive goddess. Throughout *La Gerusalemme Liberata*, for example, Tasso foregrounds the temptress Armida's siren-like voice as a signal of her duplicity. She not only seduces the hero Rinaldo with her own bewitching words, but trains the birds on her enchanted island to sing them as well:

> *Vola, fra gli altri, un che la piume ha sparte*
> *di color vari, ed ha purpureo il rostro;*
> *e lingua snoda in guisa larga, e pârte*
> *la voce si, ch'assembra il sermon nostro.* (16.13)[10]

> Among the others flies one who has plumage scattered
> with varied color, and has a purple beak;
> and he unknots his tongue in a broad guise, and he parts
> his voice so that it resembles our speech.

Like the men transformed into animals on Circe's island, Armida's bird parodies her own dangerous confusion of human and more-than-human attributes. When she first appears in the Frankish camp, she leads the Crusaders, like Odysseus' men before them, to wonder whether she is a goddess:

> *donna, se pur tal nome a te conviensi;*
> *ché non simigli tu cosa terrena,*
> *né v'è figlia d'Adamo in cui dispensi*
> *contanto il Ciel di sua luce serena.* (4.35)

> Lady, if such a name can suit you,
> you whom no earthly thing resembles,
> nor is there a daughter of Adam to whom
> heaven dispenses so much of its serene light.

Echoing Venus' lines in the *Aeneid*, Armida defers the compliment and insists that she is a mere mortal. As a sorceress with supernatural abilities, she occupies a middle ground between mortal and immortal experience. Unlike Venus, she really is a

---

10 *La Gerusalemme Liberata*, ed. Lanfranco Caretti (Milan: Arnoldo Mondadori, 1983). All references are to this edition; translation mine.

human being, but nothing else that she says is true. As her story unfolds, her associations with Circe eclipse her more superficial resemblance to the Virgilian Venus. The woman who transforms a band of Crusaders into fish and plots to murder Rinaldo is not merely deceptive but malicious.

Situating Armida within the emphatically dualistic landscape of the Christian supernatural, Tasso set an important precedent for Milton by equating her haunting ambiguities with evil. But Armida is not the only figure in the *Liberata* who inherits the Circean confusion of human and divine attributes. In other sections of the poem, words that sound more-than-mortal are not necessarily diabolical. Tasso contrasts Armida's seductive songs with the speeches of the Sage of Ascalon and the holy hermit Piero, his complementary embodiments of human wisdom and supernatural understanding. In counseling Rinaldo after his escape from Armida, the Sage urges him to heed his words:

> . . . *contrari al canto*
> *de le Sirene, e non ti sian molesti;*
> *ma gli serba nel cor, fin che distingua*
> *meglio a te il ver più saggia e santa lingua.* (17.60)

> . . . which are contrary to the song
> of the Siren, and they should not be troublesome to you;
> but keep them in your heart, until a wiser and holier tongue
> will better clarify for you the truth.

If the Sage's words are worthy of preservation because they represent the noblest human sentiments, the "wiser and holier" remarks of Piero are even more valuable. Marking God's direct intervention in human affairs, they move their auditors more effectively than any other discourse in the poem. Piero not only brings Rinaldo to complete repentance for sins with Armida but purges all the Crusaders of the "inborn affections of sovereignty, liberty, and honor" (*gl'innati affetti / di sovrastar, di libertà, d'onore*) that threaten to divide them (1.32). The Holy Spirit itself both inspires Piero's words and impresses them on the Crusaders' hearts (*Inspiri tu de l'Eremita i detti / e tu gl'imprimi a i cavalier nel core* [1.32]). As the narrator apostrophizes when Piero convinces the Crusaders to unite under a single commander, "What thoughts, what breasts are closed to you, Sacred Breath and Divine Ardor?" (*Quai pensier, quai petti / son chiusi a te, Sant'Aura e divo Ardore?* [1.32]).

[19]

La Gerusalemme Liberata became one of the primary influences mediating later writers' responses to the woman speaking with a more-than-mortal voice. Tasso reinforced a gender bias, already present in Virgil, that associated reason and divine wisdom with men and duplicity with women. The commentary tradition had modified this bias by offering alternative readings of Virgil's Venus as lust and as heavenly wisdom. When Tasso incorporated the commentators' reading into his own poem, he gave to the female Armida those associations of Venus with deception and illicit desire, while the male Piero became the poem's primary instrument of divine illumination. For post-Tassean writers, imitations of Venus' encounter with Aeneas—and the more distant encounter between Odysseus and Circe that inspired it—registered their sense not only of the relationship between humanity and divinity, but between men and women. Parallel representational hierarchies joined maleness, sincerity, and Christian truth in an alliance against femininity, deceit, and pagan fictions.

No writer responded to the Tassean hierarchies in a more complex way than Edmund Spenser, the poet whom Milton, in an often-quoted phrase, proclaimed his own "great original." Filtered through Virgil and Neoplatonic commentary and Italian epic-romance, Homer's goddess with the woman's voice provided Spenser a vehicle to honor his sovereign while simultaneously testing the moral and aesthetic limits of absolutist figuration. His several imitations of Aeneas' encounter with Venus signal the ambivalence toward Elizabeth I that soon provoked antithetical readings of his poetry as servile flattery and as a voice of thinly veiled dissent.[11] In general, his revisions dissociated Venus from the duplicity that might compromise her identity as a prototype of the queen. The goddess who presided over the "Aprill" Eclogue of *The Shepheardes Calender* and Belphoebe's first epiphany in Book Two of *The Faerie Queene* was not a trickster but the *Venus coelestis* who ought to lead her interlocutors to heavenly contemplations. But in shielding her against Circean associations with carnality and deceit, Spenser

11 For an exhaustive treatment of Spenser's imitations of Venus' epiphany, see di Matteo, "Spenser's Venus-Virgo." While di Matteo focuses on the figure's juxtaposition of Venerean and Dianic qualities, I focus on her blending of mortal and divine.

voiced anxieties about her exaltation beyond mortal compre-
hension. Cast either as Elisa or Belphoebe, she retains a Virgilian elusiveness that could be translated on a level of political
allegory into the monarch's detachment from the lives of her
subjects.

This ambivalence manifests itself in Spenser's earliest
engagement with the Virgilian Venus in the "Aprill" Eclogue.
Taking his motto from Aeneas' proclamation of Venus' divinity
"*o quam te memorem, virgo?. . . . o, dea certe*"—Spenser refigured
Venus' alienation from Aeneas as the queen's elevation above
her subjects. The Venerean interplay of mortal and divine
attributes offered him a model for the relationship between the
queen's public and private bodies. Like the Virgilian Venus,
Elisa inhabits seemingly unbridgeable worlds. Beyond the appearance of a beautiful but mortal woman lies the enduring, divinely
ordained sovereignty celebrated by Spenser's poetry: "So sprong
her grace / Of heauenly race: / No mortal blemish may her
blot" (52–54).[12] As in the *Liberata*, the manifestation of divine
truth behind the appearance of mortality supported an argument for political centralization. Just as Piero led the Crusaders
to rally around a sole commander, Elisa imposes a centripetal
order on everyone else in the poem. The figure of her surrounded by nymphs, muses, and shepherdesses became one of
the period's most striking images of a society in which authority radiates from the monarch.

Elisa retains nothing of Venus' deceptiveness, and she disciplines rather than licenses springtime's Venerean energies.
Although she stands at the center of a vernal festival charged
with erotic associations, Spenser insists not only on her chastity
but on that of everyone who approaches her: "Let none come
there, but that Virgines bene" (129). As I have argued in
another context, this urgency suggests in part Spenser's sense
of a fundamental instability in the distinction between the natural and heavenly Venuses of Neoplatonic commentary. But
this urgency ultimately shadows his celebration of Elizabeth.
As much as the Eclogue contributes to her mystique as the
Virgin Queen, it links her elusiveness as a type of the Virgilian

12 *The Works of Edmund Spenser: A Variorum Edition*, ed. Edwin Greenlaw
    et al., 9 vols (Baltimore: Johns Hopkins University Press, 1932–49).
    All subsequent references to Spenser are to this edition.

Venus to a consciousness of her coercive powers as a reigning sovereign. The Elisa ode is one of the period's most delicately poised instances of royal compliment, and its prohibitions against non-virgins who might dare to appear in the queen's presence hardly coalesce into a programmatic statement of opposition.

As critics have long recognized, Spenser's most complex rewriting of Venus' epiphany occurs when Belphoebe, another representative of Elizabeth, encounters the scoundrel Bragga-docchio, a coward who apes Aeneas' heroism.[13] In this treat-ment, Spenser does not abandon Venus' trickery altogether but transfers it instead to the male interlocutor. In Virgil, Venus is the poseur pretending to be just another Tyrian girl; in *The Faerie Queene*, Braggadocchio is the poseur, a *miles gloriosus* who responds to Belphoebe's inquiry about a missing deer with a parody of Aeneas' self-introduction as one whose fame is known "*super aethera*" (1.379). The scene ends abruptly when this mock hero tries to rape Belphoebe, who rebuffs him and retreats into the forest. As a compliment to the Virgin Queen, the passage reverses the gender ratios that Virgil introduced and that Tasso preserved. Whereas the *Aeneid* used Venus' duplicity as a foil to the integrity and *pietas* displayed by Aeneas, a surro-gate for Augustus, *The Faerie Queene* establishes the integrity of Belphoebe, an Elizabethan surrogate, against a backdrop of male duplicity.

Spenser's own left-leaning Protestantism may have set him against the more moderate Elizabeth on many issues, and critics have detected ambivalence in *The Faerie Queene*'s representa-tions of Belphoebe.[14] His co-religionists, for instance, typically

13 For previous discussion of the episode's Virgilian origins, see Edgar Wind, *Pagan Mysteries in the Renaissance* (New York: Norton, 1958), pp. 76–80; Harry Berger, Jr., *The Allegorical Temper: Vision and Reality in Book II of Spenser's* Faerie Queene (New Haven: Yale University Press, 1957), pp. 157–58; Barbara J. Bono, *Literary Transvaluation: From Vergilian Epic to Shakespearean Tragicomedy* (Berkeley: University of California Press, 1984), pp. 71–74; di Matteo, "Spenser's Venus-Virgo," pp. 56–59; Theresa M. Krier, *Gazing on Secret Sights: Spenser, Classical Imitation, and the Decorums of Vision* (Ithaca: Cornell University Press, 1990), pp. 66–82.

14 See Judith H. Anderson, "'In lliuing colours and right hew': The Queen of Spenser's Central Books," *Poetic Traditions of the English Renaissance*, ed. Maynard Mack and George deForest Lord (New

asserted women's subservience to men in ways that qualified Elizabeth's virginal independence as a model for other women to follow. When Belphoebe reappears in Book III, a book devoted to the Protestant idealization of marriage, her Virgilian elusiveness manifests itself as an indifference to her suitors that borders on cruelty. Spenser recasts the classical subtext yet again when Timias first sees her and falls in love:

> Angell, or Goddesse do I call thee right?
> .   .   .   .
> Not Goddesse I, nor Angell, but the Mayd,
> And daughter of a woody Nymphe. . . .   (3.5.35, 36)

Belphoebe's repudiation of Braggadocchio may have under-scored Elizabeth's virginity, and hence commitment to her Protestant subjects. But her inability to return or even to com-prehend Timias' love suggests that the sovereign's elevation might blind her to their needs and longings.

If Spenser felt that the actual queen fell short of his ideals, he did not abandon monarchy in principle or espouse republican-ism. Throughout *The Faerie Queene*, he imagines an aristocratic order rallying behind the Crown to advance a pan European Reformation. By the time Milton read the poem, however, a Stuart dynasty that appeased Catholic Spain while refusing to aid central European Protestants in the Thirty Years War had rendered an imagined alliance between Crown, aristocracy, and left-flank Protestantism utterly untenable. As the commer-cial class to which Milton belonged developed fiscal and legis-lative strategies for shifting political power from the Crown to an elected House of Commons, Milton himself began writing poetry that shifted epic authority from the older royal order to God's Englishmen. This transformation brought the woman who spoke with a more-than-mortal voice to the center of his poetry. As both a Protestant and as a member of an emergent bourgeoisie, Milton was inspired by Virgil's figure of a simple Tyrian huntress who spoke with divine authority. But that Vir-gilian image was contaminated for him by its original fictional

---

Haven: Yale University Press, 1982), pp. 47–66; David Lee Miller, *The Poem's Two Bodies: The Poetics of the 1590 Faerie Queene* (Princeton: Princeton University Press, 1988), pp. 224–35.

context and by intervening poetic imitations. Like Spenser, Milton imagined a Venus who retained the heavenly associations of her classical prototype, but nothing of her deceptiveness. But Milton went beyond Spenser in distancing his imagined heroine from any pretensions to divinity or mortal sovereignty. His ideal women are godly, but not divine and certainly not regal in any monarchical sense.

When Milton first revised the classical encounter between a numinous woman and an awestruck interlocutor, he recast the woman as neither a goddess nor a queen but as a fifteen-year-old girl. Like *The Faerie Queene*, the 1634 mask *Comus* reverses the Virgilian gender dynamics so that male fraud sets off female integrity. Just as Venus' voice first signals her disguised divinity to Aeneas, Comus senses something beyond the human order when he first hears the Lady sing:

> Can any mortal mixture of Earth's mold
> Breathe such Divine enchanting ravishment?   (244–45)

Like Venus, the Lady disclaims the praise, but unlike Venus, who only pretended to have been separated from her sisters, she really has lost siblings in the forest, the two brothers who are desperately worried about her safety. But while the Lady is honest, Comus is not. In promising to lead her to two boys whose "port was more than human" (297), he takes on the role of classical dissembler.

Although Comus inherits Venus' deceptiveness, his malice and his offers of false hospitality link him less to her than to Circe. Milton explicitly identifies him as Circe's son, and Comus himself associates the Lady's songs with those his mother sang "with the Sirens three," while "culling their Potent herbs and baleful drugs" (253, 255). His recollection serves as a metacommentary on Milton's poetic revisions. According to Comus' own account, Circe's siren-songs took "the prison'd soul" and wrapped it in an illusion of "Elysium," one that "in pleasing slumber lull'd the sense / And in sweet madness robb'd it of itself" (262–63). In contrast with her dangerous enchantments, the "sacred and home-felt delight" stirred by the Lady's song fills the auditor with a "sober certainty of waking bliss" (256–61). The Lady becomes a kind of Puritanized *Venus coelestis*, who leads her admirers to a contemplation of "sober" joys that reinforce, rather than unsettle, the soul's integrity.

Since Comus' literary ancestry also includes Braggadocchio, the Lady's resistance to him defines Milton against Spenser, his principal English precursor. In rewriting *The Faerie Queene*, Milton repudiates Spenser's monarchical and courtly biases. As critics have often noted, *Comus* challenges its own genre's association with aristocratic values.[15] Alice Egerton, who performed the Lady in the mask's original production, may have been the daughter of an earl. But although Milton praises her bloodlines, he honors her most for the values of temperance, prudence, and thrift that the commercial classes advocated against the alleged decadence of the ruling elite. Milton especially divests the central Elizabethan virtue of chastity of its royalist pretensions. The Lady establishes her "serious doctrine of Virginity" on bourgeois rather than courtly, Neoplatonic foundations by equating promiscuity with fiscal extravagance (787).[16] Her rejection of Comus' offer gestures toward a complete repudiation of mortal sovereignty. When Comus first hears her singing, he boasts that she "shall be [his] Queen" (265). Resisting that offer distances the Lady from Belphoebe, the Spenserian version of a chaste Venus, who appeared as an explicit type of Queen Elizabeth. The Lady owes her extraordinariness neither to allegorical sovereignty, like Belphoebe, nor to inherent divinity, like Venus, but to a soundly Protestant moral education.

One aspect of Protestant teaching that played an especially prominent role in Milton's revision of Spenser was its emphasis on wifely submission and the universal vocation to marriage. Spenser proclaimed the principle in Book V of *The Faerie Queene*, but also asserted that Elizabeth's identity as a monarch exempted her from it:

> But vertuous women wisely vnderstand,
>   That they were borne to base humilitie,
> Vnlesse the heauens them lift to lawfull soueraintie.   (5.5.25)

---

15 See especially Leah S. Marcus, *The Politics of Mirth: Jonson, Herrick, Milton, Marvell, and the Defense of Old Holiday Pastimes* (Chicago: University of Chicago Press, 1986), pp. 169–212.

16 See Christopher Kendrick's discussion of the confluence of political and libidinal meanings in the mask in "Milton and Sexuality: A Symptomatic Reading of *Comus*," *Re-Membering Milton: Essays on the Texts and Traditions*, ed. Mary Nyquist and Margaret Ferguson (New York: Methuen, 1987), pp. 43–73.

As an armed virgin wandering alone in the forest and repeatedly rebuffing male overtures, Belphoebe embodied Elizabeth's exemption from patriarchal expectations. Within the fiction of Milton's mask, the bookish Elder Brother conspicuously recalls Spenser's idealization of Belphoebe when he argues that the Lady's chastity will protect her from the dangers of the forest:

> 'Tis chastity, my brother, chastity:
> She that has that, is clad in complete steel,
> And like a quiver'd Nymph with Arrows keen
> May trace huge Forests and unharbor'd Heaths
>
> . . . .
>
> . . . with unblench't majesty.   (420–23, 430)

The Brother's tribute combines recollections of Belphoebe, and of the Virgilian Venus that lies behind her, with memories of the steel-clad Britomart, arguably Spenser's most complex and compelling challenge to Protestant conventions. But as the plot unfolds, the Brother's idealism proves naive. The Lady is less secure and less capable of active resistance to evil than he suggests. She rebuffs Comus' overtures in a brilliant rhetorical performance, but she is finally dependent on others for her rescue from his spells. In defending her virginity, her words may recall Belphoebe's, but instead of racing from her Braggadocchio-like abductor back into the privacy of the forest, she returns to her father's home with her brothers. There she will presumably remain until her future husband takes her not for his queen but for his chaste wife.

If the Lady loses something of Belphoebe's majestic independence and Venus' mystery in this poetic descent, she acquires a moral earnestness to which ordinary mortals can aspire. This democratization marks Milton's most significant revision of the *topos* that I have been examining. For Homer, Virgil, Tasso, and Spenser, the confusion of divine and human aspects signaled the exceptionalness of the characters they portrayed. For Milton, it suggested a righteousness that was potentially available to anyone who chooses to live in accordance with God's laws. In the optimism that characterized much of his writing in the late 1630s and 1640s, he imagined a figure like the Lady as a paradigm for all godly people.

As Milton's republicanism matured, he became more resolute than ever in separating the numinous woman from her Elizabethan associations with female sovereignty. Milton, along with other anti-royalist writers, rarely mentioned Elizabeth. When they did, they often followed Lucy Hutchinson's lead in praising her not as a divine woman but as one who showed "submission to her masculine and wise counsellors."[17] As a lit crary complement to this silence, Spenser's prototypes of Elizabeth, such as Belphoebe and the woman-warrior Britomart, have no place in *Paradise Lost*. Singing "the better fortitude / Of Patience and Heroic Martyrdom" (931–32) for men, Milton exchanged the active heroism of the huntress, the woman warrior, and the virgin queen for the more passive virtues of the wife. By the end of *Paradise Lost*, he offered Eve as a pattern for future English heroines. In transforming the classical and Elizabethan paradigms, he redefined female heroism as the private but significant influence that women might have over their husbands and sons within the domestic sphere.

As scholars have often observed, this privatization of female influence constitutes an important phase in an emergence of the novel that is inseparable from the eclipse of epic.[18] In the rest of this essay, I want to suggest how Milton's transformations of the woman with the more-than-mortal voice advanced that larger process of generic evolution. Throughout *Paradise Lost*, aspects of the Virgilian Venus dominate Milton's characterization of Eve at precisely those moments when she appears torn between novelistic domestication and an epic yearning to be more than mortal. Just before her temptation occurs, Milton compares her to a series of classical figures: an "*Oread* or *Dryad*," Pales, Pomona, and Ceres (9.387). But her comparison to a "Wood-Nymph light . . . / . . . of *Delia*'s train," one who "*Delia*'s self / In gait surpass'd and Goddess-like deport" (9.386–89), signals the dominant Virgilian subtext by echoing Aeneas' assumption that Venus is Phoebus' sister or one of her

---

17 *Memoirs of the Life of Colonel Hutchinson* (London: J. M. Dent, 1995), p. 70. For further discussion, see John Watkins, "'Old Bess in the Ruff': Remembering Elizabeth I, 1625–1660," *English Literary Renaissance* 30 (2000): 95–116.

18 See especially Nancy Armstrong and Leonard Tennenhouse, *The Imaginary Puritan. Literature, Intellectual Labor, and the Origins of Personal Life* (Berkeley: University of California Press, 1992).

nymphs (*an Phoebi soror? an Nympharum sanguinis una?* [1.329]).[19]
The episode begins as a reenactment of Virgil along Spenserian
lines. Like Belphoebe, Eve is a virtuous woman who enters
into conversation with a corrupt male interlocutor, Satan. Yet
Milton diabolizes certain aspects of the original Virgilian scene
to produce a horrid rather than ludicrous effect. The confusion
of human and divine aspects resurfaces as a confusion of angel
and reptile. The female deity disguised as a mortal becomes the
male devil disguised as a snake but speaking with a human
voice. Much as Aeneas wondered at the apparent Tyrian maiden's
divine voice, Eve wonders at the apparent snake's voice: "What
may this mean? Language of Man pronounc't / By Tongue of
Brute, and human sense exprest?" (9.553–54). Eve's vulnerability lies in her failure to grasp the full significance of the ser-
pent's uncanny confusion of attributes. Overlooking the real
conjunction of fallen spirit and mortal creature in her fascination with the merely apparent conjunction of human and reptile, she mistakes a diabolical plot for a natural wonder.

In a characteristic demonization of the classical past, Milton
recasts Venus' recommendation that Aeneas find shelter among
Dido's Carthaginians as Satanic temptation. As in *Comus*, he
transforms the compliments Aeneas pays Venus into a tempter's
flattery. Satan mimes the awestruck hero's initial apostrophe to
the goddess in human disguise:

> Wonder not, sovran Mistress, if perhaps
> Thou canst, who are sole Wonder . . .
>
> .   .   .   .
>
> . . . who shouldst be seen
> A Goddess among Gods, ador'd and serv'd
> By Angels numberless, thy daily Train.   (9.532–34, 547–48)

Aeneas merely acknowledged a fact: Venus really is a goddess.
But by telling Eve that she ought to be a goddess, Satan infects

19 As Barbara Pavlock notes, Milton also echoes the Virgilian comparison of Dido to Diana when she is first seen supervising the construction of Carthage. See *Eros, Imitation, and the Epic Tradition* (Ithaca:
Cornell University Press, 1990), p. 194 ff. As Pavlock argues, Milton
develops Eve's tragedy as a reenactment of Dido's. Significantly, Milton follows Virgil in presenting Eve as a temptation and as an object
of sympathy. But he conspicuously deletes any recollections of Dido's
sovereign independence.

her with pride. Her temptation is to become her Virgilian prototypes, a Venus or a Dido who distracts a man from his divine
destiny. By hailing her throughout the episode as "sovran Mis
tress," "Sovran of creatures" (9.611), Satan also tempts her to
become Elizabeth, or at least to acquire the royal dignities that
Spenser gave to such Elizabethan surrogates as Elisa, Belphoebe,
and Gloriana.[20] Much as Milton unmasks the classical gods as
demons-in-disguise, *Paradise Lost* exposes a diabolical narrative
hiding beneath his predecessors' tales of epic and monarchical
heroism. From Milton's perspective, both the Virgilian goddess
and the Spenserian virgin queen appear as belated, fallen versions
of Eve in their pretensions to divinity and sovereignty. The second chapter of Genesis, where a disguised devil lures an unsus-
pecting woman to destruction, emerges as the un-narrative behind
Virgil's and Spenser's compliments to their imperial sovereigns.

Milton completes his anti-feminist version of Venus' appearance by restoring the Virgilian gender ratios that Spenser
reversed in deference to Elizabeth. The moment Eve falls, her
temptation of Adam casts her as the dissembler luring a virtuous man into danger. When Adam sees her carrying a bough of
the forbidden tree, his response recalls but significantly revises
the Virgilian subtext. Like Aeneas, he attributes to her an awe-
some mixture of human and divine attributes: "O fairest of
Creation, last and best . . . / Holy, divine, good" (9.896, 899).
Now, however, the confusion rests in the speaker's mind rather
than in the woman's nature.[21] Eve is neither holy nor divine.
Adam retains enough moral intelligence to recognize her as a
creature, but his insistence that she is simultaneously holy and
divine suggests the willful self-delusion that brings about his
own fall.

In tempting Adam, Eve joins her epic predecessors in speaking with a voice that does not sound entirely human. The

20 For further discussion, see Albert C. Labriola, "Milton's Eve and the
    Cult of Elizabeth I," *Journal of English and Germanic Philology* 95
    (1996): 38–51; Katherine Eggert, *Showing Like a Queen: Female Author-
    ity and Literary Experiment in Spenser, Shakespeare, and Milton* (Phila-
    delphia: University of Pennsylvania Press, 2000), pp. 169–200.
21 As Quint notes, Adam overestimates Eve throughout the poem and
    ascribes "to her a perfection that verges on idolatry" (*Epic and Empire*,
    p. 293).

reader, if not Adam himself, recognizes Satan's influence in her words. Yet after the fall takes place, Eve seems to regain her full humanity when she repents her sin and begs Adam's forgiveness:

> Forsake me not thus, *Adam*! witness Heav'n
> What love sincere, and reverence in my heart
> I bear thee.   (10.914–16)

As critics have often noted, her repentance inspires Adam's suggestion that they subject themselves in a similar fashion to God.[22] If Eve first led Adam to sin and death, she also leads him to the repentance that enables his eventual salvation. Abandoning all pretensions to royalty and divinity, she resembles Venus solely in guiding the beleaguered sojourner toward refuge.

But as soon as Milton seems to have situated epic motivation decisively on a human plane, the exchange between the Father and the Son at the opening of Book XI reveals that the "humanity" of Eve's remorse is in part an illusion. Her apparently spontaneous repentance turns out to mark a final instance of the woman speaking with a more-than-mortal voice. In a passage that has long troubled the poem's readers as a sudden intrusion on the plane of human narrative, Milton asserts that divine influence prompts Adam and Eve's change of heart:

> See Father, what first fruits on Earth are sprung
> From thy implanted Grace in Man, these Sighs
> And Prayers, which in this Golden Censer . . .
> . . . I thy priest before thee bring.   (11.22–25)

If Eve's words once betrayed diabolic influence, they now reveal heavenly inspiration. "Prevenient Grace descending" (11.3) authorizes her repentance and Adam's ability to discover in it a model for his own renewed relationship with God. This unsettling reminder that Eve's words still occupy an ambiguous place between divine and human realms underscores the fact that Milton's own poem holds an ambiguous place between residual and emergent modes of narration. Despite the novelistic

---

22 See especially Kevis Goodman, "Wasted Labor? Milton's Eve, the Poet's Work, and the Challenge of Sympathy," *English Literary History* 64 (1997): 430–36.

directions of Adam and Eve's post-lapsarian conversations, they remain grounded in the epic bifurcation of natural and supernatural experience. Eve's failure to speak an entirely human discourse signals Milton's reluctance to renounce his classical inheritance for a more novelistic insistence on exclusive human agency.

Milton's commitment to classical antiquity persists in his final transformation of Aeneas' meeting with Venus, the Son's encounter with Satan in *Paradise Regained*. The Virgilian underpinnings are less apparent here than in *Comus* or *Paradise Lost* because Milton no longer follows his precursors in gendering the opposition between mortal and immortal realms as a conflict between male and female interlocutors. Satan voices the representational logic governing this departure from epic precedent in the poem's second hell council. When he informs the demons that the Son might prove harder to seduce than ordinary mortals, Belial urges him to entrap the Son in a virtual reenactment of the Virgilian scene that Milton had previously used as the basis for Adam's temptation:

> Set women in his eye and in his walk,
> Among daughters of men the fairest found;
>
> . . . .
>
> . . . more like to Goddesses
> Than Mortal Creatures, graceful and discreet,
> Expert in amorous Arts. . . . (2.153–58)

But what worked for Adam—and for Aeneas in Milton's more distant classical subtext—will not work for the Son. As Satan notes, the Son's mind is "too exalted" (2.206) to succumb to women, even ones with a goddess-like demeanor.

The Son's superiority to prior epic heroes provides an interior argument for Milton's own superiority to prior epic writers. If "Beauty stands / In th' admiration only of weak minds" (2.220–21), the Virgilian conflict between duty and sensual desire seems retrospectively trivial. By using "manlier" objects to "try [the Son's] constancy" (2.225–26), Milton creates a new, more morally compelling kind of epic temptation. The elusive woman whose voice betrays a secret kinship with divinity has no place in a poem whose lures are civic rather than erotic. Milton accordingly replaces the disguised goddess with a disguised devil who tempts the Son with masculine spectacles "of worth, of honour, glory, and popular praise" (2.227).

From the moment Satan first appears as an Archimago-like "aged man in Rural weeds," Milton seems to have abandoned Virgilian precedent (1.314). But something of the *Aeneid* still colors the exchange between a spirit "following, as seem'd, the quest of some stray Ewe" (1.315) and a human hero who immediately sees through the disguise: "Why dost thou then suggest to me distrust, / Knowing who I am, as I know who thou art"? (1.355–56). As the poem unfolds, Milton draws on a Neoplatonic tradition of allegorizing the *Aeneid* that provides striking analogues to the temptations narrated in Luke's Gospel. Cristoforo Landino, for example, anticipated Milton's substitution of the active, civic life for sensuality as the greatest temptation facing the hero in his quest for the highest good. In Landino's frequently reprinted commentary, the Carthage to which Venus directs Aeneas embodies nothing less than a temptation of kingdoms, the pursuit "of worth, of honour, glory, and popular praise" at the expense of the higher good of heavenly contemplation.

Despite *Paradise Regained*'s explicit rejection of the classics, Virgil's portrayal of the woman speaking with an immortal voice provided a departure point for Milton's reflections on the Incarnation. If the Son plays Aeneas to Satan's transgendered but still dissembling Venus, Satan also takes on Aeneas' role in trying to unravel the Son's identity as Son of God and Son of Mary:

> Who this is we must learn, for man he seems
> In all his lineaments, though in his face
> The glimpses of his Father's glory shine.   (1.91–93)

Time does not permit me to join Satan in pondering the mysteries of Milton's Christology.[23] I simply want to conclude by suggesting that Satan's Aeneas-like bewilderment before a being who seems to cross the boundary between human and divine experience travesties centuries of theological commentary. For the Milton of *De Doctrina Christiana*, who rejects the

---

23 For the best sustained account of the poem's Christology, see Barbara Kiefer Lewalski, *Milton's Brief Epic: The Genre, Meaning, and Art of Paradise Regained* (Providence: Brown University Press, 1966), pp. 133–63.

homoousianic fusion of mortal and divine essences as an absurdity, the Virgilian myth of a goddess who disguised herself as a human being without surrendering any of her divine attributes provided a compelling parody of prevalent but mistaken beliefs about Christ's two natures.

From the expulsion of the pagan gods in the "Ode on the Morning of Christ's Nativity" to the repudiation of classical learning in *Paradise Regained*, Milton explicitly contrasted Christian truths with the fictions of Greco-Roman antiquity. If we take him at his word, classical figuration survives in his poetry at best as an *integumentum* cloaking doctrines derived ultimately from Christian scripture. But the persistent presence of the Virgilian Venus even in his most assertively anti-classical poetry suggests that pagan fictions played a greater role in shaping his moral and theological imagination than either Milton himself or his later readers have dared to admit. The old gods and their interactions with mortals haunt even his thinking about such seemingly Christian issues as the nature of grace and the Incarnation. By listening more carefully to his poetry's pagan echoes, we may think of him less as a poet whose fictions begin in theology and more as one whose theology begins in fictions.

In each episode, a male figure characterizes a female figure as immortal. This chart shows how different writers develop the polarities of male/female, mortal/immortal, sincere/deceptive identities.

Homer

| Deceptive, Immortal Female | Deceptive, Mortal Male |
| CIRCE | ODYSSEUS |

Virgil

| Deceptive, Immortal Female | Sincere, Mortal Male |
| VENUS | AENEAS |

Tasso

Deceptive, Mortal Female ARMIDA	Sincere, Mortal Male RINALDO
Sincere, Inspired, Mortal Male PIERO	Sincere, Repentant, Mortal Male RINALDO

Spenser

Deceptive, Mortal Male BRAGGADOCCHIO	Sincere, Quasi-immortal Female BELPHOEBE

Milton, COMUS

Deceptive, Immortal Male COMUS	Sincere, Mortal Female LADY

Milton, PARADISE LOST

Eve's Fall, Book Nine:

Deceptive, Immortal Male SATAN	Sincere, [Mortal] Female EVE

Adam's Fall, Book Nine:

Deceptive, Mortal Female EVE	Sincere, [Mortal] Male ADAM

Adam and Eve's Regeneration,
Book Ten:

Sincere, Mortal Female EVE	Sincere, Mortal Male ADAM

Adam and Eve's Regeneration,
Book Eleven:

Sincere, Inspired Female EVE	Sincere, Mortal Male ADAM

Milton, PARADISE REGAINED

Deceptive, Immortal Male SATAN	Sincere, Mortal (?) Male SON
Sincere, Mortal (?) Male SON	Puzzled, Immortal Male SATAN

5

When to Stop Reading
The Faerie Queene

JEFF DOLVEN

How do you know when to stop reading *The Faerie Queene?* The title of Jonathan Goldberg's 1981 book *Endlesse Worke* seems like it could aptly name any number of studies of the last forty-five years or so (perhaps particularly the *magnum opus* of his predecessor James Nohrnberg, *The Analogy of The Faerie Queene*). Spenser may not be the only inexhaustible Renaissance poet, but there is something distinctively exhausting about reading his romance, a sense peculiar to him of wandering in a vast, interinanimated landscape within the bounds of which nothing can be understood without understanding everything. This almost paranoid response is the heightening—by means of sheer length, complexity, and an interlaced romance narrative—of an effect that Angus Fletcher describes as general to allegory, its construction of a *kosmos* or "total figure"[1] within which every part is implicated in the whole. Unlike a realist novel, which characteristically takes as a premise the selection of details out of an implicitly indifferent larger world, an allegory (on this account) wholly orders and constitutes its world. This is its contract with the reader, its promise of system or, failing that, at least of conspiracy: there is nothing left outside it that could be inside, nothing inside that is irrelevant, and nothing that is merely ordinary. Having articulated the contract this way, however, I want to take the two terms I have just excluded—irrelevance and ordinariness—and make an essay at describing the limits, or at least some limits, of reading *The Faerie Queene.* Always in some sense reading itself, the poem also develops ways of figuring doubts about that interminable project, doubts particularly about the relation between reading and virtuous action. At these moments it entertains the idea that what may save us—characters and readers—is a kind of metaphorical putting down the book.

1 Angus Fletcher, *Allegory: The Theory of a Symbolic Mode* (Ithaca: Cornell University Press, 1964), p. 85.

It will already be apparent that the concept of allegory I am adopting here is more Fletcher's than, say, Paul De Man's: I will talk in terms of daemons and the spaces they transgress, rather than about the rhetoric of temporality.[2] This means assuming the general integrity of the project of transcendental reference that Spenserian allegory advertises. I do so not because I take allegorical bivalence to be an adequate theory of meaning for general purposes: it disintegrates quickly for us in the solvents of deconstruction or ordinary language philosophy. It is rather because I am interested here in the poem's projected understanding of its own intelligibility, and how it may stage failures of that intelligibility not as a universal and inevitable condition but as particular events that we may learn to recognize and perhaps categorize. Understanding what Walter Benjamin describes as the "ruins"[3] of allegory means investing something in the dream of their former wholeness. Such an investment allows us to see that *The Faerie Queene* can be every bit as fearful — or weary — of that wholeness as it is of the mode's disintegration.

Taking the allegory at its word, then, exposes impasses that are staged within the poem's own myths of reading. These are moments when the interpreter's sword halts above the text: not only interpretive difficulties, but crises in the possibility of reading. "Irrelevance" I will use to describe occasions when aspects of the allegory that typically interact in significant ways — in particular, characters and houses — fail to mean anything to one another, when the unified *kosmos* seems to split into what we might think of as distinct and mutually

2 Ibid., p. 207, "The meaning constituted by the allegorical sign can then consist only in the *repetition* (in the Kierkegaardian sense of the term) of a previous sign with which it can never coincide, since it is of the essence of this previous sign to be pure anteriority. . . . renouncing the nostalgia and the desire to coincide, it establishes its language in the void of this temporal difference." De Man, "Rhetoric of Temporality," *Blindness and Insight*, 2d ed. (Minneapolis: University of Minnesota Press, 1983), values allegory for its acknowledgment of this difference, which he understands the Romantic "symbol" — with its ideal of the identify of signifier and signified — to mystify and deny.

3 Walter Benjamin, *The Origin of German Tragic Drama*, trans. John Osborne (London: Verso, 1998), p. 178.

unenlightening allegories. "Ordinariness" identifies an opposite phenomenon, the inarticulate detail and its consequences, the apparent lapse out of allegory altogether into the everyday. The latter I will pursue with special reference to the ubiquitousness of punishment as an anchor of the moral allegory; but irrelevance first.

Irrelevance

The word "irrelevance" will remind Spenserians of an argument from Harry Berger's pioneering study *The Allegorical Temper*, where he introduced the phrase "conspicuous irrelevance." His aim was to show how passages of *The Faerie Queene* that appear to be mere ornament — where the narrative is conspicuously pushed aside by what he called the larger "poetic action," be it descriptive or allusive or mythographic — in fact function as "nodal points of meaning, moments in which the larger significance of the narrative is compressed, illuminated, altered."[4] Nothing about the poem, in short, is really irrelevant: where it seems most distracted, it is often thinking hardest. The close readings sponsored by this claim made the vastnesses of Spenser's romance safe for the New Criticism. In revisiting his term I want to explore another kind of irrelevance, without performing the reversal — irrelevant to superrelevant — that Berger carries off.

Let us imagine for a moment what Spenser never gives us, an ideal book of *The Faerie Queene*. Such a book unfolds its titular virtue for the reader while preparing its hero, who labors under the sign of that virtue, to exemplify it in the action of the final cantos. The business of the intervening quest is to explore some of the characteristic errors and obstacles that might impede the realization of that virtue, and suggest strategies for overcoming them. The ultimate end is knowledge, indeed self-knowledge: an ever-higher integration of the *materia poetica* that will redeem the confusions of a fallen world and allow for a new clarity of moral judgment. (This is more or less the evolutionary dynamic Berger proposes for the whole poem in his later essays, though he stops short — and takes Spenser's strength to lie not least in stopping short — of forecasting a

4 Harry Berger, Jr, *The Allegorical Temper* (New Haven: Yale University Press, 1957), p. 133.

final reconciliation of its perpetual *discordia concors*.[5]) In this ideal book the reader's understanding and that of the hero converge in the completion of the quest. It might be objected that it is a category mistake to speak of an allegorical agent's self-knowledge, but one might argue in response that there is a Platonic version of ideal knowledge-as-action that such an agent is ideally suited to embody, or enact. If to know the good is to do it, we might be forgiven for inferring that an agent who does good univocally must be perfect in his self-knowledge; in our own doubts and inward blindnesses we are only striving toward that pure, unreflexive purposiveness. Such assumptions ascribe to the poem a teleology that we moderns might as well call Hegelian, developing toward an ideal of self-consciousness somehow shared by hero, text, and reader. Such a *telos* is consonant with a persistent strain in Spenser criticism that describes *The Faerie Queene* as a mimesis of thinking, or even as a mind itself. For Isabel MacCaffrey the poem is "a model of the mind's life in the world"[6]; Gordon Teskey calls it "a heuristic instrument for exciting the mind to activity."[7] Perhaps we do not read the poem so much as think it; realizing the poem's spectacular interrelatedness in our own mind is an exemplary integration of consciousness.

This account represents Spenser as a kind of Neoplatonic idealist, dedicated to the perfection of what James Nohrnberg calls the "duodecimal Arthur," the hero whose summary of the

---

5 Berger describes this dynamic concord as a progressive force for Spenser, applied not only to psychic but to cultural and historical development; a movement (quasi-Hegelian) from consciousness to self-consciousness. As examples he cites the "amorphous or polymorphous chaos" (Harry Berger, Jr, "The Spenserian Dynamics," *Revisionary Play* [Berkeley: University of California Press, 1988], pp. 19–35, 31) in which Book Three begins, and its gradual stabilization of elemental, sexual, and psychic contraries. It is a poem of *evolution*: "In spite of Spenser's frequent interest in depicting interruptions, failures, countermovements, and counter-statements (such as the myth of decline from golden antiquity), this evolutionary model remains fundamental in his thought, at least as a theoretical ideal that eros at all levels of existence tries to actualize" (p. 27).

6 Isabel MacCaffrey, *Spenser's Allegory: The Anatomy of Imagination* (Princeton: Princeton University Press, 1976), p. 6.

7 Gordon Teskey, *Allegory and Violence* (Ithaca: Cornell University Press, 1996), p. 99.

private and the public virtues "in his person, after that hee came to be king" (737) is projected by the "Letter to Raleigh."[8] The poem as we have it may balk such a scheme in uncountable ways, but the dream haunts its extant six-and-some books like Arthur's fleeting vision of the Faerie Queene herself. Even in its nightmare form, as a broken promise, it has a remarkable syncretic power. When the *telos* is obscured by the wandering wood there remains a pervasive sense of conspiracy, spurred by the doublings and parodies that wire episodes of the poem together across or in spite of narrative or obvious causal sequence. Relevance in the poem may be pursued in a spirit of syncretic confidence or of paranoia, but the practical effect is similar: keep reading, keep connecting, keep interpreting. Be bold, be bold, be bold. Then again, as every reader of the poem knows, this triple exhortation in the House of Busirane is qualified by a caution: "Be not too bold" (*The Faerie Queene*, ed. A. C. Hamilton [London: Longman, 1977], 3.11.54). It is this episode that I want to read as a case study in how the poem constructs irrelevance in the midst of its own intense and programmatic (if often dark) interrelation.

What is Britomart to the House of Busirane, or the House of Busirane to her? The Knight of Chastity ends up in its precincts because she pledges to help the hapless Scudamour recover his beloved Amoret from the wizard who has imprisoned her. It has three parts: a room lined with Ovidian tapestries, depicting mostly mortals raped by gods, at the far end of which stands an idol of Cupid; a room of "monstrous formes" (3.11.51) in metal frieze, festooned with the arms of warriors felled by Cupid; and finally the chamber where Busirane tortures Amoret, from which once a day Cupid's procession issues forth. Thomas Roche's reading of the episode — itself departing from C. S. Lewis — has been generative for many subsequent critics. He takes the varieties of antierotic propaganda Britomart encounters to be "an objectification of Amoret's fear of sexual love in marriage," though at the same time he insists that the description is mediated "through the eyes of Britomart."[9] Taken all together the compound space represents the

8 James Nohrnberg, *The Analogy of the Faerie Queene* (Princeton: Princeton University Press, 1976), pp. 39–42.

9 Thomas Roche, Jr, *The Kindly Flame* (Princeton: Princeton University Press, 1964), pp. 77, 75.

sorts of anxieties that could derail the Knight of Chastity from a quest that can only be fulfilled in marriage (a marriage that has the highest dynastic stakes for the poem as a whole). Harry Berger more or less follows this line while ascribing greater agency to Busirane himself as the spectacle's architect: "in showing Britomart what and how Amoret suffers, Busirane tries to dissuade both from their promised futures."[10] This sense of the house as a particularly apt test for the knight — or apt manifestation of her virtue — is an assumption that has become widespread, and indeed it is the assumption most native to the poem.[11] The two, house and guest, must be made for one another.

The first challenge that this line of interpretation encounters is that Britomart herself conspicuously does not recognize it. If we see the tapestries through Britomart's eyes, over nineteen stanzas her reaction is never once described: the mix of moralizing and delectation in the narrator's tone seems to be independent of the character whose physical progress from one tapestry to the next ostensibly strings the images together. This tacit disengagement becomes explicit when she comes to the idol of Cupid at the chamber's far end. She pays attention, but to no obvious effect:

> That wondrous sight faire *Britomart* amazed,
> Ne seeing could her wonder satisfie,
> But euer more and more vpon it gazed,
> The whiles the passing brightnes her fraile senses dazed.
>
> (3.11.49)

---

10 Harry Berger, Jr, "Busirane and the War Between the Sexes: An Interpretation of *The Faerie Queene* III.xi–xii," *Revisionary Play* (Berkeley: University of California Press, 1988), pp. 172–94.

11 See, for example, MacCaffrey, *Spenser's Allegory*, p. 112, John Watkins, *The Specter of Dido: Spenser and Virgilian Epic* (New Haven: Yale University Press, 1995), pp. 171–74. For a nearly opposite reading see Lauren Silberman's *Transforming Desire: Erotic Knowledge in Books III and IV of The Faerie Queene* (Berkeley: University of California Press, 1995), p. 66, where she treats the house as an interpretive contest between the authority of poet (Busirane) and reader (Britomart): "By imprisoning Amoret in the Masque of Cupid, Busirane attempts to assert the power of the poet to be supreme arbiter of meaning. By thwarting his attempt, Britomart reaffirms the view of allegory as a shared enterprise figured by the hermaphroditic embrace."

This combination of avid spectatorship and incomprehension is repeated several times, with the "be bold" legends ("she oft and oft it ouer-red, / Yet could not find what sence it figured" [3.11.50]; "That much she muz'd, yet could not construe it"; "whereto though she did bend / Her earnest mind, yet wist not what it might intend" [3.11.54]) and again with the spectacle of the next room ("beholding earnestly" she "Did greatly wonder ne could satisfie / Her greedy eyes with gazing a long space" [3.11.53]). John Watkins shrewdly notes the Virgil lurking privily under all of this Ovid: Britomart's reverie recalls Aeneas before the murals of Troy in Carthage.[12] Spenser's metaphors of feeding and his language of wonder perhaps both originate there: Aeneas "feasts his soul on the unsubstantial picture [*animum pictura pascit inani*]" and sees "wonderful things [*miranda*]" (*Virgil*, trans. H. R. Fairclough, 2 vols. [Cambridge: Harvard University Press, 1994], 1.464, 1.494). *The Faerie Queene* recombines the two to define the kind of reading taking place, or not taking place, in Busirane's house. Wonder, Aristotle claims influentially in his *Rhetoric*, is the beginning of understanding.[13] It is the open-mouthed, exhilarating blankness of confronting something for which we have no categories; it becomes understanding (and ceases being marvelous) as we assimilate its novelty to our existing, and ideally adapting, structures of knowledge. Hence it is one affective sign of what I am calling irrelevance — though its very intensity may suggest that an unexpected relevance awaits when it is overcome. The problem for Britomart is that she seems to idle at that threshold, feeding herself continuously without digesting anything. She is a hedonist of what ought to be a merely propaedeutic thrill. It may be that Spenser is pointing to a mode of misreading his poem, for wonder is also an affect commonly associated with romance as a pleasure that threatens to be sufficient unto itself.[14]

12 Watkins, *Specter*, pp. 170–74.
13 Aristotle, *The Basic Works of Aristotle*, ed. Richard McKeon (New York: Random House, 1941), *Rhetoric*, 1371a31–b10; on Renaissance ideas of wonder and the Aristotelian tradition see James Biester, *Lyric Wonder* (Ithaca: Cornell University Press, 1997), pp. 1–66.
14 Biester, *Lyric Wonder*; on the debate over wonder in Italian criticism of the *romanzo* (much better developed than in England), see Bernard Weinberg, *A History of Literary Criticism in the Italian Renaissance* (Chicago: University of Chicago Press, 1961), ii.1050–55.

Of course, Britomart's ignorance of the meaning of her surround could count decisively against its "relevance" to her only in that perfect poem where the hero's and the reader's understandings must converge. *The Faerie Queene* is not such a poem; unresolved dissonance between these perspectives is one of its characteristic devices.[15] There are, however, also other grounds for challenging the seasoned reader's reflexive quest for Britomart's implication in Busirane's designs. We might begin with the tapestries. They depict the monstrous, painful, and debasing shapes the gods take in their pursuit of mortal women. At first, there is some attention to the subjectivity of these women, especially an enigmatic Leda who seems to share a smile with the onrushing swan.[16] But the emphasis in everything that follows is on Cupid's triumphs over the gods, all of them male (save Venus—"ne did he spare . . . His owne deare mother" [3.11.44] — with whom no particular story is associated). The boy god again and again asserts himself over his older brothers. The second chamber's bearing on Britomart is even more tenuous, filled as it is with the spoils of Cupid's victories over "mighty Conquerours and Captaines strong" (3.11.52). One might argue that because Britomart has adopted masculine armor for her quest—a metamorphosis of sorts—she is the proper audience for an ekphrastic lecture on the violence and humiliations of male desire. But still the rhetorical focus seems misplaced, for the room's ironies are pointed at leaders of men and conquerors of land rather than at solitary questers like the Knight of Chastity.

15 MacCaffrey, *Spenser's Allegory*, p. 102, "The fact that a character's experience occurs in a particular setting and a particular pattern that is allusive *need not* (and ordinarily *does* not) signify its dramatic meaning in the character's consciousness." Susanne Wofford offers a sterner version in *The Choice of Achilles: The Ideology of Figure in the Epic* (Stanford: Stanford University Press, 1992), p. 259, "The Faerie Queene affirms that the quest endows the lives of its principal protagonists with meaning, yet consistently shows, as we have begun to see with Arthur, that this quest does not change the defining conditions of action or lift the mortal limitations that prevent the fuller understanding essential for the moral life as the poem defines it."

16 "She slept, yet twixt her eyelids closely spyde, / How towards her he rusht, and smiled at his pryde" (3.11.32). Does Jove smile? Does Leda? Do both, in a conspiracy of unrefused ravishment?

This project of disentanglement would seem to reach its limit at the masque that processes through the second room while Britomart watches from the shadows. If the tapestries and reliefs ridicule men who have become slaves to love, surely Cupid's parade — traditionally read as the course of a rash love affair from Fancy and Desire to Reproach, Repentance, and Shame — is meant for a woman's eyes. But perhaps we should take literally Kenneth Gross's clever suggestion that the pageant is "all antimasque."[17] The backstage horror of the third room is not the intended end: the masque proper may be yet to come, waiting on Amoret's surrender. Busirane is after all not another one of *The Faerie Queene*'s rapist knights, a single-minded paynim: the spells and tortures he inflicts on Amoret are "all perforce to make her him to loue" (3.12.31). This is neither simple sexual desire, nor any recognizable kind of mutual love. Perhaps what Busirane is seeking, almost like King Lear, is some kind of more or less public profession. This would make sense of the House of Busirane as a grand gesture in the game of love as male rivalry. Errant visitors to its completed form would ultimately pass through its lessons in erotic tyranny and humiliation, view an antimasque exposing the suffering their attentions usually visit on women, and finally confront a masque proper — yet to be constructed — showing Busirane triumphant in his marriage to Amoret. This would make the sorcerer a sinister master of the turn from courtly to romantic love that C. S. Lewis described as the subject of these cantos: he wants Amoret's *consent*, and he wants it because this ideal of marriage represents the most thorough victory over rival lovers, and over Cupid himself.[18] It is a strategic perversion of the dream of mutuality. Britomart just happens to stumble into the whole enterprise before it is open for business.

This last turn is obviously the most tendentious. It solves, I would argue, some durable puzzles in an episode that has attracted more than its share of commentary; it also implies an

---

17 Kenneth Gross, *Spenserian Poetics* (Ithaca: Cornell University Press, 1985), p. 164.
18 In telling the story of a shift from courtly love to romantic love and marriage that is the subject of *The Allegory of Love* (Oxford: Clarendon Press, 1936), p. 298, C. S. Lewis takes Spenser to be "not so much part of my subject as one of my masters or collaborators."

investment in narrative contingency—what would happen if—that the poem does not always warrant.[19] Even if Busirane's dream house remains a matter for speculation, however, the combination of Britomart's ostentatious imperviousness and the oddly misdirected rhetoric of the house itself, the obscurity of its address, raises the question of whether she really belongs there. And if she does not—if this is truly a case of mutual irrelevance, or rather the staging of irrelevance— what would *that* mean? For however inarticulate and unarticulated Britomart may be in these cantos, her success is straightforward. She accomplishes the obvious goal of liberating Amoret with uncommon dispatch and efficiency, and with none of the repeated self-overcomings that mark the last cantos of the previous two books (Red Cross falling and rising again, Guyon resisting temptation after temptation). Perhaps this is the point: she succeeds precisely because she understands nothing, recognizes nothing, learns nothing. Instruction as it is represented in *The Faerie Queene* is always some kind of self-diagnosis or critique; readers in the poem are always reading about themselves. Understanding itself seems to be a disabling recognition of unfitness and impediment. The key to success, perhaps, is not reading at all.

This is not to say that Britomart's untutored instincts are altogether irreproachable. Her wrath kindles immediately at the sight of Busirane torturing Amoret, and she strikes him so mightily "that to ground / He fell halfe dead" (3.12.34). Another stroke would finish the job, but Amoret hastily explains that her torments will end only if the enchanter lives to undo them. The knight stays her hand while Busirane begins "backe

---

19 The strongest reproach to imagining as I do here that *The Faerie Queene* gives us a fictional world within which cause and effect, narrative consistency, even counterfactuals are meaningful—whether they are upheld or violated—remains Paul Alpers's *The Poetry of* The Faerie Queene (Princeton: Princeton University Press, 1967) with its fundamentally rhetorical conception of Spenser's art. In some ways his conception operates harmoniously with those scenes where I diagnose irrelevance; but of course I am dependent on the tenacity of narrative for the interest of my claims. I am not prepared to accept Alpers's account of the poem as a whole, but I do believe that in a poem that is constantly playing with the *kinds* of reading it solicits, Alpers's cautions and antidotes have recently been underexploited.

to reuerse" his charms: "Full dreadfull things out of that bale-full booke / He red, and measur'd many a sad verse . . . And her faire lockes vp stared stiffe on end, / Hearing him those same bloudy lines reherse" (3.12.36). It is clear that he is read-ing poetry ("verses," "lines"), indeed doing what readers of *The Faerie Queene* are forever asked to do, reading the poem back-ward in order to make a "perfect hole" (3.12.38)—as the recovered Amoret is described—out of its scattered materials. Britomart's sword hangs above this scene of reading as an emblem of inaction and bafflement, and when she leaves the house Spenser tells us, in a perverse aside, that she is "much dismayd" to see the "glory" of the first two chambers "quite decayd" (3.12.42).[20] She is protected from understanding by an irrelevance constructed on both sides: the obliquity of the house's rhetorical address to her, and her own unconquerable wonder. Rather than making her unsuccessful there, this frac-ture in the poem's *kosmos* is the condition of her curious tri-umph. She is undistracted, uncompromised, unenlightened. I do not want to argue—it would be ridiculous to do so—that the relation between the two, place and character, is therefore somehow uninterpretable. But the poem seems to propose the breakdown of expected interplay as a particular limit of reading. Commentary on the episode that treats Britomart's victory as a further unfolding of her cardinal virtue—even accounts that emphasize the possibility, or danger, that chastity is purely negative—risks missing how she is enabled by being somehow beside the point, by the fact that nothing happens to her. What does this have to teach but the prudence of not reading?

Ordinariness

What I have been trying to describe by the term "irrelevance" is a rift in allegory: two aspects or elements of the fiction, each bearing allegory's outward limbs and flourishes, whose failure to interact when the plot brings them together questions the

20 This is the moment that transfixes Hamlet in the story of Pyrrhus' rampage (2.2.480–82), and that Aeneas must overcome when he unleashes the tempest of his wrathfulness on Turnus (12.939). In both cases it is preparatory (ultimately, in Hamlet's case) to violent and decisive action. Here Britomart's only role is to stand by and threaten.

integrity of the system and *figures* the dead end of reading itself. The second kind of limit or caution to reading has to do with the faltering of allegory, with lapse rather than with internal conflict or contradiction. For this I want to venture the term "ordinariness." It is a familiar move in the game of allegory to disrupt its mediation by an irruption of the noumenal, for example Red Cross's vision of the New Jerusalem or Arthur's night with the Faerie Queene, or by a collapse into mere matter, as in such jokes as the deflation of Orgoglio or Disdaine's severed limb becoming a "lumpe of durt" (6.8.16). I am after something different, something struggling to escape dependence on the way allegory carves up the world: a straying into the everyday, even something like realism. Once again this is not a matter that can be defined with categorical rigor, for how could we ever find a moment in *The Faerie Queene* that definitively exempts itself from allegorical reading, or definitively represents the everyday?[21] But Spenser nonetheless has distinctive ways of raising these as problems to think or worry about. The approach I will follow here is by way of punishment, or rather what might be called "unpunishment." There is a deep connection in the poem between punishment and allegory itself. What happens when the prosecutorial rigor of the mode abates—when a character seems to sin against its virtues and gets away with it—will help us see other ways in which *The Faerie Queene* seeks to shrug off the burden of its own didactic authority.

I have written elsewhere about the matter of punishment and allegory: the element of emblem-making in public justice's display of the criminal; how the decorum or "poetic justice" of a particular penalty (for instance, cutting out a slanderer's tongue) might be confused after the fact with evidence of guilt; how allegory's radical contraction of identity—think of the inmates of Dante's hell, condemned to testify endlessly to the sin that has become their cardinal attribute—makes the mode itself into a punishment.[22] I might have added there the simple problem for

---

21 Teskey, *Allegory and Violence*, p. 3, reminds us of the distinction between a text interpreted allegorically and one written as allegory (the latter of which "contains instructions for its own interpretation").

22 See my article "Spenser's Sense of Poetic Justice," *Raritan* 21.1 (2001): 127–40; on allegory, punishment, and Dante see also Teskey's *Allegory and Violence*, pp. 25–31.

a moral allegory of creating a crime-emblem that does not inter-polate any element of criticism or rebuke: such an allegory will be dependent on events in the narrative to identify it as taboo, meanwhile flourishing as a kind of unregulated advertisement for its own depravity. The most ostentatiously allegorical epi-sodes in the poem embody the association with punishment most clearly, as for example the self-revenging sins that parade out of Lucifera's castle. In other cases the plot maneuvers an evil character into a condition of suffering and unfreedom that is rec-ognizable as the fullest (or most decisive) realization of his nature: we never see Pyrochles more clearly or understand him better than when his name is explained by the flames of Furor's provocation. This is all to say that it is easy to associate the func-tion of allegory with an emblematic justice, whether that justice is imposed as we watch or is always already a condition of repre-sentation. It is accordingly disorienting when the mechanism of punishment fails to operate: we may be led to ask if something fundamental in the text's representative mode has changed.

A brief example from the neighborhood of Busirane's House will serve to illustrate unpunishment's unsettling effect. After Britomart's encounter with the miser Malbecco the narrative digresses to follow the misadventures of his wife Hellenore, a Helen seduced away by her parody Paris, the knight Paridel. Paridel loves her and leaves her, and for a few lines she seems destined to follow the tragic path toward shame and death that is laid out by the masque in Canto Twelve. In short order, however, she falls among a tribe of satyrs:

> Her vp they tooke, and with them home her led,
> With them as housewife euer to abide,
> To milke their gotes, and make them cheese and bred,
> And euery one as commune good her handeled.   (3.10.36)

Malbecco disguises himself as a goat to try to win her back, only to discover her in the arms of an energetic satyr: "Nine time he heard him come aloft ere day . . . But yet that nights ensample did bewray / That not for nought his wife them loued so well" (3.10.48). His pleas to return are "refused at one word" (3.10.51) and at daybreak the satyrs run him off. Helle-nore's place in the larger allegorical scheme of the book is clear enough: if Malbecco's hoarding represents the perils of love-as-possession, then this is its opposite, a kind of erotic communism in which she is a freely shared good. But Malbecco is subject to one of the poem's most detailed episodes of allegory-as-punishment, ultimately so consumed and reduced by "selfe-murdering thought" (3.10.57) that he is rechristened *Gealosie*. Hellenore, on the other hand, seems to settle blithely into her new life: it is not without allegorical articulations (the "nine times" as a prophecy, or parody, of fertility) but it seems exempted from judgment. Going beyond the witty and provisional triumphs of the *fabliau*, this episode ends—if it really ends—in a new society with its own rhythms of work and pleasure, apparently perpetual, free and undaemonic.[23] When Malbecco laments "th'vnkindnesse of his *Hellenore*" (3.10.45) his word acknowledges that it is almost as though she has become a different species, no longer kin to the poem's humans, faeries, or, more to the point, its allegories.

Why call this "ordinariness"—why not simply say that Hellenore has become an allegory of natural love?[24] I borrow my sense of the term very loosely from Stanley Cavell, who has carried it from Austin and Wittgenstein backward to Shakespeare (as well as to many other literary and philosophical places). Ordinariness on his account is to be understood over and against skepticism, as the acknowledgement of what skepticism denies: the accessibility of the world to knowing and feeling. Epistemology itself, arising from doubts about our ability to know, is accordingly regarded as a strategy for evading what otherwise we would have no excuse but to allow. As Cavell writes, "The power of this recognition of the ordinary for philosophy is bound up with the recognition that refusing or forcing the order of the ordinary"—turning either to skep-

---

23 On Hellenore's escape as Chaucerian *fabliau* see Watkins, *Specter*, pp. 163–67.

24 Nohrnberg, *Analogy*, p. 602, reads the episode this way: "An intimation of this kind of fulfillment is present in the story of Hellenore and the satyrs. A relation of 'natural' love is not ordinarily accessible to waking experience, where sexuality does not remain morally neutral, like stimulus and response, but either degrades or elevates"; see also p. 642. I do not disagree, but I want to explore the consequences of this "fulfillment" for the allegory: in a poem underwritten by the quest of Arthur for the Faerie Queene it may be that any fulfillment may threaten (especially threaten to obviate) the mode.

ticism or to metaphysics—"is a cause of philosophical emptiness (say avoidance) and violence."[25] I want to position his
term not against skepticism but against allegory itself, which is
to say, I want to consider allegory as a species of skepticism,
refusing the order of the ordinary, a mediating language
intended not so much to access the truth as to keep the world
at bay. At moments such as Hellenore's idyll with the satyrs the
repressed sufficiency of the world threatens the conceptual
architecture of the poem and everything it knows about virtue
with just this kind of adequacy of experience. The episode is
not an *allegory of* ordinariness. (Whatever that would be: for us,
a man in a gray flannel suit, face and fingertips white and
smooth? Which would be anything but ordinary.) It is the representation of pleasures that do not mean but simply are. The
immediacy of eros contributes to this dismantling; the everydayness of domestic routine—milking the goats and baking
the bread—helps too.[26] Of course, as soon as we identify such
a moment, the estrangement of representation itself intrudes,
and both eros and the domestic return to us as tropes, *topoi*. (If
it seems peculiar to speak of tropes of ordinariness, these are
the wages of speaking of ordinariness at all.) But even if there
is something ultimately paradoxical about representing the
ordinary, the fantasy is established. Hellenore is somehow
beyond or beneath the reach of allegory: going about her
chores and her sports, she seems to realize Hazlitt's notorious
remark that if readers "do not meddle with the allegory, the
allegory will not meddle with them."[27]

To understand the implications of this alternative mode, or
lapse, for *The Faerie Queene*, I want to turn to Book Six, the
chief analogue in the 1596 triptych to Book Three in 1590.[28]
Prince Arthur has a particularly large role there—Arthur who

25 Stanley Cavell, "Declining Decline," *The Cavell Reader*, ed. Stephen
   Mulhall (Cambridge: Blackwell, 1996), pp. 321–52, 322.
26 On the domestic, and particularly marriage, as a figuration of the
   ordinary see Cavell's book on the Hollywood comedy of remarriage,
   Pursuits of Happiness (Cambridge: Harvard University Press, 1981).
27 William Hazlitt, *The Complete Works of William Hazlitt*, ed., P. P. Howe,
   21 vols (London: J. M. Dent, 1930–34), v.38.
28 On such structural correspondences generally see, of course, Nohrnberg, *Analogy*, especially Chapter 5 (pp. 653–733) on the relation
   between Books One and Six.

is seemingly the least ordinary of the poem's characters, the most central to that grand, duodecimal order forecast in the "Letter to Raleigh." His particular antagonist in the middle cantos is the base knight Turpine, who feigns reformation when Arthur shames him for his cowardly conduct, then recruits two credulous young knights to pursue the prince into the forest. Arthur kills one and learns of Turpine's plan from the other; he sends the survivor back to lure the traitor to him. Then, unaccountably, he takes off his armor and falls asleep, "Loosely displayd vpon the grassie ground, / Possessed of sweete sleepe, that luld him soft in swound":

> Wearie of trauell in his former fight,
> He there in shade himselfe had layd to rest,
> Hauing his armes and warlike things vndight,
> Fearelesse of foes that mote his peace molest;
> The whyles his saluage page, that wont be prest,
> Was wandred in the wood another way,
> To doe some thing, that seemed to him best,
> The whyles his Lord in siluer slomber lay,
> Like to an Euening starre adorn'd with deawy ray.   (6.7.19)

The warning signals for the by-now-experienced reader are deafening: the echo of Red Cross at the fountain, "Pourd out in loosnesse on the grassy grownd" (1.7.7), the perils of sleep more generally, and what is well established in Book Six as the disastrous mistake of taking off your armor. Is this then an attitude of total mastery, the prince secure enough in strength and virtue to break the poem's rules with impunity? Or is it an unexpected vulnerability? As he sleeps the imagery that gathers around him seems almost protective. The dewy rays last fell on Chrysogone as she conceived Amoret and Belphoebe, her "wombe of Morning dew" (3.6.3) impregnated "Through influence of th'heauens fruitful ray" (3.6.6). The dews of the Garden of Adonis may be in play as well. It is a subtle prophecy of rebirth, and washed in these pure waters—like Red Cross drowned in the "dreame of deepe delight" (1.1.50) from which he will wake to slay the dragon—Arthur becomes for a moment the king of the Tudor mythology who slumbered centuries under the hills of Wales. *Rex quondam rexque futurus.* The evening star is also the morning star: allegory wheels above him like a guarantee of his millennial destiny.

There is, however, a countercurrent to this prophetic strain. As Arthur sleeps the salvage man is wandering, if not aimlessly, then to no purpose the narrator bothers to discern. There may be no more offhanded line in the poem than "To doe some thing, that seemed to him best." This kind of wandering is what Arthur more than anything cannot do. He cannot just sleep, cannot just saunter off to do whatever seems best to him. The poem cannot be indifferent to his aims because he *is* the poem. This predicament makes some sense of the darker side of his repose. He has *laid* himself *to rest*, a funereal phrase, in the *shade*, this in spite of having summoned his enemy to the scene of his silver slumber. It is almost as though he wills—or prefigures?—his own death. This impulse to self-negation is a recurrent strain in Spenserian allegory, perhaps the extension of its relation to punishment (so often figured as some kind of self-punishment). Malbecco again is a paradigmatic instance: as he approaches the condition of pure Gealosie, he approaches, asymptotically, his own demise ("Yet can he neuer dye, but dying liues" [3.10.60]). The extent to which he suffers the idea he represents is the extent to which one might say he is still recalcitrantly human; the mercy of pure abstraction is denied him Arthur too suffers: melancholy from the outset, his career of courtesy in Book Six is marked by diminishing returns, and his brush with catastrophe in this episode is the final failure of the project of reforming Turpine. The cosmic imagery of rebirth gathered in the alexandrine cannot redeem his abdication from a sense of weary contempt for all the poem's counsels of prudence. It is as though he were trying to sleep off the allegory. The salvage man functions in this scene not only to wake him up, happening back just as Turpine arrives; he is also a kind of unsupervised or unregarded antithesis, a lapse into the ordinary that points up the prince's imprisonment. He is ordinary not because he is natural, or even because of the apparent everydayness, or at least unremarkableness, of what he gets up to in the forest (though this helps link him to other fleeting idylls of domesticity), but because the poem almost loses track of him, just as it lets Hellenore slip out of its didactic and punitive designs.

The pressure exerted here on the eschatological Arthur might be said to be figured on a larger scale in Book Six by its generic modulation into pastoral. *Otium* threatens the quest (where we can understand the quest as the narrative impulse to close the rift that defines allegory[29]). But *otium* is not ordinariness. It is too dialectical: its sports are over against labor, its idle songs against the prose of *negotium* or the hexameters of epic. The salvage man's amble is indifferent to either, and Arthur's sleep seems to be a longing for surcease from both—just sleep. What follows next is a strong indication of how deeply this negligent interlude undermines the poem's discipline. Arthur humiliates Turpine and strings him up by his heels "that all which passed by, / The picture of his punishment might see, / And by the like ensample warned bee" (6.7.27). Inverting him is the sort of schematic gesture—a fundamental, graphic trope— at the heart of emblematic allegory, a lesson against his treason and his usurpation of courteous knighthood. It is the minimal move in the game of allegorical punishment: we know because he is upside down that he has opposed himself to virtue, or at least to whatever order instituted the penalty. And Arthur as punisher is restored to that order, his blunt reprisal—after so many failed attempts at reform—a kind of rebuilding of allegory and his role in it from the ground up. In the meantime, we have glimpsed what happens when the poem relaxes its vigilance. When Red Cross falls asleep by the fountain, the consequences follow him for the rest of the book; Arthur goes unpunished, which is to say, his sleep doesn't seem to *mean anything* to what follows. Character and text figure one another's exhaustion. The temptation in middest of the race is not the erotic but the ordinary, and beyond that, even death.

Conclusion

After Arthur has finished with Turpine, he does not wander far before he encounters the penitent Petrarchan Mirabella. She is the center of a creaky allegorical procession constituted to punish her fatal disregard for her lovers; she rides an ass, attended by

---

29 See, e.g., David Lee Miller, *The Poem's Two Bodies* (Princeton: Princeton University Press, 1988), p. 4, with his account of how *The Faerie Queene* is "organized with reference to the anticipated-but-deferred wholeness of an ideal body, which serves to structure the text in a manner comparable to the use of a vanishing point to organize spatial perspective in drawing."

the giant Disdaine and the dwarf Scorne, and Timias, her
would-be rescuer, is led alongside "like a dog" (6.8.5). Arthur
deplores this shameful spectacle and makes short work of her
guardians, but when he stands above Disdaine to deliver the
second, terminal blow, Mirabella begs him to stay his hand.
The reminiscence of Amoret's desperate plea to Britomart is
unmistakable (one way, of course, in which that episode *is* relevant to the rest of the poem, its internal strategies of schism
notwithstanding). At the end of Book Three, however, the
enchanter reads from his books while Britomart suspends her
sword mutely and uncomprehendingly above him. In Book Six,
by contrast, it is Mirabella—the victim herself—who speaks,
and she not only tells her story but unfolds the emblematic
punishment to which Cupid's justice has consigned her:

> Here in this bottle (sayd the sory Mayd)
> I put the teares of my contrition,
> Till to the brim I haue it full defrayd:
> And in this bag which I behinde me don,
> I put repentaunce for things past and gon.
> Yet is the bottle leake, and bag so torne,
> That all which I put in, fals out anon.   (6.8.24)

Walter Benjamin writes that the allegorical figure carries "a
scroll in its mouth, which the observer was supposed to read
like a letter"[30]: Mirabella is a full participant in this regime,
reading her own motto and glossing her parts. Most remarkably, she refuses Arthur's offered rescue, choosing rather to
serve her term "Least vnto me betide a greater ill" (6.8.30).
She seems to be the final perfection of allegorical punishment.
Or then again, perhaps not quite: Malbecco-as-Gealosie suffers
the pains of his nature without abating his sin; Mirabella no
longer plays the part of the callous cruel-fair (her compassion
for Timias gives every impression that she has reformed—an
unusual, perhaps unique event in the books of 1596), but she
still pays the price for it. Moreover her punishment has the
quality of parody. Disdaine—wont to stand "on his tiptoes, to
seeme tall" (6.8.26)—loses his leg in the fight and has to be
propped up by Scorne in order for the whole apparatus to

30 Benjamin, *Origin*, p. 197.

hobble off at the episode's end. With its bags and bottles and dwarfs and giants it must be Allegory. And if Allegory (or its travesty) has exited, where are we then? I take this episode to be a kind of last, comic stand of the promises of the "Letter to Raleigh." *The Faerie Queene* often figures, critiques, even ridicules its own mode within itself, and having done that begs the question of what to call—and how to read—the rest of it. The two strategies that I have elaborated are only two ways of thinking about what it means to stand outside, or somehow between, what had promised to be the essence and the medium of the fiction.

I began by anticipating that these strategies would disappear under the scrutiny of a methodology that presumed allegory's structural incoherence. I have accepted a more stable account of the mode in order to distinguish such strategies from more general effects of, for example, deconstructive reading. But my intent is not therefore to dismiss the usefulness of those approaches. Among the glories of *The Faerie Queene* is that it is relentlessly attentive to the kinds of reading that may be brought to bear upon it. It solicits, rewards, confutes, and ridicules our methods by turn, playing them off one another with a sophistication that criticism will always be catching up to. None of our schools but has its part in the endless work. What I have tried to do here is to describe the consequences of allegiance to what I take to be a particularly prominent and tenacious set of assumptions about the *kosmos* of the poem. These consequences are impasses of two kinds: the failure of expected relation, a rift in allegory; and the lapse out of allegory into the everyday. The value of "irrelevance" and "ordinariness" as terms in practical criticism can only be measured by the number of further episodes, some of which I have suggested, where they have explanatory power. But together they also imply something about the nature of the poem as a whole. It is a work of such extraordinary internal complexity that it always threatens to come to nothing, or nothing beyond itself. Its wilderness of parody and qualification may be how Spenser chose to teach virtue, or perhaps more accurately, how he confronted the cultural imperative that he use poetry to teach virtue. But reading itself cannot be the extent of virtue's practice. *The Faerie Queene* is never finally ready to tell us how to live; it does, however, have ways of telling us to stop reading.

6

Satire and Epyllion: Hermaphroditic Forms

MATTHEW GREENFIELD

The term "antigenre" offers a useful although potentially mis-leading clue to the evolution of systems of genres. Picaresque, in Claudio Guillen's account, develops as an antigenre to romance, and the novel from *Don Quixote* onwards develops as an antigenre to picaresque.[1] Alastair Fowler adds that works like *Tristram Shandy*, *Ulysses*, and *Gravity's Rainbow* attack and invert the conventions of the novel; some of these experiments spawn new subgenres of the novel, while others retrospectively appear to be evolutionary dead ends, unrepeatable monstrosi-ties.[2] One can question the details of these narratives and still grant the point that the history of literary forms advances by a series of antagonisms, often against caricatured and over-simplified opponents. But sometimes two antagonistic genres will develop in parallel, in a curious symbiosis. Elizabethan verse satire frequently invokes Ovidian erotic narrative as its antagonist form, but the two genres often co-exist within the same book or even the same poem. In verse satire, the hybrid body of the hermaphrodite becomes an emblem of these uncomfortably intimate encounters between genres.

I

George Gascoigne's *Steel Glas* (1576) occupies a liminal posi-tion in the development of English satire. The poem is often said to be thoroughly and unimaginatively medieval, but it is in fact a strange hybrid of classical and medieval materials.[3] It

1 Claudio Guillen, *Literature as System: Essays Toward the Theory of Liter-ary History* (Princeton: Princeton University Press, 1971).
2 Alastair Fowler, "The Future of Genre Theory: Functions and Con-structional Types," *The Future of Literary Theory*, ed. Ralph Cohen (New York and London: Routledge, 1989), pp. 293–95.
3 Dismissals of the poem include Hugh Walker, *English Satire and Sati-rists* (New York: E. P. Dutton, 1925), pp. 62–63; and Angela Wheeler,

begins with an Ovidian myth about the origins of satire, an early example of what some critics now call the Elizabethan "epyllion" (little epic): a narrative poem based on an episode drawn from the *Metamorphoses*.[4] Examples include Marlowe's *Hero and Leander* and Shakespeare's *Venus and Adonis*. Like Ovid's poem, Elizabethan epyllia were typically playful, teasing the reader with interpretive difficulties as well as, often, with a narrative of deferred erotic release. Gascoigne follows his miniature epyllion with a specimen of the vernacular medieval genre we now call "estates satire" (its authors, when they labeled it at all, tended to call it "complaint"): it itemizes the vices of society, one profession at a time. The poem demonstrates at several points an uneasy consciousness of the deficiencies of complaint, distancing itself from the categories and techniques of the medieval genre. Although *Piers Plowman* makes a guest appearance in *The Steel Glas*, the poem's hybrid form reflects a conception of the function of literature entirely different from that of the plowman tradition.

The poem is spoken by Satira, the embodiment of satirical poetry. Satira begins her myth of origin with a curious assertion: "I n'am a man, as some do thinke I am, / (Laugh not good Lord) I am in dede a dame, / Or at the least a right Hermaphrodite" (143). Satira then narrates a history based on that of Procne, Tereus, and Philomela in Ovid's *Metamorphoses*. In Gascoigne's version, the Procne figure is Poesys, or lyric poetry, and Satira is her brother: at the beginning of the story, this Philomela figure is male. Poesys marries a Tereus-like foreign king named Vayne Delight and accompanies him back to his court, where he is attended by a group of courtiers like the vice figures of Skelton's morality play *Magnyfycence*: Gascoigne's courtiers have names like False Semblaunt, Flearing Flattery, Detraction, Deceite, Sym Swash, and False Witnesse. After a

---

English Verse Satire From Donne to Dryden: Imitation of Classical Models (Heidelberg: Carl Winter, 1992), p. 32.

4 I am using the term to refer to the Ovidian etiological narratives of the Elizabethans. Some critics use the word in other ways, and some suggest that the term is anachronistic and should be abandoned. For a discussion of the issues, see Elizabeth Story Donno's introduction to *Elizabethan Minor Epics* (New York: Columbia University Press, 1967), pp. 1–20.

few years have passed Poesys develops a desire to see her brother again, and Vayne Delight sails to her parents' home and returns with Satira. On the high seas, Vayne Delight becomes aroused by Satira's singing and rapes him. Vayne Delight tries to persuade Satira not to reveal the rape, but, finding him incorruptible, eventually cuts out his tongue "with Raysor of Restraynte" (146). In a transformation borrowed from another Ovidian tale, the story of Salmacis and Hermaphroditus, Satira becomes woman-like, forced to rely on tears rather than weapons to avenge herself. She sings with the stump of her tongue, "in corner closely cowcht, / Like Phylomene, since that the stately cowrts, / Are now no place, for such poore byrds as I" (146). Only intermittently is she permitted to answer the attacks of her enemies. Her androgyny reflects an association of masculinity with political agency: to be disenfranchised is to become feminine. Because the satirist has some limited power to respond to detractors, she retains some masculine characteristics. The body of the hermaphrodite emblematizes the poem's generic hybridity, its divided sense of its own function.

Unlike the polemics of the Wycliffites and the Tudor gospellers, *The Steel Glas* dwells obsessively on the poet's vulnerability and the frustration of his secular hopes. The poem envisions no apocalyptic destruction of the courtly vices: it situates its speaker in a world where defeat results in simple oblivion rather than a glorious martyrdom. Satira feels a vestigial impulse to correct vice wherever it might be found, but employs her song primarily for revenge and self-defense. The poem makes satire into a courtly genre, the twin or double of the erotic lyric with which Philomela was conventionally associated: "This worthy bird [the nightingale], hath taught my weary Muze, / To sing a song, in spight of their despight, / Which work my woe . . ." (143). When he published *The Steel Glas*, Gascoigne appended a poem called *The Complaynt of Phylomene; an Elegye compyled by George Gascoigne Esquire*. He also dedicated the poem to Lord Gray de Wilton, who later appeared in Book V of *The Faerie Queene* as Artegall. The story of the rape of Satira represents the poem's secular, courtly ambitions as the result of a fall from grace, a debilitating contamination by the very vices the poem attacks. The use of Ovid itself suggests the poet's implication in the pursuit of "Vayne Delight":

the Elizabethans associated Ovid with erotic writing, the "court" of Augustus, and the city of Rome, with all of its exotic pleasures. The parents of Gascoigne's Satira, "Playnedealing" and "Symplycitie," had lived in the countryside. They represent a literary mode impossible to practice at court, a mode that appears in only a cautious and compromised form in the estates satire that constitutes the body of the poem. Piers Plowman, for example, enters the poem but remains voiceless: "Stand forth good Peerce, thou plowman by thy name. . . . Behold him (priests) & though he stink of sweat / Disdaine him not. . . . Such clime to heaven, before the shaven crownes" (167–70). The poet invokes the apparition of the Wycliffite plowman but strips him of his aggressive evangelism. Rather than denouncing the priests or engaging them in dialogue, this Piers is passively displayed as an exemplar of humility, a simple representative of his estate.

Where the Wycliffite and their Tudor heirs set out to restructure society, *The Steel Glas* proposes only to reform the conduct of individuals, leaving the institutional shape of the church intact. The poem works to preserve a fixed social hierarchy, lamenting (in terms that anticipate the speech of Ulysses on "degree, priority, and place" in Shakespeare's *Troilus and Cressida*): "The country Squire, doth covet to be a Knight, / The Knight a Lord, the Lord an Erle or a Duke, / The Duke a King, the King would Monarke be, / And none content, with that which is his own" (153). The poem reflects an uneasy awareness, though, that inexorable social changes have created new professions and altered the old ones. Nobles, for example, no longer invariably profess arms: ". . . by the Knights . . . Is ment nomore, but worthy Soldiours / Whose skil in armes, and long experience / Should still uphold the pillers of the worlde. / Yet out of doubt, this noble name of Knight, may comprehend, both Duke, Erle, lorde, Knight, Squire, / Yea gentlemen . . ." (155). Gascoigne wrote during the century in which a new class of professional bureaucrats began to receive aristocratic titles, and when magnates gradually stopped leading bands of their own retainers to war. Over the course of the sixteenth century military activity became a less central feature of aristocratic identity.[5] *The Steel Glas* has no ready explanation

---

5 See Wallace T. MacCaffrey, *Elizabeth I: War and Politics,* 1588–1603

of the social function of those other, non-martial nobles. Similarly, Gascoigne explains that by "peasant" he means "he that labors any kind of way, / To gather gaines, and to enrich him selfe. . . . All officers, all advocates at lawe, / All men of arte . . ." (160). The medieval schema of the four estates — king, knight, priest, and peasant — no longer serves as an adequate description of the way society is organized. The schema may not ever have had much explanatory power, and in fact many medieval writers employed other schemata, with larger numbers of estates.[6] *The Steel Glas*, though, imagines a fall from simplicity, a complication and degeneration of the social structure. The poem attempts to preserve or restore that original simplicity, but it labors under the oppressive sense that its conceptual tools are inadequate.

The poem's central trope, the "steel glas," imagines a weaker disciplinary apparatus than that of prophecy. Unlike the works of the Wycliffites and the Tudor gospellers, Gascoigne's poem ignores the questions of faith, repentance, and interior experience in its focus on social conduct. The steel glass has two functions: it displays processions of exemplary figures from the past, and it gives the present age a harsh and accurate image of itself. Satira contrasts the steel glass with the "crystal glass," a flattering mirror that emblematizes what we would call ideology: "the glasing christal glasse / Doth make us thinke, that realmes and townes are rych / Where favor sways, the sentence of the law, / Where all is fish, that cometh to the net, / Where mighty power, doth over rule the right . . ." (150). The steel glass, Satira tells us, was bequeathed to her by Lucilius, the Roman poet whom Horace acknowledged as his predecessor in the writing of satire. Lucilius' work survives only in fragmentary quotations, so he constitutes more of a mythological progenitor than an actual stylistic model for Gascoigne. Horace characterized the techniques of Lucilius as crude and

---

(Princeton: Princeton University Press, 1992), esp. pp. 467–76; and Mervyn James, "English Politics and the Concept of Honour, 1485–1642," *Society, Politics, and Culture: Studies in Early Modern England* (Cambridge: Cambridge University Press, 1986), pp. 308–415.

6 See Jill Mann, *Chaucer and Estates Satire: The Literature of Social Classes and the General Prologue to* The Canterbury Tales (New York: Cambridge University Press, 1973), pp. 1–25.

claimed to have refined them, so Gascoigne's choice of Lucilius rather than Horace seems to have a polemical point: Gascoigne wanted to represent his own satire as rough and archaic, perhaps as a rebuke to the advocates of a more Latinate style. Elsewhere in his writing Gascoigne explained his homely and archaic diction as serving a linguistic nationalism:

Next unto this, I have always been of opinion, that it is not unpossible eyther in Poemes or in Prose to write both compendiously in our Englishe tongue. And therefore although I challenge not unto myselfe the name of an English poet, yet my reader may find oute in my writings, that I have more faulted in keeping of the olde English wordes (*quamvis iam obsoleta*) than in borrowing of other languages such Epithetes and Adjectives as smell of the Inkhorne.[7]

Although the parenthetical remark in Latin undermines the point of the passage, this is a fairly accurate characterization of Gascoigne's writing. *The Steel Glas*, though, manifests something less than a strident nationalism. The poem suggests that the English could learn from the simple virtue of the Moors: "How live the Mores, which spurne at glistring perle, / And scorne the costs, which we do hold so deare?" Without the benefit of Christianity, Gascoigne adds, the Moors already live "in better wise, / Than we" (153). Similarly, when the steel glass presents a series of exemplary figures, all of them come from classical rather than English history: "Behold behold, where Pompey comes before, / Where Manlius, and Marius insue, / Aemilius, and Curius I see . . ." (155). In the well-ordered state displayed by the steel glass, "al men feare, the scourge of mighty Jove. / Lo this (my lord) may well deserve the name, / Of such a lande, as milk and honey flowes" (150). Gascoigne uses the biblical imagery of the milk and honey of the promised land in an encomium to the Roman empire.

When Gascoigne temporarily abandons the persona of the hermaphroditic Satira, he presents himself as a repentant

---

7 From *The Epistle to the Reverend Divines*, cited in Ronald C. Johnson, *George Gascoigne* (New York: Twayne, 1972), p. 75. The Latin phrase in parentheses means "although now obsolete."

prodigal.[8] Looking into the steel glass, he sees his own image:
"An age suspect, bycause of youthes misdeedes, / A poets
brayne, possest with layes of love, / A Caesars minde, and yet
a Codrus might, / A Souldiours hart, supprest with feareful
doomes . . ." (149). After a long litany of failures, he concludes with a strange meditation on personal identity:

> And to be playne, I see my selfe so playne,
> And yet so much unlike that most I seemde,
> As were it not, that Reason ruleth me,
> I should in rage, this face of mine deface,
> And cast this corps, down headlong in dispaire,
> Bycause it is, so farre unlike it selfe.   (149)

Like the story of the rape of Satira, this passage has an Ovidian
sub-text, the story of Narcissus. Gascoigne describes himself as
having a specular relationship to his identity: he becomes visible to himself in mirrors. Where Ovid's Narcissus identified his
own image as a separate person, Gascoigne finds his reflection
in the steel glass transforming or distorting his self-understanding.
In the *Metamorphoses*, the reflecting pool allows Narcissus to
fall in love with himself in an evasion of self-knowledge; in *The
Steel Glas*, the mirror floods Gascoigne with a painful self-
knowledge. Like Ovid, Gascoigne uses *polyptoton*, or repetition
of different senses of the same word, as a trope for the relationship between self and reflection. In the *Metamorphoses*, Narcissus recognizes himself and cries out, "*iste ego sum: sensi, nec me
mea fallit imago* (I am that person: I have felt it, nor does my
image deceive me)."[9] Narcissus' language echoes or reflects on
itself: he suffers from a pathology related to that of Echo, the

---

8 For a discussion of the figure of the prodigal and its use by writers of
Gascoigne's generation, see Richard Helgerson, *The Elizabethan Prod-
igals* (Berkeley: University of California Press, 1976). Gascoigne's
invocation of the convention was not purely conventional: in 1570
he was jailed for failure to pay his debts, and in 1574 his *An Hundreth
Sundrie Flowers* was called in for libel and immorality. For Gascoigne's
life, see C. T. Prouty, *George Gascoigne, Elizabethan Courtier, Soldier,
and Poet* (New York: Columbia University Press, 1942).

9 *Ovid III: Metamorphoses, Books I–VIII*, ed. G. P. Goold, Loeb Classical
Library (Cambridge, Mass.: Harvard University Press, 1994), 3.463. I
have modified Frank Justus Miller's translation.

nymph who loves him. In *The Steel Glas*, Gascoigne imagines a specular relationship that involves a form of undoing: he expresses an impulse to "this face of mine deface."

Gascoigne's self-denunciation has a practical function: as he suggests in a marginal note, "He which will rebuke other men's faults, shal do wel not to forget hys owne imperfections" (149). Admitting his own past failures improves the credibility of his denunciations. Gascoigne's horrified vision of his shape in the mirror also resonates, though, with the imagery of Calvinism's stern call for self-obliteration. Sacvan Bercovitch has argued that the Reformation called for the effacement of individual identity, a wiping away of the encrustations of self that obscured the divine spark within. Bercovitch traces this hostility to the individual self back to the New Testament and the church fathers: "The soul is like a mirror turned toward the sun, wrote Gregory of Nyssa: it images not itself but the Son's rays; and it does so most brilliantly on a surface 'pure and shining,' cleared of all 'stains of dirt.'" Bercovitch points out that in the rhetoric of Puritanism the word "self" almost always has a negative valence: phrases like "self-affection," "self-credit," "self-fullness," "self-intended," and "self-sufficiency" constitute powerful indictments, while the elect are characterized by phrases suggesting the obliteration of the self—phrases like "self-emptiness," "self-revenging," "self-trial," and "self-denial."[10] In *The Steel Glas*, the radiant ideal form glimpsed in the crystal mirror is not Christ but a collection of largely classical values. Gascoigne's unpleasant glimpse of his true form in the steel mirror, though, reflects the Calvinist image of the self.

II

Unlike *The Steel Glas*, the verse satire of the 1590s set out to create firm generic distinctions and boundaries. Turning their backs on the history of English satire, Donne, Hall, Marston, and Guilpin reanimated what they imagined as the pure and original form of a classical genre.[11] They were forced to repress

10 *The Puritan Origins of the American Self* (New Haven: Yale University Press, 1975), p. 14.

11 On Elizabethan verse satire as imitation of the Roman genre, particularly helpful works include Heather Dubrow, "'No Man is an Island': Donne's Satires and Satiric Traditions," *Studies in English Literature* 19.1 (Winter 1979): 71–83; James S. Baumlin, "Generic Con-

the classical idea of verse satire as a genre defined by impurity and mixture.[12] The fantasy of a purified classical genre, distinguished by clear boundaries from other literary kinds, was linked by analogy to a restricted social group distinguished by education and ability. This social group, the community of the verse satirists, was roughly coterminous with the Inns of Court. Hall was a fellow of Emmanuel College, Cambridge, but Lodge, Donne, Marston, Middleton, and Guilpin were all law students.[13] Hall, Lodge, Marston, Middleton, and Guilpin chose to print their satires and, with great anxiety and ambivalence, reach out to a larger audience, but their work, like Donne's, was incubated in a coterie environment. Elizabethan verse satire thus centers on the concerns of this community and its troubled relations to the larger world around it — the urban environment around the Inns and the court and government within which students sought patronage and employment. Unsurprisingly, the work of these law students displays an obsessive interest in the cultural function of the law. All of them imagined satire as a supplement to or substitute for the legal system. In a community whose regulatory mechanisms

---

text of Elizabethan Satire: Rhetoric, Poetic Theory, and Interpretation," *Renaissance Genres: Essays on Theory, History, and Interpretation*, ed. Barbara Lewalski (Cambridge, Mass.: Harvard University Press, 1986), pp. 444–67; and J. B. Leishman, *The Monarch of Wit: An Analytical and Comparative Study of the Poetry of John Donne* (London: Hutchinson, 1965). Leishman argues that despite the various features it imitated, the Elizabethan genre is actually quite different from the Roman one: the Elizabethan poems are less epistle-like and present a much more extravagantly uncontrolled persona, at pages 111–12.

12 Juvenal famously described his satires as a "farrago" (1.75), and the word "satura" itself, meaning "stuffed" or "mixed," may have implied the notion of satire as a sort of stew.

13 On the literary sociology of the Inns and the peculiar place of satire in the literary career of a gentleman, I am particularly indebted to Philip Finkelpearl, *John Marston of the Middle Temple: An Elizabethan Dramatist in His Social Setting* (Cambridge, Mass.: Harvard University Press, 1969); Richard Helgerson, *Self-Crowned Laureates: Spenser, Jonson, Milton, and the Literary System* (Berkeley: University of California Press, 1983), pp. 122–45; Arthur Marotti, *John Donne, Coterie Poet* (Madison: University of Wisconsin Press, 1986); and Lawrence Manley, *Literature and Culture in Early Modern London* (Cambridge: Cambridge University Press, 1995), pp. 390–409.

and norms seemed to be breaking down, the satirist had to take responsibility for punishing or curing the dysfunctional and re-establishing a system of values. The verse satirists understood themselves as diagnosing if not repairing not only damaged individuals but a damaged culture. In their more skeptical moments, though, the verse satirists imagined that they themselves had degenerated into biting, growling animals with potentially infectious saliva. They wondered whether art could represent filth without becoming itself filthy, and they worried that satire might work to contaminate rather than to purify. The Bishop of London and the Archbishop of Canterbury must have developed similar anxieties about the potential contagiousness of satire: when they called in and burned a pile of satirical works in June 1599, they added a sort of ritual disinfection to an act of censorship.

Both Roman and Elizabethan verse satire treated other literary genres as degenerate, as the carriers of a potentially infectious cultural damage. Juvenal declared epic bankrupt and asserted that only satire was adequate to the challenge of representing, responding to, and castigating urban Rome.[14] Horace in his satires had practiced a more delicate form of literary criticism, chastising other writers for local failures of taste rather than rejecting whole genres. He suggested that, for all his virtues, his satiric predecessor Lucilius had written a rough and unpolished verse. Following the Roman model, Joseph Hall wrote a systematic denunciation of the rest of Elizabethan literature, devoting a poem to each genre.[15] Donne, Marston, and Guilpin also attacked other genres as outmoded, hackneyed, and morally dangerous.[16] All four satirists display a particularly strong aversion to the various genres of erotic poetry,

---

14 See Juvenal's first satire. Juvenal admits the excellence of Virgil but asserts that epic can no longer be written in his own degenerate era.

15 See the first book of his *Virgidemiarum* (1597).

16 See Donne's second satire, lines 5–30, and his "Upon Mr. Thomas Coryat's Crudities," *The Verse Satires, Epigrams, and Verse Letters*, ed. W. Milgate (Oxford: Clarendon, 1967); the sixth satire of Marston's *Scourge of Villainy*, in *The Works of John Marston*, ed. A. H. Bullen, 3 vols. (London: John Nimmo, 1887); and Guilpin, "Satyre Preludium," in *Skialetheia; or, A Shadowe of Truth, in Certaine Epigrams and Satyres*, ed. D. Allen Carroll (Chapel Hill: University of North Carolina Press, 1974).

perhaps because of an uncomfortable resemblance or affinity between the two modes. This aversion and this affinity are especially evident in the work of John Marston. In 1598 Marston published *The Metamorphosis of Pygmalion's Image and Certain Satires*. "The Metamorphosis of Pygmalion's Image," as its title suggests, is an epyllion that expands an episode from Ovid's *Metamorphoses*. Marston claimed that his contribution to the genre was a parody, and appended a savagely dismissive afterword called "The AUTHOR in praise of his precedent Poem": the poem "wantonly displays / the Salaminian titillations, / Which tickle up our lewd Priapians"; although "Glittering in dawbed laced accoustrements, / And pleasing suits of love's habiliments," the poem's stanzas are "Patch'd like a beggar's cloak, and run as sweet / As doth a tumbril in the street."[17] The clothing imagery hints that the poem itself has a human body, which it lasciviously displays to the reader. Giving a text human or animal flesh is a recurrent gesture of the materialist imagination of satire. A "tumbril" is a dung-cart, and the line suggests not only that the poem's versification is execrable (which it does not seem to be) but that the erotic has been infected by the excremental — a contamination or reduction that also occurs frequently in verse satire. This afterword carefully distinguishes between the projects of the two literary modes: the function of epyllion is to arouse desire, while the function of verse satire is to eliminate desire and to make its objects repulsive. Positioned as it is between the epyllion and the verse satires in the volume, this recusatio serves, in effect, to prevent the infection of satire by erotic poetry.

The narrative of epyllion moves toward the fusion of bodies. In some epyllia the romance is never consummated, but the forward movement of the poems depends on the space between bodies or on the gravitational forces that cross that space. As Hallett Smith first noted, epyllia frequently borrow from the

---

17 Lines 5–6, 21–22, 25–26. As Bullen's footnote points out, Salamis was a town on Cyprus, and thus associated with Venus. Critics have disagreed about whether Marston is to be trusted when he claims that his *Metamorphosis* is erotic poetry or a satire against erotic poetry. Philip Finkelpearl sensibly suggests that the poem contains elements of both, like Ovid's own mythological narratives; *John Marston of the Middle Temple*, pp. 94–104.

myth of Salmacis and Hermaphroditus, even when their narratives center on other Ovidian episodes. Marlowe, for example, compares Hero to Salmacis: "Therefore unto him hastily she goes, / And like light Salmacis, her body throws / Upon his bosom, where with yielding eyes / She offers up herself a sacrifice."[18] Similarly, the Ovidian passage that closes the 1590 *Faerie Queene*, a sort of inset epyllion, ends with an image of two lovers fusing: when Amoret and Scudamour embrace, "Had ye them seene, ye would have surely thought, / That they had beene that faire *Hermaphrodite*, / Which that rich *Romane* of white marble wrought, / And in his costly Bath causd to bee site."[19] Here the body of the hermaphrodite functions as an emblem of the aesthetic object and of narrative closure: the drive to bring the bodies of the two lovers together produces the narrative, and when they are reunited the story ends. The comparison to a statue rather than to a living body has a threatening quality, as if closure could petrify the characters of a narrative, transforming flesh into stone. The word "costly" adds a further moral question, suggesting that a reader might make excessive or self-indulgent demands on a narrative, or that narrative might seduce a reader into regarding other people as aesthetic objects. The central fact about the body of this statue, though, remains its compelling beauty, its ability to give as well as to represent pleasure. In the 1596 *Faerie Queene*, Spenser eliminated the meeting of the lovers and the image of the hermaphrodite, and the narrative continued into Book IV. Other Spenserian hermaphrodites, like the figure of Venus in Book Five of *The Faerie Queene*, also function as emblems of self-sufficiency and perfection.[20]

In verse satire, the hybrid body of the hermaphrodite also occupies a central symbolic location, but it becomes an object of horror, an image of a threat to the integrity of the self.

18 2.45–48, cited and discussed in Hallett Smith, *Elizabethan Poetry: A Study in Conventions, Meaning, and Expression* (Cambridge: Harvard University Press, 1952), p. 74. In 1602, an anonymous poet who may have been Francis Beaumont published an epyllion called *Salmacis and Hermaphroditus*, in a further demonstration of this myth's central place in epyllia.

19 3.12. 46.1–4.

20 See James Nohrnberg, *The Analogy of* The Faerie Queene (Princeton: Princeton University Press, 1976), pp. 604–08.

Guilpin's "Satyre Preludium," for example, begins "Fie on these Lydian tunes which blunt our sprights / And turne our gallants to Hermaphrodites" (1–2). These lines suggest that the softer varieties of music can feminize men, contaminating them with the qualities of the female objects of their desire. Guilpin goes on to accuse erotic poetry of having a similar effect. For Guilpin, the hermaphrodite represents not completion but debility, a deadening of the male impulse toward action that creates heroic narrative. Similarly, in the second satire of *The Metamorphosis of Pygmalion's Image and Certain Satires*, Marston describes a cross-dressing female prostitute and then addresses an effeminate courtier: "Nay, stead of shadow, lay the substance out, / Or else, fair Briscus, I shall stand in doubt / What sex thou art, since such hermaphrodites, such Protean shadows so delude our sights." The "substance" that the satirist wants to inspect is Briscus' "codpis." As Guilpin's editor suggests, the unusual spelling of "codpis" seems intended to create a punning reference to urine.[21] The pun infects the aggressive erotic symbolism of the codpiece with a reminder of the link between the erotic and the excretory. The protean figures and the hermaphrodites of this passage resist definitions and categories, and they threaten to destabilize the verse satirist's understanding of his own body and its relation to other bodies. In verse satire, the hermaphrodite is situated not at the end of a story but at the beginning of an anxious analysis: the onlooker is forced to ask what sort of response the ambiguous body demands. When verse satire has any narrative shape, when it presents more than a sequence of portraits of deformity, closure involves not erotic union but the return of the satirist to the safe, solitary enclosure of his study.[22] In Elizabethan verse satire's paranoid anthropology not only sexuality but any human contact has the potential to contaminate. Roman verse satire was closely allied with the verse epistle, and frequently featured an exchange with a friendly interlocutor or respected teacher.[23] Elizabethan verse satire, on the other hand, presents a persona who remains essentially solitary.

21 *Certain Satires*, 2.123–26.
22 See Donne's first and fourth satires and Guilpin's fifth, for example
23 See, for example, the fifth satire of Persius, in which he addresses his mentor, the stoic philosopher Cornutus.

Despite their antithetical projects, verse satire and epyllion frequently appeared together in the same volumes. Marston chose to package satire and epyllion together in *The Metamorphosis of Pygmalion's Image and Certain Satires*, and Lodge's *Scillaes Metamorphosis* (1595) also contained a poem called "The Discontented Satyre."[24] This unnatural intimacy may help explain the hostility of verse satire toward erotic poetry, and toward the various genres of Ovidian poetry in particular: verse satire and erotic poetry have different relationships to the system of literary patronage and imply different versions of the career of the writer. Each mode could be seen as undercutting the ambitions associated with the other. Most epyllia were dedicated to aristocratic patrons and presented as having been designed for the refined erotic and artistic tastes of such men. Shakespeare famously dedicated *Venus and Adonis* to the Earl of Southampton. Verse satire, on the other hand, typically rejected the patronage system. Hall began *Virgidemiarum* with "His Defiance to Envy" in the place of a dedication; Marston dedicated *The Metamorphosis of Pygmalion's Image and Certain Satires* to "Opinion" and *The Scourge of Villainy* to "Detraction," and in the 1599 edition of *The Scourge of Villainy* added a second dedication reading "To his most esteemed and best beloved Self dat dedicatque" (he gives and dedicates); and Guilpin chose not to dedicate *Skialetheia* at all. Later, the Stuart satirist George Wither dedicated his *Abuses Stript, and Whipt* to himself.[25] Arthur Marotti has persuasively suggested that the wits of the Inns of Court turned to verse satire at moments of thwarted ambition: when flattery failed them, they turned to reckless criticism.[26] Verse satire's rejection of epyllion and erotic poetry derives in

24 The title page of Lodge's book reads, in part, *SCILLAES Metamorphosis: Enterlaced with the Unfortunate Love of Glaucus. Whereunto is Annexed the Delectable Discourse of the Discontented Satyre: with Sundrie Other Most Absolute Poems and Sonnets.* See *The Complete Works of Thomas Lodge*, vol. 1, ed. Edmund Gosse (Glasgow: The Hunterian Club, 1883).

25 "Let me advise my deare selfe then; to make use of this thine own worke, it will be better to thee then all the world. . . ."; George Wither, *Abuses Stript, and Whipt. Or Satyrical Essayes* (1613), A3r.

26 Arthur F. Marotti, *John Donne, Coterie Poet* (Madison: University of Wisconsin Press, 1986), p. 39.

part from a frustration with the patronage system and the social conventions that gave it shape.

One could also without too much whimsy imagine verse satire as claustrophobic, as wanting to possess its neighborhood and police its borders more effectively than the proximity of epyllion would allow. The two genres not only frequently inhabited the same printed book, they also shared a repertoire of literary techniques, including their analytical approach to the conventions of other genres. Epyllion is itself an extremely subversive form, one that gleefully inverts many of the conventions of the Petrarchan sonnet sequence — itself a genre that frequently examined or subverted its own conventions. In epyllion, the woman is frequently the wooer, as in Heywood's *Paris and Oenone* and *Salmacis and Hermaphroditus* and Shakespeare's *Venus and Adonis*; the blazons catalogue the body parts of the men as well as the women; the blazons of both men and women frequently seem excessive and even parodic; and the deaths of the protagonists and their metamorphoses into flowers and other non-human forms have a strange and elaborate beauty, as they do in Ovid, rather than the genuinely tragic quality of the transformation of Sidney into a flower at the end of Spenser's *Astrophel*. Like Ovid's *Metamorphoses*, the Renaissance epyllion has a playful and critical relationship to other genres.[27] One could say that epyllion has already traveled more than half of the distance from the erotic to the satirical. Once one has recognized the gold, honey, snow, rubies, and roses of the erotic blazon as the colors of rhetoric rather than those of the body, one has come close to verse satire's horrified insight into the materiality of flesh, with its secretions, its orifices, its vulnerability to infection, and its inevitable decay. Epyllion argues for the usefulness of fictions as antidotes to difficult truths. Maintaining the distinction between the two genres

27 For useful discussions of the conventions of epyllia, see Elizabeth Donno's introduction to *Elizabethan Minor Epics*, ed. Elizabeth Story Donno (New York: Columbia University Press, 1967), pp. 1–20; Clark Hulse, *Metamorphic Verse: The Elizabethan Minor Epic* (Princeton: Princeton University Press, 1981), pp. 3–34; and William Keach, *Elizabethan Erotic Narratives* (New Brunswick: Rutgers University Press, 1977). For discussions of inset moments of social satire in epyllia, see Hulse, *Metaphoric Verse*, pp. 65–74, and Keach, *Elizabethan Erotic Narratives*, pp. 204–05.

thus requires a special vigilance on the part of the satirist. The satirist insists on the need to probe beneath the metaphors to the actual body, to the world as it is. Satire's hostility toward erotic poetry provides an occasion for the expression of a more general distrust of fiction.

John Weever wrote an especially strange meditation on the relation between the two genres: his *Faunus and Melliflora: Or, the Origin of Our English Satyres* (1600) begins as an epyllion and ends with a myth of the origin of satire. Weever's Melliflora is a nymph who incurs the wrath of Diana by marrying the young Latin prince Faunus. Diana curses Melliflora, and the nymph's child emerges from her womb as a goat-like monster, horned and precociously hairy, who instantly runs off into the woods and becomes an enemy to amorous love. Weever gives a spurious etymology for the monster's name: because he satisfies Diana's ire, he becomes known as a "satyre." Like Marston, Weever imagines satire as developing out of a sort of allergic reaction to erotic poetry. Adding a footnote to the favorite origin-myth of the Tudors and the Stuarts, the poem then explains how satire came to England: when Brut, the mythical Trojan ancestor of the British, embarked from Italy, he carried a group of fairies and satyrs with him. This myth links Spenser's *Faerie Queene* to verse satire: both participate in the same massive cultural translation. Despite its purported antiquity, this transfer of energy from Rome to England seems to belong to the final decades of Elizabeth's reign. Unlike most versions of the Brut myth, the poem does not seem concerned to establish a continuous genealogy for British literature from Brut's time to the present. Weever's two representative satirists are Hall and Marston, so he apparently accepts Hall's narrow definition of satire as the imitation of Roman verse satire that began in the fifteen-nineties. The poem ends with a modal shift from erotic narrative to satire. After praising the satires of Hall and Marston, Weever enters the controversy between the two, apostrophizing the latter: "But I was born to hate your censuring vaine, / Your envious biting in your crabbed straine."[28] With its fusion of two antithetical literary modes, Weever's poem is itself a monstrous hybrid like the satyr figure whose birth it narrates. The satyr's hairiness and goat-like

28 Sig. F2r.

lower body, the marks of an exaggerated masculinity, also serve
to characterize the poem and its genre. In epyllion, even the
male protagonists have a feminine beauty, and the recurring
image of the hermaphrodite suggests that erotic love threatens
the masculine body with a softening, weakening transformation. Weever's myth makes epyllion a female or feminizing
genre and satire a masculine one, imagining their antagonism
as a gendered one.

In the final poem of Weever's book, this gendered antagonism becomes the basis for a small myth about why satire was
banned the previous year. The final poem follows translations
of the first satires of Horace and Persius and the first ten lines
of Juvenal's first satire. The poet explains that he has been asked
to abandon his translation of Juvenal: "Venus (to whom it is
dangerous denying any reasonable request) hearing glowming
Juvenall threaten so great a punishment, entreates my Muse
that for a while she would leave him in his English tongue
unperfect."[29] Weever follows this note with a daring allegorical
account of the Bishops' ban of 1599. The allegory takes the
form of a visit by Venus to England:

> Her journey tended to our English clime
> And here she hovered and remaind a time.
> Hearing before the satyres emnitie,
> Gainst her proceedings and her deitie,
> Using all mischiefe gainst her enemies,
> Thrusting her selfe in baudy elegies,
> Polluting with her damned luxury,
> All eares which vowed were unto chastity,
> And evermore thus on fel mischiefe bent,
> Until she found (she never was content:)
> Some of her saints (belike) who every day
> Unto her shrine their orizons did say:
> Who fore she askt, this boone to her was giving,
> That all the satyres then in England living
> Should sacrifisde be in the burning fire,
> To pacifie so great a goddesse ire,
> And from their Cyndars should a Satyre rise
> Which all their Satyricke snarling should despise.[30]

29 Sig. H4v.
30 Sig. I2r.

This little myth audaciously suggests that the Bishop of London and the Archbishop of Canterbury banned satire as a gesture of fealty to Venus—that is, out of devotion to lechery. The word "saints" was often used to refer to "Puritans," and here it seems to suggest that the bishops acted hypocritically, as Puritans were often accused of doing. The passage imagines Venus as a dangerous foreign contaminant: she invades "ears which vowed were unto chastity," as if the entry of an erotic poem into an ear were a rape-like penetration with the potential to feminize a male listener. This fear of contamination is a signature of verse satire, and Weever's poem might thus be said to continue the work of the banned satires. Accusing the bishops of erotic license also constitutes a sort of revenge for the ban. The "Satyre" that rises phoenix-like from the ashes of the bonfire, though, seems to be Weever's own poem, and this imaginary figure despises its forebears and in effect joins with the bishops in attacking the verse satire of the fifteen-nineties. Weever keeps shifting his ground: the volume begins with an erotic narrative and then attacks both satire and its enemies as well as erotic poetry. The volume imagines epyllion and satire, desire and anger, as locked in an intimate antagonism, each threatening the other with a contamination or exchange like that of sexual intercourse.

Bad genre-oriented critics produce sterile taxonomies, often quite unrelated to the interpretive frames of authors or audiences. Alastair Fowler is perhaps our preeminent advocate for the study of the subtler, more local uses of genre. I have tried here to map one such micro-generic effect. This effort seems appropriate for a volume celebrating the achievement of John Hollander, who has championed Fowler's work. Hollander's own work has frequently demonstrated that other critics have been insufficiently interested in the non-obvious imaginative consequences of literary form. We are just beginning to understand the deep work of genre, and Hollander's work, particularly *The Gazer's Spirit*, helps illuminate our path.

7

The Bible, Coriolanus, and Shakespeare's Modes of Allusion

HANNIBAL HAMLIN

I

Coriolanus, like other plays by Shakespeare, contains numerous echoes of the Bible. Its author was steeped in biblical language, as were his contemporaries, listening to the Bible read aloud weekly in compulsory church services, reading and translating it in school, and probably, given the plentiful number of biblical references in his plays, reading it on his own as well.[1] Such "references" in *Coriolanus* have been catalogued extensively by Naseeb Shaheen and, before him, Richmond Noble and Thomas Carter, and some are noted by Philip Brockbank (Arden), R. B. Parker (Oxford), and other editors of critical editions of the play.[2] The fact of the biblical language is, then, more or less accepted. The problem of its explanation remains, however. Did Shakespeare deliberately incorporate biblical language in order to supplement the meaning of particular passages or scenes? Would an audience attuned to such biblical

---

1 As Naseeb Shaheen has demonstrated (see below, note 2), the translation Shakespeare knew best was that of the Geneva Bible (1560), whose language appears most often in echoes and allusions in the plays. Accordingly, all biblical citations will be from the Geneva Bible (1560), in the Lazarus Ministry Press facsimile (Columbus, Ohio, 1998), unless otherwise indicated. Original spelling has been maintained, except that *u/v*, *i/j*, and long *s* have been modernized and contractions have been expanded.

2 Naseeb Shaheen, *Biblical References in Shakespeare's Plays* (Newark: University of Delaware Press, 1999); Richmond Noble, *Shakespeare's Biblical Knowledge* (1935; reprint, Folcroft, Penna.: The Folcroft Press, 1969); Thomas Carter, *Shakespeare and Holy Scripture* (London: Hodder and Stoughton, 1905); Philip Brockbank, ed., *Coriolanus*, by William Shakespeare (London and New York: Routledge, 1976); R. B. Parker, ed., *Coriolanus*, by William Shakespeare (Oxford and New York: Oxford University Press, 1994).

language recognize these allusions and shape their understanding of the play accordingly? Shaheen typically suggests only that his reader "compare" a certain passage in Shakespeare to one in the Bible. Brockbank finds the allusions in *Coriolanus* intriguing, but remains noncommittal about their significance. For example, he notes of the phrase "widow'd and unchilded" (5.6.151), an echo of Isaiah 47.9, that, "like other Biblical echoes in the play, this one is highly suggestive without being in any way a controlled allusion."[3] Stanley Cavell, who takes the biblical allusions more seriously than many, is reluctant to commit himself, noting allusions that seem to suggest parallels between Coriolanus and Christ but calling such parallels "shadowy matters."[4]

One explanation for critics' reluctance to move beyond suggestions and shadows may lie in the play's subject matter: *Coriolanus* is set half a millenium before the birth of Christ, so to read the play as alluding to the Gospels seems anachronistic.[5] For Shakespeare and his audience, however, it was not only permissible but customary to read the history of pre-Christian Rome from a Christian perspective. The English appropriation of the Roman classics, as Robert Miola points out, was generally "acquisitive and undiscriminating," with the result that "English classicism came to be ahistorical and eclectic in character, little concerned with understanding the past on its own terms."[6] An "ahistorical" approach to the past was also traditional in the Christian view of history, especially in its typological interpretation of the Bible, in which the primary importance of Old Testament types like Adam, David, and Jonah was that they prefigured Christ, just as Eve and "the Beloved" in the Song of Solomon anticipated the Virgin Mary. Luther and other sixteenth-century exegetes were intellectually untrou-

---

3 Brockbank, *Coriolanus*, p. 311.

4 Stanley Cavell, "*Coriolanus* and the Interpretations of Politics," *Disowning Knowledge in Six Plays of Shakespeare* (Cambridge: Cambridge University Press, 1987), p. 157.

5 A similar problem confronts the critic of *King Lear*. See the challenge to Christian readings of the play by William R. Elton, King Lear *and the Gods* (San Marino, Calif.: Huntington Library, 1968).

6 Robert S. Miola, *Shakespeare's Rome* (Cambridge: Cambridge University Press, 1983), pp. 9–10.

bled by reading many of the Psalms as foreshadowing Christ (especially since Christ himself encouraged the practice: in Matthew 27.46, for example, by reciting Psalm 22.1—"My God, my God, why hast thou forsaken me"—he retrospectively appropriates the psalm as a prophecy of his own Crucifixion). Modern readers naturally define echo as a phenomenon that works forward in time: the originating sound must precede its echo. From a Christian, typological perspective, however, it is more common for the echo to precede the sound that originates it, if we apply these terms (figuratively) to the type and antitype, respectively.[7] It is in this syncretistic, ahistorical, and anachronistic context that one can approach the biblical echoes in *Coriolanus.*

Yet, obviously, *Coriolanus* is not a biblical drama. It is a play representing a critical period in the history of Rome, when it developed from an aristocracy into a republic, and the tragedy of Coriolanus lies partly in his inability to adapt to this fundamental political change. Coriolanus is the epitome of the old-fashioned Roman soldier, a paragon of what Plutarch describes as *Virtus:*

Nowe in those dayes, valliantnes was honoured in ROME above all other vertues: which they called Virtus by the name of vertue selfe, as including in that generall name, all other speciall vertues besides. So that Virtus in the Latin, was asmuche as valliantnes.[8]

In a republic, however, political leaders must have the favor of the common people and require tact and diplomacy (which may shade into flattery and deceit) as much as "valliantnes." In Plutarch's view, Coriolanus brought ruin upon himself by his failure to adapt to the new political values of the nascent republic. In a famous phrase from the first book of the *Politics,*

---

7 This may be partly what W. S. Merwin has in mind when he asks, "How did we sound to the past?" He looks forward too, noting that "there are sounds that rush away from us: echoes of future words," cited in John Hollander, *The Figure of Echo* (Berkeley and Los Angeles: University of California Press, 1981), p. 62.

8 Plutarch, "The Life of Caius Martius Coriolanus," from *Lives of Noble Grecians and Romans,* translated by Thomas North (1579), cited from the reprint in Brockbank, *Coriolanus,* pp. 314–15. All further citations will be from this edition.

Aristotle described the man who, like Coriolanus, is unable to function within the *polis*. Man is by nature a social animal, essentially interdependent with his fellow men,

> But he that can not abide to liue in companie, or through sufficiencie hath need of nothing is not esteemed a part or member of a Cittie, but is either a beast or a god.[9]

Since Coriolanus' downfall derives largely from his dogged self-sufficiency and inability to "liue in companie," and since in Shakespeare's play he is consistently described in terms of both beasts and gods, we may suspect that Shakespeare had Aristotle in mind as he adapted the story from North's Plutarch.[10]

In Shakespeare's play, unlike Plutarch's *Lives* (his principal source), Coriolanus is frequently described as aspiring to godhood or as actually exhibiting godlike powers. He is in fact associated at different points in the play with three models of divinity. The first, and most expected, is Roman: Coriolanus is described as both Mars and Jupiter, the Roman gods of war and storm. In act 2, a messenger describes how, upon Coriolanus' arrival in Rome, "the nobles bended/ As to Jove's statue" (2.1.263–64).[11] Menenius says that Coriolanus is so proud "He would not flatter Neptune for his trident, / Or Jove for's power to thunder" (3.1.254–55), but Titus Lartius' earlier account of the "thunder-like percussion of [his] sounds" suggests that Jupiter has nothing Coriolanus doesn't already have (1.4.59). Cominius describes how "like a thing of blood" Coriolanus "struck Corioles like a planet"—presumably the planet Mars, Caius *Martius* Coriolanus' namesake (2.2.109, 113–14). Indeed, in act 4 one of Aufidius' servants states that the Volscians treat Coriolanus "as if he were son and heir to Mars" (4.6.197). More anachronistic, if one forgets the Renaissance tendency

---

9 *Aristotles Politiques*, translated by I. D. from the [French?] of Loys Le Roy (1598), cited in Miola, *Shakespeare's Rome*, p. 192.
10 Conclusive evidence of Shakespeare's reading is wanting, but, as evident in the citation above, the *Politics* was available to Shakespeare in a 1598 English translation, and Aristotle was certainly, along with Cicero, the preeminent classical authority on political theory. Miola, *Shakespeare's Rome*, p. 165n8 cites several studies of Coriolanus' debt to Aristotle.
11 All citations of *Coriolanus* will be from Brockbank's Arden edition.

toward syncretism, are comparisons between Coriolanus and the types of divinity represented in the biblical Old and New Testaments: Jehovah, a destructive God of wrath who floods the world and burns Sodom and Gomorrah, and Christ, who embodies humility and mercy. Whereas Coriolanus' comparison to the Roman gods is explicitly stated by characters in the play, his comparison to Jehovah and Christ is necessarily confined to the level of allusion, both verbal and visual. Such echoes are obviously unconscious ones for the speakers, but, from the Christian perspective of the author or the audience, they are, nevertheless, conscious allusions.

These allusions to divinity, both explicit and implicit, provide a supplementary context for Shakespeare's exploration of the conflict between aristocratic and republican political values in terms of a conflict between antithetical models of godhood. The military values of Coriolanus' Roman *Virtus*, embodied in the Roman pantheon by Mars the war god and Jupiter the god of thunder, are quite compatible with certain "virtues" of Jehovah: wrath, judgment, and vengeance. As a politician, however, Coriolanus must demonstrate an entirely different set of virtues. He is called upon to demonstrate humility to the common people, and mercy to the city of Rome, qualities embodied by Christ, a god who was also, significantly, human.

II

Coriolanus is in his element in battle, and it is in this milieu that he is likened to the fierce Roman gods by whom he himself swears, but his anger and violence also evoke the wrathful god of the Old Testament more familiar to Shakespeare's Christian audience. The tribune Sicinius states that Coriolanus' hatred of the people

> will be his fire
> To kindle their dry stubble; and their blaze
> Shall darken him for ever. (2.1.255–57)

Though the tribune is of course unaware of it, his language echoes Isaiah's description of the judgment of Jehovah:

Therefore as the flame of fyre devoureth the stubble, and as the chaffe is consumed of the flame.... Therefore is the wrath of the

Lord kindled against his people, and he hathe stretched out his
hand upon them.... (Isa. 5.24–25)[12]

The godlike Coriolanus' wrathful disposition toward the people
of Rome thus parallels that of the god of Isaiah toward the
people of Israel. A similar parallel is suggested by the echo of the
Psalms in the description of Coriolanus by the Fourth Citizen:

You have been a scourge to her enemies, you have been a rod to
her friends. (2.3.90–91)

The allusion is to Psalm 89:

I will visit their offences with the rod, and their sin with scourges.
(Ps. 89.32)[13]

In both cases, the allusions are subversive. In the first instance,
Sicinius suggests that it is Coriolanus who will ultimately be
destroyed; the implication of the metaphor seems to be that, as
a man, unlike Isaiah's god, Coriolanus must stand in the midst
of the human "stubble" he is setting alight. In the second allusion, Coriolanus' rage seems antithetical to the psalm's statement of divine Justice, since Coriolanus punishes indiscrimi-
nately both "enemies" and "friends" alike.

Coriolanus is compared to multiple divinities throughout
the play, but the allusions that prompt comparisons to Christ
are concentrated in several key scenes: 2.3, in which he must
humbly seek the favor of the people; 3.3, when the crowd
turns on him and calls for his death; 5.3, when he returns to
Rome in judgment but shows mercy after the intervention of
his mother; and 5.6, which returns to the situation of 3.3 but
with quite a different outcome.

The allusive connection between Coriolanus and Christ is
suggested early in the play. After Coriolanus charges headlong

12 The allusion (or reference) is noted in Noble, *Biblical Knowledge*, p.
241, and Shaheen, *Biblical References*, p. 662. Shaheen suggests that
Shakespeare's immediate source of this language is William Averell's *A
Meruailous Combat of Contrarieties*, but since Averell is obviously himself alluding to Isaiah or similar biblical passages, no clear distinction
seems either possible or necessary.
13 The 1535 Coverdale translation later incorporated into the Book of
Common Prayer. See Noble, *Biblical Knowledge*, p. 241.

through the gates of Corioles, one of his cowardly soldiers reports of his commander that "he is himself alone / To answer all the city" (1.4.51–52), echoing a passage from the Gospel of John:

When Jesus therefore perceived that they wolde come, and take him to make him a King, he departed againe into a mountaine him self alone.   (John 6.15)[14]

The echo may be too faint on its own to constitute an outright allusion, but it takes on significance in the context of later allusions, and may have occurred to Shakespeare because of the parallel between Christ's rejection of kingship and Coriolanus' (later) attempted rejection of the Consulship, a political office for which he is unsuited. Allusive comparisons between Coriolanus and Christ intensify as he is persuaded to enter the political arena. Brutus, for instance, describes the "pother" the citizens are making about Coriolanus in terms that to a biblically educated audience would surely have suggested Christ's unique combination of the human and divine:

> Such a pother
> As if that whatsoever god who leads him
> Were slily crept into his human powers,
> And gave him graceful posture.   (2.1.216–19)

Later in this scene, Brutus describes the ritual Coriolanus must enact in order to gain the Consulship. According to the tribune, Coriolanus must don "the napless vesture of humility" and show "his wounds / To th' people" (2.1.232–34). In North's Plutarch, the clothing required by the ritual is a "poore gowne," a "simple gowne," and "mean apparell" (North, p. 331). By contrast, Shakespeare's "vesture of humility" points to the Bible rather than Plutarch's *Lives*. "Humility" may recall the injunction of 1 Peter, to "decke your selves inwardely in lowlines of minde: for God resisteth the proude and giveth grace to the humble" (1 Pet. 5.5), or the description of Christ in Philippians 2.8, "He humbled himself, and became obedient

---

14 Brockbank notes the allusion indirectly, citing R. H. Case's commentary in the 1922 Arden edition.

unto the death." "Vesture" alludes more specifically to the Crucifixion, when the soldiers cast lots over the "vesture" of Christ (Matt. 27.35).[15] Though accurately a Roman practice according to Plutarch, to a Christian audience the showing of the wounds echoes the passages in the Gospels (Luke 24.39–40 and John 20.20–28) where Christ must show his wounds to the disciples in order to gain their trust.[16]

Alexander Leggatt writes that when Coriolanus is "translated from war to politics, he loses in translation."[17] While, as a soldier, Coriolanus can be an "army of one" (to cite the latest U.S. Army recruitment campaign), as a politician he must interact with and be responsible to and for others. This dilemma is represented partly in terms of contrastive, even parodic, allusions to Christ. The Messenger to the tribunes describes Coriolanus' entry into Rome:

> I have seen the dumb men throng to see him,
> And the blind to hear him speak.　(2.1.260–61)

As Brockbank notes, there is no equivalent for this passage in North. The description echoes that of Christ's miraculous healing in Matthew 15.30:[18]

And great multitudes came unto him, having with them, halt, blinde, domme, maymed and manie other, and cast them downe at Jesus fete, and he healed them.

15 Shakespeare does not use the word often. Most notable, perhaps, is the reference to "Caesar's vesture wounded" in Marc Antony's speech in *Julius Caesar* 3.2.198. The reference to clothing, wounds, and tongues both here and in *Coriolanus* suggests that Shakespeare had this scene from his earlier Roman play in mind as he wrote the later one. Even in the earlier play, though, the use of "vesture" may echo the Crucifixion, though more faintly. This would accord with Harold Fisch's interpretation of *Julius Caesar* in terms of Christian ideas of and attitudes toward sacrifice. See *The Biblical Presence in Shakespeare, Milton, and Blake* (Oxford: Clarendon Press, 1999), pp. 3–34.

16 Cavell, "*Coriolanus*," makes the same comparison, p. 158.

17 Alexander Leggatt, *Shakespeare's Political Drama* (London and New York: Routledge, 1988), p. 192.

18 Brockbank, *Coriolanus*, p. 168. See also Shaheen, *Biblical References*, p. 662.

Matthew in turn alludes to Isaiah's messianic prophecy that "in that day shal the deafe heare the wordes of the boke, and the eyes of the blind shal se out of obscuritie, and out of darkenes" (Isa. 29.18). The echo in Shakespeare's passage is parodic: if Coriolanus' "blind" listeners had seen and his "dumb" viewers spoken, his entry into Rome might have seemed more divine. As it is, the event, unlike the account in Matthew, is decidedly unmiraculous. Coriolanus' dissimilarity to Christ is also evident in Cominius' praise of his valor and rejection of booty. According to the general, Coriolanus "look'd upon things precious as they were / The common muck of the world" (2.2.125–26). Shaheen cites this passage as a reference to Philippians:[19]

I have counted all things losse, and do judge them to be dongue, that I might winne Christ.   (Phil. 3.8)

Yet Coriolanus in his proud disdain of what he refers to as a "bribe" for his services is not motivated by Christian self-denial (1.9.38).

Coriolanus' pointed silence through act 2, scene 2 recalls another deliberate silence, that of Christ at his trial before Pilate:

And when he was accused of the chief Priests and Elders, he answered nothing. Then said Pilate unto him, Hearest thou not how many things they lay against thee?

But he answered him not to one worde.   (Matt. 27.12–14)

Further parallels between *Coriolanus* 2.2 and Christ's trial are indicated by specific verbal allusions, and by visual allusions made through staging, costume, and gesture. As with all of the allusive parallels between Coriolanus and Christ, the differences between *Coriolanus* 2.2 and Matthew 27 are marked. For example, Coriolanus is up for nomination to the Consulship and is listening to his own praises being sung, while Christ is accused as a criminal and is listening to false charges made against him. Nevertheless, the two scenes have strong similarities. Coriolanus must sit against his will to hear his "nothings

19 Shaheen, *References*, p. 662.

monstered," and the Consulship is a position he is most reluctant to assume (2.2.77). Like Christ facing his trial and Crucifixion, Coriolanus dreads the forthcoming ritual in which he must submit to the people. Coriolanus begs Menenius (an obvious surrogate for Coriolanus' strikingly absent father), "Please you / That I may pass this doing" (2.2.138–39). In the garden of Gethsemane, Christ pleads, "O my Father, if it be possible, let this cup passe from me" (Matt. 26.39).

In the mandatory ritual, Coriolanus is, visually, at his most Christlike.[20] His emblematic clothing is again referred to as a "gown of humility" (2.3.41). Coriolanus' "Look, sir, my wounds!" (2.3.53) is a phrase analogous to Christ's "Beholde mine hands and my fete" (Luke 24.39), though Coriolanus speaks the phrase only in sarcastic mockery, stating that "I cannot bring / My tongue to such a pace" (2.3.52–53). Coriolanus' own description of the garment he must wear as a "wolvish toge" (2.3.114) alludes to the warning from Matthew so familiar from anticlerical satire like Spenser's "Maye" eclogue in *The Shepheardes Calender*:

Beware of false prophetes, which comme to you in shepes clothing, but inwardely they are ravening wolves.   (Matt. 7.15)

The allusion is again contrastive: Coriolanus is wearing, by his own account, wolf's clothing, yet in 2.1 Menenius, Brutus, and Sicinius wrestle with the wolf-sheep metaphor and, although the tribunes prefer the application the other way around, Menenius describes Coriolanus as the lamb to the citizens' wolves, which resonates with the biblical metaphor of Christ as the sacrificial Lamb of God (John 1.29 and elsewhere). A "gown of humility" is appropriate clothing for a lamb, but for Coriolanus the gown is a "wolvish toge." Perhaps, from Coriolanus' perspective, the clothing is "wolvish" in devouring its wearer in the same way that Nessus' robe did Hercules (Menenius explicitly connects Hercules and Coriola-

20 Parker suggests that, at least in terms of the description of the "vesture of humility," Shakespeare has in mind the public humiliation of penitents in Elizabethan times (see *Coriolanus*, p. 219). The more obvious association seems to me the humiliation of Christ, on which the Elizabethan imitations were surely based.

nus at 4.6.100). In any case, the incompatible wolf and lamb remain unreconciled, as one would expect if, like Shaheen, one heard Ecclesiasticus in Menenius' and Sicinius' discussion of the question, "who does the wolf love?":[21]

Everie beast loveth his like. . . . How can the wolfe agre with the lambe?   (Eccles. 13.16, 18)

The wolf and the lamb—Coriolanus and the Roman populace, however configured—may indeed be irreconcilable, and certainly Coriolanus is partly to blame, because of his utter lack of humility. The tribunes are also responsible, however, and their role in 2.3, as in others, is that of the "chief priests and elders" in the Crucifixion narrative, the manipulators behind the scenes who "had persuaded the people that thei shulde aske Barabbas, and shulde destroy Jesus" (Matt. 27.20). The people condemn Coriolanus, but only after being persuaded to do so by Sicinius and Brutus, the "herdsmen of the beastly plebeians" (2.1.94–95 and also 3.1.32). This "priestly" role of the tribunes is confirmed in Coriolanus' "Crucifixion" scene. Like Christ's, Coriolanus' sentence has been predetermined. The people play the part of the biblical mob, crying, "To th' rock, to th' rock with him" (3.3.75; compare "Crucifie, crucifie him," Luke 23.21). The voices of the people continue in the same fashion throughout the scene. The tribunes, specifically Sicinius, state:

We need not put new matter to his charge.
What you have seen him do, and heard him speak . . .
Deserves th'extremest death.   (3.3.77–78, 83)

This speech corresponds to (and echoes, in the variations on "What need we") the speech of the High Priest in Matthew:

He hathe blasphemed: what have we any more nede of witnesses?   (Matt. 26.65)

Given the parallels to Christ's trial, we expect Coriolanus' trial to lead to execution. Indeed, this is what the people and their tribunes initially insist upon. It is also what Coriolanus

21 Shaheen, *References*, p. 661.

invites, daring the people to give him "Death on the wheel, or at wild horses's heels" or on the "Tarpeian rock" (3.2.2–3). But Coriolanus is denied martyrdom. Although he has failed to be humble in begging the people's voices (2.3), and he has failed to speak "mildly" against their accusations (3.3), he is not killed but banished. Still, even his final words are allusive: he reverses the verdict against him, crying "I banish you!" and he condemns the people for their "ignorance" (3.3.123, 129). In his procession to Calvary, Christ similarly "reverses" his sentence:

Daughters of Jerusalem, wepe not for me, but wepe for your selves, and for your children. (Luke 23.28)

Christ, however, is sorry for those who condemn him, and even though he, like Coriolanus, calls them ignorant, he forgives them for it:

Father, forgive them: for they knowe not what thei do.
(Luke 23.34)

In both 2.3 and 3.3 the biblical allusions, echoes, and parallels add a dimension to Shakespeare's play not found in Plutarch. For example, the petition scene is different in the two versions: Plutarch writes that Coriolanus goes through the ceremony dutifully, showing his wounds to all the people (North, p. 332). In Plutarch's depiction of Coriolanus' banishment, charges are brought against him by the tribunes that are not mentioned by Shakespeare. The verdict is assigned to the "voyces of the Tribes," but Plutarch does not note the actual words of the judgment (North, p. 341). Nor, in Plutarch, does Coriolanus have anything to say after his sentence is passed.

Coriolanus presents a poor imitation of Christ, yet these parodic allusions in acts 2 and 3 may serve to underscore the reason for Coriolanus' political failure. As Brutus remarks, Coriolanus lacks the necessary humility, since "With a proud heart he wore / His humble weeds" (2.3.151–52). The tribune astutely reads Coriolanus' true character in terms of divinity:

You speak o'th'people
As if you were a god to punish, not
A man of their infirmity. (3.1.79–81)

Brutus is correct: Coriolanus fails because he is unable to abase himself to the common people. Christ, on the other hand, is the god who so humbled himself as to become human; Coriolanus is the man so proud that he behaves like a god. And the kind of god on which he models his behavior is, as Brutus recognizes, a "god to punish," a god of vengeance and of warfare, like Mars or the Old Testament Jehovah.

Comparisons between Coriolanus and the latter types of divinity intensify following his banishment, as he becomes increasingly solitary and inhuman, ultimately being described as an "engine" or "a thing made for Alexander" (5.4.19, 22). In the last two acts, he abandons political aspirations and becomes a soldier again, obsessed by a desire for vengeance on Rome. Cominius reports Coriolanus' position with respect to the Volsces:

> He is their god. He leads them like a thing
> Made by some other deity than nature, . . .   (4.6.91–92)

Aufidius' Lieutenant has the same opinion of his new commander, remarking that he inspires such awe that the "soldiers use him as the grace 'fore meat" (4.7.3). Cominius returns to the biblical harvest metaphor, reporting that Coriolanus no longer cares even for his friends and "could not stay to pick them in a pile / Of noisome musty chaff" (5.1.25–26). The allusion builds on the earlier echo of Isaiah, likening Coriolanus to the wrathful Jehovah, except that in this case the language points not to Isaiah but to John the Baptist's modified use of the same metaphor to describe the coming of Christ,[22]

Which hathe his fanne in his hand, and wil make cleane his floore, and gather his wheat into his garner, but wil burne up the chaffe with unquenchable fyre.   (Matt. 3.12)

Unlike Christ's, Coriolanus' fire is undiscriminating. As Cominius further reports, "He said 'twas folly, / For one poor grain or two, to leave unburnt" (5.1.26–27). As most editors

---

22 Noted by Brockbank, *Coriolanus*, p. 277, and Parker, *Coriolanus*, p. 322. For the passage from Isaiah, to which Cominius alludes, see above, pp. 77–78.

note, this passage echoes the agreement of Abraham's God to spare Sodom for the sake of a few righteous men (Gen. 18.23–33).[23] The significant point for the attentive listener is that Coriolanus is here even more vengeful than the Old Testament Jehovah at his angriest. The fire of Coriolanus' anger, a metaphorical expression of his literal plan to burn Rome, is a recurring image in acts 4 and 5. Although Plutarch writes of "the fyer of his choller" (North, p. 343), echoes of the divine retributive fire of the Old Testament are exclusive to Shakespeare's version.

Act 5 scene 3, like the pivotal scenes, 2.3 and 3.3, combines verbal and visual allusions, primarily to Christ. First, the key image of the scene is Coriolanus enthroned, a visual tableau anticipated by Cominius' earlier description:

> I tell you, he does sit in gold, his eye
> Red as 'twould burn Rome; . . .   (5.1.63–64)

Cavell suggests an allusion to the figure of Christ in Revelation, who sits on a throne in heaven, and whose "eyes were as a flame of fyre" (Rev. 4.2, 1.14).[24] In this case, Coriolanus is likened to Christ in a manifestation that better suits his wrathful nature, that of his Second Coming on the Day of Judgment. Second, in an earlier anticipation of Coriolanus' arrival, Cominius returns to the wolf-sheep metaphor, though his application of it is as unexpected as was Menenius' in 2.1. Cominius states of Coriolanus that

> the people
> Deserve such pity of him as the wolf
> Does of the shepherds.   (4.6.111–12)

One expects Coriolanus to be the wolf, yet the term is applied to the Roman people. The comparison of Coriolanus to a shepherd recalls Christ the "good shepherd" of John 10:14, but in the Gospels the shepherd represents care and protection, not punishment. (As Christ says, he "giveth his life for his shepe.") Third, Coriolanus's rejection of family ties also echoes Christ:

---

23 Brockbank, *Coriolanus*, p. 277; Parker, *Coriolanus*, p. 322.
24 Cavell, "*Coriolanus*," p. 159.

> Wife, mother, child I know not. My affairs
> Are servanted to others. (5.2.80–81)

Christ asks, "Who is my mother? and who are my brethren?" (Matt. 12.48). Of course, while Coriolanus aims to renounce all ties to family (and Rome, and, despite his claim to be "servanted to others," to humanity in general), Christ is embracing a more universal notion of family, extended to all mankind, marking a contrast between the latter's broad humanity and the former's desire to "stand / As if a man were author of himself / And knew no other kin" (5.3.35–37).

The last act's critical moment is Volumnia's petition to Coriolanus for "mercy" on behalf of Rome (5.3.137). Cominius sees Rome as entirely dependent upon Coriolanus' granting the request:

> We are all undone unless
> The noble man have mercy. (4.6.108–09)

Later, Menenius states that Coriolanus "wants nothing of a god but eternity, and a heaven to throne in." But the ever-perceptive Sicinius replies, "Yes, mercy, if you report him truly" (5.4.24–26). Noble notes two references to Isaiah in Menenius's statement:[25]

For thus sayth he, that is hie and excellent, he that inhabiteth the eternitie, whose Name is the Holie one.... (Isa. 57.15)

Thus saith the Lord, the heaven is my throne. (Isa. 66.1)

These references constitute faint, though perhaps genuine, echoes, but the emphasis on mercy certainly evokes an attribute of New Testament divinity, whether of Christ the Son or of God the Father. Brockbank compares Sicinius' response to the words of the Communion Prayer: "But thou art the same Lord, whose property is always to have mercy."[26] By contrast, Coriolanus seemingly has no such property.

---

25 Noble, *Biblical Knowledge*, p. 242.
26 Brockbank, *Coriolanus*, p. 299. The example from the Communion Service is a good one, but the language of mercy runs throughout the services of the Book of Common Prayer.

Unbeknownst to Menenius and Cominius, however, Coriolanus has in fact already demonstrated the very quality Sicinius accused him of lacking. Volumnia is jubilant at the turn of events, and she predicts an exclamation from the people, "'Be blest / For making up this peace!'" (5.3.139–40), strongly echoing the Beatitudes' declaration, "Blessed are the peace makers" (Matt. 5.9).[27] This act marks a change for Coriolanus from wrath to mercy, making comparisons to Christ seem, for the first time, apt. Saint Paul's letter to the Ephesians also seems to lie behind this scene of transformation, signaled by Menenius' comparison of Coriolanus to the "cornerstone" of the Capitol (5.4.1–6). His intention is to emphasize Coriolanus' immovability, as well as his inhumanity (analogies to a "dragon," an "engine," a "tiger" follow), yet, ironically, in the previous scene Coriolanus *has* been moved, and has demonstrated human sympathy after all. Shakespeare's use of "cornerstone" (the only one in his plays) echoes the metaphor of Christ as the "chief corner stone" (Eph. 2.20). Perhaps the echo is an ironic one, but for once the irony may actually work in Coriolanus' favor, since his "movement," his act of mercy is, finally, behavior that the audience can recognize as genuinely Christian. Furthermore, Christ is the "corner stone" not of a stone building but of a "householde," a family of "Saintes." The Christian metaphor, unlike Menenius', suggests not inanimate immovability but human interdependence (and especially human dependence upon Christ). The general emphasis in Ephesians 2 is on conversion, and Saint Paul welcomes the Ephesians, who are "no more strangers and foreigners: but citizens with the Saintes, and of the householde of God" (Eph. 2.19). The transformation from "stranger" to "citizen" is precisely the one Coriolanus himself undergoes at this point.

As Aufidius remarks, Coriolanus has also undergone a transformation of values from "honor" to "mercy." But this shift, Aufidius recognizes with delighted self-interest, will be Coriolanus' undoing:

> I am glad thou hast set thy mercy and thy honour
> At difference in thee. Out of that I'll work
> Myself a former fortune.   (5.3.200–02)

27 Shaheen, *References*, p. 667.

In fact, Coriolanus predicts his downfall himself:

> Behold, the heavens do ope,
> The gods look down, and this unnatural scene
> They laugh at. O my mother, mother! O!
> You have won a happy victory to Rome;
> But for your son, believe it, O, believe it,
> Most dangerously you have with him prevail'd,
> If not most mortal to him.   (5.3.183–89)

Shaheen notes in the opening lines of this speech a reference to Acts: "Behold, I se the heavens open, and the Sonne of man standing at the right hand of God" (Acts 7.56). If this is what Shakespeare had in mind, the allusion is highly appropriate, since these are the final words of Saint Stephen the martyr. For Coriolanus at least, this "mortal" moment is a kind of martyrdom, sacrificing himself for the good of Rome, or at least his family. For the audience, however, the meaning of the allusion— whether it points to similarity or difference—is difficult to gauge. Although the word "mortal" is used by Plutarch in Coriolanus' speech to his mother (North, p. 363), it acquires a different connotation in Shakespeare's *Coriolanus*, with its allusive subtext. Volumnia has, on the one hand, persuaded her son to a "mortal" action (since, as Coriolanus senses, it will lead to his death). But she has also forced him to concede his common humanity, making him, rather than godlike, merely "mortal." Finally, Coriolanus returns to Antium to be cut down by the mob, led on by Aufidius and his fellow conspirators, in a repetition of his earlier "Crucifixion" scene in Rome. The parallels this time seem more genuine: Aufidius, whom Coriolanus trusted, has betrayed him and made false charges against him, and, like the crowd in Luke 23.21 ("Crucifie, crucifie him"), the Volscian crowd chants for his death: "Kill, kill, kill, kill, kill him" (5.6.130).

III

Why would Shakespeare compare this paragon of Roman aristocratic *Virtus* to competing models of divinity? Possible answers may lie in act 5 scene 3, the confrontation between Coriolanus and Volumnia, and in Aristotle's description of the solitary man. *Coriolanus* deals in part with the political problem of accommodating the exceptional individual—especially an outstanding warrior, whose skills are essentially antisocial— within an increasingly egalitarian society. Certainly, such accom- modation is the last thing Coriolanus himself wants, and he struggles against community, against his humanity, against his ties to other people. In a sense, Sicinius is right when he accuses Coriolanus of wanting to "depopulate the city and / Be every man himself" (3.1.262–63). Furthermore, Coriola- nus' monolithic integrity, his inability to "seem / The same you are not" (3.2.46–47) not only renders him politically impotent (the great politicians in Shakespeare—Richard III, Henry V, Marc Antony—are always great actors), it makes him seem inhuman. When Coriolanus asserts that he can only "play / The man I am" (3.2.15–16), although he expresses precisely the opposite of Iago's nihilistic "I am not what I am,"[28] both state- ments nevertheless echo the same biblical passage: God's state- ment of absolute self-sufficiency, "I am that I am" (Exod. 3.14). A man cannot be entirely self-sufficient; if he cannot be "part or member of a Cittie," he must be either a beast or a god. Aristotle's point, of course, is that men cannot be gods, just as they cannot really be beasts. Men are inescapably, unavoidably human, and to be human means to be socially interdependent. As John Donne wrote, "No man is an island, entire of itself; every man is a piece of the continent, a part of the main."[29]

Like Christ, Coriolanus is "too absolute" for the world of politics (3.2.39). Certainly, like Christ, Coriolanus shows mercy to those who hate him when he halts his campaign against Rome. Like Christ, Coriolanus is finally a victim of the mob (set on by the conspiring Volscian "Pharisees"), killed after false accusations have been laid to his charge. Despite similarities suggested by Shakespeare's biblical allusions, Cori- olanus is not a god and never can be. His defiant cry, "There is a world elsewhere!" (3.3.135) recalls Christ's answer to Pilate, "My kingdome is not of this worlde" (John 18.36), but with consider- able irony. Coriolanus' kingdom—his republic, anyway—is very much of this world, and, for him, there is no world elsewhere, at least not a transcendent one. And without a heaven, dying

28 *Othello*, 1.1.65.
29 John Donne, *Devotions Upon Emergent Occasions* (Ann Arbor: Univer- sity of Michigan Press, 1959), p. 108.

with a curse rather than a blessing on his lips, Coriolanus makes an unconvincing martyr. Kenneth Burke argues nevertheless that Coriolanus is a scapegoat sacrificed to ease "the pervasive unresolved tension typical of a given social order," an acute tension for Shakespeare's audience, after recent grain riots in response to the Enclosure Acts.[30] Coriolanus is ultimately destroyed by the people (though he may seem less a sheep devoured by wolves than, more pathetically, a wolf devoured by sheep). But even if this is the case, a scapegoat is a lesser creature than the sacrificial Lamb, the latter a manifestation of God, the former just a beast. Since Coriolanus is not a god, must he die a beast?

The problem with such an interpretation is that Coriolanus' downfall is the result of his one genuinely human gesture. What Harold Bloom calls Coriolanus' "solipsism" is defeated only by Volumnia, who alone is able to avert Coriolanus' attack.[31] Coriolanus never demonstrates fellow-feeling with the common people, but Volumnia prevails with him because she is his mother, his one undeniable link to humanity. Volumnia, who draws Coriolanus' attention to his "mother's womb / That brought thee to this world," is the physical proof that he is not "author of himself" (5.3.124–25, 36) By turning aside his attack, Coriolanus acknowledges her claim on him, but the acknowledgment of kinship has wider implications as a tacit recognition of his kinship with his fellow Romans and with humanity as a whole. (In this context, Sicinius' earlier question to Volumnia, "Are you mankind?" takes on added significance [4.2.16].) It may be, therefore, that Coriolanus finally dies as neither a god nor a beast, but as a man. However reluctant, partial, and contentious his admission of unself-sufficient humanity, Coriolanus does make such an admission; perhaps his tragedy and his achievement are that this admission makes him finally, and in all senses, "mortal."

30 Kenneth Burke, "*Coriolanus*—and the Delights of Faction," in Harold Bloom, ed., *Modern Critical Interpretations: William Shakespeare's Coriolanus* (New York: Chelsea House, 1988), pp. 33–50, 48–49.

31 Bloom, *Interpretations*, p. 5.

8

Timing Redemption in the Early Modern Devotional Lyric

JOHN ROGERS

The seventeenth-century English devotional lyric broods like few other early modern literary modes on the relation of time to literary form. Time, of course, had always been, and will always be, a subject not only of lyric poems, but of all discursive genres and modes. But the devotional lyric came to lend itself especially well to the newly urgent, fractious considerations of time occasioned and intensified by the Reformation. The religious lyrics of seventeenth-century England (by John Donne, George Herbert, and dozens of their poetic imitators) worked hard to accommodate the traditions of lyric to the new demands of Protestant theology. Luther, and especially Calvin after him, may not have invented the temporal inversions at the heart of Christian history, but surely they are responsible for Western culture's unprecedented focus on the Christian rethinking of temporal sequence. The conceptual revolutions introduced at the Reformation are familiar, and so I will simply summarize a single aspect of the so-called shift in consciousness triggered by the Reformation. In its unyielding rejection of the role of *works* as a means to salvation, Protestantism, in its purest form, robbed the individual of any immediate control over or participation in his salvation. "Works," of course, is the theological term referring not only to the participation in the Church's sacraments, but essentially any form of virtuous human activity, undertaken as a means to redemption and salvation. In the derogation of *works*—what was often taken to be a derogation of the value of human endeavor, of human activity generally—the Reformers rendered meaningless the traditional, temporally bound understandings of cause and effect that structured the Christian experience. Our salvation was to come about not by our present *doing*, not by the actions undertaken even in a life devoted wholly to the pleasing of God; but our salvation was to occur by means of a decision by God made inestimably prior to even the most obedient and pious of our actions. With the doctrine of predestination, Protestantism located the most significant cause of our salvation at the beginning of time, at a moment before not merely God's creation of the earth, but the much earlier event of God's creation of Heaven. Concomitant with this unprecedented pre-dating of the causes of salvation was a newly intensified understanding of the temporality of human sin and its atonement. The sins we do by two and two were of as little significance as the pious acts of virtue we perform one by one: the only sin that can be meaningfully said to have caused our damnation is the *original sin*, Adam's eating of the fruit which necessarily preceded in time any action undertaken by his sons or daughters. The only action that can be said to have meaningfully atoned for that sin was the Crucifixion of Christ, an event that necessarily occurred *after* what were arguably centuries of meaningful human progress, and that necessarily occurred *prior* to any of the pious or obedient actions performed by Christians. Max Weber forwarded his notorious theory of the cultural dialectic that pushed Protestant Europe, seized by the theological derogation of works, to pursue an unprecedented (and paradoxical) commitment to the practical activity of work. And surely this dizzying inversion, if we are able (as I think we are) to credit some of Weber's thesis, was enabled by Protestantism's relocation of all significant causes away from the time line of any given person's lived experience. In a world in which the Christian was everywhere obliged to forswear sin and pursue righteousness, the chief instantiations of both sin and its atonement were always already completed events. The Reformation forced the Christian to look backward to see the origins of his future.

It was a profound and sophisticated appreciation of the ironic timing of sin and atonement that Protestantism bequeathed to the seventeenth-century lyric poem in English. The devotional lyric, for the first generation of "metaphysical" poets, John Donne and George Herbert, often centered on the revelation of the inescapable belatedness of the speaker's own sin and the speaker's own virtue. In his late lyric, "A Hymne to God the Father," Donne puns cleverly on his own name, to exploit the tension between the sin he is doing and the more consequential, original sin already "done":

Wilt thou forgive that sinne where I begunne,
Which was my sin, though it were done before?
 Wilt thou forgive that sinne; through which I runne,
And do run still: though still I do deplore?
  When thou hast done, thou hast not done,
    For, I have more.   (1–6)[1]

The sin that requires forgiveness has a personal origin both in the speaker's past and in the present, "that sin where I begun" and "that sin, through which I run, / And do run still." But that sin, according to the traditional paradox, can also be identified with the original sin that long predated ("done before") the speaker's own life. Laboring under the burden of the temporal paradox informing the relation of personal to original sin, the speaker seems willfully to blind himself to the more consequential paradox of God's justification of the sinner. Through Christ's atonement for man's sin, a guaranteed forgiveness of sins predates their commission: God had by means of the mechanism of the Christian atonement already bestowed the forgiveness for which the speaker is asking at the present moment. Dwelling on the temporal paradox of sin to the neglect of the temporal paradox of justification, Donne's speaker violates all Reformation orthodoxies as he concludes with a desperate, theologically misguided attempt to compel the Father to promise that the already guaranteed justification of Christ will extend to the death of the speaker: "But swear by thy self, that at my death thy son / Shall shine as he shines now, and heretofore." Like the sun that rises the next day regardless of a petitioner's request, Christ's justification of the sinner is a completed fact that renders superfluous the speaker's present imperative to "swear."

George Herbert would similarly stage the revelation that he has already been forgiven, and already redeemed, for sins he is committing at the present moment and that he will continue to commit in the future. In a cluster of poems in *The Temple*— "The Thanksgiving," "The Reprisal," "The Agony," "The Sinner," "Good Friday," "Redemption," "Sepulchre," and "Easter"— Herbert broods on the strained, even competitive relation of the pious individual to the all-encompassing theological struc-

1 *The Poems of John Donne*, ed. Herbert J. C. Grierson (Oxford: Clarendon Press, 1912).

ture of grace, the divine source of action that at once preempts and supersedes the pious man's virtuous actions.[2] The speaker of "The Thanksgiving," for example, hopelessly seeks a mode of piety appropriate for a savior whose Crucifixion has already rendered all pious actions supererogatory: "O King of wounds! How shall I grieve for thee, / Who in all grief preventest me?" (3–4).[3] Through the Crucifixion, Christ "prevented"—both came before and hindered—the speaker's own gestures of sympathetic suffering, robbing them in advance of any prayerful efficacy. So troubling is the passion's interruption of the linear expectations of a pious cause and a redemptive effect that Herbert ingeniously permits the speaker's recognition of that "prevention" to interrupt the otherwise logical progression of his systematic plans for a virtuous response to Christ's love:

> As for thy passion —But of that anon,
>   When with the other I have done. (29–30)
> Then for thy passion—I will do for that—
>   Alas, my God, I know not what. (49–50)

Just as Christ's suffering prevented the redemptive efficacy of the speaker's own, so the poem's recognition of this central Protestant tenet prevents its linear progression to a definitive theological conclusion. Where "The Thanksgiving" focuses on the frustrating uncertainty with which the pious Protestant approaches the problem of pious action, the next poem in Herbert's atonement sequence, "The Reprisal," examines the competitive structure of the relation of man to a God who seems always already to have redeemed him:

> I have considered it, and find
> There is no dealing with thy mighty passion:
> For though I die for thee, I am behind;
>   My sins deserve the condemnation. (1–4)

In measuring his own sacrifice, as well as his own virtue, against Christ's, the speaker of "The Reprisal" finds the most

2　See Richard Strier, *Love Known: Theology and Experience in George Herbert's Poetry* (Chicago: University of Chicago Press, 1983), pp. 48–60.

3　Herbert's poems are cited from *The Works of George Herbert*, ed. F. E. Hutchinson (Oxford: Oxford University Press, 1941).

fitting statement of the theological problem of "dealing with [Christ's] mighty passion": "I am behind."

One of the poetic strategies Herbert employs to accommodate Protestantism's insistence on the structural belatedness of human action is the surprise ending. The surprise is the clever revelation that the seemingly reasonable course of virtuous action proposed and plotted over the course of the lyric's progress is purposeless, since the atoning action of Christ's passion has already prevented, and rendered meaningless, any human attempt to respond to, take advantage of, or "deal with" the passion. One such poem is "Redemption," a brief allegorical sonnet illustrating the paradox of the necessity and superfluity of man's petition to God for justification and salvation. The narrator, a "tenant long to a rich Lord," resolves to find the lord and "make a suit unto him, to afford / A new small-rented lease, and cancell th' old" (3–4). His attempt to make the suit, however, is preempted by the lord's sudden and unexpected granting of it:

> At length I heard a ragged noise and mirth
>> Of theeves and murderers: there I him espied,
>> Who straight, *Your suit is granted*, said, & died.

The speaker's understandable assumption of a diachronic spiritual history that places prayer and response, or repentance and forgiveness, in a familiarly linear causal and temporal scheme, is the theological mistake unveiled at the poem's brilliant poetic accommodation of the Reformation inversion of traditional diachrony.

Herbert would take the theological problem of belatedness a step further, suggesting in other lyrics, as Stanley Fish has argued, the supererogatory status of the poem itself: the devotional poem itself, Herbert seemed to reflect in dozens of lyrics, was superfluous in a world in which no communication between a creature and his God could affect or alter the facts of sin and atonement, long since established.[4] Herbert goes so far to suggest at the end of "A True Hymn," that the only true

4 See Fish's chapter on Herbert in *Self-Consuming Artifacts: The Experience of Seventeenth-Century Literature* (Berkeley: University of California Press, 1972), pp. 156–223.

poem is the one already written, or at least completed, by God:

> As when th' heart sayes (sighing to be approved)
> *O, could I love!* and stops: God writeth, *Loved.*

The sighing poet's protestation of love for God will always be superseded, Herbert is continually learning, by God's previous inscription of his own poem: God's *already having loved* man renders unnecessary the frenzied poet's desperate search for divine approval. And it is a conviction of the poem's belatedness, of its nonnecessity, that Herbert is seeking. The startling revelation, staged throughout Herbert, that God has already written the poem, is as comforting as the knowledge that God has already redeemed the otherwise unredeemable poet.

No seventeenth-century poet feels the ironies of the Protestant rethinking of time more keenly than John Milton. But the discontinuous interruptions of the narrative of redemption that were dictated by the Reformers do not, as they did for the Calvinist Herbert, surface to offer consolation. The disruptions of the Miltonic lyric, whose relation to Calvinism is tense even at its most orthodox, voice disappointment or anxiety far more often than solace. Milton's early religious lyrics are typically structured by a diachronic narrative of redemption: the birth of Christ, in one poem, or Christ's circumcision, in another, are seen as events that begin a long, ongoing process of purification that can from one perspective lead seamlessly to an apocalyptic future of new heavens and earth. The natural world and the natural man overcome the effects of the fall by means of a slow cultivation of virtue and purity, a process seen eventually to burst out into a glorious ending. This is the dominant image—we can call it a fantasy—behind all of Milton's most powerful early poems. A fantasy, because at some point or other in nearly every one of Milton's lyrics, there comes the recognition that this narrative of a temporally sequential virtuous progress is at odds with the Reformation re-dating of the causes of sin and atonement.

As in many of the early religious lyrics, the human narrator of Milton's "At a Solemn Musick" both imagines, and seems actively to participate in, an ambiguous union with a higher, divine source of the poem. As William Kerrigan has argued in

The Prophetic Milton, the human persona of these lyrics often imagines and sometimes actually enacts the "forfeiting" of his poetic voice to that of a divine author, variously figured as the heavenly choir and the music of the spheres. Like the Miltonic narrator of *Paradise Lost*, whose voice is for nearly 45 lines indistinguishable from that of the celestial choir he is describing (3.372-415), the lyric speakers of some of Milton's poems seem to use the authority of the divinized human voice to represent a provisional narrative of redemption that bypasses entirely the temporal discontinuities occasioned by the Protestant understanding of original sin and redemption. In "At a Solemn Music," the speaker, at least initially, exploits the potentially angelic status of his voice to promulgate a narrative of salvation that short-circuits any Reformation understanding of the atonement and redemption; his is a slow redemption of human experience that swells to a glorious image of man and angels singing together before the heavenly throne:

> Hymns devout and holy Psalms
> Singing everlastingly;
> That we on Earth with undiscording voice
> May rightly answer that melodious noise
> As once we did.

With those last four words, Milton shifts tense to accept an orthodox version of Reformation theology, and permits the beloved image of a gradual continuous purification to be seen as a lie. With this eleventh-hour reminder of the perfect, melodious life before the fall, Milton asserts the unavoidable fact that the original sin prevents all human attempts in the present to participate in a redemption of man and nature. The original sin, temporally prior and logically superior to any one act of human experience, renders impossible any narrative that sets forth the redemptive potential of virtuous action, or virtuous poetry, at the present moment. The violent switch to the past tense reveals the idea of a self-directed, autonomous human or natural human progress as an unsustainable fantasy.

Milton will in all of the early poems perform versions of this same trick to accommodate the forward motion of the lyric's chronological redemption narrative to the temporal discontinuities essential to Protestantism. The forward movement of the redemptive narrative is invariably interrupted by an abrupt grammatical switch away from the dominant tense. The temporal discontinuity often takes the form of a sudden turn to the past, as in the obstacle to self-redemption introduced in "At a Solemn Musick"—"as once we did." If, as in Milton's poem "Upon the Circumcision," the poem is narrating a redemptive action, like circumcision, that took place in the past, the speaker can burst into a present tense, to remind us of an original fallenness that lives beyond that redemptive act. The Son of God, in that poem,

> For us frail dust
> Emptied his glory, ev'n to nakedness;
> And that great Cov'nant *which we still transgress*
> Entirely satisfied.

But just as often, as elsewhere in "Upon the Circumcision" and the "Nativity Ode," the recognition or remembrance of Protestantism's temporal discontinuities comes in the form of a disconcerted turn to the future. Both of those odes take heterodox positions and assume that earlier events in the life of Christ might have initiated the redemption of fallen man. For the "Nativity Ode," it is the incarnation of the Son of God as Jesus that is seen, for the first 150 of that poem's lines, as the sacrificial beginning of the gradual return of humanity to glory. The poem proceeds, for the vast majority of its lines, to narrate in chronological order the purificatory effects of the incarnation, a purgation from the earth of pagan sinfulness that leads, ultimately, to an apocalyptic close, at which "Heav'n as at som festival, / Will open wide the Gates of her high Palace Hall." At this image of the progressive movement to glory, the poem stops to catch itself. Recalling the Reformation insistence that atonement can never come through a gradual purification of sin, but by means of the sacrificial mechanism of Christ's death, the poem aborts the onward rush of its image of glory:

> But wisest Fate sayes no
> This must not yet be so,
> The Babe lies yet in smiling Infancy,
> That on the bitter cross
> Must redeem our loss;

A closely related tic interrupts the speaker's musings in "The Passion": "Yet more; the stroke of death he must abide" (20). Nearly all of Milton's religious lyrics feature some version of this gesture, the speaker's alarmed, eleventh-hour recollection of the necessity of Christ's atonement for the speaker's own sin. Each poem stages the surprised realization that the glorious end of Christian history must hinge on the brutal sacrifice of the Son of God. This trick, or surprise, may well be the strongest of the dramatic elements Milton brings to the seventeenth-century religious lyric. But, at least in the context of Milton's early verse, it becomes perhaps one of the most predictable. Milton self-consciously, perhaps even stagily, recoils from the full formulation of an atonement achieved without the mortal cost of Christ's crucifixion, that position identified by E. M. W. Tillyard as Milton's heterodox theological desire for a salvation unaided by Christ's substitutive sacrifice.

As will happen throughout Milton, even as late as *Paradise Lost*, the poem recoils from the chronologically organized narrative of redemption that supplies its glorious vision. The Father in Book Three of *Paradise Lost* will reluctantly remind himself of the crucifixion with his "But yet all is not done" (3.204), just as the speaker of the "Nativity Ode" would concede that "wisest fate says no," a full redemptive glory "must not yet be so" (150), until justice is satisfied by Christ's execution. As so often, Milton punctuates the poem with the concern that any narrative of a gradual redemption, any representation of a purificatory process, smacks of a Catholic faith in the efficacy of works. Milton interrupts the narrative, switches tense, and permits Protestantism's temporal dislocation of sin and atonement to disrupt and reorient the poem's otherwise diachronic representation of the unfolding of time.

Every one of Milton's religious odes is structured by this tension between a chronologically organized narrative of redemption and a sudden and unexpected recognition of a competing time frame, the Protestant time line that removes the chief causes of sin and atonement from the parameters of the speaker's experience or vision. Every one of Milton's religious odes, that is, but one, is so structured. At some point in the mid 1630s Milton penned the brief Ode "On Time." And here, quite stunningly, he offers a narrative of a redemptive purification that admits of no interruption:

Fly, envious Time, till thou run out thy race,
Call on the lazy leaden-stepping howrs,
Whose speed is but the heavy plummets pace;
And glut thy self with what thy womb devours,
Which is no more than what is false and vain,
And merely mortal dross;
So little is our loss,
So little is thy gain. (1–8)

Remarkably, given the consistent treatment of time and atonement in the other religious lyrics, Milton permits in this poem no intrusion of Protestant orthodoxy to disrupt its platonic, temporally seamless vision of a gradual progress from the mortal dross of man's earthly existence to the beatific sight of the soul's arrival at the heavenly court.

The fallen state of both man and nature at the present time is taken, in this poem, for granted. There are no delusions here of a present perfection that must be corrected with a reminder of a fateful fall into original sin. And there is similarly no sudden recognition of the impossibility of gradual progress: no last-minute orthodox reminder of an atonement that is yet to occur, or that occurred long ago, and that had the power to determine in an instant, and without any reference to human action or behavior, the ultimate disposition of souls at the end of time. The engine behind this temporally continuous redemptive process is none other than Time itself, the envious abstraction apostrophized at the poem's opening that is seen sometimes as running, some times as leaden-stepping, but always moving forward without cessation or backward glance.

If the surprised interruptions of Milton's other religious odes work to voice Milton's disappointment with the constraints of orthodoxy, then the uninterrupted redemption painted in "On Time" gives us an extraordinary glimpse into the workings of Milton's fantasy theology. Here the religious vision is fantastical, for its essentially classical, Platonic image of cosmic perfectibility, which gives no quarter to the unique sacrificial atonement necessitated by nearly every stripe of Protestant Christianity: without a nod to the asynchrony behind the Reformation understanding of either original sin or redemptive sacrifice, the poem imagines a purgative process of purification that issues gradually in a state of glory.

The poem's vision qualifies as fantasy, too, for the way it manages, as none of the other religious odes do, to eroticize the soul's ascent from earth to heaven:

> For when as each thing bad thou hast entomb'd
> And last of all thy greedy self consum'd,
> Then long Eternity shall greet our bliss
> With an individual kiss;
> And Joy shall overtake us as a flood.

Scholars have argued about the meaning of "individual" here: does the eternal God single out each individual soul for this special show of affection? Or is the kiss between man and eternity "individual" in the original sense of "indivisible," a sign that salvation brings with it a liquefaction of previously discrete human identities? Whatever the meaning here of that particular word, the image of any type of kiss, accompanied by an overwhelming flood of joy, situates this vision (certainly in relation to Milton's other poems) outside the generally dour walls of seventeenth-century English Protestantism.

The poem continues, in fact, its narrative of redemption, with a view quite astonishingly attuned to a Catholic doctrine of works; not the passive faith in the vicarious atonement of Christ, but a life of goodness, entitles the soul in this poem to its blissful rewards:

> When every thing that is sincerely good
> And perfectly divine,
> With Truth, and Peace, and Love shall ever shine
> About the supreme Throne
> Of him, t' whose happy-making sight alone,
> When once our heav'nly-guided soul shall clime,
> Then all this Earthy grosnes quit,
> Attir'd with Stars, we shall for ever sit,
> Triumphing over Death, and Chance, and thee, O Time.

How could Milton justify this lyric of redemption, which unfolds without halting to concede to Protestant orthodoxy any of its temporal dislocations? It is possible, of course, that he would not have wished to justify this vision, which any contemporary student of Calvin would have to have dismissed as scandalously pagan, or worse, papist and mystical. But if there is any aspect of this poem that could have permitted Milton to relax his generally unswerving commitment to the fits and starts of Reformation redemption, it was the particular figuration of time that dominates the poem's long conceit. The apostrophized Time that is pushing the redemption along is self-consuming, a force whose only true value lies in its ultimate self-vanquishing. Further, the Time that is running its race, no less fast than slow, appears to be running, or consuming, backwards. I am thinking, of course, of the poem's most striking line, line four: "And glut thy self with what thy womb devours." The conventional womb of time is not here seen to give birth to the future, allowing each moment in time to create the possibility of the next. The future seems already to have been born—by what means of parturition we are not told—and the march of time involves a decidedly grotesque reversal of that birth: the womb of time's abortive, murderous ingestion of an already living present and future.

Milton was able only in this one, relatively short poem to countermand the Reformation insistence on looking backward. Luther and Calvin had taught early modern England to contradict lived human experience and to antedate the causes of sin and atonement—isolating all meaningful causes of damnation or salvation in an unrecoverable, unrepeatable past. But Milton is able in the lyric "On Time" to assert a fantastical vision of uninterrupted virtuous self-redemption only by aligning that redemption with an inverted, perversely dislocated image of time. Proceeding forward, by proceeding backward, the lyric "On Time" works in its small way to undo or at least question Milton's many other concessions to the temporal jerks of Protestant orthodoxy. But it works, too, to explore the larger question, as important to Donne and Herbert as to the later, more radical Milton, of the special role played by the devotional lyric in the early modern meditation on time.

9

Tennyson and the Rapture
of "Tithonus"

CORNELIA D. J. PEARSALL

Among the murals in the Jefferson Building of the Library of Congress in Washington, D.C., is a series produced in the 1890s by American painter Henry Oliver Walker, depicting scenes from British literature. The images appear below the names of major English poets. The majority of the figures are prepubescent boys: slim, lithe, beardless ephebes. Under the name of Keats appears Endymion, stretched out, asleep, a cloth barely covering his loins, a thin crescent moon in the distance behind him. In another mural, Adonis, having just been killed by a wild boar, also lies supine, backwards, head towards us, limbs stretched out, back arching up, his genitals scarcely covered by a diaphanous swatch of material. Figured similarly as boys on the edge of puberty (though arrayed in more fabric), are the Boy of Winander, in a cloak, and Comus, in animal skin, each in a separate arch under the names "Wordsworth" and "Milton." Under the arch titled "Tennyson" appears another naked ephebe, barely adolescent, and again barely covered across his groin, in a waft of fabric that stretches around and floats behind him as he is raised aloft into the sky on the wings of Zeus, appearing in the form of an eagle: an image of Ganymede.

One would search in vain for a poem of Tennyson's featuring the figure of Ganymede in any central way; in this, the figure is unlike the young men representing the other English poets named in these murals.[1] And yet, despite the predilec-

---

1 There are scattered references to Ganymede in Tennyson's work. For example, "The Palace of Art" (1832, 1842) depicts a young man with "his rosy thigh / Half-buried in the Eagle's down" (121–22). In "Will Waterproof's Lyrical Monologue" (1837, 1842), the "plump head-waiter" at the Cock Tavern in Fleet Street, a favorite watering place of Tennyson's friends in this period, is compared to Ganymede, although instead of serving ambrosia, he serves pints of stout.

Ganymede, H. O. Walker, Tennyson Arch, Library of Congress.

tions of a muralist who appears to have searched for boys, rather than poems, to illustrate, Ganymede is a curiously appropriate figure to represent Tennyson and his work. Like his great-nephew Tithonus, Ganymede was a beautiful youth, a member of Troy's ruling family, who was rapt away by an immortal. Toward the end of his life, during an illness that his family feared might be fatal, Tennyson woke from a dream to announce to his son Hallam, "Priam has appeared to me in the night." But Tennyson's consciousness had long been visited by members of the Trojan royal family, headed by Tithonus' brother Priam during the Trojan War. Tithonus, beautiful human lover of the dawn, asked the gods for immortality, which he was granted. According to myth, what he meant to say was "Give me eternal youth"; instead, Tithonus' lot is to age, to increase in decrepitude hour by hour for all time, unlike his eternally youthful lover Aurora. This essay considers the rapture of Tithonus and some of its direct if complex implications for Tennyson's poetic practice. In the dramatic monologue "Tithonus," Tennyson uses the story of the beautiful Trojan who coupled with the goddess of the dawn for a radical imagining of the processes of identification and transformation, and a searching examination of the most extreme perils and pleasures of imperative, efficacious monologic speech.

"Rapture" is a word that signifies aggressive acts of seizure or rapine, as well as submission to ravishing transport or exaltation. Tennyson's major dramatic monologues, I argue, can be seen to explore these and other mechanisms of radical transformation. At the same time, we may track certain processes of rigorous ratiocination in these poems, as dramatic speakers deliberately effect, rather than undergo, sequential transformation. In viewing Tennyson's speakers as agents of conscious transformation, I read against a critical tradition that too often views Tennyson himself as overwhelmed by his own rapturous lyric abundance, unknowing in his affect and his effects, stupefied. This claim finds its analogue in the virtually unwavering claim offered by critics regarding the genre of the dramatic monologue. The speech of dramatic monologists in Tennyson, Browning, and other Victorian poets is invariably considered gratuitous and unintentionally self-revealing, accomplishing nothing but the unwitting subversion of the speaker's position or aims. I argue instead that these poems forward a fiction of deliberative, efficacious lyric: something is accomplished during the course of a dramatic monologue, because of the dramatic monologue itself.

Tennyson returned obsessively, in a wide range of poems, to the greatest example Western literary history offers us of lyric efficacy, of a poet's song inducing monumental effects, namely, Apollo's musical raising of the walls of Troy. This myth of civic foundation underwrites, I believe, some of Tennyson's most representative works, including the dramatic monologue "Tithonus." And Tennyson returned again and again not only to the walls of Troy, but to its most beautiful male inhabitants, who, we shall see, were unusually prone to the complex experience of rapture.

Ganymede's rapture by Zeus, his translation into a realm of perpetual pleasure, establishes important patterns for a certain line of Trojan men. In his three-volume 1858 work titled *Studies on Homer*, William Ewart Gladstone observes that beauty is ascribed to Achilles and other Achaeans, but "of the Trojan royal family it is the eminent and peculiar characteristic."[2] Gladstone in his 1869 *Juventus Mundi* further remarks,

2 Gladstone also claims, unconvincingly, "The great Greek heroes are also called beautiful, but their mere beauty, particularly in the *Iliad*, is

"Among the bodily qualities of the Kings, one is personal beauty. This attaches peculiarly to the Trojan royal family, and is recorded even of the aged Priam in his grief." Forwarding a genealogy of morals, Gladstone everywhere debases and feminizes this patriarchal line, insisting upon "a more base and less manly morality among the Trojans." Walter Pater in his 1880 essay "The Beginnings of Greek Sculpture" notes a similar pattern, calling the Trojans "superior in all culture to their kinsmen on the Western shore, and perhaps proportionally weaker on the practical or moral side, and with an element of languid Ionian voluptuousness in them, typified by the cedar and gold of the chamber of Paris." What Gladstone calls "peculiar," Pater calls "superior," yet the voluptuous sensuality of the inhabitants of Troy is seen by both critics to carry a proportional weakness in practical or moral sense. What is the significance for Tennyson of this line of extraordinary male beauty, one "peculiar" in its consistency?

While on the subject of Trojan male beauty, I must acknowledge what anyone familiar with Tennyson's own appearance as a young man will recall, namely what one Tennyson biographer, R. B. Martin, refers to as Tennyson's own remarkable "physical beauty." In a letter to Ralph Waldo Emerson, Thomas Carlyle called the young Tennyson "One of the finest looking men in the world"; his is only one of many contemporary accounts of the young Tennyson's often stunning visual impact. And, indeed, he was of a beautiful line; virtually all the members of the poet's large family were renowned for being, as Martin puts it, "exceptionally handsome."

Hartley Coleridge told Tennyson upon meeting him in 1835 that he "was far too handsome to be a poet." Yet Tennyson had already articulated in the unpublished 1833 dramatic monologue "Tithon," a precursor of the 1860 "Tithonus," a keen intimacy between beauty and poetics, one that followed closely not only the line of Trojan kings, but also the line of Apollo, beautiful god of poetry, and composer of Troy's walls.

---

for the most part kept carefully in the shade." Gladstone, who met Tennyson when both were college-age through their mutual friend Arthur Henry Hallam (the subject of Tennyson's 1850 *In Memoriam*), published more books on Homer than any other author of the Victorian period.

Indeed, we may trace Tithonus' self-construction partly by way of Tennyson's related representations of Paris, in "Oenone," and of Tithonus' and Aurora's extraordinarily beautiful son, Memnon, himself killed in the Trojan War, who is figured curiously in a number of Tennyson's early poems, predating the dramatic monologues.[3] Tithonus' kin include generations of beautiful Trojan men, godlike in their beauty and desired by the gods; this is part of this dramatic monologist's complex patrimony and a context that criticism of this poem has entirely overlooked. The images of these beautiful young men at once enchant and trouble perception, and it is important to follow their contours, because they are for Tennyson, I argue, figures of incarnate poetics.

Ganymede, Tithonus, Paris, Memnon, and other Trojan princes can all be charged with what Gladstone calls a superflux of beauty, but the accusation of perhaps possessing too much beauty has long been addressed to Tennyson's poetry more generally. Douglas Bush in *Mythology and the Romantic Tradition in English Poetry* casts a bemused eye upon the many lines in Tennyson's poetry that "constantly call attention to their beauty," and it is their apparent aesthetic self-consciousness, a necessary subject of any critical study of Tennyson, that renders them problematic for, even offensive to, many of this poet's nineteenth- and twentieth-century readers. Such exhibitionism appears to be characteristic of the Trojans, as conceived of by the Victorians. Gladstone in *Juventus Mundi* explains, regarding Paris, "One solicitude only he cherished: it is to decorate his person, to exhibit his beauty." Tennyson's great profusion of glorious images, and the density of what Bush calls his "beauty of verbal ornament," correspond to the attraction to gorgeous display that we might label a Trojan aesthetic.[4] The Trojans were notorious for their love of luxurious decoration,

3 For a fuller accounting of these connections and of the argument in this essay as a whole, see Pearsall, *Tennyson's Rapture: Civic Transformation in the Victorian Dramatic Monologue*, forthcoming, Oxford University Press.

4 Even Priam, acknowledged as genial and kindly by Gladstone, is prone to what he terms "overindulgence." While Gladstone in *Studies on Homer* must admit the "capacity of the Homeric Greeks for acquisition," he sees in them nevertheless "a remarkable temperance, and even detestation of excess, in all the enjoyments of the senses."

of embellishment, and here too this culture provides a relevant and surprisingly far-reaching context for the reading of a poet whose works were from the start either valued or dismissed on the grounds of their aesthetic richness. This tendency to prodigious, even prodigal, spectacle came early to be attributed to the poet, and was encouraged by his intimate friend Arthur Henry Hallam. At the outset of his seminal 1831 review essay on Tennyson, "On Some of the Characteristics of Modern Poetry, and on the Lyrical Poems of Alfred Tennyson," Hallam insists that the "predominate motive" of the artist must be "the desire for beauty." For the critic and friend whose opinion was of paramount importance to Tennyson, beauty was paramount for poetics, so much so that its apprehension and indeed manufacture were held to be the prerogative and the obligation of the poet.

A comprehensive review of Tithonus' kind can follow lines literally drawn by Tennyson. In an 1806 edition of Homer's *Iliad* in Greek and Latin owned by the poet's father and used by the young Alfred Tennyson for his lessons are many marginal notes and drawings on the front boards and flyleaves. As a child, he doodled a number of genealogical diagrams, some extensive, some brief. The most extensive of these family trees chronicles the line of Troy, from its founding by Saturn through multiple generations descending from Aeneas. Abbreviated diagrams center on Ilus (father of Priam and Tithonus) and Assaracus, both sons of Tros. (I have added, in italics, the placement of Tros and Ganymede, who appear on longer tables charted by Tennyson, in order to show the relation more clearly between Ganymede and the Trojan male line.)

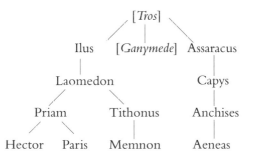

In these particular generations, Ganymede, Tithonus, Paris, Memnon, and Anchises were so notable in their beauty as to have been desired or loved by a range of divinities, while of course Priam, Hector, and Aeneas were hardly considered to have disappointed the familial expectations of male pulchritude.

Tennyson's primary source for "Tithonus" is the *Homeric Hymn to Aphrodite*, which recounts the seduction of Anchises by that goddess. In the story recounted in the *Hymn*, Aphrodite is caused to desire the beautiful herdsman Anchises by Zeus. After their lovemaking, she reveals her true identity to her human lover, informing him that they will have a son, Aeneas. Perhaps with an eye to their son's genetic inheritance, Aphrodite links her lover with his kind, telling him "of all mortal men these who spring from thy race are always nearest to the immortal gods in beauty and stature." She gives as an example "golden-haired" Ganymede, carried away "for his beauty's sake." He remains, she reports, "a marvelous thing to behold, a mortal honoured among all the Immortals."

Aphrodite next cites the hideous example of Tithonus' perpetual aging to explain why she will not attempt to make Anchises immortal. Tennyson's chief literary source for this dramatic monologue thus wholly embeds the story of Tithonus within a network of direct familial association. Having described the abduction of Ganymede, Aphrodite continues, "So too did Dawn of the Golden Throne carry off Tithonus, a man of your lineage, one like unto Immortals." It is vital to note that Ganymede and Tithonus have, as Aphrodite describes, parallel raptures: however much Tithonus may come to desire her ravishment, he had initially been taken forcibly by the Dawn. K. J. Dover in *Greek Homosexuality* describes ancient representations of this seizure of Tithonus, pointing to images showing that Dawn "lays violent hands" on Tithonus. Some images of the "rape," as Dover calls it, show Tithonus "brandishing a lyre" in his struggle against her.

We have established the extreme particularity of Tithonus' line, comprising not only Troy's royalty but also its beautiful men who are like gods and desired by gods. When Tithonus begins his monologue, though, he appears to express nostalgia for a broader sense of his former kind:

> The woods decay, the woods decay and fall,
> The vapours weep their burthen to the ground,
> Man comes and tills the field and lies beneath,
> And after many a summer dies the swan. (1–4)

In these opening lines, Tithonus raises the question of finality, of the mortal ends to which all these other entities turn. We can hear this finality in the first four end-stopped lines, sounding out definitive closures, which are in sharp contrast to the extravagant, theatrically enjambed lines that follow: "Me only cruel immortality / Consumes" (5–6).[5] The self-referential enjambment acknowledges and even glories in Tithonus' sense of himself as straddling two worlds, ongoing, unstoppable. For all his recognition of the decisive ends vouchsafed these other beings, however, the simultaneous and countermanding pattern he discerns here and is still more drawn to is that of the *processes* or transformations they are undergoing. All move through successive stages: the woods decay, and then further decay; the vapors drift, falling downward; man labors toward death; and the swan floats from one summer to another and "many" another. Tithonus seeks an analogue for his own transformations in these ongoing processes, being himself both attracted to and disturbed by these examples of progressive alteration. In seeking a category of *being* with which he might identify, in any state, Tithonus enters into the knotty subject of what Hallam called "sympathy."

Arthur Hallam delivered his essay titled "On Sympathy" to his friends the Cambridge Apostles, a group of which Tennyson was an honorary member, on 4 December 1830; Tennyson had ample opportunity to study this essay, as Hallam presented him with a copy of it. While one can clearly hear in the essay debts to the philosophical and literary traditions of which Hallam was such a brilliant student, this is nevertheless an accomplished and even profound performance for a youth of nineteen. He begins by noting that the definition of "sympathy" is necessarily a "fluctuating" one, but includes in his definition the increased ability to be "pleased with another's pleasure and pained with another's pain, immediately and for their own sakes." He ultimately finds this standard account of what he calls "the machinery of sympathy," though, inadequate to explain "the peculiar force of sympathy itself."

5 I'm grateful to John Hollander for an illuminating recent conversation regarding these opening lines. Among other insights, he asked a question of them that applies to this monologue as a whole: "In what does the beauty of these lines consist?"

Hallam acknowledges that the "notion," as he calls it, which his essay goes on to develop, "will be thought to border on mysticism." But he maintains that his listeners must all have felt moments "in which he has felt it miserable to exist, as it were, piece-meal, and in the continual flux of a stream; in which he has wondered, as at a new thing, how we can be, and have been, and yet [are no longer] that which we have been." "So also," he continues, is the soul disturbed "in its eager rushings towards the future, its desire [for] that mysterious something which now is not," by the knowledge that she cannot maintain her past, present, and future states as one coherent and singular entity. The problem with existing, as one necessarily must, in what he stresses are "innumerable successive states" is that one cannot be a unified self. With each transition in time, the self alters.

As an antidote to this perpetually dividing self, Hallam comes to posit that "sympathy" with another in its deepest form makes possible something akin to a reunion of the self with itself. Through sympathy, the self or soul "absorbs" the other being "into" her own identity, as if that other person were the equivalent of her own past or future experience. Sympathy with another allows one to reunite the divided facets of a self always undergoing alteration, which in any given moment is different from what it has previously been, and what it will momentarily be. The other consciousness is absorbed into the self as a temporal figure, as one of the self's own "innumerable successive states." Rather than constituting the contemplation of a separable person, sympathy makes possible the soul's "identifying the perceived being with herself." Hallam proposes that it is through this *identification* that another being becomes inseparable from a temporal state in one's own ever-shifting consciousness.

Hallam recognizes that this "amalgamation," in which two separate entities mix into simultaneous successive states of one perceiving consciousness, can seem unimaginable: "But," he insists, "were these impossibilities removed, were it conceivable that the soul in one state could coexist with the soul in another, how impetuous would be the desire of reunion, which even the awful laws of time cannot entirely forbid!" It is just such a situation of what Hallam terms "innumerable successive states" that Tithonus in his monologue both remembers and desires, seeking vainly for analogues to himself with his opening words, and finding none.

"Impetuous" is the word Hallam uses several times to characterize the desire for an innumerable succession of temporal states—within and especially between selves— which the "awful laws of time" "forbid" but cannot entirely prevent. And certainly Tithonus describes his request for immortality in terms that suggest the headlong; presumably a moment's hesitation or reflection would have enabled him to ask for eternal youth rather than eternal life. Yet Hallam's essay helps us to understand that Tennyson's Tithonus asked for precisely what he desired. Here is the speaker's account of the progression of thought that led to his apparently heedless outburst:

> Alas! for this gray shadow, once a man—
> So glorious in his beauty and thy choice,
> Who madest him thy chosen, that he seemed
> To his great heart none other than a God!
> I asked thee, "Give me immortality."
> Then didst thou grant mine asking with a smile,
> Like wealthy men who care not how they give. (11 17)

Doomed to bear perpetual witness to his body's ruination, Tithonus claims here to be bodiless, now only a "gray shadow." As he reveals, however, he has always been entirely absorbed in his own materiality. He implicitly insists that, although he was "once a man," he is one no longer. Indeed, so far is he from that status at this moment that he is divorced too from any previous experience of human subjectivity. Recalling of himself, "his beauty," he can only judge his former appearance objectively. Tithonus' moment of most acute self-perception, then, is the moment of his sharpest self-destruction, because as he perceives his own beauty he destroys it.

Tennyson's Ulysses acknowledges himself to have been "made weak by time and fate." The depredations that time and fate have wrought on Tithonus' form are still more harrowing, and promise to be continually so. Yet Tithonus did not always lament change, but rather found in the sensations of physical transformation his most extreme pleasure. He recalls,

Ay me! ay me! with what another heart
In days far-off, and with what other eyes
I used to watch—if I be he that watched—
The lucid outline forming round thee; saw
The dim curls kindle into sunny rings;
Changed with thy mystic change, and felt my blood
Glow with the glow that slowly crimson'd all
Thy presence and thy portals.   (50–57)

In other days, with another heart, and other eyes, another self watched Aurora's daily alterations, and, he tells her, altered with her. He oscillates in his memory from watching her extraordinary transformation to watching himself watch her, marveling, "if I be he that watched." Describing his conjugal pleasure, he speaks as one wholly divorced from his former beautiful self, as earlier he acknowledged an identity articulated in the third person. This objectifying self-regard tells us again that his beauty has long played havoc with his subjectivity.

This temporal division of himself from himself is the state on which Hallam premises his argument in "On Sympathy." The process Tithonus describes moves from his watching of his own watchfulness of her to his incorporation within her, in a union that another of Hallam's essays can illuminate. His 1831 "Theodicæa Novissima," much admired by both Tennyson and Gladstone (who singled it out for praise in a reminiscence of Hallam written more than sixty years later), builds on Hallam's earlier work. After presenting this essay to the Apostles on 29 October 1831 he sent the notebook containing it to Tennyson and his sister Emily. In the essay, he remarks, "Philosophers who have fallen in love, and lovers who have acquired philosophy by reflecting on their peculiar states of consciousness, tell us that the passion is grounded on a conviction, true or false, of similarity, and consequent irresistible desire of union or rather identification." While Tithonus now feels divorced from his former self, he recalls the intensity of union with Aurora, as he merged with her altering form: changing with her mystic change, glowing with her glow, feeling his own blood warm with her crimsoning. What so overwhelms him, of course, are not only her numinous changes but also his concurrent participation in them. In the intensity of their lovemaking, he felt what it was like to become her, which is to say, to become her becoming, to change with her, a change in himself that is also a change of and *into* her: this simultaneity of innumerable successive states is the impossible sensation he seeks now to regain.

In the earlier 1833 version, "Tithon," the speaker claims that he can no longer "know / Enjoyment save through memory" (*1833*, 14–15), and in the deleted passages in which Tithonus conveys the experience of being lover of the dawn we witness more fully the enjoyment with which his memory taunts him. Their union is represented in the 1833 *T. MS B* and "Tithon" as a wholesale melding: "my mortal frame / Molten in thine immortal, I lay wooed." In an insight that elucidates the attraction of divine and human commingling, Tennyson makes clear that Tithon was a mortal at their intensest merging. Engulfed, encircled, enraptured, molten, Tithon suggests that the pleasure they took in their integration was itself dependent upon the temporal dissonance be-tween them, a division in this moment at once breached and affirmed.

Tithonus forged himself, his earlier avatar Tithon tells us, in the smithy of Aurora's molten embraces. In *T. MS B* he describes how he was "By thy divine embraces circumfused," as her embrace becomes indistinguishable from what it encircles. *T. MS B* also describes his mortal heart as "Drowned deep in rapturous trances, beating fast." Also called "rapturous" in the *Homeric Hymn to Aphrodite*, their lovemaking is a process of transportation, as his physical sensations take him out of his body but also house him more certainly there. Given that Tithonus' dramatic monologue is informed, given form, by one of the most intense descriptions of sensation ever produced by a poet who had been introduced in Hallam's ground-breaking essay on Tennyson as a "Poet of Sensation," we are obliged to specify still further the nature and kind of these sensations.

We recall that when Tithonus makes his demand, "'Give me immortality,'" his speech is immediately efficacious: he reminds her, "Then didst thou grant mine asking with a smile, / Like wealthy men who care not how they give" (16–17). Enigmatic as is Aurora's expression, we must look beyond it to note that his asking was granted not only with a smile but also, as he describes it, with a *simile*, an enormously revealing and appro-

priate figure of speech at this moment. The simile that Tithonus invokes in order to understand what happened at the precise moment when he was granted his request—a request to
continue in a simultaneity of successive states—points also to a
wide network of tropological identifications. The beauty of
Trojan men is so rich as to put into question not only divisions
between gods and mortals, but between the categories of masculine and feminine. It is here, in the course of this simile, that
his break with having been "once a man" is twofold: he was
once a mortal, and also once a member of the male sex. Tithonus' own relation to "masculinity" is vexed; as Michael Greene
notes, the "words 'man' and 'men' appear six times in the
poem, but he does not use them of himself, except to recall
that he was 'once a man.'" Indeed, it is Aurora who is most
often associated with manliness by Tithonus, whose similes
compare her repeatedly to male figures: she is "like a
wealthy man" and her whispers are like the song of the
male sun god Apollo. In the moment of Tithonus' becoming still more like an immortal, she becomes like a wealthy
mortal, as he (as Trojan royalty) once was; the simile neatly
reverses their temporal positions. And the simile acknowledges the reversal of their gender positions as well; certainly
their lovemaking itself put him in the traditionally feminized role as passive recipient to her "wooing" (a word Tennyson omitted in revision; "I lay wooed," he recalls in *T. MS
B* and "Tithon").

The pattern of seduction and rapture of these Trojan princes
points to what Gladstone in *Studies on Homer* considers a dis-
concerting, entirely feminized "sensuality" and vulnerability to
rapture. Gladstone remarks, "whereas in Greece we are told
occasionally of some beautiful woman who is seduced or rav-
ished by a deity, in Troas we find the *princes* of the line are
those to whose names the legends are attached." Tithonus'
identity as he remembers it has always been based on a fairly
active passivity. He knew himself, he tells his auditor Aurora,
only as "thy choice," and "thy chosen," referring diplomatically
to her (by some accounts, violent) sexual aggression, as if rapture by another were a self-defining act.

It is possible, indeed, it may be unavoidable, to read Tithonus and Aurora in terms of roles characterized most commonly
as masculine or feminine. But I would like also to take their

circumfusion literally, and to take seriously the blurring of binaries (mortal/immortal, male/female) that Tithonus reports as having been the highlight of their luminous union. The categories of sex and gender identification get confounded deliberately by Tithonus, blurred as impetuously by him as he blurs the distinction between mortals and immortals. "Why should a man desire in any way / To vary from the kindly race of men," Tithonus asks and also answers in his monologue. While his question is generally assumed to refer to mankind or humankind, from whom he with his immortality comes to vary, it is also sex-specific, since his monologue outlines precisely why a man might desire acutely to vary from men.

Tithonus seeks to compound his identification with his immortal lover, taking on the transformation of the dawn, itself necessarily an event of successive stages. The Dawn is indisputably a figure of time, and the time that she keeps becomes a measure of the successive stages of his altering self. This is why he asked her so specifically, in demanding immortality, for still *more* of her time. Rather than desiring to enter into the stasis implied by immutable and unchanging eternal youth, his request for immortality expressed a specific desire to prolong the infinitely ongoing transformative state his monologue chronicles and indeed re-enacts.

In light of the reading I have forwarded of Tithonus' desire for wholesale absorption into Aurora's being and becoming, his closing question, "How can my nature longer mix with thine?" can be interpreted literally. With this phrasing, he acknowledges that their relationship has been founded entirely on his dialectical "mixing" with her, on an implicit absorption of his "nature" (mortal, male) into hers (immortal, female). And his rejection of that synthesis, or mix (a word that connotes both a thoroughgoing amalgamation and a mix-up), signals this dramatic monologue's final turning point. What the gods have joined, Tithonus would now put asunder.

In his decisive leave-taking, Tithonus enjoins his auditor:

> Release me, and restore me to the ground;
> Thou seëst all things, thou wilt see my grave:
> Thou wilt renew thy beauty morn by morn;
> I earth in earth forget these empty courts,
> And thee returning on thy silver wheels.   (72–76)

These lines have invariably been read not as Tithonus' farewell to her arms, as they are, but as a claim that he will persist in attempting to die, in spite of his clear recognition, in a line he earlier recited by rote, that "'The Gods themselves cannot recall their gifts'" (49). I have been arguing that Tennyson's Tithonus is in command of what he asks for at all points. His demand for immortality, for instance, was a specific bid for an unending experience of simultaneous states of successive identity, not a misstatement. This final command is as specific, serious—as intentional—and as possible to fulfill, as the earlier one. Indeed, what he wants is for Aurora to see not only his grave but also his *gravitas.*

In closing, Tithonus expresses his desire to become particulate. Tennyson's expansive Ulysses desires too to be "a part" of all he has met, but for Ulysses this will enable the appropriation of the world by the self, while for Tithonus, to become a part is to dissolve the self, to merge the "I" with soil. Tennyson names his source for the phrase "earth in earth" as Dante's "terra in terra"; clearly, Tithonus envisions an afterlife of compost. This merging of self is not predicated on death, however. As we saw in his opening lines, Tithonus refers more to a process than to a final outcome, and it is a process that resembles the experience of lovemaking that his monologue records. With the phrase "earth in earth," he invokes the process of one entity ("earth") being incorporated, merging wholly into another, virtually identical, and yet infinitesimally separable one ("in earth"). With Dante's help, Tennyson's Tithonus is able to view this relocation to the grave as a restoration, not to human mortality, but to intense identificatory mingling or "mixing." And if he is restored to an infinitude of simultaneous successive states (the eternity of decay that his monologue evokes in its opening line), then he will indeed be spared bearing witness to Aurora's sunny court, while she will have to carry the burden of witnessing his ongoing alterations, or at least the location of them: "Thou wilt see my grave." Like the sexual union his monologue details, decay, too, can be conceived of as a dialectical process, and in his monologue's closing Tithonus hints that perhaps the rapture of their lovemaking was not for him, in retrospect, unlike being decayed. Both experiences involve for him the slow and staggered diffusion of the self into another entity, a submission of physical control or agency over one's corporal body, an enveloping synthesis.

Tithonus, I hope to have shown, seeks to enter into an identificatory relation to Aurora, to become "like" her in all the ways he can, structuring his identity and his figurative language on Hallam's logic of sympathy or identification. In stressing their present difference, he laments, "Ever thou growest beautiful, / In silence"; he now seeks to grow beautiful again himself, but to do so in and through speech. The monologue must enact his beauty, which thus becomes the provenance not of appearance but of articulation. His dramatic monologue is a performance, a return for this speaker to the state of being apprehended and honored on aesthetic grounds, a return to his prior joy in being taken as "glorious in his beauty." But the monologue is also performative: his words attain for him a set of specific goals, which we have only begun to name.

As we have noted, Gladstone and others charge the Trojans with a "redundancy" of beauty—they possess more than is necessary, more than one can use. But Tithonus' beauty has been for him wholly necessary, virtually a condition of his existence. His overabundance of beauty is a privilege he was born to, and he knows no identity apart from this birthright. We have seen that Tennyson's poetics were met with a similar accusation of excess. I should also note that the charge of discursive superfluity, of speech being divorced from any discernible use, has long been leveled at the genre of the dramatic monologue more generally, as we can hear in Robert Langbaum's influential claim that the speech of any dramatic monologuist is "superfluous," and "need never have taken place."

The beauty of the dramatic monologue "Tithonus" has long stood as a matter of critical consensus, even critics who might not be seen to agree with each other on much can agree on this. Christopher Ricks writes of the "superbly mellifluous movements of the verse," and stresses in his reading the "fineness of musical verbalism that makes "Tithonus" [Tennyson's] most assuredly successful poem." Harold Bloom praises the "surpassingly beautiful opening passage" of the poem, and concludes his reading with what he calls its "glorious closing lines." It is not happenstance that "Tithonus" is surely one of

Tennyson's most aesthetically pleasing poems, that like Tithonus among the Trojans, it is one of the most beautiful among a beautiful kind.

Tithonus' words bear the tremendous burden of representing a beauty now discursive rather than visual, and part of what the dramatic monologue effects for him is the re-attachment of the concept of beauty to his own name. This accounts for his need of the monologic, as Aurora must be transformed from the viewer who chose him into the auditor who releases him. In replacing physical with rhetorical beauty, he is becoming a figure of speech, renewing his beauty word by word. If what he intends is for his words to accomplish his release from immortality, they must surely fail; this is no swansong. But if what he intends is his release from the spectacle of her beauty, and, more, the recapturing of his own aesthetic predominance, then his aim is accomplished in the monologue, by way of the monologue. He is indeed, as ancient images depict him, defending himself against Aurora by way of, in effect, brandishing the lyre.

Tithonus' chief ambitions, then, are formal ones, just as form is his chief predicament. His once physically beautiful form is now degenerate, a physical mass losing all definition and even such agency as he, "chosen" and rapt away by an immortal, enjoyed. The form into which he would now metamorphose is that of the dramatic monologue; before our eyes he is transfigured from an ancient form to a new kind, from the mythical Tithonus to the monologic poem titled "Tithonus." Tithonus' dramatic monologue has need of, makes use of, its beauty, because it seeks to effect rapture; the speaker knows that its glorious form will attain for him release, or nothing can. He renews his beauty in the monologue, by way of the monologue, since while losing bodily form he takes poetic form. The poem's beauty, then, itself constitutes the speaker's central rhetorical strategy. And while the only closure possible to this speaker is poetic closure, in the transfer of his beauty from his corpus to his monologue even his infinitude may be an advantage. In the 1841 essay "The Poet as Hero," Carlyle considers the distinction between "true Poetry and true Speech not poetical," noting that much had been written on this subject in recent years by "German Critics": "They say . . . that the Poet has an *infinitude* in him; communicates an

Unendlichkeit, a certain character of 'infinitude', to whatsoever he delineates." T. S. Eliot in an essay in his 1933 *The Use of Poetry and the Use of Criticism* also suggests that advanced age, regardless of one's term of years, might be a defining mark of a poet: "hyperbolically one might say that the poet is *older* than other human beings."

In his essay on Tennyson and contemporary poetry, Arthur Henry Hallam contrasts the artist who, pursuing "the pleasure he has in knowing a thing to be true," will "pile his thoughts in a rhetorical battery, that they may convince," with the artist who takes "pleasure" in knowing a thing to be "beautiful," and so lets his thoughts "flow in a natural course of contemplation, that they may enrapture." Tithonus, battered himself, rather than convincing by a battery of arguments, seeks rather to enrapture his auditor by way of his dramatic monologue, even as he was enraptured by the strange songs of Apollo and Aurora. Readers have long recognized the aesthetic and rhetorical elements of this transport. Referring to the passage in which Tithonus is rapt by his lover (beginning "while I lay"), Ricks calls it a "moment of uttered audible beauty," while Bloom also remarks Tithonus' "heightened powers of aesthetic perceptiveness while being embraced." Tithonus has been rapt in the sense of having been physically translated or removed to Aurora's courts, as Ganymede was rapt to the heavens and Persephone rapt to Hades. And Tithonus came to be enraptured in the discursive sense of Hallam's use of the term, both by Apollo's song and Aurora's whispers. Hallam places this "beautiful" discursive excess, efficacious because overwhelming, in opposition to oratory, establishing it, in effect, as a substitute for oratory. Aurora's seduction, we recall, was not only labial (her kissing lips) but also linguistic (her whispers). The monologuist Tithonus reminds her that he once was her auditor, that he too once knew, as she does now, the experience of being silent and beautiful: in this also they have inverted their previous positions. Her whispers recall to him his earlier audition of Apollo's song, during which "Ilion like a mist rose into towers" (63), since both of these were efficacious performances, causing myriad radical transformations. Having experienced it in many forms, Tithonus makes rapture his own discursive aim: what Tithonus has sustained, his monologue must now perpetually perform.

10

Audible Ecphrasis: Songs in Nineteenth-Century Fiction

JENNIFER LEWIN

And yet it is perhaps a little soon for my song. To sing too soon is a great mistake.

BECKETT, *Happy Days*

This essay is about songs that occur in novels—songs that are alluded to, quoted from, misquoted, remembered, or performed. Following Auden, whose "Music in Shakespeare" claims that Shakespearean drama always contains at least two kinds of song, the "called-for" and the "impromptu," I am going to argue that moments of singing in some British novels extend the implications of Auden's categories by becoming inset narratives within larger plots, instances of what one might call "audible ecphrasis." Audible ecphrasis occurs when characters intentionally or unintentionally reveal themselves through song, diverting the reader's attention from the main plot and turning to a performance that comments on as well as advances knowledge of the character, novel, author, and so on. Although a singer can masquerade as an "impromptu" artist, someone who "stops speaking and breaks into song, not because anyone else has asked him to sing or is listening, but to relieve his feelings in a way that speech cannot do or to help him in some action," the songs and the tableau that the performance creates have always been "called-for" by various fictive and non-fictive agencies.[1] They differ from other moments of quotation and allusion in their inherent performativity; to my knowledge, no one "breaks into" a remembered passage from Aristotle's *Politics.* They appear to be spontaneous, yet their

I thank Lisa Zunshine and Brenda Weber for helpful comments on an earlier draft of this essay.

1 W. H. Auden, *The Dyer's Hand and Other Essays* (London: Faber and Faber, 1963), p. 522.

presence has been carefully structured and sometimes calculated to miss the mark.

Thus novels make it difficult to distinguish the "impromptu" song from the "called-for" song that Auden considers a more self-conscious performance: "a called-for song is a song which is sung by one character at the request of another who wishes to hear music, so that action and speech are halted until the song is over."[2] In them, listening or performing rarely entails the pausing of action and speech; the song itself performs an action and becomes a form of communication. After exploring examples of novelistic music-making that do not involve specific songs, my main discussion turns to an instance in which Cervantes incorporates balladry in *Don Quixote* and thereby creates the kind of generic self-consciousness I mention above, and then focuses on songs in British fiction from the eighteenth to the twentieth centuries in an attempt to explain how musical performance allows authors to test their strategies for raising questions about the relationship between song, singer, narrator, episode, and larger narrative.

Especially for women in the eighteenth and nineteenth centuries, training in accompanying and playing musical instruments was a common feature of life in genteel households. Recommended to young people in advice manuals dating back to the Renaissance, such as Castiglione's popular *The Courtier*, one of the proper social ornaments of a well-educated and gracious person has long been musical ability. In the eighteenth and nineteenth centuries, women were encouraged to play and sing as an "accomplishment."[3] When novels highlight this ability with scenes of entertainment among family and friends after a meal or on a leisurely afternoon, they create dynamic social situations in which various aspects of the performance context take on great importance in developing plot and character. These aspects can include the performer's talent or motives, her style of playing, the song or settings chosen, the attention or mood of the audience or performer(s), and so on, combining to offer richly nuanced portraits of the role of

2 Ibid., p. 511.

3 For an informative discussion of this historical development, see Arthur Loesser, *Men, Women, and Pianos: A Social History* (New York: Simon and Schuster, 1954), pp. 267–83.

song in suggesting and enacting relationships. Songs are never heard exclusively with one interest in mind; they serve multiple purposes and open up several avenues of exploration. Auden writes that in Shakespeare, "a called for song" entails "that the character called upon to sing ceases to be himself and becomes a performer; the audience is not interested in him but in the quality of his singing."[4] In the novel, the quality of singing is only one part of the story that songs tell.

Two examples of the degree to which scenes of music-making matter in novels, whether or not they include the words of the songs themselves, are found in *Sense and Sensibility* and *Jane Eyre*.[5] In Austen's novel, unsurprisingly it is Marianne whose musical talent serves as an early, crucial point of contact between herself and Colonel Brandon. The recent film adaptation makes some changes in the scene worth noting. Her first encounter with the colonel involves his watching her play:

Marianne's performance was highly applauded. Sir John was loud in his admiration at the end of every song, and as loud in his conversation with the others while every song lasted. Lady Middleton frequently called him to order, wondered how any one's attention could be diverted from music for a moment, and asked Marianne to sing a particular song which Marianne had just finished. Colonel Brandon alone, of all the party, heard her without being in raptures. He paid her only the compliment of attention; and she felt a respect for him on the occasion, which the others had reasonably forfeited by their shameless want of taste.[6]

The musical performance that ends the evening at the Middletons not only confirms the Dashwood sisters' emerging opinions about their hosts, but it allows them to deepen their understanding of Colonel Brandon's personality. Readers are also able to witness the formation of Marianne's compassion

4 Auden, *Dyer's Hand*, p. 511.

6 Jane Austen, *Sense and Sensibility*, ed. Claudia L. Johnson (New York: W. W. Norton & Co., 2002), p. 28.

for him and her steady resistance to his charms. In the next chapter, Mrs. Jennings starts to suspect Brandon's attraction to Marianne because of his attentiveness during her performance. Obviously the musical interlude is not the only kind of scene Austen could have invented in order to establish these various developments, but it does become an incredibly economical way to reveal characters' feelings for one another and the directions in which those feelings may lead them.

In Emma Thompson's film version of the novel, two significant performances of song appear. One is an adaptation of the scene I have described, and both fascinatingly are related to one another in terms of theme. Marianne asks to play the pianoforte to defuse a moment of tension in the dinner table conversation; no such request appears in the novel. Brandon hears her from outside the house where he is getting ready to make a late entrance: "His head snaps up to the windows. An expression of pained surprise comes into his melancholy, brooding eyes."[7] He makes his entrance while she is in the middle of the second stanza of John Dowland's "Weep You No More Sad Fountains," a popular English Renaissance ayre (newly set by Patrick Doyle, the film's composer). The setting is as sorrowful as the original without retaining any recognizable elements of it. In the verses that we hear Marianne sing, a woman is noticed "while she lies sleeping." The song itself seems to correspond more to the emotional state that Thompson creates for the Colonel than that which Marianne experiences in either film or novel. In the second performance, Marianne plays Jonson's "The Dream" just before Edward Ferrars appears to attempt to win Elinor's hand in marriage. The song fits the melancholic mood we see Elinor in, but its subject really differs—the poem concerns guilt and shame felt by a speaker who has awoken to find that an elusive, erotic dream has just aroused him. Still, the line "I am undone tonight," which is more audible than the rest of the song, nicely anticipates her reaction to Edward's clarification that it is his brother who has married, and not himself. Having been performed by Marianne, both songs can be said to be consistent with Mari-

---

7 Emma Thompson, *The Sense and Sensibility Screenplay and Diaries: Bringing Jane Austen's Novel to Film* (New York: Newmarket Press, 1996), p. 71.

anne's association with "sensibility," and their mournfulness and emphasis on the passivity of the speaker also succeed in reminding us of the sisters' sheer lack of control over their circumstances. While sadness about the impossibility of finding waking satisfaction is a common topic in both songs, their language of sleep and dreams works to opposite effect: in Dowland's ayre, sleep is peaceful; in Jonson, its receptivity to an affecting dream instills anxiety.

In *Jane Eyre*, another kind of knowledge is revealed through song, establishing *perceived* relationships between characters. Mrs. Fairfax reports to Jane that Rochester tends to accompany Blanche Ingram on the piano as she sings, and knows himself to show off his singing voice. Jane's acknowledgement of their shared penchant for musical performance leads her to conclude that she is not a legitimate contender in the competition for Rochester's affections, although it does not deter her from closely watching them when they are together at Thornfield. Her telling Mrs. Fairfax that she "was not aware he could sing"[8] begins the process of turning a realized connection into an excuse for self-deprecation. She twice calls Blanche "accomplished," a word used specifically in reference to musical training and other female pursuits. Her mental picture of Rochester and Blanche suffices to convince Jane of her meaninglessness in his world.

Protagonists and narrators and the songs and music they recall can also reflect on the work that they mutually ask each other to perform. Proust, for example, writes of "the little phrase" of a sonata that to Swann sounds like a human voice that "spoke to him of the vanity of his sufferings":

It was the charms of an intimate sadness that it sought to imitate, to re-create, and their very essence, for all that it consists in being incommunicable and in appearing trivial to everyone except him who experiences them, had been captured and made visible by the little phrase.... Swann had regarded musical motifs as actual ideas, of another world, of another order, ideas veiled in shadow, unknown, impenetrable to the human mind, but none the less perfectly distinct from one another, unequal among themselves in value and significance.[9]

8 Charlotte Brontë, *Jane Eyre* (New York: Bantam Books, 1986), p. 149.
9 Marcel Proust, *In Search of Lost Time*, translated by C. K. Scott Mon-

The life of their own that musical motifs accrue in the novel
not only advance our understanding of relationships between
characters and the gap between knowledge and perception, as
the instances discussed thus far suggest, but they almost allow
for moments of pure performance, acts of aesthetic appreciation whose ramifications extend beyond their immediate contexts. Applicable here is an observation made by John Hollander
about refrains in poetry, which perform the work of memory in
more than one way: "refrains are, and have, memories—of their
prior strophes or stretches of text, of their own preoccur-
rences, and of their own genealogies in earlier texts as well."[10]
In the novels I discuss below, the loneliness that preoccupies
Proust intersects with the sociability of the texts themselves,
making songs into catalysts for intensely realized moments of
generic self-consciousness.

Like the recitative in opera, the ballad is a genre that covers
a lot of narrative terrain in a few lines. Like Goldsmith and
Fielding after him, both of whom include or allude to ballads
in meaningful ways, Cervantes stages a generic confrontation
between the novel and the ballad in the master-puppeteer
scene in *Don Quixote*, where we learn the story of Master
Pedro, who entertains guests at an inn. The puppet show's boy-
narrator explains that he draws upon a "true history" of the
star-crossed but ill-fated lovers Don Gayferos and Melisendra,
"taken word for word from the French chronicles and Spanish
ballads,"[11] yet the boy repeatedly resists relating his tale "word

crieff and Terence Kilmartin and revised by D. J. Enright, volume 1
(New York: Modern Library, 1992), pp. 495–96.

10 John Hollander, "Breaking into Song: Some Notes on Refrain," *Melodious Guile: Fictive Pattern in Poetic Language* (New Haven: Yale University Press, 1988), p. 138.

11 Miguel de Cervantes, *Don Quixote de la Mancha*, translated by
Charles Jarvis, edited by E. C. Riley (Oxford University Press, 1992),
p. 709. Other quotations are cited in parentheses in the text of the
essay. Several versions of the pseudo-Carolingian story of Gayferos
and Melisendra were widely anthologized in Spain in the mid-sixteenth
century. Germán Orduna traces at least three extant versions of it in
each of the following: *Cancionero de Romances sin año* (1548) and *Cancionero de Romances de 1550*, both edited by Martín Nucio; and *Silva de
Varios Romances* (1550–51), edited by E. de Nájera (*Selección de Romances
viejos de España y América* [Buenos Aires: Editorial Kapelusz, 1976], p.

for word." As he digresses, he shows himself to be mindful and indeed obsessed to the point of incomprehensibility with the very tales he attempts to push away from his narrative ken.

The shadows cast by the source ballads dominate the scene in several ways. As he introduces the story, the boy refers to a ballad's version to justify the set design: "there you may see how Don Gayferos is playing at tables, according to the ballad: Gayferos now at tables plays, Forgetful of his lady dear, &c." He then quotes some lines from another ballad's dialogue between Melisendra's father, Charles the Great, and Don Gayferos, but tries to obscure their origins by stating that the conversation simply "is reported." As he meanders from one excursus to another, even Don Quixote scolds him: "Boy, boy, on with your story in a straight line, and leave your curves and transversals," to which Master Pedro adds, "Boy, none of your flourishes, but do what the gentleman bids you; for that is the surest way; sing your song plain, and seek not for counterpoints; for they usually crack the strings" (pp. 710–11). The last ballad excerpts appear as he describes the conversation between the captive Melisendra and Gayferos, whom she mistakes for a passer-by. He unimaginatively reports that Melisendra "talks to her husband, believing him to be some passenger; with whom she holds all that discourse and dialogue in the ballad. . . ." Refusing to repeat more than a few lines from their speech, he tells his audience that he is engaging in a form of *occupatio*: "the rest I omit, because length begets loathing" (p. 711). The snatches of popular balladry he has quoted are more concise than his tale, of course, and the juxtaposition would have been apparent to his contemporary audience. The swift movement of the source ballads from one scene to the next and their concentration on specific events contrast with the boy's "curves and transversals." As he becomes increasingly digressive, therefore, the boy wanders further from the ballads.

In his discussion of the novel, Robert Alter describes this scene of narrative imbedding in terms of a conversion of "the fictional world . . . into a multiple regress of imitations that call

---

121). For an abbreviated English translation, see "Melisendra" in John Gordon Lockhart (1794–1854), *The Spanish Ballads* (London & New York: Frederick Warne & Co., n.d.), pp. 126–32.

attention in various ways to their own status as imitations."[12] Alter notes that the story points self-consciously to its status as a combination of previous texts: "Imbedded in the boy's manifestly fictional narrative—which is, of course, enclosed in turn within the Second Author's version of a narrative by Cid Hamete Benengeli—are lines of old ballads, that is, fragments of another, preexistent body of literature."[13] Cervantes not only "encloses" one narrative within another, but he stages a moment of auditory ecphrasis that humorously confronts the differences between those narrative forms; they are not merely "preexistent," they point to their own conventions and subvert them. While the overall premise of the novel parodies the chivalric romance with its famously absurd hero's adventures, this episode's use of the ballad adds an additional generic component to the novel's satirical elements.[14] Cervantes juxtaposes the structure of the novel's own circuitous, delaying, and, indeed, *anti-balladic* narrative strategies, with the ballad's directness of speech, intensity, and suspense. He brilliantly shows one possibility for incorporating ballads in other narrative genres.

By contrast, the major eighteenth-century British novelists who learned so much else from Cervantes rarely mention or use ballads or songs. Except for an occasional, passing refer-

---

12 Robert Alter, *Partial Magic: The Novel as a Self-conscious Genre* (Berkeley: University of California Press, 1975), p. 11.

13 Ibid., p. 12.

14 Gerould's discussion of the matter is particularly insightful: "This way of telling a story in terms of its crucial or concluding incident, to the neglect of the chain of events that precedes it, and of permitting the action to interpret itself with the minimum of comment and descriptive setting, is quite characteristic of ballads on the Continent as of those sung in England and Scotland. This is strikingly illustrated by Spanish ballads, the material of which is derived from earlier, extended narratives. The ballads themselves are completely centralized, episodes no longer, but stories of a single dramatic situation briefly but independently developed. . . . Ballads, however, are not merely short: they are compressed," *The Ballad of Tradition* (Oxford: Clarendon Press, 1932), pp. 5–6. See also M. J. C. Hodgart, *The Ballads* (New York: W. W. Norton & Co., 1962), pp. 27–45. Hodgart's use of Eisenstein's concept of *montage* is also relevant here: "[Ballads] present the narrative not as a continuous sequence of events but as a series of rapid flashes, and their art lies in the selection and juxtaposition of these flashes," p. 28.

ence, Defoe, Richardson, Fielding, Smollett, Sterne, and Burney did not seem to find many appropriate places for songs or ballads in their novels.[15] Their heroines' singing voices often are praised, but readers rarely encounter episodes in which performances of songs occur. We read that Pamela and Clarissa play the lute to solace themselves privately, like Queen Elizabeth with her virginals, but we never hear or see them nor do we expect to.

Tom Jones is the exception here, and in a brief scene Fielding parodies the social function of song as a form of rhetorical persuasion by showing his heroine skillfully using it to her advantage. Early in the novel, Tom convinces Sophia to petition her vengeful father to relieve from prosecution the trespasser Black George. She decides to soften him by playing some of his favorite songs on her harpsichord. These songs include vulgar drinking songs that make Sophia wince: "*Old Sir Simon the King, St George he was for England, Bobbing Joan*, and some others," and he is so overjoyed that he decides to grant all her wishes: "If she would give him t'other bout of *Old Sir Simon* he would give the gamekeeper his deputation the next morning. *Sir Simon* was played again and again, till the charms of the music soothed Mr. Western to sleep."[16] This scene reveals Sophia's eagerness to obey Tom's wishes, and exposes her father's gullibility and lack of true interest in the music itself. The episode on the whole does not do much more than what it accomplishes at that moment. For the most part, it is a closed system of explication.

The Vicar of Wakefield, however, follows *Don Quixote* in its use of popular balladry to confront other kinds of verse and those who write them. Ballads are part of Goldsmith's use of the novel as a staging ground for judging the poetic merits of his contemporaries.

15 For an interesting discussion of a related matter — Sterne's use of quotations in *Tristram Shandy*—see Herman Meyer, *The Poetics of Quotation in the European Novel*, translated by Theodore and Yetta Ziolkowski (Princeton: Princeton University Press, 1968), pp. 72–93. On Samuel Richardson, see Michael Austin, "Lincolnshire Babylon: Competing Typologies in Pamela's 137th Psalm," *Eighteenth-Century Fiction* 12 (July 2000), pp. 501–14.
16 Henry Fielding, *Tom Jones*, edited by R. P. C. Mutter (New York: Penguin, 1985), p. 166.

At first the narrative situations in which songs occur seem conventional. In the vicar's "little republic,"[17] his children are frequently entreated to sing for their parents during Sunday afternoon picnics: "Sometimes, to give a variety to our amusements, the girls sung to the guitar," he reminisces, "and while they thus formed a little concert, my wife and I would stroll down the sloping field, that was embellished with blue bells and centaury, talk of our children with rapture, and enjoy the breeze that wafted both health and harmony"(pp. 26–27). Songs are included among the ordinary features of the family's picturesque tranquillity, but two specific situations in which Olivia and Sophia perform songs readily resist creating a sense of *otium*. Instead they show the ultimate futility of the vicar's attempts to influence his daughters' behavior, thus becoming associated with a sexual maturation that the vicar cannot control.[18]

During one of their outings, for example, a large hunting party led by Squire Thornhill stumbles upon the family's recreation. The vicar reacts bitterly to the aristocrat's intrusion, silently disdaining Thornhill's "careless superior air" and his brash declaration "that he was owner of the estate that lay for some extent round us" (p. 27).[19] By gazing flirtatiously at Olivia and Sophia and asking for a song, he tarnishes their innocent, familial self-containment. The sisters' enthusiastic compliance

17 Oliver Goldsmith, *The Vicar of Wakefield*, edited by Arthur Friedman (New York: Oxford University Press, 1974), p. 24. All subsequent references to the novel are indicated by the page numbers in the text of the essay.

18 The vicar's general ineffectualness is discussed by David Durant, who observes that "what defeats the Vicar is the unruly actuality of experience" ("*The Vicar of Wakefield* and the Sentimental Novel," *Studies in English Literature* 17 [1977]: 477).

19 Goldsmith's depiction of the vicar's resentment of aristocratic entitlements seems to anticipate the narrator's address to nature in "The Deserted Village" (1770), in which a similar "tyrant" intrudes upon and destroys a pastoral landscape:

> Sweet smiling village, loveliest of the lawn,
> Thy sports are fled and all thy charms withdrawn;
> Amidst thy bowers the tyrant's hand is seen,
> And desolation saddens all thy green;
> One only master grasps the whole domain,
> And half a tillage stints thy smiling plain   (35–40)

removes them from the rule of his "little republic." Singing establishes some aspects, then, of the vicar's Job-like journey—namely, his family's deterioration and his increasing powerlessness. It also foreshadows the novel's association of singing with the perils of seduction.

This moment joins with the scene in which Olivia sings "When lovely woman stoops to folly," to set song against the ballad, which is presented as a more innocuous and community-oriented form of entertainment. In one scene early in the novel, the Vicar is delighted that his new, rustic neighbors appreciate the ballad: "these harmless people had several ways of being good company, while one played, the other would sing some soothing ballad, Johnny Armstrong's last good night, or the cruelty of Barbara Allen" (p. 24). The vicar's taste is a thinly disguised version of Goldsmith's own—an essay in the *Bee* (1759) and Reynold's description of Goldsmith in his *Portraits* confirms that he had a particular affection for those particular ballads.[20]

Ballads are also often accompanied by a character's reflections on the relative superiority of the ballad to poetry, another position famously associated with Goldsmith himself, and placed in the mouth of Burchell in the novel. He disliked Collins and the archaisms in the odes of Thomas Gray in particular. Just after the scenes I have mentioned, Burchell sermonizes on contemporary English poetry and attributes its poor quality to the rise of "epithetic language." He claims that poetry "is nothing at present but a combination of luxuriant images, without plot or connection; a string of epithets that improve the sound, without carrying on the sense" (p. 38). He then provides a counterexample by reciting Goldsmith's popular ballad, "Edwin and Angelina." The ballad tells the story of a maid, dressed as a boy, who is lost in the forest and rescued by a hermit, to whom she reveals both her sex and the love-sickness that has caused her miserable wandering. The hermit, realizing that he is the rejected suitor of her narrative, reveals himself and they live happily ever after. Robert Hunting is probably

---

20 Goldsmith, *Vicar*, pp. 201, 204n. For the view that Goldsmith intended his allusions to ballads and his insertions of his own compositions as satiric attacks on rural mores, see Robert Hunting, "The Poems in *The Vicar of Wakefield*," *Criticism* 15 (1973): 234–41.

correct in noting that Sophia's fall into Burchell's strategically placed lap at the end of this episode makes him seem manipulative.[21] A second ballad is summoned when a similar opinion on modern poetry is espoused at a family gathering days before Olivia is to marry farmer Williams. The vicar's youngest child Bill sings the balladic "Elegy on the Death of a Mad Dog," and his father appreciatively comments that "the most vulgar ballad of them all generally pleases me better than the fine modern odes, and things that petrify us in a single stanza; productions that we at once detest and praise"(p. 86).

These two episodes contrast sharply with the two performances of non-balladic songs in the narrative. As I have noted, in the first scene Olivia meets the squire, singing an air of Dryden's with her sister. The second scene allows the sub-plot of Olivia's rebellion against her father's republic to achieve closure by returning us to the same locale in which she first saw and sang for Thornhill. Olivia rejoins her family after her failed affair, in a self-conscious re-creation of their first entertainment: "it was in this place my poor Olivia first met her seducer, and every object served to recall her sadness" (p. 133). Timothy Dykstal characterizes this moment as the "single most memorable feature of [Olivia's] presence in the novel" because she is able "to impose that moral judgment on herself, not to have it imposed on her, from her father."[22] The song criticizes her rather sharply:

> When lovely woman stoops to folly,
> And finds too late that men betray,
> What charm can soothe her melancholy,
> What art can wash her guilt away?
>
> The only art her guilt to cover,
>   To hide her shame from every eye,
> To give repentance to her lover,
>   And wring his bosom—is to die.

The former incident is also recalled when Thornhill surprisingly reappears, abruptly ending the scene. The song performs

21 Hunting, "Poems," p. 239.
22 Thomas Dykstal, "The Story of O: Politics and Pleasure in *The Vicar of Wakefield*," *English Literary History* 62 (1995): 337, 340.

a ceremonious recognition of and apology for her wayward activities, although the solution it proposes—"to die"—certainly is not a premonition of Olivia's end.

Incidentally it is worth noting that over a century and a half later, T. S. Eliot transforms this moment of remorse into an equally theatrical one of repeated solitariness:

> When lovely woman stoops to folly and
> Paces about her room again, alone,
> She smoothes her hair with automatic hand,
> And puts a record on the gramophone.
> ("The Waste Land," lines 253–56)

After Eliot's poem, Olivia's song would never sound the same, because Eliot has yoked together the melancholy of the original and an erotic coolness that would have been unthinkable to Goldsmith.[23]

Although the narrative contexts in which Goldsmith quotes from songs and ballads do not stray far from the conventional associations of music-making with light entertainment, the novel presents us with an interesting perspective on the ballad. Because Goldsmith's critique of his contemporaries' poetry is directly connected to his preference for the ballad (as in Sir Philip Sidney's *Defense of Poetry*, in which Sidney acknowledges his love for "the old song of Percy and Douglas"), it is no coincidence that the opinions which most closely resemble the author's own are placed in the mouths of the novel's most bathetic characters—Primrose and Burchell. The simplicity of Goldsmith's ballads and their happy endings (in "Edwin and Angelina" the long-lost lovers reunite; in "Elegy on the Death of a Mad Dog" the bitten man survives) intimate a faith in human goodness.

---

23 An amusing parody of the song was written nearly a century after Goldsmith's novel by Phoebe Cary (1824–71). In Cary's poem the much less penitent "lovely woman," in search of a "favor" from her obstinate lover, is advised:

> The only way to bring him over,
> The last experiment to try,
> Whether a husband or a lover,
> If he have feeling, is, to cry!

After Goldsmith, ballads and songs do not occupy an unde-
niably prominent place in British fiction until Sir Walter Scott's
Waverley (1814). Yet one earlier novel contains unexpectedly
rich and innovative quotation—and misquotation—of song.
In two central chapters of *Belinda* (1801), Maria Edgeworth
incorporates songs from two popular Jacobean dramas: Jonson's *Epicoene* and Shakespeare's *The Tempest*. In misquoting
Ariel's song in Act Five she raises fascinating questions about
issues of intentionality and consciousness also associated with
the "called-for" song that Maria sings, and gets wrong, in
Joyce's "Clay."[24]

The first song that Edgeworth quotes from is *Epicoene*'s "Still
to be neat, still to be drest" (1.1.91-102). A closer look at the
song reveals a hitherto unexamined source—Jonson's lady
Haughty—for her characterization of Belinda's guardian, lady
Delacour, the "dissipated" and artful aristocrat who is estranged
from her husband and daughter (through Belinda's benign
domestic influence she later reconciles with them; this reconciliation will bring in the second instance of song that I consider). Among numerous similarities between lady Haughty
and lady Delacour, one is particularly central: the open secret
of their dependence on "paint," or what Pope calls "the cos-
metic powers."[25] The song in the novel epitomizes the contrast
between Delacour's physical and verbal use of artifice and
Belinda's "simplicity" in the eyes of Clarence Hervey.[26]

24 For a persuasive explanation of Maria's performance, see Philips
George Davies, "Maria's Song in Joyce's 'Clay,'" *Studies in Short Fiction* 1 (1964): 153–54.
25 Additional comparisons between Delacour's attitudes toward her toi-
lette and True-wit's bold recommendations are fascinating. True wit
suggests, for example, that "they must not discover, how little serves,
with the helpe of art, to adorne a great deale" and "a wise ladie will
keepe a guard alwaies upon the place, that shee may doe things
securely" (1.1.120-21, 128–29). In *Belinda*, one of the major themes
is the complex relationship between Delacour's "secure" use of cosmetics, her secret and locked boudoir, and her belief that she has
breast cancer. Unfortunately, because most of these facets of her
character do not directly relate to Edgeworth's use of Jonson's song,
they will not be discussed in the present context.
26 It is important to note the frequency with which Hervey uses the
word "simplicity" in praising Belinda, because the same word appears
as a "grace" in the quoted snatch from the *Epicoene* song. Before the

Early in the novel Belinda does notice Delacour's compulsion to use "rouge" that is "so glaring" and "pearl powder" that is "so obvious."[27] Although we discover it stems from serious illness, her need for cosmetics becomes an unattractive trait for Clarence Hervey, her "admirer" rather than a lover. He almost states as much when he sings three lines from Jonson's song to Delacour:

> Give me a look, give me a face,
> That makes simplicity a grace;
> Robes loosely flowing, hair as free—

We are then told that "Belinda recollected the remainder of the stanza":

> Such sweet neglect more taketh me
> Than all th'adulteries of art,
> That strike mine eyes, but not mine heart.[28]

Considering that Delacour is well aware of her own use of "all th'adulteries of art," Hervey's singing is quite a risky move, but either the allusion is lost on Delacour or she chooses (or Edgeworth chooses) not to respond to it. Belinda's readiness to follow Hervey's less than subtle hints about dress soon appears: "it was observed, that miss Portman dressed herself this day with

---

song appears, however, Hervey uses it when he seeks to amend his poor treatment of Belinda at lady Singleton's masquerade ball. When the ball ends he asks lady Delacour to convey to Belinda his esteem of her "dignity of mind, and simplicity of character" (*Belinda*, edited by Kathryn J. Kirkpatrick [Oxford: Oxford University Press, 1999], p. 77), a compliment that Delacour immediately throws back to him in mock admonishment. He then repeats the epithet as if in defense of it. The following chapter begins thus: "When lady Delacour repeated to miss Portman the message about 'simplicity of mind, and dignity of character . . . '" (p. 81). The phrase gets somewhat forgotten for some pages, since the jealous Delacour intentionally neglects to mention it during her next conversation with Belinda. In addition, Hervey immediately regrets having complimented her for "dignity of mind" (p. 81) but he does not take back the "simplicity" comment. In fact, one could argue that pages later, the song acts as a reminder to the reader of Hervey's earlier judgment.

27 Edgeworth, *Epicoene*, p. 21.
28 Ibid., p. 169.

the most perfect simplicity." Like Jonson's lady Haughty, Delacour is criticized by the man she attempts to attract. Finally, the unuttered song lyrics act as a secret exchange between Hervey and Belinda, causing Hervey's esteem for Belinda's "simplicity" and "sweet neglect" to affect her dress.

Edgeworth's use of Jonson's song allows Hervey's championing of Belinda's "simplicity" to acquire a unique literary precedent and to be conveyed to her in a direct fashion. In another scene, a song from *The Tempest* is quoted, or, rather, misquoted. The two women are arguing when Delacour's young daughter Helena enters the room, singing a version of the final lines of Ariel's song (5.1.92-94). Until this point Delacour had thought herself an unfit mother and had sent Helena away to her aunt, but she summons her daughter under Belinda's urgings and resumes a traditional maternal role. Helena indeed seems reminiscent of the representations of "tricksy" Ariel, which became increasingly popular in late eighteenth-century engravings, paintings, and theatrical productions. As the nineteenth century approached, Ariel evolved into a character more and more diminutive and feminine.[29] Like this newfangled Ariel, Helena is obedient, affectionate, and charming; she is also as love starved as her namesake in *A Midsummer Night's Dream*. She becomes both a symbol and the direct beneficiary of the family harmony that Belinda realizes. She dramatizes this role upon interrupting the quarrel between Belinda and Delacour by singing Ariel's song, which in its context celebrates his liberation and a different kind of family reconciliation.

Helena sings "Merrily, merrily shall we live now, / Under the blossom that hangs on the bough."[30] Edgeworth's changing of "I" to "we" does not have precedent, to my knowledge, either in extant pre-1800 copies of *The Tempest* or in musical settings that have survived from the same period.[31] If the varia-

---

29 For an account of the historical depiction of Ariel, and in particular of Ariel's eighteenth-century acquisition of femininity, see the introductory discussion and accompanying engravings in Stephen Orgel's edition of *The Tempest* (Oxford: Clarendon Press, 1987).

30 Edgeworth, *Epicoene*, p. 208. Kirkpatrick notes the excerpted song's origin but does not mention the difference between the two versions.

31 See *A Shakespeare Music Catalogue*, edited by Bryan N. S. Gooch and David Thatcher, volume 3 (Oxford: Clarendon Press, 1991), pp. 1505–1670.

tion is Edgeworth's own, is Helena supposed to be mistaken, or aware of her slip? Since she has just returned home and is excited by the prospect of her mother's care, Helena's "we" seems to celebrate the imminent "merriment" of the family reunion. Unlike Ariel, whose "I" suggests that he is eager to begin an idyllic existence *alone* after being given his long-awaited freedom from Prospero's command, Helena voices enthusiasm for domestic bliss with family.

While Goldsmith wrote his own songs and ballads and Edgeworth exclusively quotes from familiar contexts, Sir Walter Scott brings into his novels both his own poetry and traditional Scottish balladry. In *The Heart of Mid-Lothian* (1818), ballads appear in a variety of contexts, most often in the development of the character of Madge Wildfire and, to a lesser extent, Effie Deans, and tend to signify society's inability to control female madness or aberrant behavior. Women in this novel sing when they have rebelled against social norms, and when they fail to survive the society that has ostracized and tortured them. Madge Wildfire dies singing—her rendering of "Proud Maisie" acts as an eerie, powerful swan song. Like Ophelia, one of Scott's models, she offers a series of memorable performances of songs.

Effie Deans also uses song to intimate her affair with George Robertson-Staunton and to taunt her sister. Jeanie hears Effie singing the ballad that celebrates the love of the "elfin knight" for his lady as she dances home from a tryst. Jeanie scolds her for singing a song that their father would object to. When she questions Effie about her secret activities, Effie teases her about her friend Butler. Then Effie "looked at her with a sly air, in which there was something like irony, as she chaunted, in a low by marked tone, a scrap of an Scotch song"[32] about a promiscuous woman who meets men for clandestine romantic adventures. Effie interrupts herself in the middle of the fourth line when, not having reached the bawdy lines, she sees that she has made Jeanie cry; the implications of the song have already been strongly suggested. Jeanie again chides her for singing "fulesongs" and Effie responds by regretting that she

---

32 Sir Walter Scott, *The Heart of Mid-Lothian*, edited by Tony Inglis (New York: Penguin, 1994), p. 101. All subsequent references to the novel are indicated by the page numbers in the text of the essay.

had ever "learned ane o'them" (p. 102). She also distinguishes herself as bolder and cruel. The "impromptu" nature of the performance, however, allows her to retain the veneer of innocence.

Madge Wildfire's association with ballad-singing is the stronger of the two. The epigraph to the chapter in which we meet Madge is a snatch of dialogue from *Hamlet* in which Ophelia's speech that "is nothing" is described. Our introduction to her is through song, specifically one that acts as a mysterious warning. During Jeanie's meeting with the stranger who wants her unlawful cooperation to free her sister from jail, they hear two ballad stanzas being sung "in a wild and monotonous strain." The first of them, written by Scott himself, discusses the separation between the predator and the prey in the animal world:

> When the gledd's in the blue cloud,
>   The lavrock lies still;
> When the hound's in the green-wood,
>   The hind keeps the hill.   (p. 161)

The following stanza, a version of which exists in Child's collection, warns a character named "Sir James" more explicitly about approaching men. Immediately upon hearing the songs, the stranger flees. It is not until three chapters later that we learn that the singer of these stanzas is Madge Wildfire, who has been prompted to warn the stranger (who turns out to be Effie's George) by the humming of Ratcliffe, her former companion currently being bribed by the police to betray his friends. Her songs are not mad at all, then, but make complete sense. He had hinted that she begin singing by starting "to hum, but in a very low and suppressed tone, the first stanza of a favourite ballad of Wildfire's, the words of which bore some distant analogy with the situation of Robertson, trusting that the power of association would not fail to bring the rest to her mind" (p. 181). Robertson's rationale is crucial to our understanding both of mad song in general and its function in this scene. One of the characteristics of mad song that frightens listeners is, in fact, its intimation that the singer is able to bring ideas together through singing or hearing songs, ideas that are often logically linked but that may not appear to be in the minds of those beholding a deranged person. As a final example, the narrator notes that the songs she sings as she dies retain an astounding coherence and applicability to her situation: "And it was remarkable, that there could always be traced in her songs something appropriate, though perhaps only obliquely or collaterally so, to her present situation" (p. 414).

Perhaps the most striking aspect of Madge's singing is the fact that Scott attributes the authorship of several of Madge's autobiographical ballads to George Robertson-Staunton, who has not only wooed and fathered an illegitimate child with Effie Deans but also with Madge. He has taught her songs that identify her as a madwoman who believes herself to be exempt from the social conventions that define the community. She sings snatches of the songs frequently: "I maun just sing a bit to keep up my heart—it's a sang that Gentle George made on me lang syne, when I went with him to Lockington wake":

> I'm Madge of the country, I'm Madge of the town,
> And I'm Madge of the lad I am blithest to own—
> The Lady of Beever in diamonds may shine,
> But has not a heart half so lightsome as mine.
>
> I am Queen of the Wake, and I'm Lady of May,
> And I lead the blithe ring round the May-pole today:
> The wild-fire that flashes so fair and so free
> Was never so bright or so bonnie as me.   (p. 316)[33]

Songs allow Madge to imagine herself in a position of female power that she never can occupy in reality.[34] Just as her songs

---

33 See also page 169, where she sings "I glance like the wildfire through country and town; / I'm seen on the causeway—I'm seen on the town" (lines 5–6) and replaces "wild-fire" in line 7 with "lightning." Another variation occurs on page 294: "With my crutch on my foot, and my shoe on my hand, / I glance like the wildfire through brugh and through land."

34 Two other readers find similar features in Madge's songs. Although he does not characterize Madge's fantasies of power as signs either of madness or femininity, Ian Duncan argues in *Modern Romance and Transformations of the Novel* (Cambridge: Cambridge University Press, 1992) that her songs are important for understanding her character: "Madge's possession by the ballads and lyrics of folk romance signifies

intimate the strength of her self-delusions and her confidence that she can overcome adversity, they also powerfully display her weakened state as she dies.[35] On her death-bed Madge famously sings one tune after another, in a sequence that indicates her steady deterioration, and in which the songs are also "set" by the narration. Madge is "no longer overstrained by false spirits, but softened, saddened, and subdued by bodily exhaustion." When "she began again to sing in the same low and modulated strains" in her next excursus into song, Scott more specifically evokes a particular setting: it "rather resembled the music of the Methodist hymns, though the measure of the song was similar to that of the former" (p. 413–14).

Another of Scott's most histrionic madwomen, Lucy Ashton, curiously is silent after going mad and stabbing her husband. While Donizetti and Cammararo's Lucia encapsulates her entire history with Edgardo in the prolonged mad-song she performs ("Il dolce suono") after leaving the bloody bridal chamber, one of Lucy's most striking features is that she dies "without her being able to utter a word explanatory of the fatal scene."[36] But Lucy does perform a song early in *The Bride of Lammermoor*, before her troubles begin. The song is a set-piece within the narrative, an instance of impromptu audible ecphrasis. Lucy's father was "walking through the house when

---

her delusion, her aptness for seduction" (p. 152). Judith Wilt, in *Secret Leaves: The Novels of Sir Walter Scott* (Chicago and London: University of Chicago Press, 1981) makes a similar point from a feminist perspective: although it "appears to construct a world of efficacious action for women over against the stubborn, blocking inertia of the world of men and their laws" (p. 116) women have no real power without the political clout of husbands (i.e., Queen Caroline) or the cold cash of benefactors (Jeanie).

35 I am reminded here of Elspeth's singing of "The Ballad of the Red Harlaw" as she dies. We are told that as the Antiquary overheard her, "he was surprised to hear the shrill tremulous voice of Elspeth chanting forth an old ballad in a wild and doleful recitative" (*The Antiquary*, chapter 40). Indeed, her visionary last words, "We are coming, my lady!" are similar to the owl's greeting at the end of Madge's recitation of "Proud Maisie": "Welcome, proud lady."

36 Scott, *The Bride of Lammermoor*, ed. Fiona Robertson (Oxford: Oxford University Press, 1991), p. 339.

suddenly he heard the sound of his daughter's lute."[37] He pauses outside and listens:

> Look not thou on beauty's charming, —
> Sit thou still when kings are arming, —
> Taste not when the wine-cup glistens, —
> Speak not when the people listens, —
> Stop thine ear against the singer, —
> From the red gold keep thy finger, —
> Vacant heart, and hand, and eye, —
> Easy live and quiet die.

Following the song are several paragraphs of description focused on Lucy's physical and psychological features. The song is revelatory: "the words she had chosen seemed particularly adapted to her character; for Lucy Ashton's exquisitely beautiful, yet somewhat girlish features, were formed to express peace of mind, serenity, and indifference to the tinsel of worldly pleasure." Thus she is characterized and beheld for a moment, while the possibility that she'll break free from the ecphrasis looms.

Lucy's song becomes an important example of a kind of relationship that can be forged between a prior song and its narrative context, and a subsequent novelist's careful use of the song when E. M. Forster uses Lucy Ashton's song in *A Room With a View*. Forster quotes not only the song but Scott's particular mode of framing it. In doing so, he reimagines the novelistic possibilities for musical performance. Forster's heroine, another Lucy, sings Ashton's song at the end of the novel, when she is between men—just after rejecting Cecil and before marrying George Emerson. The Reverend M. Beebe, like Sir William Ashton, "opened the door, and heard the words of a song."[38] In the middle of the song, the scene is described from the point of view of the different characters. Beebe asks himself, "Why should Lucy want either to marry or to travel when she had such friends at home?" and tells her, "It's a beautiful song and a wise one."[39] The conversation and the

---

37 Ibid., p. 41.
38 Forster, *A Room With a View* (New York: Vintage Books, n.d.), p. 220.
39 Forster, *Room*, p. 221.

song continue to occur simultaneously, one informing, critiqu-ing, and glossing the other. While her performance is made to seem less formal by the breakup of the lines and the interspers-ing of conversation, a narrative technique that probably would not have occurred to Scott, it becomes more integral to the sense of informality and familiarity between the characters.[40]

Finally, Thomas Hardy, like Scott, commonly incorporates songs and ballads into many of his novels. Donald Farfrae in *The Mayor of Casterbridge* (1886) sings frequently, charming the townspeople with his performances of songs such as "Oh Nan-nie," "Auld Lang Syne," and "Bonnie Peg." It is not until his last novel, *Tess of the d'Urbervilles* (1891), that Hardy employs the greatest range of allusion to and quotation of songs. He draws on local, oral ballads and songs as well as two Renais-sance sources.

The sophistication of the Renaissance songs is juxtaposed against Tess herself, whose rustic family draws upon the oral tradition of ballads and folk songs. When Alec D'Urberville uses the melody line of "Take, O Take those Lips Away" to teach Tess to whistle, for example, his cunning choice of tune secretly thrills him, and tension builds as readers are told that "the allusion was lost upon Tess."[41] A later reference to Cam-

---

40 As the final lines "Vacant heart and hand and eye / Easy live and quiet die" are sung, Beebe describes the setting as having a "soaring accompaniment." What setting could Beebe have had in mind? In his edition of the novel, Oliver Stallybrass is skeptical that Forster has an actual setting in mind at all; in a note on the passage he writes: "the only known non-fictional setting of these words is by Henry Bishop (1786–1855). . . . The accompaniment of rippling arpeggios can hardly be said to 'soar' and the song—a most improbable gift from Cecil Vyse—is unlikely to have been in Forster's mind if indeed he even knew it." In addition to raising the fascinating issue of the difference between fictional and non-fictional settings, Stallybrass's search for a suitable "non-fictional" setting might not have been com-plete. While I have been unable to locate the Bishop setting, I have found one by Eliza Flower whose accompaniment indeed "soars," and it does so, for nearly two octaves, at the phrase "easy live"—about where the description would seem to call for it. Perhaps Forster had known and remembered her 1835 setting.

41 Thomas Hardy, *Tess of the d'Urbervilles*, edited by Simon Gatrell and Nancy Barrineau (Oxford: Oxford University Press, 1988), p. 63. In *Hardy's Use of Allusion* (Lawrence: University Press of Kansas, 1983)

pion would have also been lost on Tess; similarly, it relates to
the gap in knowledge between Tess and her lovers. Unlike the
boy's song from *Measure for Measure*, it is remembered and not
performed. The narrator describes Tess's most cherished physical features in the mind of Angel Clare: "He had never before
seen a woman's lips and teeth which forced upon his mind,
with such persistent iteration, the old Elizabethan simile of
roses filled with snow" (p. 152). This image appears in Campion's "There is a Garden in Her Face," which describes a
mouth like "cherries" with teeth of "orient pearl": "Which
when her lovely laughter shows, / They look like rosebuds
filled with snow."

By contrast, ballads belong in the domestic space of Tess's
family. Her mother is "a passionate lover of tune" (p. 25), and
she sings "The Spotted Cow" while rocking her newborn in
its cradle. For Tess, her mother's singing gives the modest
cottage's "unspeakable dreariness" some intimations of happiness. It also enhances what Jane Millgate calls the novel's
"transposition of romance." Millgate claims that the novel
becomes almost emblematic in its use of the romance motifs
Hardy learned from Scott: "the depiction of the countryside,
of Tess's family, and of her daily life, is realistic and particular-
ized, but an effect very close to that of romance is achieved
by the frequent heightening of the individual and local
almost to the level of the symbolic."[42] Ballads in Tess seem to
achieve this particularization. Although common traits of the
ballad are their impersonality and the absence of a first-
person narrator, Tess personalizes and allows them to haunt
her conscience.

Another significant instance of the link between the ballad
and personal history is Tess's sudden recollection of lines from
'The Boy and the Mantle,'" a popular Arthurian ballad anthol-

---

Marlene Springer reads this allusion in the context of Alec's relationship to Shakespearean comedy: "For Alec is consistently associated
with Shakespeare's comedies, allusively preparing the reader for the
game he is playing with her" (p. 131).

42 Jane Millgate, "Two Versions of Regional Romance: Scott's *The Bride
of Lammermoor* and Hardy's *Tess of the d'Urbervilles*," *Studies in English
Literature* 17 (1977): p. 731.

ogized and revised by Percy and M. G. Lewis respectively.[43] It concerns a boy who has arrived at Arthur's court with a mantle to test the women's fidelity; if they have been unfaithful, as they adorn the mantle the cloth shrinks or disintegrates in front of their husbands and other onlookers. It shrinks for Guinevere and for Sir Craddock's wife, although as soon as the latter confesses her peccadillo (she kissed her husband before marriage), it fits. As she tries on wedding clothes, Tess remembers the song as one her mother sang when she was little: "Alone, she stood for a moment before the glass looking at the effect of her silk attire; and then there came into her head her mother's ballad of the mystic robe, 'That never would become that wife / That had once done amiss'" (p. 205). Until this point in the narrative Tess has been able to suppress her feeling of ambivalence toward withholding her secret past from her husband. As soon as she recollects the ballad, her brave new world begins to deteriorate. She insists on confessing to Clare, and he permanently estranges himself from her. The ballad acts almost as a charm or a momentary spell, compelling her to be truthful; its consequences, however, are more monumental and devastating than she had imagined.

Songs in novels, from Cervantes to Forster, have a wide range of functions. Ballads, as we have seen, can act as magical spells cast on a character or a narrative. Sometimes the consequences of their utterance are clear to the reader but remain private knowledge within the narrative. As oral narratives they can also serve as minimalist outlines for novels; in Scott, the stories that characters tell through singing ballads are often, simultaneously, stories about the ways in which ballads themselves—like the quotations used as epigraphs—control, shape, and haunt the characters in the narrative as well as the author himself. They can also rebel against conventional uses of language, as do the songs of Madge Wildfire.

Songs can also act as secrets shared between characters, private systems of signification meant for the ears of only one or a few. Like all allusions, they carry their previous contexts with them in various ways, and they can remind the reader, on a

---

43 See Thomas Percy, *Reliques of Ancient English Poetry*, edited by Henry B. Wheatley (London, 1877), pp. 3–12; M. G. Lewis, *Tales of Wonder* (London, 1801), *English Literature* pp. 398–408.

more didactic level, of values or sentiments shared between the present context and the previous one. Or, as in T. S. Eliot's rewriting of Olivia's song, they can parody the original text, even scandalously. They have agencies of their own and are capable of affecting their singers and listeners on any number of unconscious and conscious levels. The narrative context always frames the song in ways that move the song from performance into action.

"Reason Also Is Choice": Reflection, Freedom, and the Euthyphro Problem

JOHN BURT

Mechanism and Value-Positing

Milton's God says, "Reason also is choice," in one of those prickly asides in *Paradise Lost* in which he curtly replies to a skeptical reader (he is ostensibly addressing the Son, but in fact he is speaking over the Son's shoulder to us) before rushing on to his main point. There is a "take that" quality about his remark, and a sense, on his part, that it settles the question so thoroughly that he need say no more about it. His immediate argument is that the rebel angels were not constrained by necessity to their revolt, and Adam and Eve will not be constrained by necessity to their fall, and that had either been constrained by necessity to obedience their obedience would have been meaningless, because not free. His subsidiary argument, which is the one that interests me here, is that even if obedience were the only reasonable course, the compulsion of reason is totally unlike the compulsion of necessity, and those who order their conduct as reason requires cannot be said to have sacrificed their freedom, even if reason dictates only one course, because reasons are different from causes, and persuasion by reasons is different from compulsion by causes:

> I made him [Adam] just and right,
> Sufficient to have stood, though free to fall.
> Such I created all th'Eternal Powers
> And Spirits, both them who stood and them who faild;
> Freely they stood who stood, and fell who fell.
> Not free, what proof could they have givn sincere
> Of true allegiance, constant Faith or Love,
> Where onely what they needs must do, appeard,
> Not what they would? what praise could they receive?
> What pleasure I from such obedience paid,

When Will and Reason (Reason also is choice)
Useless and vain, of freedom both despoil'd,
Made passive both, had serv'd necessitie,
Not mee.

What does it mean to say that reason also is choice? The claim seems to point to something stronger than to the distinction between causes and reasons, to argue not just that freedom is the ability to follow a law one gives one's self through reason, but also that the dictates of reason are somehow matters of choice. One is tempted at first to deny that: if reason really declares something, then it's *not* a matter of choice, only the conclusion of a train of argument, perhaps in ideal cases the conclusion of a kind of deduction a machine can do.

Does one have to imagine moral reasoning as being in crucial ways like calculation? Suppose one imagines moral reasoning (more plausibly) as something less mechanical, as something more phronetic, as something different not only in degree but in kind from calculation. Suppose we conceive of moral reasoning as something in which both thought and feeling are in play, something tied not only to regulative abstractions but also to implicitness (the sense that one's values are never exhausted by one's formulations of them and always retain that power to deliver rebuking surprises, despite our cleverness, that Socrates embodied in his *daimon*), and to situatedness (the sense that we can only understand a value in its implicitness once we have played it on the pulse of actual living). Although what the deliverances of a phronetic moral reasoning will be ceases to be totally predictable, even in this case one never quite wants to say that the deliverances of practical reason are subject to choice, else they cease to be deliverances.

On the other hand, a vision of the moral life in which choice does not matter, because reason dictates what one must do down to the smallest details, is in many ways unattractive, partly because the experience of choice is valuable, and partly because moral experiences are only made possible under circumstances where other people are recognized as having freedom. It matters that you love me, for instance, because it is possible that you might not, and unless I have somehow won your free assent what passes between us cannot be called love. Indeed, I can't really call it love if I am sure that you are driven to me even by *inner* compulsions, never mind by outer ones. Even having persuasive reasons to love someone is a necessary but not sufficient condition of love, since the *choice* of giving one's self to love is the crucial thing, and if one gives the trump to the reasons one has for loving one is bound to treat love as venal and interested ("I love her because she is good for me") or a little bit unreal ("When I tallied up her moral attributes, I realized that she would be the person it would be wisest for me to love"). One may have reasons, but one loves from choice, not from reasons, and the gravity and depth of that choice sometimes remains even when the reasons dissipate. It's easy enough to see in the case of love what it means to say, "Reason also is choice," because in that case reason and choice are so entangled with each other that they are hard to tease apart.

Can we say the same about other areas of moral experience? We think of the moral law as commanding, but we also expect that obedience to that law will be free, and we mean by "free" something stronger than merely "not extorted by threats or seduced by bribes." We mean that following a moral law realizes expressive possibilities of freedom in the way that falling in love does. Which, again, means that obedience to that law must involve both reason and choice.

When we insist that others follow a course whose morality is clear to us but not to them (let's suppose that the reasoning is so clear to us that it no longer seems to be a question of choice, for us or anybody else), we not only risk becoming a kind of moral tyrant, we also risk losing that respect for the freedom of others without which we cannot find meaning in our own freedom and in our own moral acts. There is an inevitable tension, which under certain circumstances rises to the level of a stark contradiction, between the fact that it is the work of moral reflection to give binding law, and the fact that the proper element of that reflection (and of that law) is freedom. Although I do not sacrifice my freedom but discover its meaning when I follow a law I have given myself through reason, I cannot exactly say the same thing about the act of imposing that law upon others against those others' considered judgments. I may reason with myself, but I must persuade others, which is to say that I must woo their own free choice, not merely have at my disposal what seem to me to be trumping arguments for my views (or be able to win a verdict from

an impartial spectator, say), and if I neglect the duty of persuading others, it scarcely matters that the reasoning may be
sound that supports the course of action I compel them to.
The moral life cannot long survive a state of affairs in which
reason is not also choice.

But even here there are limits. There must be some positions
that we cannot imagine any person reasonably holding, else
there is no distinction between accepting the responsibility
of persuading (which means also accepting the responsibility of
opening one's self up to persuasion), and accepting at face value
any brutality or cruelty some other person proposes, merely
because they have so invested themselves in doing it that they
can't be talked out of it; there must always come some occasion where the dictates of practical reason bind the self and
demand the compulsion of others, else what we are talking
about is neither ethics nor a theory of justice. And once one
reaches that line, it would seem that reason no longer also is
choice: there is at least one act X such that if you really insist
on choosing to do X, you and I will have to engage in a contest of force. All too often, of course, when we draw in the
sand the line of a non-negotiable demand, we do that merely
as a way of stiffening our own backs, impressing our allies or
constituents, or bluffing down our opponents. But that is not
to say that the occasion never arises when a line in the sand
must be drawn. And where lines in the sand have to be drawn,
we cannot say that reason also is choice.

We have a habit of thinking of reason and choice as opposites. What is true or good or beautiful, if we mean those
words with seriousness, is true or good or beautiful without
our say-so. If we really take those terms at their worth, we seek
a sense of those terms that allows us to be rebuked by them,
not a sense that serves our (ulterior or unconscious) ends. We
may, of course, not in practice find a specific use of those
terms that is free of our temptations to special pleading. But
we mean by each of those terms to attend to something that
does not depend merely on our choice, because it is the thing
that is always in a position to rebuke our choices. One of the
reasons we know that there is a difference between conventional and absolute senses of terms like these is that when we
discover that one of our own uses of these terms is merely
conventional we are disappointed and ashamed, and when we

discover that someone else's use of such a term is merely conventional we expect that person to be taken aback by the disclosure. We can imagine ourselves conceding upon reflection that we were mistaken about whether something was beautiful. If we can at all imagine conceding upon reflection that we were mistaken about whether something was pleasant, we nevertheless imagine a concession that takes place under very different rhetorical circumstances and under very different rules from the concession that we were mistaken about whether something was beautiful or not. Similar arguments can be constructed about aesthetic value and about ethical value.

"Reason also is choice" means two related things: first, that moral reason does not work the way deduction works but works instead the way reflection works, and second, that free choice is not arbitrary selection among indifferent ends, but the discovery, through the elaboration of rules, of the expressive possibilities of freedom. When the will holds itself responsible to a law given to it by reason it does not invent that law at will and it does not internalize a law imposed upon it from without by tutelage or by someone else's will. At the same time the contents of that law do not declare themselves except in the unfolding of experiences that follow from the act of giving one's self that law as a law. Values, this is to say, share with persons the attribute of implicitness. Knowing a person is different from knowing all the facts about a person; knowing is a species of recognition, not of cognition, since what one knows when one knows a person is that one will never know them all the way down. The implicitness of persons does not inhere in some set of facts that can't be discovered but in the sense that knowing those facts deepens rather than forecloses further questions about that person. We know persons by opening ourselves to the experience of unknowing about them; we see someone as a person to the extent that we resist the temptation to see that person as someone whose story is already over. A value has implicitness of the same kind: we know in advance that every conception we formulate of that value is inadequate to its concept, that it will always be saturated with entailments and consequences that we cannot anticipate fully and that will continue to surprise and rebuke us as Socrates' *daimon* rebuked him. Values oblige us, but they also remain implicit, and therefore, inexhaustibly, they unfold in ways we can neither anticipate nor satisfy nor evade. The live unfolding of a value from its implicitness, something that happens, as I will describe, at the exact limit of identity, and at the exact limit of will, is also the live experience of moral freedom, that freedom in which reason also is choice.

I don't want to say, however, that reason and choice come together in the act of discovering one's inner nature and destiny, for that is merely a way of saying that freedom is the illusion one feels when one fully gives one's self over to one's obsessions. And surrendering to one's obsessions in the final analysis is neither reason nor choice.

The identity of reason and choice is something one aims for but never possesses—we are led to it intuitively by our very act of taking values, real values, seriously, and of imagining those values, those transcendentals, as concepts that inform but are not constrained or defined by what we do on their account. The identity of reason and choice is not a fact in the world or a truth of deduction. It is always not quite here but yet at hand, an intuition that inspires us once we begin to believe that there is a truth, and that we are never even in principle in full possession of that truth; that there is a good, but that at the same time our moral life is still an unsettled question; that there is beauty, but it is not captured in our own private tastes.

I have resisted the idea that freedom is a name for unconditioned arbitrariness because it does not seem to me that freedom and reflection are opposites. Indeed, each is the condition of the other. Any argument that imagines that there is one reason governed by a kind of iron logic and another region in which anything goes ultimately treats freedom in a decisionist way. If, for instance, with Weber I imagine a world rigorously organized by causality, and by instrumental reason (which is simply a redescription of causality in order to render comprehensible a world in which people have strategic intelligence but not practical reason), I place the human being in a world in which there is a complete rationality about the compulsions to which we are subject (and to which we subject others), but no rationality about ultimate ends, about the meaning and purpose of lives. As Gadamer complained about Weber, this methodological rationalism ends in crude irrationalism. But a similar devil's bargain between rationality and irrationality applies also to the conviction that reflection applies only within some spheres of action and in other spheres reflection does not apply at all. Such an understanding is unfair to reflection (because it imagines it only as a brutally reductive kind of calculation) and unfair to freedom (because it imagines it only as nonsense and white noise). "Reason also is choice" means that people reflect about what they do in every sphere of action, and that reflection is a human assay, a playing on the pulse, of the infinite implicitness of values, not merely calculation from propositions.

The Euthyphro Question and the Fragility of Goodness

Milton's God's assertion is intended as a sweeping answer to what might be called the "Euthyphro Question," the question of how much primary values depend upon free acts of will (whether the will of God or the will of the people), and how much upon abstractions that exercise a compelling force from some depth to which will is irrelevant; it is the question of the vexed relationship between morally certain principle and moral freedom, between a vision of the moral life that imagines it as rational, capable of being captured in binding rules, and a vision of the moral life that turns on human capacities such as loyalty and gratitude, capacities that from a purely rational ethical standpoint seem only to offer temptations to heteronomy, temptations to love one's own in ways very unlike how one loves humanity, and temptations to love an irascible and human God in a human way, rather than admire a philosopher's God who contains all the perfections but who seems completely abstract.

When Socrates asks, "Is what is pious pious because it is pleasing to the gods, or is it pleasing to the gods because it is pious?" he asks about the role of choice and the role of principle in mores and in morals. If something is pious just because the gods happen to like it, then it does not matter what that thing is; what's more, we cannot tell in advance what those things will be. And we cannot rule out that the gods might demand something awful (indeed, the fact that that kind of demand is awful is evidence that it is in earnest: we don't need a command from God to love our children, and it would take a command from God, if even that, to make us kill them). As Abraham learned, if not in Genesis

then in *Fear and Trembling*, what God can demand can be anything, including not only destroying what one rightly loves
and has a duty to protect (as Agamemnon was also required
to do), but also breaking (as only Abraham had to) what God
Himself had set up as a law. If, on the other hand, piety is
something we can understand a rule about, then piety can be
subject to a kind of calculation that would enable us to give
laws to the gods: Zeus is *supposed* to be pleased by this, and
it's his problem if he's not. (Half of the comedy of *Religion
within the Limits of Reason Alone* comes from the spectacle of
Professor Kant lecturing God about what God had jolly well
better honor if he wants anybody to think of Him as a proper
God.) Indeed, if piety is purely a matter of rule, then there is
no reason to imagine anything personal about Zeus at all,
and there is no reason to see in piety any relationship to those
precious things that have in them anything of the personal,
whether values like loyalty and respect, or feelings like love
and wonder. And there would be no room in the concept of
piety for awe and terror, what Rudolf Otto called the *myste-
rium tremendum et fascinans* that seems to be an indispensable
part not only of religious feeling but also of a fully human
life. To give trumping power to only one side of the Euthyphro Question, to argue that value must inhere in rules
and that moral reasoning must be like calculation, is to argue
that there is no place for these specifically human virtues in
moral living.

That values must be applied through phronesis, and that
phronesis is an accommodation to situatedness, to the partly
heteronomous life we are already leading, is in my view the
chief of the critiques of absolute morality proposed by Carol
Gilligan in *In a Different Voice*, and it is to answer a critique
like Gilligan's that I seek to develop the related concepts of
implicitness and situatedness. The problem is that situatedness seems to require both a step forward and a step back
from absolute morality: it is awfully difficult to tell in particular cases whether the attempt to situate a moral theme is
the attempt to play it on the pulse, or is merely the attempt
to qualify away its prophetic criticism of practices by insisting upon maintaining an inside view of local mores. In the
first case, one seeks the good, but seeks to deepen one's allegiance to the good by bringing nuance to one's understand-

ing of it. In the second case, one seeks to abandon the good in favor of the nice by invoking the power of affiliation and connectedness in ways that are not far different from special pleading. The still unsolved problem raised by Gilligan's book is that special pleading and respect for nuance are almost impossible to tell apart. My argument that the theme of situatedness is a consequence of the deeper theme of implicitness is an attempt to work out a solution to that problem: we must see our values in situated ways because crucial things about our values will always remain unknown to us in explicit abstract examinations of them, and examining them in situated ways is likely to bring to light some of the unarticulated features of our values, is likely to surprise us with what we didn't know we were already committed to. That said, the theme of implicitness does not provide us with more than a rough and phronetic guide to telling the difference between respect for nuance and relativist special pleading.

Gilligan's argument about situatedness is related to the critique of Enlightenment ethics proposed by philosophers of the Romantic era. Gilligan's critique of Lawrence Kohlberg's stages of moral development is similar to Herder's critiques of d'Holbach and Helvetius, in that both find the generality and abstractness to which their opponents are committed in some way brutalizing and less than fully human. Moral commitments at the highest level of abstraction, while removed from special pleading and partiality, are too bare a thing to support a livable moral life: one does not love humanity with the same warmth that one loves one's family, or even one's country, since one loves humanity only in a rather skeletal way, but one loves family or country in flesh and blood ways (except if one abstracts one's country, in the fashion of high nationalism, which is inconsistent with love of country although sometimes hard to tell from it—Virgil's patria, Willa Cather reminds us in an aside in *My Ántonia*, is his neighborhood, not his nation, obscure Mantua rather than world-historical Rome).

The attachments that most matter to us ethically are not attachments that are the product of rationality anyway: one does not love dogs the way one loves Toto, and when Toto dies one can't quite replace him with Lulu, even if Lulu is a better dog in every way. Such an attachment only has ethical meaning because of its slight irrationality, and to attempt to find a rational basis for it is to compromise fatally its importance.

Gilligan, like Herder (and like Martha Nussbaum), proposes to put flesh on the bones of moral convictions by seeing them in the context of dense networks of affiliations. Both, in so doing, run the risk of using affiliation to stampede judgment. Certainly the ideal of country that Herder invokes—I don't use "nation" because "nation," as Benedict Anderson argues, turns out to be a possessing abstraction, not a network of local affiliations—has turned out more often than not to be what people invoke when they wish to engage in special pleading of a more or less obviously immoral sort, and even these concrete local affiliations keep sliding into horrifying abstractions, country into nation, *sittlichkeit* into heteronomy, *gemeinschaft* into *volk*. Even internally fractured, self-consciously fictive, social-energy-circulating, and restlessly self-undoing postmodern conceptions of the social frame resolve themselves under pressure into drearily familiar forms of identity politics and loyalty politics, often in the very face of the explicit intentions of the authors who develop those conceptions. The insistence upon seeing one's values in a situated way slides all too easily into the insistence on "me first, and people like me first, too." There is no immediate and obvious way of telling the difference between local attachments that are simply heteronomous, that cloud the moral judgment by throwing loyalty politics and tribal identity politics in the eye, and local attachments that are the necessary furniture and equipment through which moral commitments may be realized. One might treat with less suspicion local attachments that make global promises—as for instance when deutero-Isaiah makes special claims for Israel, but makes those claims not on the basis of simple tribal loyalty but on the basis of a redemptive mission aimed at everyone. But even though the ethos of deutero-Isaiah is more attractive than the "kill the Amalekites because God commands it" morality he displaces, one still has to be on guard against redemptive missions that have too coercive a feel: If I say that "all men *shall* be brothers, and it is my mission to make them so," you have reason to worry about what I will do, particularly if I turn out to be in the habit, as we Americans all too often are, of making all men brothers at gunpoint.

A similar argument for concrete and contingent attachments

not already given by reason is made by Martha Nussbaum in *The Fragility of Goodness*. Non-fragile goodness, such as in their different ways Kant and Plato strive after (in Nussbaum's reading of them), are also in some way non-human. Esteem for non-fragile goodness underestimates, in her view, the tragic complexities of moral experience, because those who strive after durable forms of the good, in their quest to provide an account of the moral life which enables them to solve all imaginable cases of moral conflict (a rule by which one can reliably determine what is pious, for instance), produce a stunted and foreshortened account of the entailments of different entangled allegiances (entangled allegiances such as one feels if one seeks to do what pleases the many gods with their many different ideas of what is pleasing—the burden of Greek tragedy, although it is treated only as a matter of low comedy in the *Euthyphro*).

The two arguments (that non-fragile visions of the good are non-human and brutalizing, and that non-fragile visions of the good provide a false account of human allegiances to incommensurable values) do not necessarily imply each other, since there is no necessity to the claim that high abstractions must be expected to sort with each other. Isaiah Berlin, no less than Nussbaum, argued that we have no reason to believe that all of our key values sort with each other, but that did not necessitate for him a retreat to a lower level of abstraction in which one cannot tell situated allegiances from heteronomous ones. (And he was not driven by this recognition, as, say, Sartre was, to embrace an ethos of value-positing.) Nor do we have any reason to believe that respect for the fragility of goodness will make our behavior in the moral or political world less brutal. To recognize that we are always caught in a tangle of opposed demands and that those demands are so embedded in situatedness that it is nearly impossible to get an abstract purchase on them without playing them false may give us a more accurate sense of what it is to be human in a fragile and multifarious world, but it will not make tragic conflicts less tragic or in practice less brutal, since in concrete conflicts the narcissism of small differences has proven just as bloody as the titanic clash of opposed or mutually unintelligible world-views, particularly since closely related cultures struggling over ways of being (to say nothing of water and land), know each other well enough to see each other with the kind of contempt that continued experience of each other only further ratifies. The hard part for such peoples is not to dispel their ignorance of each other but to get past their knowledge, since neither may know the whole story, but what they know of each other is in each case true enough and bad enough. Situatedness of Nussbaum's kind may tempt one to see a conflict in terms of concrete allegiances—to "our kind" and against "their kind"—in ways that obscure rather than clarify the stakes of the moral tragedy, since if one knows that one's claims are really only intelligible within the horizon of one's own kind one still has no reason not to favor one's own kind over any other. If we are ever going to stop killing each other, there has to be some way that you can show me that what I want to do to you really is wrong, and not just relatively. Hostility to the pretensions of world views with universalizing ambitions seemed to be an intellectual hallmark of the late years of the Cold War, when a little doubt about whether one really had God on one's side might well have made one hesitate before pushing that big red button. In an era of vicious little ethnic conflicts like our own the idea that values are context dependent seems a lot less attractive.

Nussbaum also ties the quest for non-fragile good to the quest for a coherent notion of personal identity, which defines its integrity in its hard-spheres separateness from others; attention to the fragility of goodness is in her view a way of attesting to a less egocentric notion of identity, one that discovers its nature in investments and relatedness. Again, the necessity of the connection between a quest for a regulative abstraction and a hard-spheres notion of personal identity eludes me: Nussbaum can connect them by plausible retrospects made more plausible by the mid-1980s hostility to both the concept of a stable and coherent personal identity and to the concept of regulative abstractions with absolute force, but this still seems to me more a case of guilt by association than of genuine necessity, and the relation of the themes could have plausibly been worked out in far different ways. And to lament the coldness and foreshortenedness of the available abstractions is not to make allegiance to the available concrete affiliations any less heteronomous in character. The constellation of antifoundationalist relativism about the incommensurability of values, hostility to the idea of the coherent and autonomous self, and attraction to heteronomous communitarianism, seemed a tightly connected one to thinkers of the 1980s, but in fact all three themes are independent; they appear bound together tightly only if situatedness is the deepest theme about values, but if, as I argue, situatedness is a practical consequence of implicitness, each theme is susceptible of a different development from the one that seemed so inevitable fifteen years ago.

The desire to honor the power of local affiliations may lead one in the direction of Burkean conservatism, which offers at least that one might be able to free one's self of the idea-madness that is completely imprisoned by its own take upon its obsessing abstractions and cannot see that when it has deduced some horrible consequence from those abstractions it is not duty-bound to carry them through. But this same conservatism pays for that sanity by imprisoning itself in unreflected allegiances. If what genuine freedom we enjoy must ineluctably seek a basis in reflection, this style of conservatism sacrifices that freedom; it buys warmth and safety at the price of conformity and loyalty politics.

But Burkean conservatism is not the inevitable or only course that that desire to honor local investments can motivate. For while it is possible to be invested in one's own folkways so completely that one cannot imagine the case of others in other conditions, it is also possible that those investments can have a broadening rather than a narrowing effect: if I love my family it might seem reasonable for me to recognize that others love their own and therefore that they should not be made to sacrifice them to my family's advantage, or perhaps even to the interests of Humanity (if one ever understands such a thing clearly). If I love my country I can possibly be brought to see that other people love theirs as well. I may never have a sufficiently lively appreciation of their condition to enable me to stand in their place. But I may have a lively enough sense of the vulnerability of my own position to know what I should hesitate to ask of them.

Rawlsian Liberalism is often understood as if it were motivated by a doctrine of the person that requires one to imagine that one is without affiliations: the liberal citizen is a generic person, on this reading, not a flesh and blood human with powerful attachments to fragile things. This is Sandel's famous argument from *Liberalism and the Limits of Justice*, and the fact that it issues from a thorough misreading of *A Theory of Justice* has somehow not, in the current cultural milieu, prevented Sandel's charge from sticking, perhaps because Sandel's real target is not Rawls at all but a cruder although more common form of liberal culture and politics. The argument resembles the attack on Liberalism from the cultural left in the 1980s in the name of "difference," which treats Liberalism as a form of cultural homogenization that assimilates and evaporates humanly dense affiliations into a deracinated consumer culture. But it also resembles the attack on Liberalism from the cultural right, from Donald Davidson, say (the poet Donald Davidson, not the philosopher), or Wilmoore Kendall, in the 1950s, which argued, for instance, that the price of remedying the social ills of the South would be to destroy its southernness, creating a culture in which all American places are as alike and as sterile as their airports. While cultural homogenization is a force to be reckoned with and has a high cost, it is not the necessary consequence of Liberalism, and the generic person is not the ideal liberal citizen. (Properly speaking, cultural homogenization is a consequence of modernization, and modernization and Liberalism are not necessarily the same thing, as the recent history of China should demonstrate.)

The Rawlsian original position, in which one is required to imagine one's self as standing behind a veil of ignorance that prevents one from knowing one's specific place in a society one is examining (even as one knows what the range of possible places in that society is), is, these writers forget, only an imaginative construction, not a description of an ideal of human nature. From behind the veil of ignorance, we know that actual human beings are densely situated in affiliations; all we are prohibited from knowing is which affiliations will be our own. Rawlsian Liberalism neither requires nor promotes the homogenization of culture in the service of an ideal of abstract, generic citizenship. It requires only that one recognize that others are as attached to their own ways of doing things as we are to ours. (If there is a better way of putting respect for cultural difference into practice, I'd like to know what it is.) It does not require us to have no affiliations, no convictions, no history. It only requires us not to treat those things as stampeding obsessions in our dealings with each other. (This is not to say that Rawlsian Liberalism is or ought to be a doctrine that is universally tolerant: it cannot tolerate views that can only be maintained by the repressive use of state power, at least if those who maintain those views are in a position to make good their demand for that repressive power.)

Rationality as Repression

Another matter at stake in the Euthyphro Question, the question of whether at the deepest stratum our common moral and political life stands upon grounded principles or upon ungrounded choices, is the role of philosophy as a guide to life, as the love of wisdom. Both of the obvious alternative answers to the Euthyphro Question are for different reasons unsavory. The examined life is a life in which one's courses have passed through the refining flame of reflection, and the alternative seems to be a life dominated by power or by special pleading. But the examined life shades into the calculated life, the life that James Mill tried to impose upon his son and which John Stuart Mill found impossible to lead as a human being; rationality frees us from the tutelage that authority imposes upon us, but rationality itself seems to have a brutalizing side, a side captured in Dickens's Professor Gradgrind or Blake's Urizen. Whatever wisdom is, it must be responsible both to principle and to freedom, both to regulative ideas and to the human lifeworld. Whatever wisdom is, it involves the recognition that the reasonable and the rational are not always the same.

For example: if, to protect ourselves from sophistry and illusion, we had indeed committed to the flames all of the books that David Hume told us to burn at the end of the *Inquiry*, we would have reason to complain of rationality as redeeming its promise of liberation only by inventing new varieties of repression, what Adorno and Horkheimer call the Dialectic of Enlightenment. One of the reasons we are so often driven to the distinction between wisdom and knowledge, or the related distinction between reasonableness and rationality, is that we do not want to suppose that the commitments reflection imposes upon us are so specific that experience cannot open us to new possibilities.

To divide the world into one region, where our proper conduct is declared with apodictic certainty, and another region, where we are free because our actions in that region can only be arbitrary, is to get the nature of moral freedom exactly backwards. To see how wrong this is, we need to remind ourselves of what the great promise of the Enlightenment was, the promise of release from tutelage by public use of reason that Kant described in "What is Enlightenment?" Reason liberates even or rather especially when it proclaims law. For one thing, our sense of what we are required to do has a claim on us because it is at least in part the issue of a process of free reflection; the deliverances of practical reason have power because, ideally, left to ourselves and freed from the ulterior compulsions of Priest, King, Need, and Desire, we ultimately come to those deliverances under our own power. And for another thing, ethical rules seek also to express, not to repress, moral freedom, in the way the rules of prosody open new expressive possibilities in poetry or institutions like marriage seek to make possible a more variegated and meaningful experience of love and passion.

The founding claim of Liberalism is the claim Kant makes in "What is Enlightenment?" that convictions must arise from reasonable grounds rather than from tutelage. Reasonable grounds liberate because they enable one to construct an alternative to the *diktat* of those in power as the origin of conviction and the motor of action. Reasonable grounds are liberating to the extent that grounds for action depend upon something other than a Big Somebody's *ipse dixit*. (And that Big Somebody can as well be King Mob as King George. It can even be my needs and desires, if I am alone with them and inclined to give them the upper hand. Someone who is, after all, capable of anything, is not really somebody who is free but somebody who just can't help himself.) It is only because it depends upon something—reason—that enlightenment can provide an alternative to power's *ipse dixit*. If reason did not dictate (if strong relativism applied rather than, say, pragmatism), there would be no alternative to the say-so of the strong, and conviction or action would be the outcome of a contest of force among authorities who have no common unit of measure other than force. Strong relativism is not only not a necessary part of Liberalism, it is a principle actively hostile to Liberalism.

Liberalism combines the Enlightenment faith in reason as a liberator with a sense, derived from the state of affairs at the close of the wars of religion, that matters of faith should not be subject to state compulsion because nothing done under state compulsion can possibly count as faith. This claim at first seems in some tension with the Enlightenment faith in reason, since reason after all does dictate (and may possibly dictate to the state that certain religious tenets are dangerous to the health of the state), and faith also, whatever it is, is not something that reason can develop from within reason's own first principles, which is not to say that religious considerations are in every case and in every respect irrational. These two moments within the heritage of Liberalism, religious toleration and respect for the regulative power of reason, need not starkly contradict each other, since on the one hand one need not imagine faith as something about which reflection has nothing at all to say (as if it were a species of demonic possession or hysteria that can be tolerated only in the way other irrationalities can be tolerated, which is to say, only so long as it makes no difference to anything), and on the other it is not necessary to view respect for reason as requiring that it plumb every aspect of life with constructions from first principles. Indeed, the kind of rationality that could not coexist with faith (or at least with many kinds of faith) is the repressive kind, the kind that confuses the examined life with the calculated one. (This strain of enlightenment thinking was after all strong enough to richly deserve the rebuke Schleiermacher delivered to it in *On Religion: Speeches to its Cultured Despisers.*) But enlightened reasonableness can leave plenty of room for actual living, and need not treat what goes on in that room as arbitrary and so permissible (but only to the extent that it is trivial). Enlightened reasonableness differs from exhaustive calculation in that it can broadly recognize significant and non-trivial areas of spontaneity, one of which is the world of faith.

Crucial Moral Experiences and the Limit of the Will

It is not merely because it is a valid deduction from first principles we accept that a moral demand is compelling upon us; the force of a moral demand is not merely that it is valid but that it has a *claim* on us, and it has that claim upon us because it issues from our own freedom, and is so deeply rooted in our freedom that we cannot be ourselves or be free unless we meet that claim. The force of a moral claim is not merely, "this proposition is valid; do therefore as it recommends." The force of a moral claim is its ability to make us say, "Here I stand; I can do no other." To say that the compelling force of a moral claim is different from the validity of an ethical proposition is not to say that moral compulsion is arbitrary, is the end product of what is ultimately rather amoral decisionism. For the ability to stand reflection is a necessary if not sufficient condition of moral compulsion. And the compulsion itself is not merely something arbitrary, like demonic possession or obsession. But the compulsion of a moral idea is still something far different from agreement with a proposition or recognition that a deduction is valid.

When a pious Jew keeps the halakhic laws, he or she comes to a deeper consciousness of the meaning of Judaism, and exercises the kinds of religious choice that would not have been available without submission to the Law. The refinement of the law is the refinement of the expression of piety, and the refinement of freedom, too, since it enables one to express things that, lacking the refinements of the law, one could not have expressed because one lacked the means of expression. Law enriches the field of distinctions from which expression derives, and each new layer of distinctions makes possible further layers of distinction and the richly articulated piety that those further distinctions make possible.

The compelling force of a moral idea is like the compelling force of love or of faith. It is compelling because it is an expression of freedom—not merely of the fact that we are free, but of the meaning of that freedom. The compelling force of a moral idea is not something that is totally beyond the will, but it is also not something that is totally subject to it. It arises neither from within nor from beyond the will: like all crucial things that have the air of a calling about them, it arises at the exact limit of the will. The most central moral experiences— falling in love, going through a religious conversion, discovering one's profession—are as much things that happen to one as things that one does. They are certainly not only things one does after calculating the alternatives, and indeed one would begin to doubt such an experience if it were too completely the subject of choice, as one doubts the act of someone who chooses to fall in love with someone just because that person's love would be good for him. At the same time, one also doubts this kind of experience if it is obviously unreflected upon—as one doubts religious conversions that look too much like guilty obsessions or doubts whether the story is really all about love when his neurosis and her neurosis get up on their hind legs together and howl. A calling vitalizes the will, but it cannot itself be willed; it cannot be summoned up by main force, and its deliverances, however surprising, never seem arbitrary in retrospect but keep revealing new ways in which they are all of a piece.

This is not to say that callings are utterly unresponsive to the will. I can sometimes acquire a taste, over the long term, for instance, and certain kinds of spiritual exercise intensify and shape and differentiate the experience of faith. (Indeed, without such exercises, faith tends to remain amorphous and flabby and begins to lose its seriousness as faith.) The morally crucial things both are and are not chosen, both are and are not reflected upon, both are and are not prepared for. They happen, as I say, at the exact limit of the will, because they don't happen without the will, but the will itself cannot make them happen by main force any more than you can will yourself to sleep by gritting your teeth and trying.

James's paradoxical concept of the Will to Believe captures the sense in which deep exercises of the will happen at the will's exact limit. What is the Will to Believe? Clearly it is not just a main-force overbearing of the intellect by the feelings: "I will believe X, damn it all, despite what I believe" (or "You will love me, and of your own free will, damn it"). But willing one's self into belief (perhaps by clicking one's ruby slippers three times) isn't really what William James meant by that term anyway. James was concerned to provide an alternative to W. K. Clifford's evidentialism, which would have narrowed what one can affirm to a compass so small that the life lived on its basis would not be a human one. The question was not one of willing one's self into a state of belief from a state of unbelief but was rather one of not rejecting beliefs out of hand simply because they are not already beyond question. James doesn't seek to whip up belief from air. He seeks to restrain the empiricist habit of mind from laying waste to the human personality, to give one's self license to follow out an intuition into belief (whose force one already feels) in order to see where it leads.

We traditionally ask two contradictory things of moral commitments, things that tie them on the one hand to feelings and on the other to ideas. Feelings are not subject to will, but can be shaped by will. Of them we ask whether they are *genuine*, although that is a question that immediately places us in quandaries, because we don't know how to assure ourselves of an answer to that question. Ideas by contrast are subject to critique, examination, thought: I can determine whether they are right or wrong, sense or nonsense, and so on, and I can rationally affirm or deny them. I ask about an idea not whether it is genuine but whether it is correct, whether it has grounds reason might respect.

Values seem to partake at once of feelings and of ideas. They have an inward quality—say "allegiance"—about which we can ask the question of whether it is genuine. And they have an outer quality—call it "truth"—about which we can ask whether it is correct. Adhering to one's values both is and is not an act of will. A value does not simply seize the mind in an unmediated way. It is not something like demonic possession (always the unbeliever's idea of what belief looks like). Indeed, I want to say about values that it is possible to be "partially invested" in them—to try them on, to see how they look, to see how the world looks illuminated in their light. Moral imagination is after all the ability to enter seriously if provisionally into other conditions, and exercising that imagination is the ethical work we expect art to enable us to do. It is possible to have some distance upon one's values—distance enough at least to weigh different developments of them that all claim derivation from the same value concept, if not to enable us to enter moral worlds that are entirely foreign.

The double aspect of value—its affinity to feeling on the one hand and to thought on the other—is like the double aspect of legitimacy in politics, its affinity to will and consent on one hand and to judgment and integrity on the other.

Values as thoughts require the kind of analysis that sees human beings as purposive: we have ends, a *telos*, we act from grounds. But values-as-feelings tie us to the world of causality: we are driven by urges behind which we cannot go. When I treat the values of others merely as feelings, I manipulate them ("Use only positive images to shape the young," or "If I change how people *represent* I change how they *think*."). When I treat the values of others as thoughts, I reason with them. But neither reasoning nor manipulation quite captures what I mean by a living confrontation with one's own values. (Political deal-making, in fact, comes closer to it than either.)

When I treat values as thoughts, I ignore their necessary connection to felt life—a felt life that is in some ways prior to thought. The felt aspect of values is their tie to identity. Values are felt as *mine* in ways I do not necessarily think of propositions as *mine*. They tie to a "hot" sense of identity, to those things that seemed to be already part of me before I became fully aware of them (and of me), to the sense that my experience in some way that evades analysis is all of a piece and has meaning. A particular feeling may be fleeting. But a structure of feeling is not fleeting but more stable even than a thought, since a proposition is likely to be knocked over by the first person with a better argument. Values are lived-through, both in thought and in feeling. The "thought-through" aspect of values is their tie to a considered identity, the "best self" we shape through reflection and analysis of our feelings. And the "felt-through" aspect of values is their sense that they belong together and are inevitable and inescapable. (They project this feeling of belonging together and of inevitability even when they are in fact in conflict with other equally inevitable values that seem to belong to the wholeness of our experience. The feeling that they all hang together is part of our investment in them, but that they provoke this feeling in no way means that they really *do* hang together.)

These morally crucial experiences that take place at the limit of the will may be non-propositional in nature. At the end of the *Tractatus* Wittgenstein describes how someone who has gone through a period of spiritual crisis that has resolved itself will often be unable to point to what that experience taught. What it taught may be shown, but it cannot be said. If such a person did put the meaning of the experience into words, he or she might well say something that probably could have been said just as well beforehand. Born-again Christians, for instance, knew and believed all the same things before their key experiences that they know and believe afterwards, but somehow their relationship to what they know has been changed by their experiences. Such a person does not believe anything that he or she did not believe before, but he or she lives in a different world. Something of the same sort happens when one inwardly experiences a renewal in an emotional relationship of long standing. This does not mean that one has not really learned anything, only that it is something that cannot be directly articulated in propositions. Nor does it merely mean that one's emotions are aroused, that were quiescent. If I suddenly see something in my world with new clarity, I do not merely feel inspired; I feel in the presence of something that is worth the inspiration. If I lose that sight—the experience Coleridge describes in "Dejection: An Ode"—what I have lost is not merely access to the richness of my own feelings, but access to the non-propositional meaning that would have been the occasion of those feelings.

Consider the person who says, "Since I became ill with cancer, I have discovered that life, that this world, is wonderful, and I have learned to love it more deeply." Is this discovery the discovery of a propositional truth? Certainly not. What the speaker has discovered is something he or she never disagreed with, or if he or she did, then it wasn't an argument or a piece of evidence that changed the belief. That person has not come upon an argument but has opened to an experience, has discovered an existential, not a propositional, truth. Yet our most morally crucial experiences—and some of the grounds for the respect we have for each other as persons—arise from these non-propositional grounds. A similar sense of this inarticulate but urgent pressure of something meaningful inheres in all deep experiences. Something of this is what Emerson means by "being alive in the present." It is this presence, not merely an emotional lift, which Emerson describes in his famous passage in *Nature* about crossing the bare common, in snow-puddles, and suddenly seeing himself as part and parcel of God.

Non-propositional experiences of meaning are not totally beyond argument, but they are not the creatures of argument. Arguments can provide the occasion, if not the substance, of such an experience (which is what we mean when we say that an argument has a poetic structure or a poetic persuasiveness), and argumentative structures can articulate, but not really establish, the meaning of crucial but non-propositional experiences. Argument can give shape to, can develop, can bring into flower, experiences of this kind, but argument does not rule them. Argument's relation to experience is a poetic one, and logical rules have the same relationship to such experiences that prosodic rules do to the meaningfulness of poems.

The God of the philosophers, seen only as the creature of argument, who has only the attributes the philosopher can prove him to have, is of course a stick figure. God is what itches the philosopher into philosophy, not the object of philosophical proofs. And divine philosophy is a way of experience, not a way of knowledge. Does the good have the same relationship to ethical philosophy that God does to philosophical theology? The only thing that saves theology from ridicule is its ability sometimes to face one with the living God. (It does happen, really.) Does philosophical ethics likewise have one foot in absurdity—the attempt to discover the moral life by calculation—but have the other foot in poetry, in the live experience of ethical vocation? Ethics would be not the proof or disproof of moral propositions so much as the occasion of the experience of ethical calling. Logic here is not the defining ground of truth and falsity but the ritual precondition of an experience (as prayers are the ritual preconditions of transubstantiation).

Somehow the openness to this kind of experience is crucial to our sense of being human and to our sense that being a human being is a valuable thing to be. Deep experiences impose on us a moral burden and a moral project and demand realization in an honorable habit of life. The problem is that deep experiences, as Emerson and Schleiermacher knew, lend themselves to immediate self-falsification; faiths become creeds, a shared moral project becomes a destructive national mystique, a god becomes an idol, a moral calling becomes operatic moral narcissism. But the fact that these experiences almost inevitably play us false does not in itself prove that they never have any truth in them.

The Chaos of Willing

If one ever breaks out of an imprisoning formalism, an explanatory universe so complete from within its premises that it is sealed against counterexamples (Marxism, Freudianism, Darwinism, and Classical Economics each are or can be imprisoning formalisms), it is only a "visceral recognition" that enables one to do so. Our strongest moral convictions are sometimes visceral in the same way. For all of his professed skepticism, for instance, Socrates was powerfully certain of many things, and what he had the most certainty about were convictions that most of his interlocutors find so incredible that they barely take in what he means by them. None of Socrates' convictions is more unshakeable than that it is better to suffer wrong than to do it, except perhaps his equally non-obvious conviction that the satisfactions offered by love of power are ultimately not only shallow and degrading but also not really satisfactions. Not even sympathetic interlocutors such as Adeimantus or Glaucon are ever brought fully to this view (here I am assuming that there is at least a shadow of the early Socrates in the middle books of the *Republic*, even if the style of argument in that text is wholly foreign to Socrates). And yet Socrates' convictions are not irrational, even if they are not the rigorous consequence of his premises. They are not the fruit of moral calculation, but they clearly arise from somewhere only the Socratic *daimon* gives us direct access to: they do not positively circumvent reason (Socrates' position is at least no more obviously irrational than Thrasymachus' is), and they are elaborated using reason's means, but they originate from somewhere in the shadows within reason, not from somewhere beneath it. They are not held as a consequence of premises, but they are responsible for the meaning of the arguments Socrates does make from premises. Unlike dogmatic or heteronomous convictions, they are not finally limitations upon freedom, for their function is to keep the mind detached from powerful attractions (such as love of power, or ethical skepticism, with its unearned claim to superior realism) in which the mind would otherwise be imprisoned. The function of this kind of conviction is not a heteronomous one, for it keeps open a question that the mind is subject to powerful temptations to foreclose prematurely, the question of whether anything matters other than power and pleasure. The workings of such convictions take place at the limit of reason, as they do at the limit of the will.

One consequence of the fact that morally crucial experiences take place at the exact limit of the will is that such experiences, so telling and unmistakable when one is in their grip, are hedged around always with doubts and ambivalences whenever one has upon them the purchase of distance. I will call this consequence "the chaos of willing." Part of the experience of the chaos of willing is the experience of the will's always failed sovereignty over itself. Arendt, first in *Between*

Past and Future, and in more detail in *The Life of the Mind,*
describes this experience, first articulated in Paul but most
fully thought through by Augustine, who saw this opposition
between willing and nilling as the endless stalemate between
moral will and physical impulse, or between a will to do the right
and a perverse but undeniable will to destruction and death.

The impasse is a function not so much of the strength of a
contrary inner will (a nill, as it were), but of the fact that the
one thing the will cannot will is to will itself a better will.
What I want, Augustine cries, is to want better things; but
that's precisely the thing I can't do simply by wanting to, since
I may want better things for bad reasons, or have bad reasons
for wanting better reasons. If I do find myself wanting better
things, it can't be because I have been able to make myself do
so, but only because I have discovered that somehow I already
did. (This is the paradoxical logic of Donne's sonnet "Batter
my heart, Three-personed God": "For I, / Except that you
enthrall me, never shall be free.")

The transformation of the will happens only at the will's
exact limit—by grace, by the force of something both within
and beyond us, an aboriginal self unknown to my psychological or social identity and yet intimately intertwined with it.
The power of things that transform the will at the will's exact
limit will always be subject to second thoughts and will always
raise unanswerable and paralyzing questions about authenticity
and bad faith. In the heat of the moment the self-transforming
power Emerson describes in "Self-Reliance" looks at best like
antinomianism and at worst like narcissism. But, as Emerson
himself remarks, "if anyone thinks this law is lax, let him try to
live by it one day." For if we learn, in Kierkegaard's phrase, that
purity of heart is to will one thing, the next thing we learn is
that willing one thing is beyond us, that self-serving, self-
dramatization, and self-deceit always displace our morally crucial
motivations as soon as we catch sight of them, and our high profession turns out to be a kind of aria we sing on what Robert
Penn Warren calls the high secret stage of self. And indeed the
inability to face down the chaos of willing is the hallmark of
the characters in Warren's fiction who succumb to moral panic,
behaving like fanatics not because they are in the grip of a
transforming belief but because they suspect that they might
believe nothing after all. "Power ceases in the instant of repose,"

Emerson remarks in "Self-Reliance," noticing in that moment how instantly the becoming and restless, endless, self-overcoming of vocation dissolves into the chaos of willing or hardens into dogmas that betray the faith from which they sprang and which they were an attempt to express. "Power ceases in the instant of repose," falling either on one side into nothing or on the other into force.

There is a difference between opposing one's *impulses* (Homeric heroes, after all, do that, and are placed in quandaries about it), and opposing one's own *will*. The chaos of willing is a situation in which one's own will divides and confronts itself as an alien being. What Augustine learns is not that he has bad desires but that he is sick in his will. He wills to have a better will, but that is not fully in the power of the will.

The will divides only under the pressure of an absolute but inscrutable moral imperative. The division in Augustine's will is the division between the city of man and the city of God, which is to say not just between good and bad desires but between good and bad ways of seeing the world as a whole. The chaos of the will is the reflection of the pressure of a kind of ethical standard, a standard that is separate from the ethical commonplaces of a culture and which can criticize those cultures in a wholesale way, not merely as not living up to their values but as wholly devoted to mistaken values.

Conventional morality is consonance with the ruling commonplaces of a culture, alignment with the available structure of roles, duties, and responsibilities that shape a form of collective life. Prophetic morality is distinguished by its ability to stigmatize a conventional morality as *tout court* devoted to illusion. And the chaos of willing is the inevitable consequence of a prophetic morality, because prophetic morality is capable of asserting that not just conventional morality but our internalized habits through which we make our way in the world are fundamentally wrong and that the things we have most relied upon are fundamentally unreal.

The chaos of willing explains one of the paradoxes of poetic inwardness. Poets often write poems in which they confront their own experience of becoming initiated into poetry. But these poems, poems of election, often bear an uncanny similarity to palinodes, those poems in which the poet turns against his inspiration and bids farewell to poetry, as Laura Quinney points out. So, for instance, there is a close resemblance between the poetic logic of Wordsworth's poem of election, "Tintern Abbey," and his palinode, "Peele Castle," so Whitman's poem of election "Out of the Cradle Endlessly Rocking," closely parallels his palinode "As I Ebb'd with the Ocean of Life." What makes these parallels possible is that the poet at the moment of election—Wordsworth or Whitman in the examples above, or Emily Dickinson in "There's a Certain Slant of Light," or Elizabeth Bishop in "In the Waiting Room,"—is not somebody endowed with power but somebody who feels a power he or she will never control, a power which is sometimes exercised against rather than for the poet. What the poet learns from the inward experience of election is not his or her inner greatness but erotic loss, death, longing. But the places where these things happen are also the places where greatness dwells—not the greatness the poet wields but the greatness the poet serves, before which he or she must remain humble. This is why the poetic sublime confronts the poet as alien and even non-human, why the poetic moment has joy and terror at the same time. The poet is not endowed with the ability to articulate great things, but feels the pressure of something great which demands but exceeds articulation, something before which the poet always feels preterite and in the face of which the poet's consolations feel like whistling in the dark. The romantic poet does not speak the orphic word but registers the pressure that word exerts upon the language it deforms.

It is because the pressure of poetic inspiration is the pressure of something that demands but evades articulation that poetic inspiration is always subject to the paralyzing doubt that the poet is merely fooling him or her self. Imagination begins with the rejection of fancy, and it is the necessity of eluding self-deceit that makes imaginative power an austere thing, as the necessity of rejecting the idea that God is a louder-voiced version of one's self underlies the ascetic rejection of religious language that marks the truly religious sensibility. The poet must reject narcissism because whatever poetry is it is debased by being put to the service of venal needs. Skepticism about putatively imagined experiences is an ascetic way of purifying the imagination of ulterior motives and personal limitations, and it is an asceticism that proceeds infinitely, since even asceticism can be the subject of self-deceit.

[173]

The muse is not a narcissistic projection. If it were, good poetry would be a lot easier to write than it is. The muse demands an unfolding process of relationship and engagement from the poet, and like all such processes—like intimacy itself—many of its steps are false ones, and even a successful one is the upshot of a great many failures.

The risk is that in rejecting narcissism the poet also rejects selfhood entirely—hence the association between inspiration and fatal varieties of intoxication.

The fact that the will is chaotic raises the question of what gets to count as an expression of my will. Every act issues out of a welter of intentions, some of them contradictory. Each intention is entertained at a different scale of time, and perhaps with different amounts of investment. What the upshot of my intentions is is something I can only sometimes describe with assurance, not only because of the scatteredness and ambivalence of my thoughts, but also because the implications of my thoughts are not all present to me at the same time, and when I see them fully I may well change my assessment of them, an act that speaks neither for my consistency nor for my inconsistency. "My will" exists only in virtual time, not in real time. It flourishes in that time out of time when the meaning of my intentions becomes clear to me and renders a comprehensive account of my fluctuating volitions, neither reducing them to an average nor weighing momentary impulses more heavily than they deserve. What gets to represent me should be neither my spontaneity, which does not sort out what I am durably invested in from what I am momentarily seized by, nor my considered self, which plays false all of the turbulent and contradictory things of which it is made. My will, what gets to represent me, exists only in a time out of time, a present with duration, which the real present does not have. In any real present my story is still untold and any account of me falsifies some potentiality or some implication or some allegiance. My agency issues from an implicitness that nothing ever makes fully explicit.

Consider the paradoxical attraction that determinism holds for idealist sensibilities. One would think of de-terminism as a philosophy that encourages passivity, if only because it teaches that none of one's actions make a difference since the outcome of one's project is inevitable. Yet determinist theories have had an élan and a world-historical force that theories of freedom have been hard-pressed to match. Consider, for instance, the heroism older Marxists used to expend in the name of history, whose course seemed inevitable to them. My first thought was to say that the sacrifice of freedom these causes demand is the price of the grandeur they offer—that my life is a larger thing if it is swept up in History than it is if it's all spent getting pleasure and money. But that doesn't fully explain the genuine heroism such convictions sometimes called forth, even in bad causes, because those who do this do not feel themselves to be sacrificing their freedom at all. Quite the reverse, they feel themselves to be discovering it.

What people discover when they embrace determinism is an inner will deeper than their own will and thus truly themselves. They are finding a source of will at the same time powerfully intimate to them and also unknown to them, a real me who is mysterious to me but more in possession of the meaning of my being me than any version of myself that is present to my experience (the reader will notice that this is the same language one might use to describe the experience of grace, which likewise cuts the Gordian knot of the chaos of willing). Because the will is a chaos, because we do not want what we want to want, because nothing we know of ourselves satisfies our sense that we *are* selves, we reach through self to the intimate other—indeed, to the muse—that a theory of determinism proposes for us. Determinism is a way of resolving the chaos of will by, Heidegger's phrase, willing not to will.

Is determinism the only theory that enables contact with the intimate other that grounds the will beyond its own chaos? No; theories of transcendence can also do this, and theories of transcendence are available even to Liberalism. But contemporary Liberalism is embarrassed by theories of transcendence, preferring to *entertain* them—as acts of value-positing—rather than to believe them. That is why liberals so often feel small in the presence of those who are in fact finally not much better than fanatics.

To demand the purity of heart to will one thing is to propose a test that nobody can pass. Acts of this kind are supposed to spring out of a lucid and intense present in which I *am* and I *am*, and what I am is known to me in a wholly satisfactory although perhaps wholly implicit way. But the first fact one knows about one's own will is its ambivalence. What finally issues from me as an act is only what survives from a tangle of contradictory impulses, hesitations, and desires, some of which I recognize as transitory and "not really what I am about," others of which may strike me as deep but also as obscure, as things that I do not fully understand but wish to see where they lead. No will can be wholehearted in the way the test proposes. In fact, the only time my will becomes simple is not when it springs hot out of my own immediacy but when I have reflected upon it and sorted it out: it is like the poem I write once I have crossed out all the false starts and wrong turns, a poem that represents my intentions more fully than the groping draft does, because even as I take these wrong turns I recognize that there is *something* off about them, something to be "cleaned up" later. And the presentness of a poetic speaker (to pursue the metaphor) is not the actual present in which the actual poet hangs fire over a word and walks about the room or the actual present in which a reader recites it haltingly aloud, but an intensely imagined present that either of them win through to only once the poem is complete. But this achieved presentness is exactly what the notion of spontaneous, wholehearted authenticity thought it was ruling out.

My own will, that is to say, is as mysterious and as incalculable as that great abstraction "the will of the people." And the process of shaping an act is not much different from that of formulating a law in a heterogeneously divided legislature. It will reflect several different time-scales: the temporary equilibrium I have been able to work out over the time allotted to deliberation, and the longer-term homeostasis through which I shape my best self and discover what my momentary intuitions really come to.

If the necessity of standing the test of reflection distinguishes a calling at the limit of the will from arbitrary decisionism, it is still the risk of anything at the limit of the will that it can confuse the boundaries between calling and obsession, between finding one's destiny and choosing one's juggernaut. (Recognizing that risk is after all one of the things that makes the chaos of willing chaotic.)

The chaos of willing, if it takes on constitutive rather than regulative force, becomes a dark Dionysian quest for authenticity. Any theory of value that gives inwardness a constitutive power is an authenticity theory, a theory that grounds value by tying it to the dictates of a god within, who, being a god, can lead one anywhere (as the gods lead Euthyphro).

Authenticity theories resolve themselves into pursuit of an élan that possesses the mind but cannot be fathomed by it. They promise access to something deep and value-creating. But that deep thing retreats before us like the beloved of Shelley's "Alastor." Pursuit of such a source is pursuit of something that always eludes us, something that we always betray, something about which every claim we make is not even a half-truth but already a lie.

Pursuit of a constitutive inwardness is a kind of demonic possession. Or rather, it is a longing for a kind of possession, but it keeps turning into fakery and hocus-pocus. It keeps promising the ability to leap into faith. But whenever we make that leap we discover not faith but narcissism. Pursuit of a constitutive inwardness is like being swept up in a movement: one cannot say what it means, one cannot hold it to account, one merely feels it as meaningful and goes where it takes one. How many steps is it, then, from the leap of faith to the will to power? (And how many steps is it from the will to power to the dance of Shiva?)

A regulative inwardness does not have the same force as a constitutive one, for its work is to produce second thoughts, circumspection, distance on one's own intuitions, exactly the things a constitutive inwardness leads one to dismiss as signs of inauthenticity. Socrates' *daimon* has a dispossessing, not a possessing force.

Those who sacrifice themselves in the name of a great dark vision of inevitable process also, after all, think of themselves as acting in freedom and in its service, and when one builds altars to the beautiful necessity that crushes us that building is usually done by the very self that discovers the purpose of its self-reliance in building the altar upon which it is to be sacrificed. Because in practice we never really know not only how our acts will turn out but also which act is finally the right one, even what issues in reflection has something of a wager about it.

It is customary to think of the turn into the chaos of willing as an unambiguously bad thing. Arendt's Robespierre (in *On Revolution*) is drawn into a death-spiral of increasing bloodshed in order to prove, not only to the multitude but to his own unanswerable self doubt, the sincerity of his anguish for the sufferings of the poor. The counter-cultural figures Trilling rebukes in *Sincerity and Authenticity* are caught up in the same self-defeating drama, and the depressing replacement Richard Sennett describes (in *The Fall of Public Man*) of the language of public deliberation by the language of intimate expressivity (the stereotyped language, I might add—"the intimate revelations of young men are largely plagiarized," as Fitzgerald's Nick Carraway remarks) is an example of a similar dynamic. If, as Adorno claims, the jargon of authenticity obscures, perhaps strategically, what it professes to clarify, then perhaps the public world of deliberation and action, in which one plays out a persona that both is and is not one's self (as "my Hamlet" both is and is not me) offers an alternative to the chaos of willing. "Enough of this navel-gazing," one hears, "Go up into the public world of deliberation and action." ("Do that which lies nearest you," Carlyle's Teufelsdrock chants as he comes out of the Eternal No in *Sartor Resartus*, "and the next thing will be that much the clearer.") It is as if one were to reject the Thoreau of *Walden* for the Thoreau of "Resistance to Civil Government," unaware that they are not only the same man but that the one Thoreau is the condition for the other. The chaos of willing is meant to be faced, not to be blustered down, and facing it as it is ought to produce modesty, pragmatism, generosity, and worldly realism, the moral constellation of Melville's Rolfe, not Melville's Ahab.

Freedom and Pattern

The division of the world into "the place where reflection has something to say" and "the place where we are free to do whatever we will" ignores the fact that uncompelled reflection is the defining characteristic of freedom, and freedom of one kind or another is the element of reflection. But if that division misunderstands the world of Rule, it also, and about as deeply, misunderstands the world of Spontaneity. For the things we do freely, especially the things we do with a kind of virtuosity, are valuable roughly in proportion to depth of reflection out of which they proceed. That reflection need not be propositional, or even conscious—think of the subtle but intuitive sense of his or her art a great jazz musician has—but it is far from arbitrary. Freedom is not something that must be protected from the intrusive force of reflection; freedom is the water in which reflection swims, and reflection, in producing pattern (to change the metaphor), extends and deepens freedom.

One way to imagine the relationship between reflection and freedom is to consider the relationship between pattern and variation in works of art. Part of the experience of a work of art that unfolds in time (such as music or literature) is the spectator's effort to construct a representation of it in an abstract space, the space in which one speaks of the "shape" of a story or the "overarching structure" of a symphony. A work of art continuously solicits, but also continuously transforms, expectations about what that shape will be. When we notice a pattern opening, we form an expectation about how it will close, but that expectation is never satisfied in exactly the manner in which we formed it. For either that pattern is broken across a different pattern—as for instance when a story "takes a turn" or when, in Frost, the "sentence sound" of the ordinary human voice (whatever that is) plays out a kind of diffraction pattern with the regular *tactus* of the formal pentameter. Or our expectation of a closed pattern is transformed by our awareness of other patterns at different scales—as, for instance, when a little well-shaped melody begins to be seen as part of a set of variations that itself has a shape, or when one simultaneously sees a small stretch of narrative prose as part of an exchange, a passage, a chapter, an episode, and a novel.

Aesthetic experiences always happen only in those places where pattern and predictability are at odds. The retrospective sense one forms as one goes of "the story thus far" must never, for instance, be absolutely identical with the prospective sense one forms as one goes of "how this one's going to end." Or parts serendipitously fall into very different wholes at very different scales, so that the patternedness, not only the breaking of patterns, is also part of the novelty. My sense of aesthetic experiences here follows the theories the linguist Ray Jackendoff has proposed about the psychology of music. He has in mind merely our ability to recognize a series of tones as a melody, say, but also our ability to call a melody "interesting" or "novel." Jackendoff's very sophisticated model accounts not only for how musical affect is tied to the play of expectation and (not quite) satisfaction, but also how a piece of music does not lose its ability to seem meaningful to us once we already know it thoroughly.

All this is not merely to motivate the old cliché that a life well lived is a kind of work of art. (Nor is it to motivate the revolting cliché that politics should resemble art—a cliché that in our time has been used, as Benjamin described it, to replace political thought by the stampeding force of mass spectacle.) It is to say that we do not recognize the merely random and arbitrary as a kind of freedom—what has more sameness to our ears than white noise, even if white noise is in fact totally unpatterned?— but that our experience of freedom is an experience of living changingness in which pattern is always present but in which how the pattern will close is not predictable. Another way of saying the same thing is that we value other people's freedom partly because we hope that their stories will make a kind of sense to us and because upon close examination we always learn that their stories are not only not "the kind of thing we've heard a thousand times before" but are also never quite over. If there is any kinship between the aesthetic world and the political world it is that both seek to give an expressive realization to freedom through the continuously opening development of patterns. (This is what Kant seems to have in mind in the *Critique of Judgment* when he says that what one artist learns from another is not to imitate the first's technique but to imitate the first artist's freedom.) If I respect a work of art, I know that there is some depth in it not captured by my summary accounts of it. If I respect a person, I know that the more I know about that person the less likely I am to regard his or her story as already done with. Whatever else Spontaneity is, it is not mere randomness, but the sense that there will always be more to something than one has already been able to account for. Spontaneity is not the opposite of pattern but the live development of pattern. If laws of freedom are the fruit of free reflection, they are also, ideally speaking, the conditions of possibility of new kinds of spontaneity. Which is what I mean (although it may not be what Milton meant) by "Reason also is choice."

Calling and Justice

Like Burke, or like Oakeshott, I see that naked abstractions are not enough to invent a society with or to revolutionize deeply embedded social practices. But it does not follow for me, as it does for Burke or Oakeshott, that the embeddedness of those practices, and their entanglement with the many implicit threads of living, should shield those practices from critique from an abstract point of view. I concede that sometimes when we pull on the loose thread of an injustice we find ourselves unraveling the garment in which it is tangled, since that thread has unanticipated and unanticipatible connections with other things, fragile things, that matter to us. At the same time I argue also that it is a mistake to treat embedded practices as the widest horizon within which critique can take place.

The widest horizon of critique, the horizon of transcendent first principles, is not fully available to us, since those principles tend to be slippery and abstract in the first place (so that what their dictation amounts to in particular cases is not always certain), and in the second place reaching after them has a way of maddening the moral personality. But access to that absolute horizon is not the only alternative to imprisonment in the world of practice, because even from within the world of practice one keeps running up against unanticipated resistances, that sense that "there is something the matter here" with which the Socratic *daimon* is always tripping one up. The unanticipated, and unanticipatible, resistances keep forcing one out of the horizon of accepted practices, even if they do not yield one access to the absolute. My view is ultimately not Burke's, but Channing's and Bushnell's, the view that although we learn what our morals mean from the relationships in which we are already embedded, those morals themselves force us to take a critical stance toward those relationships. The critical ties of mind and heart from which moral critique proceeds, although arising from this situatedness, from the ethnic accident of being brought up in a particular time and place, are not merely ethnic accidents but also guides (if only for a few steps), into a wider region of thought and life not fully captured by ethnic accidents. We may not have easy access to values utterly detached from arrangements as we know them already. But we do have the urging of the Socratic *daimon* to keep us uneasy with those arrangements and on the lookout for a better way.

In American circumstances this concession, that we never have access to values that are completely free from our implicit practices, means that I read the American revolution, with

Arendt in *On Revolution* and with Habermas in *Theory and Practice*, as distinguished from the French revolution by its ability to call upon concrete political traditions that were already a part of the political experience of the founders. (This argument too is made in different ways by Burke and by Tocqueville, and indeed the distinction is a commonplace of nineteenth-century political thought on both sides of the Atlantic.) To make this claim is to say that the founders' doctrine of inalienable rights declared in self-evident truths was not an insight into an absolute order of being that yielded them political imperatives that they had to impose upon a completely resistant social order (as the doctrine of rights was for Robespierre), but an insight into a political life they had already lived their way into, in town government, and in colonial legislatures.

I call the founders' doctrine of inalienable rights an insight, however, and not a commonplace. If Jefferson's insight into self-evident truths about inalienable rights were a commonplace, it would make a claim that would be so obvious as not to require stating, a claim that, while perhaps itself unprovable, would be so strange to deny that one would not know what to make of someone who denied it. To declare a self-evident truth is not merely to notice a commonplace; it is to proclaim an insight. To proclaim an insight is at once a constative and a performative act, for it is performative insofar as the proclamation is meant to have force and is meant to make something happen (a revolution in mores and politics), and constative in that it claims that the insight captures the meaning of practices and institutions in which even those who deny it are already thoroughly imbricated. When I declare a self-evident truth I tell you that you have already made certain kinds of promise, even though you may not know it in any explicit way and may deny it if asked about it. I have had a powerful, if contestable, insight into the meaning of what you and I are already doing, and in proclaiming it I promise to bend myself (and maybe you, to the extent that I can persuade you) to fulfill those promises.

Jefferson's self-evident truths are insights, pinpricks of the *daimon*, not commonplaces, because although the founders' practices had put them in a position to apprehend the power of Jefferson's doctrine, it was far from being a doctrine they were fully willing or able to put into practice (or that their descendants have been fully willing or able to put into practice either). The founders were, after all, violators of those self-evident truths about rights, and so are we. In fact, by proclaiming them as self-evident truths they conceded that there are many who would not find them to be so, conceding not only that they themselves have failed to live up to the promise they are only now aware of having already made, but also that many among them might not concede that they have made this promise at all. Arendt is particularly alive to the pathos of declaring something to be a self-evident truth. She sees Jefferson's act as one of proclaiming to the world—and of reminding himself as well—a truth implicit in its practices but disavowed in those same practices. (Indeed, proslavery writers like Thomas R. Dew, or William Harper, or James Henry Hammond, routinely singled out Jefferson's doctrine for ridicule.) But Jefferson did not invent those rights, and those self-evident truths, out of whole cloth. Although, as MacIntyre insists, there is no language for rights in Hebrew, Greek, Latin, or Arabic before the fifteenth century, the founders saw that they had already lived their way into a world of rights and duties, that before they had made themselves explicitly aware of them, they were already thoroughly bound up in them, even if now as well as then they (and we) did not fully understand the entailments they engender.

The crucial claim is that investment in received practices is not under all circumstances submission to the heteronomous tutelage of habit, for those practices are haunted by insights into depths of meaning and obligation that are beyond habit. A critical insight into the meaning of practices is the only thing that can bridge the gap between a human but thoroughly heteronomous world of habits and a morally compelling but inhuman world of principles. Such an insight is a route to a transcendent value, not because that transcendence declares itself in so many words in the insight, but because one cannot tell in advance just how far that insight will lead. Jefferson's insights arose from the republican habits of life in which he was already initiated, but they led him and us far from the hierarchical and racist society in which he had that insight, however phronetically, and intermittently, and imperfectly. And for all the phronetic messiness, Jefferson's insights remain in contact with both sides of the Euthyphro problem, with both the human lifeworld and the critical and liberating but inhuman absolute.

Because Robespierre could not count on an already natural-ized tradition of self-rule, he had to assume that the public habits of the people he sought to rule were completely cor-rupt. He therefore had to adopt a strict view of the contami-nating power of interests in public life, a view very different from that of the American founders, who assumed that citizens would of course have private interests, that interests are not inherently shameful, and that fair dealing among worldly per-sons who have interests but are not prisoners of their interests is a better image of public life than mystified talk about the public interest or the general will. The Americans were free to adopt a relaxed view of interests because they did not have to invent a theory of the public good from whole cloth. Their ability to maintain this relaxed view was not a function of their rampant materialism but of their already sturdy moral consen-sus and of their traditions of public negotiation with each other over interest issues. They did not see interest and virtue as opponents because an ethos of fair dealing is not scandalized by the fact of interest. They were, in Bruce Ackerman's telling phrase, neither Public Citizens concerned only with the glory of the state, nor Pure Privatists concerned only with getting and spending, but private citizens who knew how to make promises and keep them, and who valued a culture in which the making and keeping of promises is a form of public life.

When Arendt argues for the separation of "the political" from "the social," she is often taken to mean that political insti-tutions must not concern themselves with the material condi-tions of life. This view of her claim is shared by those who reject her thought in wholesale ways and by those who have some qualified sympathy with her thinking, by Pangle, say, or Kateb, or Whitfield, or, most recently, Hanna Pitkin. Indeed, Arendt herself seems to suggest (with a certain snobbish incom-prehension of American politics that always clouded her view of current events) that politics should be above grubby things like getting and spending and that welfare-state liberalism should be regarded as venal. But surely Arendt's claim is moti-vated not by a desire that governments keep their hands out of economic matters but by a desire that governments not be so panicked by the spectacle of urgent human misery that they trample the institutional basis of fair deliberation. Arendt invented the distinction to make clear her sense of how Madison's view of politics differed from Robespierre's, and certainly Madison's politics has a great deal of concern with the social and economic life of the people. The difference is in Madison's relatively relaxed view of interest politics: he does not seek to solve social problems by repressing thought about interest in the desire to make the General Will clear to itself, but to enable people with interests to deal with each other in a fair but thoroughly worldly way. Arendt's anxieties about "the social" were anxieties about a particular kind of political panic that urgent human needs make us liable to, a kind of panic that not only winds up subjecting political institutions to the metabolism of necessity and force, but that usually undoes the attempt to meet those urgent needs that motivated the panic in the first place. Arendt is no apologist for Lochnerism, although modern Lochnerians may cite her and modern anti-Lochnerians may abuse her.

Lacking a developed tradition of self-rule, Robespierre and his like had to assume that interest only had a contaminating force, and therefore had to resort to tyranny in the interest of purity. I do not believe, as Hegel does, that the excesses of the French Revolution are somehow the consequences of the Enlightenment as a whole. But it is easy to see how the belief that a new kind of virtuous citizen would have to be created from whole cloth by means of coercion, a belief that follows immediately from the idea that virtue and interest are irreconcilable opposites, can motivate almost anything. It is this specific claim, not the more general claim against the Enlightenment, that Habermas argues Hegel had in mind in his famous denunciation of the revolutionary Terror.

A public insight like Jefferson's has some of the features of a calling. Like a calling, it reveals to us what we already were, even when we denied it. Like a calling it demands of us that we continue to become, that we continue to transform ourselves into better keepers of those promises we had already made before we saw them. But, also like a calling, a public insight remains disputable. A calling is disputed always by the chaos of the will. But even in the midst of the chaos of the will, a calling lends itself to moments of pure and indisputable clarity, in which I do will one thing and one thing purely. This never happens in the case of public insights (except in moments of mass hysteria, where what seems to clarify the will is some intoxicating confusion). There is after all no such thing as a public will. There are only the promises made by public institutions by people engaged in persuading each other about things they both agree and differ about.

Autonomy and discipline are in harmony in the concept of a calling, but the common life of citizens, particularly under conditions in which they find themselves in profound moral conflict even as they are also profoundly tied to each other, cannot be brought under the concept of a calling without transforming that calling into something repressive and heteronomous. Whatever citizenship is, it is, like a calling, something responsible both to freedom and to the constraint of principle, but it cannot bind freedom and principle into the tight unity a calling demands. For callings are the hallmark of voluntary associations, and societies are not voluntary associations: we are born into them, we are thrown into their midst. Yet on the other hand, we have a stake in each other, and a stake in our common life, even if that stake is not the same thing as a calling. The difficulty of the problem of citizenship is to define a concept that binds freedom and principle more weakly than a calling does, but does not bind them only so weakly as a mere *modus vivendi* would bind them: there is more to liberal society than the mere promise to make as little trouble for each other as we have to, but whatever moral investments citizens of a liberal society have in each other, they must not include the ability to enlist the repressive machinery of state power on behalf of a vision of the meaning and purpose of life merely because its adherents think of a particular such vision as an especially good one.

The questions raised by the problem of "calling" are transformed versions of the question of what relations liberal societies, for whom a primary value is fairness, should have to communal visions of the good. The traditional vision of Liberalism as the rule of fairness, a vision developed in Kant's political writings but articulated most recently and forcefully by Rawls and Ackerman, which requires public neutrality between competing visions of the good, has come under heavy fire in the last twenty years, although in my view not all of that fire is accurate. A defensible conception of liberal neutrality need not require citizens, when acting in their capacity as citizens (nor even the state, so long as its means are limited) to adopt a position of complete indifference on all disputed questions of value, nor need the state treat conflicts over values merely as a slightly less rational (less rational because less concrete) version of conflicts over interests.

Critics of Liberalism such as MacIntyre, Sandel, Macpherson, Wolin, Unger, and others criticize it first for being neutral, and therefore in their view amoral, but also for being not neutral enough, in not being able to stomach every imaginable point of view. A similar cleft stick has been argued from within the horizon of liberal thought by William Galston. This cleft stick argument, never very telling to begin with, has been successfully met by several strains of liberal argument, such as Galston's own straightforward denial that strong neutrality was ever a liberal postulate; or Ackerman's vision of a "dualist democracy" that establishes a procedural separation between ordinary lawmaking and higher lawmaking that, without drawing lines in the sand, functionally separates what liberal societies must be neutral about from what they must not; or Rawls's distinction between metaphysical and political Liberalism, and his argument that even the latter, while not requiring assent to liberal values in every sphere, nevertheless requires and generates an overlapping consensus of values that gives the adherents of different comprehensive doctrines, different visions of the meaning and purpose of life, reasons to deal with each other fairly, reasons that are ethical in nature, rather than merely prudential. The Rawlsian overlapping consensus, while a weaker motivation than a calling or a stirring vision of the good, is nevertheless the basis of a kind of Liberalism that is not a mere *modus vivendi* that people with different views might be willing to settle for as a second-best solution, given that they can't exterminate their enemies, but rather a first-best solution that expresses deep insights into the common moral life of persons in a political society. One way of expressing the issue is to see the Lincoln-Douglas debates not, as Sandel does, as an argument between a Liberal Douglas and a Republican Lincoln, nor (more persuasively) as Greenstone does, as an argument between a Humanist (Democratic Party) Liberalism represented by Douglas and a Reformist (Republican Party) Liberalism represented by Lincoln, but as an argument over where

Liberalism can safely argue on the basis of an overlapping consensus, and where it must retreat to arguments that assume only a *modus vivendi*.

Acknowledging an overlapping consensus is perhaps as close as a liberal society can come to discovering a calling. It is still an open question to me whether an overlapping consensus must take the form of a set of highly abstract core values to which all sides must subscribe (a view Rawls sometimes hints at but does not commit himself to); or whether it is instead a looser and more general allegiance to maintaining a world of political bargaining and engagement, in which all sides are bound together by their complicated relationships of agreement and disagreement, with many parties contending across many different and mutually entangled lines of division even if no particular claim is held by all of them in common. Or maybe, with Charles Larmore (and with Stephen Douglas) the best we can hope for is a *modus vivendi*, or maybe a modus vivendi and the hope of something more.

12

Contamination and/of "Resistance"

DAVID GREETHAM

A few years ago, I wrote a polemical,[1] take-no-prisoners introductory piece[2] to a collection I was editing on *The Margins of the Text*. While the resulting volume, with essays by

[1] To non-textuists, the polemic may seem an unexpected, almost improper mode of discourse (though anyone who has seen Tom Stoppard's recent play, *The Invention of Love*, on A. E. Housman, the most celebrated and influential textual critic of his time, will recognize that the plaintive, rustic nostalgia of *A Shropshire Lad* was replaced by an aggressive irony in his textual essays—"The Germans have mistaken textual criticism for mathematics" and so forth—). Indeed, it might be argued that the polemic is the *primary* discourse of textual criticism, from Jerome onwards, in that scholarly editing often justifies itself by an attack on precursor editors, whose inadequate or misrepresentations of their texts become the rationale for one's own work. Jerome J. McGann, in one of the most influential essays of recent years ("The Monks and the Giants: Textual and Bibliographical Studies and the Interpretation of Literary Works," McGann, ed., *Textual Criticism and Literary Interpretation* [Chicago: University of Chicago Press, 1985]), in his own "polemic," finds that the apparently objective, apparently scholarly, apparently timeless editions produced by Fredson Bowers in the previous generation were emblematic of the "polemical" edition. McGann has even disavowed his own monumental edition of Byron on ideological as well as just methodological grounds: all of which may seem passing strange in the light of my next note, but that is precisely the point of much of my work—that there is a conflict being waged for the very soul of textualism.

[2] Some context (which is in any case one of the principal modes of this current essay): the "Resistance" essay (properly "The Resistance to Philology") arose out of an MLA panel I had organized earlier on "Race, Class, and Gender in Scholarly Editing," just three of the several "non-linguistic" issues that the central tradition of textuality had preferred not to confront. The resulting *Margins of the Text* volume (part of the Michigan series on "Editorial Theory and Literary Criticism," instituted by George Bornstein), divided the study of "margins" into two classes: the margins of "discourse" (those social, non-linguistic forces that were not supposed to be

[189]

such luminaries as Jonathan Goldberg on gay textualities ("Under the Covers with Caliban"), Ann Thompson and Brenda Silver on some varieties of feminist editing ("Feminist Theory and the Editing of Shakespeare: *The Taming of the Shrew* Revisited" and "Whose Room of Orlando's Own? The Politics of Adaptation" respectively), and William L. Andrews ("Editing 'Minority' Texts") advanced the study of their various fields considerably, my own impassioned lead-off, which I playfully called "The Resistance to Philology," seems to have been folded into my general thesis for the "conflation," indeed even the "contamination" of textual

---

admitted into editorial protocols) and the bibliographical margins (titling, marginalia, glossing, and commentary) that had, of course, always been a part of the "whole book," but had been undervalued—in fact, generally ignored—during the hegemony of the so-called "Greg-Bowers-Tanselle" school of concentration on the New Critical/New Bibliographical formalist "text itself." My own contribution was to interrogate (in the "discourse" section) Paul de Man's thesis that this very focus on "the text itself" was of a piece with the "turn to theory" in the 1970s, which de Man saw as a "return to philology, to an examination of the structure of language prior to the meaning it produces" (de Man, "The Return to Philology," *The Resistance to Theory* [Minneapolis: University of Minnesota Press, 1986], p. 24). I argued that de Man's agenda or hope that "historical and philological facts [should be] the preparatory condition for understanding" (de Man, "The Resistance to Theory," ibid., p. 4) was illusory, and reinforced that too-widely-held assumption that philology was "non-hermeneutic," and thus the products of philology in such monuments to "fact" as scholarly editions were not critical, and therefore not "real" books. My "polemic" was mounted not so much against de Man and his thesis but against those textuists who "resisted" both the theory and the practice of hermeneutics (taking refuge in that very "pre-hermeneutic" *grammar* that de Man postulated for philology), and thus ghettoized scholarly editing and textualism institutionally and culturally. I claimed instead that scholarly "philologists" had to acknowledge that (like Joyce's famous comment that his work was not only "trivial," but "quadrivial" as well) philology was also rhetorical and not merely "in the service of logic" (de Man, "Resistance," p. 14); that is, textuists had to become "textually dangerous" again, even if this meant the "loss of philological face," for otherwise we would continue to be "nobodies producing nonbooks" (Greetham, "Resistance," p. 20).

theory and literary hermeneutics, and it is that "folding" (indeed "invagination"[3]) that will form one of the threads in this present essay.

In fact, I had already alerted the reader to the technical as well as the more general senses of both "conflation" and "contamination"[4] by the apparent simplicity of my title. But of course there are different classes of "alert" readers: my title depended for its conflation and/or contamination on the

3 I use "invagination" in the common Derridean sense of a linguistic double embedding and continual recontextualizing of types of discourse, a figure that will inform much of this essay on "contamination": (see, for example, "Invagination is the inward refolding of *la gaine* [sheath, girdle], the inverted reapplication of the outer edge to the inside of a form where the outside then opens a pocket. . . . Like the meaning 'genre' or '*mode*,' or that of 'corpus' or the unity of a 'work,' the meaning of version, and of the unity of a version, is over-run, exceeded, by this structure of invagination" ("Living On. *Border Lines*," *Deconstruction and Criticism* [New York: Continuum, 1979], pp. 97, 102), an essay that I believe (from *my* position on the margins) imitates (or parodies) in its very textual appearance the dual form of the page of a scholarly edition, with "text" above and "commentary" or "apparatus" below, in reduced type (see my "[Textual] Criticism and Deconstruction," *Studies in Bibliography* 44 (1991): 1–30, reprinted in *Textual Transgressions: Essays toward the Construction of a Biobibliography* [New York: Garland, 1997] and the "Supplément" chapter of *Theories of the Text* [Oxford: Clarendon Press, 1999], for a fuller commentary on what I perceive as Derrida's failure to exploit the figural and parodic interpenetrations of his two discourses). I also use "invagination" in the "conflational" sense of Irigaray's "When Our Lips Speak Together," a textual "speaking" only accomplished by the doubling of the two pairs of lips in the vulva (*This Sex Which Is Not One*, trans. Catherine Porter [Ithaca: Cornell University Press, 1985]).

4 "Contamination" strictly speaking refers to the memorial infiltration of one text by another: say, a copyist might be ostensibly following the text in witness *x*, but with a prior familiarity with witness *y*, will unconsciously (?) allow variants from this precedent *y* into the resulting text of *z*. "Conflation" is properly reserved for the deliberate construction of *z* by an active and presumably hermeneutic or evaluative criticism of the variants contained in the two texts, *x* and *y*, which lie before the copyist in this active "misprision" of the documentary authority of either one in the service of some greater good—authorial intention, social reception, and so on. As is quite appropriate, however, the two terms are often "conflated" (or even "contaminated").

forceful yoking of those two essays by de Man, "The Resistance to Theory" and "The Return to Philology," and thus on a reader's familiarity with de Man's work (though I will admit that I explicated the yoking since that was one of the themes of the piece); Brenda Silver's similar act of making strange bedfellows depended on a differently alert reader, one who not only knew that both *Orlando* and *A Room of One's Own* were by Woolf (the first slotted into the second), but, as the essay itself demonstrated, that both works had recently been themselves "contaminated" by being "edited" by other hands for different media—film, television, and stage production. Silver, I think, made her contaminations work harder than I did mine (and she did have the advantage of fairly recent performative versions of her two texts).[5]

All of this may seem to either the culture critic or the bibliographer to be much ado about (almost) nothing, for the art (and craft) of both contamination and conflation are a staple of contemporary discourse, from the posters on bus shelters, the ironic covers of *The New Yorker* and other magazines, to television and virtually every form of modern/postmodern media reception.[6] As has been often noted, even something as monu-

---

5 Such conflation *and* contamination might almost be a staple of Silver's work, as for example, in her essay, "Who's Afraid of Virginia Woolf, Part II," George Bornstein, ed., *Representing Modernist Texts: Editing as Interpretation* (Ann Arbor: University of Michigan Press, 1991), which subsumes Albee's play as its "already written" precursor text.

6 Such a cross-citational ethic is, I believe, a perfect manifestation of the very etymology of *text* as "textile" (see the historical references in my "[Textual] Criticism," esp. note 19, with the continual contest between this "Barthesian" meaning and what might appear to be its exact opposite, *text* as authority—particularly in relation to the Scriptures—as something fixed and determinate). Moreover, I have posited textual criticism as the exemplary site for a terminological and methodological interdisciplinarity (with the important qualification that textual criticism deforms and reinvents the terms it co-opts from other disciplines, making them do "other" than they would in their "home" disciplines ("Editorial and Critical Theory: From Modernism to Postmodernism," George Bornstein and Ralph Williams eds., *Palimpsest: Editorial Theory in the Humanities.* [Ann Arbor: University of Michigan Press, 1993], reprinted in *Textual Transgressions*), in response to Stanley Fish. "Being Interdisciplinary Is So Very Hard to Do," *Profession 89* (New York: MLA, 1989).

mental as Philip Johnson's AT&T building in New York is a conflation (for those who know their architectural history) of the Gothic cathedral at street level, the Chippendale grandfather clock at the pediment, and the stark geometrism of essentialist modernism (the perfected extruded cube) in the middle. When one adds to this mix an awareness of the career of the building's designer, from modernist to postmodernist architect, the "canny" reader of the intertextualities of this monument (and I use the term very deliberately, since I believe that in some way it is indeed Johnson's public manifesto of his own biography), then the "alert" reader will undoubtedly feel a sense of "mastery" over the apparent irreconcilables of the cultural icon. Case apparently closed.

But while even the most "strict and pure" bibliographer of the most positivist days of "philology" would surely not suggest that the disparate elements of this AT&T building be reconstructed to form a "text that never was" (the Holy Grail of eclectic editing of the Greg-Bowers-Tanselle dispensation) immutable in its platonic ideality, with texts existing in what have sometimes been conveniently designated as the "linear" media (literature, music, and so on) as opposed to the "spatial" (painting, sculpture, architecture) being more hospitable in their very ontology to the incursions of eclecticists, idealists, social receptionists, and other brands of the current textual potpourri, one is given pause by this overly neat dichotomy, and by its most quoted embodiment in Bateson's provocative question, "If the *Mona Lisa* is in the Louvre, where is *Hamlet?*"[7]

7 F. W. Bateson, "Modern Bibliography and the Literary Artifact," *English Studies Today*, ed. Georges A. Bonnard (Bern: 1961), pp. 67–77, 2d ed., cited by, for example, James L. McLaverty, "The Mode of Existence of Literary Works of Art: The Case of the *Dunciad Variorum*," *Studies in Bibliography* 37 (1984): 82–105, in his argument that the materiality and spatial properties Pope specifically undertook for the *Dunciad Variorum* are not simply the surface "accidentals" of the work, but its very semantic coding, and thus its meaning. (Note also that McLaverty's essay is yet another with a deliberately "contaminated" title, positing itself *against* the several, non-material "modes of existence" examined in René Wellek and Austin Warren's *Theory of Literature* [New York: Harcourt, Brace, 1956], 3d ed., and, perhaps even more tellingly, that McLaverty nowhere in his own essay feels it necessary to acknowledge the intertextual play, any more than did Silver in "Who's Afraid.")

That artful question, relying on the singularity and non-iterability of the spatial art work[8] as against the linguistic or

8 Leaving aside the "iterability" problem in textuality (for which see, for example, Joseph Grigely, "The Textual Event," Philip Cohen, ed., *Devils and Angels: Textual Editing and Literary Theory* [Charlottesville: University Press of Virginia, 1991]), where, for instance, Grigely denies that the "work is . . . equivalent to the *sum* of its texts . . . whether those texts are authorized or not," claiming instead that, since a work (of literature) cannot be "finished," and since "its boundaries are not prescribed," there can be only a "series of texts that comprise [the work's] polytext" (p. 176), the major statement on the ontology of textual repetition (especially as it relates to textuality and, inferentially, to editing," remains Walter Benjamin's "Work of Art in the Age of Mechanical Reproduction," *Illuminations: Essays and Reflections*, trans. Harry Zohn, ed. Hannah Arendt (New York: Schocken, 1968), though see also Gilles Deleuze, *Difference and Repetition*, trans. Paul Patton (New York: Columbia University Press, 1968), which lays out a thesis very similar to that in this essay on contamination and conflation: "Modern Life is such that, confronted with the most mechanical, stereotypical repetitions [I will admit that I am uncertain whether Deleuze intends a bibliographical "contamination" in this phrase, which finds emblematic historical exemplification in the shift from hot type, which although participating in a "mechanical" process, is still literally "manual" in its "composition," and the stereotype, in which the mechanical achieves its most significant textual shift, having also major cultural ramifications; see Allan C. Dooley, *Author and Printer in Victorian England* (Charlottesville: University Press of Virginia, 1992), where the social and economic commodification of an author like George Eliot can be charted by the shift from hot type to stereotype in the setting of her novels], inside and outside ourselves, we endlessly extract from them little differences, variations, and modifications. Conversely, secret, disguised, and hidden repetitions, animated by the perpetual displacement of a difference, restore bare, mechanical, and stereotypical repetitions, within and without us. In simulacra, repetition already plays upon repetitions, and difference already plays upon differences. Repetitions repeat themselves, while the differenciator differenciates itself. The task of life is to make all these repetitions coexist in a space in which difference is distributed" (p. ix). It is exactly this play and counter-play between open and secret repetitions and differences that I am concerned with in this essay.

But Benjamin's analysis of mechanical reproduction has achieved such a wide-ranging influence that it must be acknowledged as the *locus classicus* (pre-Derrida's "iterability") of textual repetition and cultural dissemination of this repetition. Thus, while I have some major notational abstraction of the linear (that is, *Hamlet* would somehow still "exist," even if it were to be found *nowhere* specifically, even if all concrete manifestations of the authoritative work were to disappear, whereas the single-state ontology of the painting or sculpture is contained and defined by its formal properties) begs far too many questions than can be answered here; for example, what is an authority, what is a work, a text, a manifestation? And these questions have been the subject of much debate in textual circles of late.[9] But it

---

reservations about Benjamin's theory—in part derived from the social and historical circumstances in which it was composed—and have dealt with them in some detail in my *Theories of the Text* (Oxford: Clarendon Press, 1999); "Benjamin and Textual Reproduction," pp. 389–97, a few remarks are still necessary for this occasional piece. For example, as I note in *Theories*, Benjamin bases his historical account on Marx's assumption that the superstructure (the thought and ideology of a culture) will change more slowly than the base (the means of production). Thus it is only several centuries after the invention of mechanical reproduction that we can begin to assess its cultural significance. And, like Deleuze, he acknowledges a difference between "simulacra" (Benjamin's *replicas*), man-made simulations or imitations of an original, and true *mechanical* reproduction, which he believes begins only with the woodcut, the first infinitely reproducible medium (pp. 218; 243n2). I find Benjamin's reliance on the concept of "infinite reproduction" to be bibliographically and historically naive (see *Theories*, p. 390), but I do accept that his key concepts of *authenticity, aura, presence, distance, cult, ritual, exhibition, exile, readership, distraction,* and *concentration* are all, to one degree or another, relevant to my current consideration of contamination and conflation. For example, Benjamin's claim that "for the first time in world history, mechanical reproduction emancipates the work of art from its parasitical dependence on ritual. To an ever greater degree the work of art reproduced becomes the work of art designed for reproducibility" (p. 224) is a concession that the *aura* of an "originary" moment of inscription may pass—through mechanical reproduction—to the derived copy, which may be culturally so disseminated that it displaces the original in authenticity. Benjamin can therefore maintain that the fact of an "authentic" print being an ontological absurdity is evidence of a complete reversal of the function of art: freed from ritual, it now becomes political (that is, part of the *polis*).

9 The two most succinct statements for, on the one hand, the platonizing/idealist position, and on the other, the materialist/socialized view of text are, respectively, G. Thomas Tanselle's *A Rationale of Tex-*

would be a safe generalization to note that over the last twenty years or so, the focus of much textual attention has shifted from the text quæ text (the "linguistic codes") to, on the one hand, the materiality of its medium and mode of production, and, on the other, to the cultural and social forces at work in both the creation (with an interest in collaboration as paradigm rather than the romantic figure of the isolated singular author) and in the dissemination of textual forms beyond the control of any author and sometimes taking on forms and usages that could never have been envisaged by such an author. As Gary Taylor, co-editor of the *Oxford Shakespeare* has often muttered, out-Barthing Barthes, "The author has *always* been dead."[10]

---

tual Criticism (Philadelphia: University of Pennsylvania Press, 1989) and Jerome J. McGann's *A Critique of Modern Textual Criticism* (Chicago: University of Chicago Press, 1983; reprinted Charlottesville: University Press of Virginia, 1992), which has primarily influenced Anglo-American textual theory, and D. F. McKenzie's *Bibliography and the Sociology of Texts*, The Panizzi Lectures (London: British Library, 1986).

10 Taylor's work on rhetoric in textuality puts in high relief the double bind de Man constructed in creating a class (for "philology") of the pre-hermeneutic, a reading of the *trivium* as being "in the service" of logic. For example, Taylor's assertion that "[t]extual criticism is about rhetoric, rhetoric is about persuasion, persuasion is about audiences" "The Rhetoric of Textual Criticism." *Text* 4 [1988], p. 47) denies any pre-hermeneutic function for foundationalist philology, but instead resituates supposed philological "facts" as part of a series of social negotiations, so that even his injection of rhetoric becomes ultimately a social construct: "A textual critic does not worry about promiscuously persuading any possible reader; a textual critic must persuade the readers who matter. We expect our intellectual actions to be judged by a jury of our peers; but who are the peers of a textual critic? The definition of that peerage fluctuates historically, and that fluctuation depends upon the perceived relationship between textual and literary criticism" (p. 47). So the relational and reflexive nature of the philological enterprise forbids any firm position in either the *trivium* or the *quadrivium*. Indeed, Taylor argues that the editorial production of text can only be a rhetorical strategy—even down to construction of a table of contents—under which an intentionalist editor commits a form of ventriloquism in moving the authority for the rhetoric elsewhere: to the author. Taylor sees this rhetorical strategy in Foucauldian terms ("to adopt the voice of power is to speak beyond oneself, to ascribe one's powers elsewhere" [Michel Foucault, *Power/*

It may therefore seem paradoxical that contemporary textuality may accept an always-dead author while at the same time beginning to move away from the positivist, technology-driven disappearance of the editor (what Talbot Donaldson dismissively referred to as the "editorial death wish"[11]) toward what Donald H. Reiman[12] has labeled a "personalist bibliography"—in parallel with the personalist criticism of some feminist critics, notably Nancy K. Miller, Hélène Cixous, and Mary Ann Caws.[13] Endorsing and playing on such an enlargement of the biographical "presence" of the textuist, I have written what (I think) I am pleased to have had called "the strangest book on text criticism."[14]

All of which can be read as both a "supplément" on that first essay on "Resistance" (in which I now provide a further glossarial context in which the clash of discourses may be read—historically, formalistically, psychologically, and so on) *and* as a textual "foreplay" on my privileged, "editorial" empowerment

---

Knowledge, ed. Colin Gordon (New York: Pantheon, 1980), pp. 93–94; Taylor, "Rhetoric," p. 43]). As I note in *Theories* (p. 145n5), even a seemingly "positivist" textual critic as Tanselle can recognize that "[i]n the end, all evidence is internal," for sooner or later one reaches a point where there is nothing outside to relate to (that is, no foundationalist philology that can provide a pre-hermeneutic grounding; and thus "[w]hat we agree to call historical knowledge is built up by the accretions of individual acts of pattern-finding, some of which invalidate previous acts and some of which confirm and extend them" ("Printing History and Other History," *Studies in Bibliography* 48 [1995], p. 283). Or, as Taylor might more cynically (or demographically) put it: "the more registered voters who support a textual proposition, the more likely it is to be true" ("Rhetoric," p. 47)

11 "The Psychology of Editors of Medieval Texts," *Speaking of Chaucer* (London: Athlone / New York: Norton, 1970).

12 *The Study of Modern Manuscripts: Public, Confidential, and Private.* (Baltimore: Johns Hopkins University Press, 1993).

13 See, for example, Mary Ann Caws, "The Conception of Engendering: The Erotics of Editing." Nancy K. Miller, ed., *The Poetics of Gender* (New York: Columbia University Press, 1986); Hélène Cixous, *"Coming to Writing," and Other Essays* (Cambridge: Harvard University Press, 1991).

14 George Bornstein's opening sally in a very perceptive review of *Textual Transgressions, Analytical & Enumerative Bibliography.*

through belatedness by making my two (now three) texts speak "otherwise."[15]

Clearly I make much of the prominence of notes, which may sometimes serve as apparent clarifications or even disquisitions on points made in the "superior" text from which they hang, but may just as frequently be cast as an *adversarius*, a feature of annotation that Heather Jackson nicely documents in her recent history and genre study of marginalia, where she adopts what I have characterized as a "nice locution" of the marginalia/annotation being a "shouting at" the dead author, from John Hollander's poem "The Widener Burying-Ground" (Jackson pp. 83, 274). I would hope that my own "alert" reader has concluded, through the title, layout, and cross-referencing between "text" and "note," that it is that "shouting" at the dead author (de Man in the original "Resistance," myself—the author

---

15 This formal property of making the "base" text (again a term conferring privilege on the belated editor, for this "base" is, like Edmund, to be considered as "bastard," the improper miscegenation and cohabitation of texts, which the purely moral acts of a platonizing editor will disambiguate) speak "otherwise" is one of those potentially figural or parodic elements that I believe Derrida does not exploit fully. I comment: "Thus, the 'lower' ('*Border Lines*') text is indeed quite properly concerned at first with discussing, allusively and figuratively, the relationship between the commentary/apparatus and 'the text itself' above. Noting (in the text of 'Living On') that the commentary is usually thought of as 'only a textual supplement,' an 'in other words' for the text proper, Derrida nowhere takes up this frequent theme of the 'other words' and applies it to the formal mechanism of an apparatus, which is constructed precisely to find a home for these 'other words' of the text. The apparatus is nothing but the text in other words (rejected words)." As I have several times pointed out, however, these "rejected" words exist *in order to be made inferior* precisely because at some point in the textual transmission (and most often in the "base" text) they were regarded as the text speaking properly and not "otherwise," *otherwise* they would not be present in any witness, and especially not the "authoritative" base text. No editor has, to my knowledge, "invented" a reading solely for the purpose of rejecting it, though the orthodox use of Lachmannian stemmatic theory might postulate non-extant "misreadings" in a medial hyparchetype to account for the transmissional degradation from the purity of the originary moment of composition to the corrupted, contaminated extant form in the "insincere" witnesses.

is *always* dead, remember, even the author writing *here* and *now*—and all texts ever edited or annotated by subsequent editors) is the motivating formal and rhetorical mode of this essay.[16]

16 Heather Jackson, *Marginalia: Readers Writing in Texts* (New Haven and London: Yale University Press, 2001); (forthcoming review-essay of Jackson in *Papers/Cahiers of Bibliographical Society of Canada*); Jackson, *Marginalia*, pp. 83, 274. At the moment of this authorial inscription, I am in much the same position as Derrida in his ignored instructions to the editors/compositors of *Border Lines* ("My desire to take charge of the Translator's note myself. Let them [the translators] also read this band as a telegram or a film for developing [a film 'to be processed,' in English?], pp. 77–78; "This would be a good place for a translator's note," p. 79; "to be quoted in its entirety," p. 135): none of these authorial "instructions" are in fact carried out in the published text. My comment on this apparent malfeasance is "[s]o by what is the authorial will countermanded? Paradoxically, by the translator's desire for fidelity to the text and therefore fidelity to the authorial will. And so here is the double bind: the translator is in the long line of descent from those early Benedictine scriptoria in which the *exact* text was to be rendered warts and all, without additions (even when, as in this case, asked for by the author), deletions, or emendations. Sometimes that desire for literal fidelity can yield wonderfully comic effects, as when the scribe of one of the manuscripts of Hoccleve's *De Regimine Principum*, on realising that he has inadvertently omitted *an entire stanza* of his copytext, subsequently writes out the missing stanza— where else but in the margins?—and then puts a rope around the stanza and draws in a figure dragging the stanza into its right and "proper" place on the text-page (though my guess is that most readers have so delighted in this spatial play that they have come to regard the margin as the "proper" place for this particular *mise-en-page*, just as in the Harley MS of the same work, Hoccleve has "caused" to be drawn a portrait of Chaucer in the margins, pointing to Hoccleve's text (see Theresa Tinkle, "The Wife of Bath's Textual/Sexual Lives," George Bornstein and Theresa Tinkle, eds., *The ICONIC PAGE in Manuscript*, PRINT, and Digital Culture (Ann Arbor: University of Michigan Press, 1998), in which she admits in the headnotes to the notes (p. 79) that there is some ambiguity as to which word exactly Chaucer's finger is pointing to (or "shouting at"?), a difference that has substantial implications in calibrating the relationship between text and commentary/margin, image and language, and originating "transdiscursive" author and diligent but subservient disciple (see Michel Foucault, "What Is an Author?" trans. Josué V. Harari, *Textual Strategies: Perspectives in Post-Structuralist Criticism*, ed.

Josué V. Harari [Ithaca: Cornell University Press, 1979], collected in Paul Rabinowitz, ed., *The Foucault Reader* [New York: Pantheon, 1984], esp. pp. 113–17, where Foucault cites Freud, Galileo, and Marx as examples of the "transdiscursive" author who will not only be "the authors of their own works. They have produced something else: the possibilities of and the rules for the formation of other texts" (p. 114). I (and obviously Hoccleve) would include Chaucer as a "transdiscursive" author, since he does not merely become the "begetter" of other works but also (graphically and substantively) retroactively co-opts the work of his disciple.

I have asked a very obliging editor, Jenn Lewin, to try to use her editorial prerogative to make sure that a) my annotations present spatially a "dialogue" with the text page by being set as footnotes (see Evelyn B. Tribble, "'Like a Looking-Glas in the Frame': From the Marginal Note to the Footnote," D. C. Greetham, ed., *The Margins of the Text* [Ann Arbor: University of Michigan Press, 1997]) rather than end notes (for which there is no excuse in these days of computer typesetting), and to try to get the compositor to reflect the typographic distinctions I am inheriting from *The Iconic Page*. But I have been told that I should not worry about formatting in general, since the copyeditor will happily take on that burden. Since this concession is offered as a palliative to the overextended author, I am supposed to take it as an act of courtesy, but of course, in my argument for the "shouting at" the dead, the dead ought properly to be alive (or present) enough for the reader to see what one is shouting *at*. At this point, I have no idea whether these (to me) important spatial and graphical distinctions will be observed or whether they will be subsumed under the protocols of the house styling of the publisher. But in either case, I would want the Derridean "instructions" to be preserved, even if (as in *Border Lines*) they are not acted upon. The absence will in this case speak to the ongoing power struggle for control of the text between author and publisher, of which the most egregiously daring I have so far encountered (as editor) has been Randall McLeod's attempt (Random Clod, "Information Upon Information," *Text* 5 [1991]: 242–85 [or possibly 286], incorporating "The Dynamic of the Actual" by Random Clovd: 279–81) to repaginate the entire volume of the journal *Text* from the point at which he was demonstrating from the evidence of analytical bibliography that there had been a pagination dislocation in the English translation of *Orlando Furioso*, a "bibliographical disjunct" that he wanted to make materially manifest by simulating it in the repagination of his own essay, which suddenly became a "new" essay with a "new" author (McLeod is continually reinventing himself with pseudonyms— Random Clod [or Cloud or Clovd], Claudia Nimbus, and so on— as he teases out the spatial "meaning" of a material object through his own idiosyncratic typesetting codes).

To my mind, there is therefore a link (or perhaps a *rite de passage*) between the currency of textual rhetorics and de Man's nostalgia[17] for a linguistic-based mode of discourse.

17 "Nostalgia" might seem a paradoxical term to apply to one of the most critically sophisticated and forcefully interrogative writers of the last century. After all, it was de Man who, in his *Allegories of Reading*, warned most severely against the metaphorical status of the "voice" of the inscribing "author," allying this metaphor along with the "metaphors of primacy, of genetic history, and most notably, of . . . the self" (*Allegories*, p. 16), figures that, as I have noted (*Theories of the Text*, p. 160 and passim) are among the staples of textual criticism. Citing de Man's interest in the *literalization* of metaphor (especially in his brilliant analysis of the "sublime simplicity" with which Archie Bunker's wife, Ethel, responds *literally* to Archie's *rhetorical* question "What's the difference?" whether his bowling shoelaces should be laced over or under" ["Semiology and Rhetoric," *Allegories*, p. 9; *Theories of the Text*, p. 160n2), I have, I will admit, made much productive use of de Man's *caveats* about the construction of a speaking subject out of the remaniements of its predicate (especially when these remaniements are scribally or compositorially "contaminated" or "conflated"); and in the discussion of "voice" as a metaphor for an absent "presence," it is to de Man that I turn: "even if we free ourselves of all false questions of intent and *rightfully* [my emphasis] reduce the narrator to the status of a mere grammatical pronoun, without which the narrator could not come into being, this subject remains endowed with a function that is not grammatical but rhetorical, in that it gives voice, so to speak, to a grammatical syntagm. The term *voice*, even when used in grammatical terminology as when we speak of the passive, or interrogative, voice is, of course, a metaphor inferring by analogy the intent of the subject from the structure of the predicate" (*Allegories*, p. 18; cited *Theories*, p. 160).

One can easily see (or hear?) why de Man was so intent on preserving the integrity (and separation) of "the structure of the predicate" from such metaphorical extensions (or, as I would put it, "contaminations") as the subject and his/her voice, but it is in this fear that such a contamination will indeed often (perhaps usually) happen—despite the moral force of his own rhetoric ("rightfully," "reduce the narrator" and so forth), de Man is in a sense aligning with pure "structural" modeling such as in Paul Maas's horror (*Textual Criticism*, trans. Barbara Flower [Oxford: Clarendon Press, 1958]) at the possible bridging of that gap between "semiosis" and "structure" that is alarmingly, even histrionically evident when Maas throws up his hands in despair in acknowledging that "Gegen die Kontamination ist keine Kraut," and, what is even more telling, when Maas admits (on purely technical, structural grounds) that but one in which ironically the "pre-hermeneutic" is its per-fected form. This rhetorical swerve is, however, itself a hermeneutic act, a declaration that the ideality of linguistic form is in a moment before the fuller expository mode of composition has been ignited (borrowing from Shelley's "burning coal" image) and of necessity long before the social acts of textual misprision have been committed by those charged with the constructivist act of creating the "contaminated" formal properties of text that Edward

---

the presence of contamination in the charting of the descent of witnesses is the equivalent of introducing female lines into family trees (see my analysis of this patriarchal prejudice in *Theories of the Text*, p. 478 et seq., where I note that [like de Man?], Maas so relies on the integrity of his "grammar" of philology, that he admits to a desire to recognize "dissident readings" (*Textual Criticism*, p. 8), to afford "[s]ome degree of protection against contamination . . . [that] makes it impossible to hope for a clear-cut solution" (p. 8). From Turing's box down to contemporary studies of chaos and complexi-fication, the distinction that de Man worries about (via Archie Bunker's shoes) between Yeats's "dancer" and the "dance," between pure structure and impure (because contaminated) semiosis, puts de Man's desire for a foundationalist "grammatical" philology in some very good company, both textual and scientific: Greg's *A Calculus of Variants: An Essay on Textual Criticism* (Oxford: Clarendon Press, 1927); Vinton Dearing's *Principles and Practice of Textual Analysis* (Berkeley: University of California Press, 1974); and Dom Henri Quentin (*Essai de critique textuelle* [Paris: Picard, 1926])—among others—have all sought, through symbolic logic or algebraic for-mulae, to fortify "structure" against "semiosis," an issue that the modeling theorems of complexification also confront (see, for example, Floyd Merrell, *Simplicity and Complexity: Pondering Litera-ture, Science, and Painting* [Ann Arbor: University of Michigan Press, 1998] or John L. Casti's *Complexification: Explaining a Paradoxical World Through the Science of Surprise* [New York: Harper, 1995], My point is that once it becomes culturally possible for, say, Bernard Cerquiglini (*Éloge de la variante: Histoire critique de la philologie* [Paris: Seuil, 1989]) to assert that contamination is the normative rather than aberrational state of dissemination (that is, convergent not divergent), and for this position to be widely embraced by practi-tioners outside its immediate audience, then the pure grammatical philology that both Maas and de Man, in their different ways, so determinedly wanted to protect, does indeed begin to look, well, "nostalgic."

Mendelson[18] has likened to the composite historical and formal syntheses of the medieval cathedral (my own postmodernist architectural exemplar has usually been the Beaubourg, where the formal properties and elements of the Centre Pompidou are literally turned inside out, as well as contaminated, with a color-coding[19] of these elements to emphasize the "invagination."[20]

18 Edward Mendelson, "The Fading Coal vs. the Gothic Cathedral or What to Do about an Author both Forgetful and Deceased," *Text* 3 (1987): 409–16.

19 To adopt one of Derrida's unfulfilled "instructions" in the *Border Lines* "commentary" on "Living On": This note should be read *after* the longer subsequent note on the Beaubourg: it is thus I think quite fitting that as a purely linguistic device color-coding can be used as a phenomenological de-coding of the *states*, or *couches*, or "guerrilla raids" on the text that Ralph Hanna III regards any form of interposition through annotation or emendation (see Anne Middleton, "Life in the Margins, or, What's an Annotator to Do?" Dave Oliphant and Robin Bradford, eds., *New Directions in Textual Studies* (Austin: Harry Ransom Humanities Research Center/University of Texas Press, 1990). Indeed, responding to the Anglo-American distaste for, and unfamiliarity with, the complex set of editorial sigla Hans Walter Gabler used on the verso pages of the three-volume "critical and synoptic" edition of *Ulysses* in charting the composition of the "single manuscript text" of that work, in a provocative response to the structuralist ("on/off switches") of these sigla, Vickie Mahaffey has proposed a color-coded system of states and variants that could overlie the abstract sigla ("Intentional Error: The Paradox of Editing Joyce's *Ulysses*," George Bornstein, ed., *Representing Modernist Texts: Editing as Interpretation* [Ann Arbor: University of Michigan Press, 1991]. And I will admit that in tabulating the manuscript variants of the extant witnesses to Trevisa's *De Proprietatibus Rerum*, I employed a similar system of color-coding to identify each manuscript's "swerve" from the copy text, without (of course) any expectation that the august Clarendon Press would ever represent variance through such visual coding. No, it was all rigorously linguistic, not graphic. It is easy to see why such a huge volume (set in Monotype if one can believe it) could not indulge the expense of color-coding (though color was used from the very beginning by the Gutenberg press and its immediate descendants), but many of the "editions" completed by my graduate students as their final assignment in the required "textuality" seminar I teach at CUNY have sought out the riches of computer setting on a web site or CD-ROM, where the spatial relations can easily assume an even greater significance (and presence) than the purely linguistic.

20 As Ivan Zaknic notes (*Pompidou Centre* [Paris: Flammarion, 1983], p.

Inside/outside, difference/repetition, textile/authority, rhet-
oric/demographics, contamination/conflation, Living on/
Border Lines: in these and many of the other contradictions
and crossings of discourse alluded to in this essay, I hope only

---

23), "All the mechanical services, as well as structural elements, are
exposed. It is like a human body with all its organs and systems exter-
nalized, including the skeleton. There is something honest and grotesque about this unmasking" (cited in my "Editorial and Critical
Theory," p. 540. Within the fading coal/gothic cathedral dichotomy
of Mendelson's theory of compositional, transmissional, and editorial
theory, I place Zaknic's analysis within the broader frame of modernist essentialism versus postmodernist citation (of which Mendelson's
cathedral partakes: This is not a matter of a chronological progression,
even though my prepositional "from" and "to" might make it seem
so, but of a series of stylistic (and thus ontological) "swerves": "Consider an architectural example—Piano-Rogers' Centre Pompidou in
the Beaubourg in Paris. While the inheritance of the Beaubourg is
eminently modernist, deriving from Le Corbusier's 'twentieth-century
museum concept' [the square spiral of 1931], and while its architects
have acknowledged their debt to other modernist precursors, including the Constructivists, Futurists, Archigramists, and Metabolists, the
'urban machine' actually produced is in conceit and use far removed
from the sleek geometrizing associated with Gropius and van der
Rohe, where function was totalized and subsumed under the 'clear
text' of pure form. Repudiating clarity (or at least exemplifying a
competing and at first disquieting mode of clarity, where color
becomes the taxonomic discriminator, not geometric form, which is
placed in the service of color), the Beaubourg's architects promoted
instead flexibility and adaptability. There is no point at which this
building *begins*, or *ends*, or has a *middle*: it is quite possible to envisage
its continual reopening of its own *text* (that is, its "textile" qualities,
its "interweavings") a figure that I use throughout *Transgressions* as
markers for the specific autobiographical "crossings" of textual
boundaries) in an infinite regress of deferral (or, I suppose spatial
différence) that takes the compositional narrative of the accretional
cathedral, but then subjects this narrative to an "inside-out" reading.
It is very different in historical conceit from the disjunctive "joining"
by a Saussurean rather than Derridean *différence* in the preservation of
the ruins of the medieval Coventry cathedral, to which is attached
(but not incorporated) the modernist "museum" (with the enormous
textile of Graham Sutherland "Christ in Majesty" over the altar, and
the nave full of the several tokens of artistic modernism) that becomes
the contemporary "completion" of the cathedral (*mis*cited from the
Transgressions version of "Modernism and Postmodernism").

to have demonstrated that my initial encounter with de Man's model for foundationalist, pre-hermeneutic philology can generate a good many *adnotationes*, and that it is in the play of rhetoric between the *adnotationes* and the (much reduced) *textus* that the anti-discipline of textuality may be most constructively observed. The annotations should indeed constrain and hedge in the "text itself" as well as illuminating and perhaps on occasion clarifying it. Derrida claims that he has "always been interested in footnotes," and it is to the notes that he will go first when encountering a book,[21] for it is there that the real "discourse" is to be found. By contaminating my text with the "exorbitance" of the annotation, I have both subjugated it and yet allowed it to participate—as provocateur, as conspirator, as addressee—with a circle of rhetoric that, while it may never hope to be pre-hermeneutic or foundational, may form a sort of "ground" for more exorbitance.

21 "This Is Not an Oral Footnote," Stephen Barney, edd., *Annotation and Its Texts* [New York: Oxford University Press, 1991], p. 204.

13

Music Is Thinking, Then, Sound:
An Aesthetic Exercise

JOAN RICHARDSON

The title of this essay plays on a line of Stevens's that has preoccupied me as part of a larger musing about thinking itself. From "Peter Quince at the Clavier," the line is, "Music is feeling, then, not sound." It opens the second tercet of the poem's first of four sections. The occasion of Stevens's poem by the speaker's account is "thinking" of a woman in her "blue-shadowed silk," which, it is noted, "Is music." This thinking brings with it, or is identical with, an extended meditation connecting the poem's "I" with the "red-eyed elders" who enter the poem by way of a variation on the Apocrypha story of Susanna. Stevens's elders, well-hidden, watch Susanna bathe and feel "The basses of their beings throb / In witching chords, and their thin blood / Pulse pizzicati of Hosanna." (It may or may not have relevance to know that in the early years of his marriage Stevens had given his then still beautiful wife a blue silk kimono and a piano, and that he knew Handel's oratorio "Susanna," with which his poem shares certain structural similarities.[1]) Having a copy of Stevens's poem at hand, as a score, will help readers in this exercise.

It will be noticed that I have somewhat misrepresented the poem's occasion: it is not simply "thinking" about this woman, but "that what" the speaker *feels*, desiring, in an ambiguous relation to "Thinking of [her] blue-shadowed silk" that is the occasion and "Is music." I call this an ambiguous relation because it is entirely unclear whether what the speaker

---

1 In Part I, Scene 3, for example, the tenor enters accompanied by the throbbing of basses and *intones* the pain of his *amorous strain*. A second elder, a bass, enters next, opening the subsequent scene and adding his voice to the deepening drama of desire. From the first elder's opening strophes, as he begins to describe his *thin blood*, and intermittently through the elders' exchange, continuing until the end of Part I, strings pulse pizzicati.

feels, desiring, precedes thinking of the figure in the blue-shadowed silk, or whether it is the image that has prompted the feeling, or whether "Thinking of your blue-shadowed silk" is in apposition to, and therefore presented as identical with "that what I feel . . . desiring you." Moreover, also uncertain is whether the "what [he] feel[s]" is identical with "desiring" the "you." What is abundantly clear, however, is that the poet has confused feeling, thinking, and desiring, or perhaps it would be better to say, confused *the relations* of feeling, thinking, and desiring. In doing this, Stevens foregrounds what has become, since Charles Darwin's unsettling news, of central concern, the origin and nature of what we call thinking. (We have only to reflect on the number of book titles including consciousness and thought in recent years to realize how pressing this concern continues to be.) Notably, in Stevens's alignment of thinking, feeling, and desiring with music, he uncovers, as the concealed spring, the same prime motive of all life that Darwin in his *Notebooks* points to again and again: pleasure, most specifically, pleasure as the satisfaction of appetites and the erotic. Oddly, in all the work that has been done on consciousness and thought since Darwin, very little, and that only of late, has been done connecting thinking, feeling, and desiring. Perhaps it is because Freud managed so effectively to separate the sexual from the rational that this is the case, something that William James realized in criticizing Freud for his reductive view, and something that James attempted to repair. As noted not long ago by James Livingston, William James "believed that sexual desire or attraction was a 'social force' that could neither be ignored nor forgotten, in part at least because it was not monopolized by men. Bodies as such were the source and site of desire, in his view, but they were also the condition—the incentive and the limit—of reason. As he put it in March of 1869, 'not a wiggle of our happiness save as the result of physical laws, and yet notwithstanding we are *en rapport* with reason.'"[2]

I shall here use Stevens's poem to examine some of the ways that thinking or reason, under the pressure of Darwinian information, has gradually been pressed to include feeling and

2 *Raritan: A Quarterly Review* 17: 2 (Fall 1997): 66.

desiring as part of its definition. To describe the work that art does, Raymond Williams uses the notion of "structure of feeling," the "particular living result of all the elements in the general organization" of any culture. "Structure," in Williams's view, suggests that any given culture is indeed a distinct entity and unity and manifests a "firm and definite" articulation and shape. But it is necessary, as Williams goes on to say, to take account of "feeling" as well. Any analysis that ignores the place of feeling remains "reductive and invalid until it incorporates 'the most delicate and least tangible parts of our activity.'" The more than rational distortion that is the work of art allows it to describe and express more adequately what cannot be described and expressed on the flat historic scale. Naturally, the more informed and attuned the poet to the myriad aspects of our human environment, the more fully will the "structure of feeling" of the work produced reflect a successful adaptation and so ensure its greater survival value. (In this context it is worthwhile to recall that Darwin revised *Origin* six times in the attempt to represent in his syntax and organization his revolutionary realization that there is no design, no teleological plan for the shape of life on earth.)

Borrowing from the aesthetics of music the basic conceptual grid of pitch as the vertical axis and time as the horizontal against which a musical composition places itself, and connecting this idea of the grid with Williams's "structure of feeling," we could say that what is communicated under "pitch" is the range of what Williams calls "feeling," while "time," parsed into tenses and other references to past, present, and future, easily enough slides into the slot of "structure." *Pitch/feeling* represents, then, those "most delicate and least tangible parts of our activity," while *time/structure* provides "firm and definite" articulation and shape. While the nuanced variety of verbal or pictorial expression cannot be plotted quantitatively like the decibels and measured phrases of a musical composition, imagining the different elements of a poem as coordinates arranged along the vertical and horizontal axes of *pitch/feeling* and *time/structure* provides a schema for the work conceived as the relation between what we could otherwise call the connotative and denotative elements of an extended historical moment: the more "primal" or inarticulate the feeling/pitch, the more immediate, spontaneous, and "simple" the cry, the less time it takes to express; the more complex the feeling/pitch, the more time. The space opened in the mapping of these complicated gestures is filled by what we call "thinking"/music/a poem. That is, thinking is what goes on in between the sounds, the images, the words. There is an infinity of possible scales or statements. The images, the words, are not in themselves important except as notes toward a supreme fiction of relationships illustrating the operation of mind in negotiation with its surroundings. Thinking is simply another instrument, transitional in its time, with its own technology in its time, limited and limiting what can be played.

Looking at the opening of Stevens's poem will help to illustrate what I am describing. We read and/or hear the title and first section, "Peter Quince at the Clavier": we imagine a man, a dandy of sorts, somewhat foppish, yet sexual because of his name with its hints of Henry James's ghostly Quint from "The Turn of the Screw" and the quiet play on slang terms for both male and female pudenda; we may also recall Peter Quince the carpenter who fashions an imaginary window—"the fitful tracing of a portal"—in Shakespeare's *A Midsummer Night's Dream.* We figure this figure sitting at a clavier, and here our trouble begins. Are we to envision a keyboard instrument capable of holding the bass continuo that will play its part in suggesting "the basses of [the red-eyed elders'] beings"? Or are we to see nothing at all, following the abstract indication of "clavier" as the generic name for any keyboard instrument, and thus take Stevens's title to point us to reading the poem as being about the pure good of theory? We go on hoping for clarification through the first stanza and on into the beginning of the second, "Music is feeling, then, not sound"; there are keys, but we still do not know whether they are sounding. And what about "then"? In the parodic syllogism the poet sets up in the second stanza, "then" equivocates any possibility of certainty since we can read it in any of three ways, which will condition how we read "not sound." (We recall another of Stevens's descriptions of the state he creates for us here: "I was of three minds, / Like a tree / In which there are three blackbirds.") Returning to "Peter Quince," if we read "then" as part of the logical statement it pretends to inhabit, we have a proposition that separates sound from feeling. Or, we have an observation that says that the experience of music is feeling not sound, not well, whole, grounded. Or, if we follow the temporal aspect of "then," we have the speaker commenting on the power of music to evoke a past, feeling *then*, not now, and "that what" is "not sound," not an appropriate response to the present. By thus disrupting our complacency in thinking we understand what we read, Stevens illustrates William James's central observation about how feelings, desires, divide us up in time, opening spaces in the conventional grammar and syntax of perception. How those spaces are themselves experienced depends on whether we can find, or ourselves shape, structures of feeling. Without structures of feeling, the spaces opened up are terrifying, the abyss of the existentialists.

It is useful here to look at the way in which Stevens in the first section of "Peter Quince" traces a structure of feeling, a way of thinking, that protects the speaker and us from falling into the abyss of uncertainty created by his having forced the realization that conventional language is inadequate to thinking, that both are instruments and exist in a reciprocal relation, like the clavier and the possible music it can or cannot produce. His score, the pattern of expression fashioned on the *pitch/time* grid, at the moment our feeling of uncertainty is most intense, moves us in time back first to a moment in the speaker's personal past by way of an image of the desired female in her "blue-shadowed silk," and then to an apocryphal historical past redolent with images drawn from a story that simultaneously distracts our attention from our discomfort at now knowing how to read and communicates most effectively "that what," the desire that is the motive and actual content of the thinking evidenced by and in the language of the poem. In plotting this section, Stevens has deployed his images to move through time in analogue to the musical composer's variations in time on a stated theme, the musical fact from which we derive aesthetic pleasure in recognizing the theme through its variation, difference in sameness, a sort of speciation. Stevens's sequence of imaging manipulates, stretches, feeling in particular ways by referencing through time by way of images that have changed from being representations or symbols of any kind to signs. The first image is soothing because derived from a lived past, the following set of images stirring because leading somewhere unexpected while elaborating a thematic connection with the first. This pattern, the feeling of knowing and not knowing at once, is familiar to us from music; we listen and anticipate, not knowing how a progression will develop yet feeling its rightness when we hear it.

Raymond Williams's focus on the place of feeling in representation results from the same post-Darwinian reorientation concerning the nature of human experience that prompts Stevens to confuse the relations of feeling, desiring, and thinking. Through the Romantic period and well into the nineteenth century in the West the opposition between feeling and thinking was maintained, feeling consistently set aside in the equations of rationality. With the growing acknowledgment of what it means to be animal, however, and what it is to exist in accidental propitiousness in an equally accidental environment, we have had to rethink thinking. Recent work by neurobiologists Antonio and Hannah Damasio, Gerald Edelman, Jean-Pierre Changeux, all following *The Principles of Psychology*, Williams James's monumental development of Darwin's outline as set out in *The Descent of Man* and *The Expression of the Emotions in Man and Animals*, consider human thinking as a species-specific negotiation with a complex environment and base it entirely in somatic processes. This is not the place to go into a recounting of the experimental evidence that these researchers have adduced to support what Darwin theorized; I mention it here only to ground what I want to argue about the nature and function of great poetry: that is, that those we come to recognize as major poets so attune themselves to the undertones of what they understand nature to be, an understanding that changes over time, that they are able to anticipate in the structures of feeling their works are what later comes to be common knowledge or common sense. As Charles Sanders Peirce reminded us, what comes to be common sense is what the species has accumulated over aeons through trial and error of one kind or another that enables it to survive. What are greeted first as examples of an avant-garde aesthetic—Milton's blank verse in the seventeenth century, Emerson's seeming logical perversity in the nineteenth, Stevens's abstract fictions in the twentieth—presciently represent actual new forms of thinking that gradually come to be a *lingua franca*, a "new vulgate of experience," once science confirms hints provided by earlier aesthetic speculation.

I am not saying anything new here. Kant made abundantly clear the place of the aesthetic in the ascent to understanding.

What has remained unclear, however, is that the aesthetic has a structure, and that this structure is identical to whatever it is we mean by thinking during a particular historical moment, even if at the time it is initially encountered it is not recognized as thinking, but rather cast as a form of feeling in opposition to or in contrast to what is then thought to be thinking. The work of poetry is to accommodate human beings to their creaturely actuality by providing space and form for the animal, for feeling, the aleatory, accidental, irrational elements. The more successful the poetry, the more it enables us to attend to those aspects and to begin to find ways to integrate and speak about them, within the parameters established by the *pitch/time* grid of our culture. With the information we have come to have about ourselves since Darwin, the opposition between feeling and thinking, which shaped our language and perception, is dissolving. The fact of feeling: we need fear it only if we do not have forms with and in which it can perform its necessary function in our lives. William James was keenly aware of this. In the grounding chapter of *The Principles of Psychology*, titled famously, "The Stream of Consciousness" (originally titled "The Stream of Thought," changed by James when he condensed his volume into a teaching text), we have the following puissant suggestion:

If there be such things as feelings at all, *then so surely as relations between objects exist in rerum natura, so surely, and more surely, do feelings exist to which these relations are known.* There is not a conjunction or a preposition, and hardly an adverbial phrase, syntactic form, or inflection of voice, in human speech, that does not express some shading or other of relation which we at some moment actually feel to exist between the larger objects of our thought. If we speak objectively, it is the real relations that appear revealed; if we speak subjectively, it is the stream of consciousness that matches each of them by an inward coloring of its own. In either case the relations are numberless, and no existing language is capable of doing justice to all their shades.

We ought to say a feeling of *and*, a feeling of *if*, a feeling of *but*, and a feeling of *by*, quite as readily as we say a feeling of *blue* or a feeling of *cold*. Yet we do not: so inveterate has our habit become of recognizing the existence of the substantive parts alone, that language almost refuses to lend itself to any other use.

The Empiricists have always dwelt on its influence in making us suppose that where we have a separate name, a separate thing must needs be there to correspond with it; and they have rightly denied the existence of the mob of abstract entities, principles, and forces, in whose favor no other evidence than this could be brought up. But they have said nothing of that obverse error . . . of supposing that where there is *no* name no entity can exist. All *dumb* or anonymous psychic states have, owing to this error, been coolly suppressed; or, if recognized at all, have been named after the substantive perception they led to, as thoughts "about" this object or "about" that, the stolid word *about* engulfing all their delicate idiosyncrasies in its momentous sound. Thus the greater and greater accentuation and isolation of the substantive parts have commonly gone on.[3]

It is to this unexplored territory that Stevens directed his attention and to which we turn ours in considering what music offered him and us as a way of beginning to understand what it would be to have forms for what William James else-where called those "recesses of feeling, the darker, blinder strata of character . . . the only places in the world where we catch real fact in the making."

We are familiar with the nineteenth-century Symbolist rubric to have all art aspire to the condition of music, a direction Stevens diligently observed. What did he understand this rule to mean? And how do we, his readers, experience it? We will address ourselves to these questions by way of William James once again. In *Science and the Modern World*, Alfred North Whitehead, invoking James's central contribution to thought, called him "that adorable genius," the one who had finally exploded the "idea idea." Whitehead significantly points out how James in his *Principles* legitimized through careful articulation what had been in the air at least from the end of the eighteenth and early nineteenth centuries when first James Hutton's and later Charles Lyell's geological speculations and findings neces-sitated an extension of imagining to include perceiving pro-cesses of change over and through time that no human being could have experience of, except in thinking. In other words, the imagining was of something wholly invisible and not rep-

3 Cambridge, Massachusetts, and London, England: Harvard University Press, 1983, pp. 238–39.

resentable, though there were and are concrete evidences of the processes imagined. (This kind of imagining is different from that of, say, Copernicus or Galileo who were also seeing movements they could not experience in fact, but of a system they conceived as nonetheless eternal and unchanging in its cyclical nature and which they could represent in mechanical models.) Replacing the earlier idea of "simple location," Whitehead termed this new function "prehension," which he later changed to "event." It was in this imagined intellectual atmosphere that Darwin was to uncover inklings of our bond to all that dust and in which William James attempted to alter our habits of mind, habits made wholly out of words.

James realized that the "idea idea" so neatly expressed by John Locke in the *Essay Concerning Human Understanding* was an inadequate description of perception. Locke's notion of the "train of ideas" figures thinking as linking up sets of images drawn from a bank of impressions derived from a lived past. But for thinkers like Hutton, Lyell, Darwin, and others this description had given way, under the pressure of having to account for the unaccountable, the evidences of change over inconceivable spans of time, to an idea of imagination emptied of image. What is "seen" under this dispensation of imagination is a movement through spacetime of a principle of organization. The work of thinking then is to provide a description of what has been "seen" in this way: *It Must Be Abstract.* The obvious analogues for this kind of description are musical composition and mathematics. An instance is Mozart's description of seeing a symphony as a whole in one moment before setting it down in time and notation. Stevens's setting down is mimetic of the same kind of apprehension as Mozart's, or Darwin's. All recorded in flawed words and stubborn sounds something capable of being perceived only in the mind as a projection through a sequence of some kind that accounts for present fact or feeling. These translations of what can imperfectly be called "insight" represent a human adjustment to an ever-changing environment, what Stevens beautifully termed "momentary existence on an exquisite plane." These adjustments have an animal, animate motive. They give pleasure because they harmonize us, for the extended moment they create, to the reality we inhabit that is and always has been a relation between, a relation between what is there outside us, what Emerson called the "Not Me," and what/how we interpret that outside to be, the "Me." These adjustments feel right because and when they provide the space for us to sense, to give attention; they restore our native, natural senses by forcing us to be silent, like Milton's angels, for as long as it takes to understand them. This is what Emerson meant when he described the difference between "Man thinking" and "Man inhabited by thought." The styles of major poetry represent the historicizing of thinking. Music became the model for all art when imagination lost the image: "The absence of imagination had itself to be imagined," the effect of time passing making the visible invisible, Cronus devouring his children. Attention had to be drawn to what happens in between facts, to the relations in spacetime, to the transitive aspects of language and experience pointed to by William James. Music replaced painting, the *ut pictura poesis* standard in place at least since the Renaissance, just as thinking gave up the register of teleology and design and yielded to the increasing evolutionary information of the nineteenth century.

I want to explain what I mean here a little more closely because the alteration in this habit of mind is something we are always at work on in some way or another, and it is difficult to see clearly a process we are experiencing. As Emerson put it, "The field cannot well be seen from within the field."[4] Moreover, conceiving of the image as discrete and corresponding and thus representing an order of things that we will be able to apprehend only if we understand the place of each thing we can image is a habit worn and practiced for at least the more than five thousand years of our recorded history; it is not a habit easily changed. As we know also from William James and the work that has been done by physiologists and neuroscientists following him, habits of mind become common sense and come to seem almost instinctual because neuronal tracks are set down in the brain pan by repeated use. In order to begin to change this hard-wiring, it is not so much that the old system has to be disrupted but sidetracked, as it were; new practices must be learned through an effort of will whose first requirement is creating the time and opening the mental space for attention. If the change is made abruptly there is system error

4 *Essays and Lectures* (New York: The Library of America, 1983), p. 409.

and breakdown. The hard drive cannot process the information on the new disk; the new information has to be read through the system code in place. A new style, a different aesthetic emerges. It is understandable that from the mid nineteenth century and into the period of early modernism those individuals who worked most deliberately at changing the grammar and syntax of perception through their work on language and thinking in fact suffered nervous collapse: Emerson, Charles Sanders Peirce, William James, Henry Adams, T. S. Eliot, and others as documented by Jackson Lears in his study of anti-modernism in American culture from 1850 to 1920.

The model of music offers structural accommodation to an evolutionary view of development. A variation on a particular melodic line will lead to other possible variations from which yet others branch, all having an organic connection with the opening theme but no one progression determined at inception. Possibilities present themselves as the composition grows. The finished piece is one of many potential forms. We can read backwards and see how the design of the piece grew from its opening, but the shape it has could have been another. Its rightness, the pleasure we derive from hearing it has to do with what we are capable of hearing, what we are prepared to hear, quite accidentally, from the relations in pitch and time that we have grown used to hearing. A new scale is a sounding of a new spatio-temporal relation, a finding of something *in between* relations that were in place before, a new adaptation, the issue of a marriage of sorts. "We have no questions to ask which are unanswerable" (Emerson, 7) As Plato so exquisitely explicated in the "Cratylus," the seed of the erotic is the question, the source without which the satisfaction of resolution would be impossible, the concealed spring of all imaginings, asking what is possible in between this and that, moving into the spaces opened, feeling at sea, responding in full attention and with the animal need to survive and come to rest for a while, pleasure, renewal. This happens beyond ourselves yet is ourselves in the most profound sense. When Stevens, coming to the end of his poem, moves the Romantic aesthetic phrased by Keats from the Grecian urn's frozen image to its grounding in the flesh—"Beauty is momentary in the mind— / The fitful tracing of a portal; / But in the flesh it is immortal"—he is addressing precisely the change in structure of thought and feeling occasioned by Darwin's having discovered our ancestor to be a small, sloth-like creature, mostly arboreal in its habits.

A new aesthetic form forces spaces of attention to open. We do not at first know what to make of what we hear or see. We are in a new territory, questioning, alert, interested, literally *inter-esse*, between being one way and another. Coming to understand a new form requires time, standing under it, suffering its discipline, asking questions of it, tracking through it again and again until we become native and fluent in its speech, dressed in a new habit of mind. We map the new space, repeat its contours, its relations. Our responsive accommodation to it is something like a template; we imitate the form while preserving the difference each of us is, theme and variation, adaptation, RNA.

Yes, all well and good, some of you will be thinking, but what about images? They persist. They form what seems to be the substance of our memories and dreams, and I would not have been able to communicate anything of what I have without them. They are to language what notes are to music; without them no relations could be perceived. Because of the primacy of sight in human experience, images hold a species-privileged, accidentally necessary, place. Images will not disappear, as long, at least, as our species continues to be sighted, but our understanding of how they process our survival, our thinking, is changing and will continue to change. We exist in a reciprocal relation to our thinking, in fugitive propinquity to things as they are, like music. "Spirit is matter reduced to an extreme thinness" (Emerson, 475). Stevens's poem illustrates the transformation of images, like the reduction on the keys of a piano into music, thinking. In a central passage from the chapter entitled "Language" from *Nature* (1836), Emerson elaborates this process:

Because of this radical correspondence between visible things and human thoughts, savages, who have only what is necessary, converse in figures. As we go back in history, language becomes more picturesque, until its infancy, when it is all poetry; or all spiritual facts are represented by natural symbols. The same symbols are found to make the original elements of all languages. It has moreover been observed, that the idioms of all languages approach each other in passages of the greatest eloquence and power. And as this is the first language, so is it the last. This immediate dependence of language upon nature, this conversion of an outward phenomenon into a type of somewhat [we should note the play on "type"] in human life, never loses its power to affect us. It is this that gives that piquancy to the conversation of a strong-natured farmer or backwoodsman, which all men relish.

A man's power to connect his thought with its proper symbol, and so to utter it, depends on the simplicity of his character, that is, upon his love of truth, and his desire to communicate it without loss. The corruption of man is followed by the corruption of language. When simplicity of character and the sovereignty of ideas is broken up by the prevalence of secondary desires, the desire of riches, of pleasure, of power, and of praise,—and duplicity and falsehood take place of simplicity and truth, *the power over nature as an interpreter of the will* [emphasis mine] is in a degree lost; new imagery ceases to be created, and old words are perverted to stand for things which are not; a paper currency is employed, when there is no bullion in the vaults. In due time the fraud is manifest, and words lose all power to stimulate the understanding or the affections. . . .

But wise men pierce this rotten diction and fasten words again to visible things; so that picturesque language is at once a commanding certificate that he who employs it, is a man in alliance with truth and God. The moment our discourse rises above the ground line of familiar facts and is inflamed with passion or exalted by thought, it clothes itself in images. A man conversing in earnest, if he watch his intellectual processes, will find that a material image, more or less luminous, arises in his mind, contemporaneous with every thought. . . . Hence, good writing and brilliant discourse are perpetual allegories. This imagery is spontaneous. It is the blending of experience with the present action of the mind. It is proper creation. It is the working of the Original Cause through the instruments he has already made. (22–23)

Emerson composed these paragraphs for an audience not yet alerted to the disappearance of God and dressed his depiction of what the Romantics called "inspiration" appropriately. His address is nonetheless precisely to the change of habit in thinking he realized to be necessary because of the new understanding of process he had come to both from his reading in natural history and a most important recent visit to the Jardin des Plantes in Paris, where, in a moment of epiphany, he perceived, almost at the same moment as did Darwin aboard *The Beagle*, the incapacity of the existing systems of classification to represent the method of nature. We should note particularly the qualifiers he uses to characterize how and when it is that images aligned with the "truth" of things arise: "The moment our discourse rises above the ground line of familiar facts *and* is inflamed with passion *or* exalted by thought, it clothes itself in images. A man conversing in earnest, *if* he watch his intellectual processes, will find that a material image, more or less luminous, arises in his mind, contemporaneous with every thought [emphases mine]." It is the transitive aspects of mind prompted by emotion and attention and indicated by the conjunctions *and*, *or*, and *if* that make all the difference here. It is as though William James in his later work responded exactly to these lines of Emerson. (Not for nothing did William James call himself Emerson's spiritual heir.) A feeling of *and*, a feeling of *or*, a feeling of *if* are moments of lived experience, far more accurately descriptive of our animal condition than substantive instances and constructions. We are most alive when *in between*, in a state of *if* or *or* or *and*. These are the places of optimal consciousness, what James elsewhere and repeatedly calls the *vague*. It is during these moments that we discover who and where we are. The images that uppour from that saltier well within us to clothe our "thought" connect what we perceive in a present with our experience of the past, whether lived in flesh or in words, and so we practice rationality, finding out what part of one thing is like another, measuring this against that. The greatest thing by far is to be a master of metaphor. "In fact, the eye,— the mind,—is always accompanied by these forms, male and female; and these are incomparably the richest informations of the power and order that lie at the heart of things" (31).

It is to be noted as well that Emerson opens his excursion by invoking infancy as the muse of language. We recall that *infans* means "without words." From this the poem springs and brings us back again, in astonishment, to attend in stillness and quiet to who we are and what is around us, which may amount to the same thing. The greater the pressure outside us, the more the noise of the world threatens, the greater the necessity for poetry that creates these moments when we can return to our primal condition, animals, infants, and know ourselves and our world more truly and more strange. In a brilliant observation stretched over thirty-odd pages, William James embellishes Emerson's poignant and powerful strain:

> Sensations are the stable rock, the *terminus a quo* and the *terminus ad quem* of thought. To find such termini is our aim with all our theories—to conceive first when and where a certain sensation may be had, and then to have it. . . .
>
> *The first sensation which an infant gets is for him the Universe.* And the Universe he later comes to know is nothing but an amplification . . . of that first simple germ which, by accretion on the one hand and intussusception on the other, has grown so big and complex and articulate that its first state is unrememberable. In his dumb awakening to the consciousness of *something there*, a mere *this* as yet (or something for which even the term *this* would perhaps be too discriminative, and the intellectual acknowledgment of which would be better expressed by the bare interjection "lo!"), the infant encounters an object in which (though it be given in a pure sensation) all the "categories of the understanding" are contained. *It has objectivity, unity, substantiality, causality, in the full sense in which any later object or system of objects has these things.* Here the young knower meets and greets his world; and the miracle of knowledge bursts forth, as Voltaire says, as much in the infant's lowest sensation as in the highest achievement of a Newton's brain. The physiological condition of this first sensible experience is probably nerve-currents coming from many peripheral organs at once. Later, the one confused Fact which these currents cause to appear is perceived to be many facts, and to contain many qualities. For as the currents vary, and the brain-paths are moulded by them, other thoughts with other "objects" come, and the "same thing" which was apprehended as a present *this* soon figures as a past *that*, about which many unsuspected things have come to light. . . .
>
> Where, then, do we feel the objects of our original sensations to be?
>
> Certainly a child newly born in Boston, who gets a sensation from the candle-flame which lights the bedroom, or from his diaper-pin, does not feel either of these objects to be situated in longitude 71 degrees W. and latitude 42 degrees N. He does not feel them to be in the third story of the house. He does not even feel them in any distinct manner to be to the right or the left of any of the other sensations which he may be getting from other

objects in the room at the same time. He does not, in short, know anything *about* their space-relations to anything else in the world. The flame fills its own place, the pain fills its own place; but as yet these places are neither identified with, nor discriminated from, any other places. That comes later. For the places thus first sensibly known are elements of the child's space-world which remain with him all his life; and by memory and later experience he learns a vast number of things *about* those places which at first he did not know. But to the end of time certain places of the world remain defined for him as the places *where those sensations were;* and his only possible answer to the question *where anything is* will be to say *"there,"* and to name some sensation or other like those first ones, which shall identify the spot (*Principles*, 657–58, 681–83).

To these places we attempt to return, in feeling one way or another, throughout life.

William James anatomized our distancing from our original habitation in the feelings, the aesthetics, of our bodies. Feelings get temporalized into thinking as we go through experience, gathering additional names for what we encounter along the way, storing the record of that experience in images. But throughout life our nostalgia for the animal condition of our beginning in the world keeps turning us, as if in gravitational compulsion, back through those images, to infancy, to being without words, reminding us that we feel things before we think them, and that following the thread of the complicate harmony we make of what we think, back to what we feel, gives pleasure, the strain of being.

14

Aesthetic Value and Literary Language: Bishop and de Man

LEE EDELMAN

for John Hollander, who noted: "All is trope save in game."

What do we make of the "literary" in "literary criticism" today? Does it serve as a disciplinary designation, one superseded perhaps by the changing emphases of contemporary cultural studies? Does it refer to a system of values, one superseded perhaps by the ongoing challenge to the ideology of the aesthetic? Or does it indicate a site of resistance to any system of values as such, one superseded perhaps by the current engagement with the politics of literary production? Is the "literary," in other words, the token—the relic—of a particular historical epoch, beyond which either the academy or the culture more generally may have moved, or is it instead the enduring ground of a history that tries to forget it, the senseless material substrate of sense that *makes* history, but always as allegory?

However we choose to interpret the "literary," it continues to function effectively as an institutional address, designating a range of projects, artistic and academic both, that find their legitimation by way of the light this name gives off. But this should remind us that the "literary" names more than a particular institution; it also names the logic essential to institutionalization. It names, that is, the logic of naming, of linguistic or rhetorical positing, responsible for instituting identities endowed with the self-evidence of the literal only insofar as they manage to repress their determining rhetoricity. And precisely because it inaugurates this production of the literal, the "literary" can't really be identified as either literal or figurative itself. "Literal" and "literary" may share a derivation from the Latin word for letter, but the "literary" eludes literality since literality depends on a prior naming for which the "literary" serves as a name. Construed as literal the "literary" would denote the effect of itself as cause; but choosing to read it as figural doesn't solve the problem either: the "literary" would then name a substitute for some literal entity only produced by means of that substitution. In either case the literary would have to come before itself, enacting the separation or division inscribed, as Barbara Johnson has reminded us, by the Greek verb in which the roots of our English word "criticism" lie.[1] If the "literary," however, like "criticism," inscribes this fundamental division, then "literary criticism" would perform the stuttering iteration of the rupture marking identity's impossibility—an impossibility it simultaneously refutes (and thus enacts) by asserting its institutional identity. And the conceptual stutter of the name responsible for securing that concept of identity might be taken to allegorize history as allegorization of the "literary," which is cognate with literature's own attempts to contain the disruptions of the "literary" by producing substitutive narratives engaging aesthetics as a system of values. The "literary," that is, takes its value from the aesthetic valuations to which it gives rise in the process of trying, by means of narrative or temporal elaborations, to coincide with itself.

To think through this issue more fully, I want to consider two sharply dissimilar texts both published in America in 1978 and both concerned with literary criticism, allegory, epistemology, and aesthetics. One, as a poem first printed in the *New Yorker*, seems uncontroversially "literary"; the other, a work of literary theory first published in *Critical Inquiry*, seems closer to philosophy than to poetry as it offers up complex readings of passages from Locke, Condillac, and Kant. Near the end of that essay, "The Epistemology of Metaphor," Paul de Man, having traced the persistent disturbance of philosophy by linguistic figure, denies that literature names "the place where the unstable epistemology of metaphor is suspended by aesthetic pleasure." Instead, he represents literature as "a place where the possible convergence of rigor and pleasure is shown to be a delusion."[2] From the outset of her

---

1 Barbara Johnson, *The Critical Difference* (Baltimore: Johns Hopkins University Press, 1985), p. 4.

2 Paul de Man, "The Epistemology of Metaphor," *Aesthetic Ideology* (Minneapolis: University of Minnesota Press, 1996), p. 50.

poem, "Santarém,"[3] however, Elizabeth Bishop freely acknowledges the possibility of delusion while recalling what she goes
on to represent as a place of pure convergence, a place that her
rigorous description defines as the site of aesthetic pleasures.
"Of course I may be remembering it all wrong / after, after—
how many years?" she writes of her visit to Santarém, a city
depicted in the poem as defining a literal "place . . . [of] convergence" since it marks the spot where "two great rivers," the
Tapajós and the Amazon, come together as if to materialize a
confluence that seems, in Bishop's retrospect, consistent in this
with pastoral, to join the particularities of nature to the formal-
izing, quasi-mathematical logic at work in aesthetic perception:

> That golden evening I really wanted to go no farther;
> more than anything else I wanted to stay awhile
> in that conflux of two great rivers, Tapajós, Amazon,
> grandly, silently flowing, flowing east.

Though the reader can be no more certain than Bishop
whether nature or trick of memory paints the evening this
shade of gold, the poem insists on wrapping the whole of the
city in its hue. Bishop, for example, evokes "a sky of gorgeous,
under-lit clouds, / with everything gilded, burnished along
one side," and she characterizes the city's street as "deep in
dark-gold river sand," an observation to which she returns
when she notes: "the people's feet / waded in golden sand, /
dampered by golden sand."

Historicist critics might quickly note that Bishop made her
visit to Santarém in February of 1960, only two years after the
discovery of gold along a tributary of the Tapajós sparked a
gold rush, the largest in Brazilian history, that lasted for many
years. And perhaps that fact does somehow inform this memorialization of a golden moment in a paradisal place; the poetic
vision of Santarém, after all, dissolves when the poet's souvenir,
an empty wasp's nest she much admired and was given as a gift,
prompts a traveling captain of industry, "the retiring head of
Philips Electric," to ask her, uncomprehendingly, "What's that
ugly thing?" But the attention to what's gilded or burnished,

---

3 *Elizabeth Bishop: The Complete Poems, 1927–1979* (New York: Farrar,
Straus, and Giroux, 1991), p. 185–87.

like the businessman's question itself, seems to center instead on a questioning of aesthetic value and aesthetic pleasure.

Like Jerusalem, Bishop's Santarém may be figured as bathed in gold, but even the poem seems not to know exactly what that means. Interpreted naturalistically, the "golden evening" refers its gold to the light of the setting sun that occasions the lambent theatricality of "gorgeous, under-lit clouds" and effects an aesthetic translation of the scene that leaves "everything gilded, burnished along one side / and everything bright, cheerful, casual." Leaves everything, at least, so burnished until Bishop adds: " or so it looked." This qualification may be casually made, but it's neither bright nor cheerful, for it reminds us that being gilded isn't the same as being gold, especially when that gilding only extends "along one side." If asked where the proper referent of the gold in this "golden evening" lies, we couldn't, then, with any assurance point to its natural source in the sun, since we couldn't rule out its reflecting the deceptive coloration of trope or lie: the falsification, perhaps, of memory or simply the distance between the scene itself and the wholly subjective, internal light by means of which it's seen. The literal status of "golden" here seems to turn on a simple conjunction, "or," a word always ready, in romance languages, to turn into gold itself. This "or" might appear to gesture toward the other side of "everything"—the side not gilded or burnished, the side that resists aestheticization—were it not for the fact that the poem identifies the mediation of formal oppositions as the very principle *of* the aesthetic. Like a version of Rumpelstiltskin, the economy of aesthetic value turns even the refusal or undoing of the aesthetic into more aesthetic gold, instructing us in a mode of perception that recognizes beauty in the "ugly" wasp's nest as well as in the formal chiasmus that places the waspish denigration of that object— "What's that ugly thing?"—in the mouth of one "Mr. Swan." "Santarém" thus enacts an allegory of literature as the gold standard of aesthetic value by tracing that value to the conjunction of linguistic possibilities *in* a conjunction. The convergence or "coming together" announced by the "conflux of two great rivers" starts to seem like a narrativization, a transposition into the order of nature, of "or," a word as good as gold, but also a conjunction exclusively confined to the order of language and to which, therefore, nothing natural is ever naturally conjoined.

Now Paul de Man's essay, as chance would have it, also speculates on "gold," pausing to consider what happens to John Locke's theory of words and language when Locke takes "gold" as his model for a substance defined as the collection of its properties. "The structure of [such] substances . . . upsets the convergence of nominal and real essences"[4] de Man tells us, and it does so because the properties that constitute those substances are able to appropriate, by means of synecdoche, the name of the substance itself. Thus "gold" can refer, as Locke himself observes, to any "shining yellow" color, though that color is only one of the many properties associated with "gold."[5] The name of the substance won't stay in one place; it wanders where it shouldn't, demonstrating, as de Man points out, the perpetual mobility of trope: "always on the move, more like quicksilver than like flowers or butterflies."[6] Citing Locke's declaration, based on the heterogeneous things to which the word "gold" can properly refer, that "no one has authority to determine the signification of the word *gold* (as referred to such a body existing in nature)," de Man proceeds to gloss it as follows:

It is indeed not a question of ontology, of things as they are, but of authority, of things as they are decreed to be. . . . We have no way of defining, of policing, the boundaries that separate the name of one entity from the name of another; tropes are not just travelers, they tend to be smugglers and probably smugglers of stolen goods at that. What makes matters even worse is that there is no way of finding out whether they do so with criminal intent or not.[7]

The critic who will conclude his essay by describing literature as a "place" here peoples that place with tropes, compellingly personified as "travelers" before making their way through the rest of his text to turn people into tropes. It wouldn't be hard to map the textual logic that gives birth to de Man's figure of

4 De Man, "Epistemology," p. 39.
5 Ibid.
6 Ibid.
7 Ibid.

figure as living and mobile, and thus as a "traveler." He travels rather quickly himself along a path that leads his thought associatively from the likening of trope to "quicksilver," a comparison metonymically motivated by Locke's own linguistic meditation on "gold," to the quickening of trope into a living being, one disinclined, like quicksilver, to remaining in any one place. The "traveler," then, is the metonymy of Locke's linguistic invocation of "gold" by way of the intervening metonymys brought together, like the conflux of two great rivers, in a single signifier: "quicksilver." And since metaphor, which succeeds by synecdoche in naming figuration as a whole, etymologically refers to the activities of carrying or transportation, there's no reason for de Man not to specify this particular trope of trope further still by making the figurative "traveler" into a "smuggler" of "stolen goods." Why not, when the very trope of trope as "traveler" has itself been taken, displaced, even "stolen" from John Locke's original "gold." The "stolen goods" smuggled by the traveler thus turn out to be the traveler as such: the figure, the metaphor, that carries nothing more valuable than itself.

But how do we read de Man's musing here on "criminal intent"? To what in the realm of language could "intent," whether criminal or not, refer since intent involves willful agency, and "criminal intent" an ethical choice? If this exten sion of de Man's own figural play intends to question *authorial* intent in the textual play of figures, then the issue should not be the "criminal intent" of the tropes themselves as smugglers, but the intent of some higher authority, a criminal ringleader or a Mafia boss, in whose hands those tropological smugglers would become mere instruments, so many pawns. Though trope may fill the space of the text with goods that are bad for its logic— importing counter-narratives, contradictions, and other scenes— that stealthy importation engages the smugglers' "criminal intent" only if the critic proposes that language has a will—and hence a consciousness: a mind, a life—of its own, or if his trope imports, through an agency here imbued with the *force* of a will, a suggestion that willful agency, the very purposiveness of intent, is born to account for the moving force, the motive, of tropic motion. In which case the concept of intent itself as the agency of the mind would function as a figure for a literal reality that would have to be purely linguistic.

This brings us back to Bishop's poem, also focused on places and travelers: back to the "golden evening" experienced at the "conflux of two rivers," that may owe its experiential coloring to the linguistic reality of the conjunction "or"; for that "or" introduces at once a protracted series of joinings or conjunctions along with a demonstration of how conjunction should be thought:

> I liked the place; I liked the idea of the place.
> Two rivers. Hadn't two rivers sprung
> from the Garden of Eden? No, that was four
> and they'd diverged. Here only two
> and coming together. Even if one were tempted
> to literary interpretations
> such as: life/death, right/wrong, male/female
> —such notions would have resolved, dissolved, straight off
> in that watery, dazzling dialectic.

Linguistic conjunctions earn that name by joining clauses or sentences, or by coordinating words in a clause, but "or" effects such a union to establish different possibilities and thereby to introduce the possibility of difference. A phonetic truncation of "other," "or" marks a structure of alterity that can open the door, as in Bishop's poem, to epistemological doubt. Her simple clause, "or so it looked," casts the golden glow of Santarém in an indeterminate relation to the reality of the place. Small wonder, then, that the poet immediately reiterates that uncertainty by joining across a semi-colon two independent clauses: "I liked the place; I liked the idea of the place." The place and the idea of it: you'd think we'd crossed the border into Wallace Stevens land. But "Santarém," like so many of Bishop's still seriously under-read poems, proves Bishop, no less than Stevens, adroit in what he once called the "theatre of trope." By collocating "I liked the place" with "I liked the idea of the place," the poet refuses to specify if the latter revises the first's imprecision (as if to say, "I liked the place, *or, rather,* I liked the idea of it") or merely adds more information (as if to say, "I liked the place *and* I liked the idea of it too"). The absence of a conjunction suspends the sense of the clausal relation between "or" and "and," as if those two conjunctions, as different ways of conjoining, were themselves here being conjoined. But

Bishop's "or" makes the place itself a little hard to see; so even if we wished to imagine the two as implicitly linked by "and," we couldn't know if the speaker knows the difference between "and" and "or." Could she ever distinguish the place itself from the idea of it that she likes in order to affirm that the relation here could be one of "and" and not "or"?

The poem, of course, explicitly scorns the reification of such binarisms, linking them to the facility of "literary inter-pretations / such as: life/death, right/wrong, male/female," as Bishop puts it. Not, of course, that Paul de Man endorsed such binarisms either; indeed, his essay explicitly scorns reliance on them too, linking them to philosophy's endeavor to cordon off and discredit trope: "the resulting undecidability," he declares of such efforts on the part of philosophy, "is due to the asym-metry of the binary model that opposes the figural to the proper meaning of the figure."[8] This leads de Man to reject the possibility of circumscribing trope as the "literary" in order to guarantee thereby philosophy's epistemological stability. Though Bishop and de Man thus both disavow the logic of either/or, each associates that logic with a different term in the binarism of literature and philosophy. In the case of "San-tarém," this means resisting "literary interpretations," where the "literary" connotes turning natural reality, as here the "two great rivers," into allegorical figures. Like the binary abstrac-tions as which the "literary" interpretation reads the rivers it construes as tropes, the "literary interpretation" itself is "dis-solved" in the conflux that the poet represents as "that watery, dazzling dialectic."

In celebrating this "dialectic," though, as the dissolution of the binary and allegorical constructs of "literary interpreta-tions," the poem seeks to dazzle us. "Dialectic" may name the process of bringing together "and" and "or," and in that way may signal the non-necessity of their binary opposition; but it also names the logic of philosophical argumentation, and, by extension, serves to designate philosophy itself. Privileging "dialectic," then, over "literary interpretations" reinscribes the binary mode of thought the poem names, and condemns, as "literary," and does so, just to make matters worse, precisely in

8 Ibid., pp. 48–49.

the mode of allegory associated with the "literary" imposition of binary abstractions upon the two rivers. But how could the "conflux of two great rivers" be seen as a "dialectic" without plunging us headlong once again into allegorical waters? Allegorizing, perhaps in its own despite, the impossibility of escaping allegory, the poem enacts the impossibility of traveling, except by means of epistemologically unreliable tropes, from the realm of the "literary" or linguistic into the "naturalized" aesthetic depicted in the quasi-paradise of "Santarém." But it does so while trying to blind us with a "dazzling dialectic" that holds out the golden promise of aesthetic totalization: an aesthetic totalization that may rest on the anamorphosis of "or."

"Santarém" thus suggests that while "literary interpretations" always take the form of allegory, allegory manages to cover up, by narrativizing, the "literary," imbuing its referential emptiness with value, spinning its straw into aesthetic gold. I've argued that the literal referent of the "golden evening" in "Santarém" can be situated, at least in part, in the wholly linguistic play of "or," which generates a figural discourse of conjunctions from which the poem and its rivers both flow. That signifier makes another appearance in the poem in a slightly different form, italicized in a passage that distracts our attention from its status *as* a signifier by embedding it in a narrative that proposes the explanatory value of historical analysis:

> Two rivers full of crazy shipping—people
> all apparently changing their minds, embarking
> disembarking, rowing clumsy dories.
> (After the Civil War some Southern families
> came here: here they could still own slaves.
> They left occasional blue eyes, English names,
> and *oars*. No other place, no one
> on all the Amazon's four thousand miles
> does anything but paddle.)

All of our critical interests *du jour* seem condensed in these few lines: questions of race, nation, economy, of colonial and post-colonial experience. The moral imperatives, themselves perhaps displaced aesthetic values, commanded by these various discourses, can make the insistence I place on "*oars*," emerging as it does both lexically and conceptually here from "dories," seem perversely beside the point. And so it is. For making what de Man called linguistic materiality *beside* the point is *itself* the point of aesthetics, and of every other allegorization of the "literary," whether we call those allegorizations history or philosophy or even literature. De Man, in a passage cited earlier from the end of "The Epistemology of Metaphor," identifies literature as "the place where the possible convergence of rigor and pleasure is shown to be a delusion." Such showing, of course, cannot escape the very delusion that it shows us, as is shown by de Man's own allegorization of literature here as "a place." But the further we go into that figural place where convergence is always delusion, the closer we come to "Santarém," and the more we find ourselves dazzled by an aesthetic logic that perpetuates itself by performing its own dissolution. However carefully we try to navigate between linguistic materiality and its allegorizations, we seem to find ourselves, in more ways than one, up a creek without a paddle. Literary criticism may name the inevitable fracture of formal identity, tracing a "golden evening," for example, to the delusions of verbal play, the plenitude of referential reality to the materiality of a conjunction, but the aesthetic always finds a way to load each rift with ore. Perhaps it's not irrelevant, then, that the logic of sublimation—often associated, as Lacan points out, with forms of "moral and spiritual elevation, that of the scale of values"[9]—designates also a process for translating the impurities of ore into gold.

---

9 Jacques Lacan, *The Seminar of Jacques Lacan, Book VII: The Ethics of Psychoanalysis, 1959–1960*, ed. Jacques-Alain Miller, trans. Dennis Porter (New York: W.W. Norton & Co. 1997), p. 87.

15

John Hollander's Spectral Emanations: The White Light of Truth

DAVID MIKICS

This essay is for John Hollander, scholarly quester and guide.

He was alone. He was alone like Harting, contraband smuggled in, living like Harting on borrowed time; hunting, like Harting, for a missing truth. . . . As he returned to the desk he nearly tripped over a green box. . . . It had the Queen's initials just beneath the handle and reinforced corners of thin steel; the locks had been ripped open and it was empty. *That's what we're all doing, isn't it: looking for something that isn't there.*

JOHN LE CARRÉ, *A Small Town in Germany*[1]

John Hollander's *Spectral Emanations* is a poem on a sacred subject: the loss and refinding of the menorah, the central holy object of Judaism. The seven sections of this remarkable work are named after the seven colors of the spectrum (Red, Orange, Yellow, Green, Blue, Indigo, Violet) and allude in their number to the seven branches of the menorah. In this essay, I will take a close look at the first three sections of *Spectral Emanations*, Red, Orange, and Yellow, in an effort to follow Hollander's idea about how poetry is related to the course of empire (as in Thomas Cole's famous series of paintings, about which Hollander has written[2]). For Hollander, poetic beauty (whose color is Yellow) tries to distinguish itself from the pursuit of success exemplified in America's imperial capitalism (Orange), but these colors nevertheless remain close, even interdependent: not thoroughly blended or dissolved, but discernable as two shades are, one from the other. But before we get to these two visions, of American capitalism in Orange and

---

1 John Le Carré, *A Small Town in Germany* (London: Pan Books, 1969), p. 258.
2 John Hollander, "Landscape's Empire," *Prose* 2 (Spring 1971): 79–94.

American imagination in Yellow, we encounter Hollander's primary color, Red, at the beginning of his sequence. Red evokes not America but Israel. As Harold Bloom has noted, *Spectral Emanations* asks what it means to be a Jewish American poet like Hollander, committed to his religious nationality within a nation that, more than any other, stands for the purely secular.[3]

First, the story of the menorah, which Hollander finds in Hawthorne's *The Marble Faun* and L. Yarden's *The Tree of Light*, among other places. For centuries the menorah remained guarded at the Holy of Holies, the inner sanctum of the temple at Jerusalem. The seven branched candlestick is familiar to everyone as a copy, having assumed many inventive variations and ingenious designs since it was taken from the temple. But what of the original?

According to legend, the menorah from the Second Temple was stolen by the emperor Titus' Roman legions in A.D. 70. A relief picture of the menorah is still inscribed on the Arch of Titus, in Rome. Supposedly, the original menorah fell from the Milvian bridge into the waters of the Tiber when a sign appeared in the sky signaling Emperor Constantine's victory over the pagan Maxentius: a cross accompanied by the initials IHSV, "*In hoc signo vinces*" (in this sign you will conquer). With Constantine's conversion of the Roman empire, Christianity becomes a means of dominion, a world-historical sign that threatens to overwhelm Judaism as it did paganism. But, as Hawthorne's character Hilda says in *The Marble Faun*, "Such a candlestick cannot be lost forever." The Midrash Rabbah on Numbers 15 states that "when in the fulness of time the Temple shall rise again, the golden menorah will likewise be restored to its place 'to gladden Jerusalem.'"[4] Hollander complicates this faith: his poetic quest for the menorah does not wait for apocalypse, the fulness of time.

What would it mean to restore or refind the menorah in a poem? What sort of project is this for a poem to set itself: national and public? esoteric and mystical? To whom is the poem's project addressed, and who will listen to it? *Spectral*

3 Harold Bloom, "John Hollander's *Spectral Emanations*: The Menorah as the White Light of Trope," in *Agon* (New York: Oxford University Press, 1982).

4 L. Yarden, *The Tree of Light* (Ithaca, N.Y.: Cornell University Press, 1971), p. 49.

Emanations has at its center the crucial idea that, as Hollander puts it in his essay "A Poetry of Restitution," the truth in poetry means wanting to say *I mean you and me, not what the others say*."[5] Every poem pursues sacredness since it quests after the committed intimacy of an I and a you, exercising a contrast between itself and the less earnest voices that surround us all the time ("what the others say"). Poetic intimacy argues against the secular events, the advent of secularity, summed up in what the words in the sky told Constantine, "*In hoc signo vinces.*" The argument is a hard one: these words are what the others say, but *Spectral Emanations* suggests that they are also what we say. We cannot refine away the secular from the sacred, material prosperity from poetic vision. We remain creatures of our historical space and time, bound by our conditions. But, in an Emersonian (and Cavellian) turn, I can also recreate these conditions by speaking them to you. The seven parts of Hollander's poem, which evoke the six days of creation followed by the sabbath (in the quiet, haunting final section, Violet), allow poetry to approach religious address by telling the reader: in these words you will, not conquer, but look for what is lost (a poetry of restitution).

Hollander's poem is antireligious in the Greek sense of *anti* (which means not just "the opposite of" but also "in place of"). It replaces religion by taking over the religious prerogative of high and holy speaking, a speaking that commands the one who hears. If poetry like religion is privileged, special speech, its specific privilege is to *take the place of* religious expression. Hollander, in the poem's subtitle, announces that his work stands "in Lieu of," in place of, "a Lamp" (117), substituting itself for the lost menorah that symbolizes Jewish observance.

The Jewish poet may be affected, more than others, by a sense of the difference between the religious and the poetic. Allen Grossman, in his essay "Jewish Poetry Considered as a Theophoric Project," suggests that Jewishness and poetry are deeply at odds. Jewish tradition, in his reading, implies a suspicion of the poet's fictive delights, his ingenious love of persuasion and enchantment. Grossman writes,

---

5 John Hollander, "A Poetry of Restitution," *Yale Review* 70 (1981): 161–86.

For the Jew *there is always a sense* (a profound understanding beneath all other understandings) *that the category of the sacred and the category of the poetic repel one another* —because the poetic defers the sacred, which is, nonetheless, the destination of all things.[6]

In moving from the idea that the sacred and the poetic "repel one another" to the idea that "the poetic defers the sacred" (as representation defers the unrepresentability of God) Grossman raises an interesting question about whether the Jewish religion and poetry are compatible, and if so, how. On the one hand, religious observance is antithetical to poetry because it honors the creation, repeating "the one Word that is," instead of inventing new fictions. The ability to make lies-that-look-true that Hesiod's muses offer him as the inducement to become a poet couldn't—so it would seem—be more different from a thoughtful Rabbi's effort to discern the true meaning of scripture. On the other hand, poetry serves the sacred by *deferring* our arrival at "the destination of all things," and is therefore a legitimate part of the journey. In one way, *Spectral Emanations* is anti-religious, a fiction in place of a truth. In another way, though, it defers to, and looks for, a truth that it cannot represent, the holiness that is the object of the quest.

But how, exactly, is pagan fiction related to sacred destiny? Can a Jewish poet's quest be both solemn enough to honor the creation, to stand in the place of religion, and at the same time playful enough to do the proper poetic work of dissimulation? The answer, Hollander's *Spectral Emanations* shows, is not a mere matter of attaining a balance between the wilderness of trope and the homecoming of final meaning, but an investigation of how these two things, finally, fit together, in the realms of hope and of survival. The investigation of our desire for a definitive coming home, a transformation into final meaning is, *Spectral Emanations* seems to argue, the quest of quests.

The quest for the menorah looks different in each of the seven sections of Hollander's poem. On the one hand, the seven spectral colors suggest the colors of rhetoric, of poetic persuasion. These seven poems embody seven different ways of urging the audience, by getting them to look at things in distinct

6 Allen Grossman, "Jewish Poetry Considered as a Theophoric Project," *The Long Schoolroom* (Ann Arbor: University of Michigan Press, 1997), p. 161.

shades. On the other hand, each of the colors is, more than a means or a perspectival lens, a realm unto itself, an adjoining country. The word "spectral" suggests a certain ghostliness: each quest, taken separately, may seem a mere shadow of itself. If, together, they could be blended into wholeness, combining to make what Hawthorne's Hilda, in *The Marble Faun*, calls "the white light of truth" (117), then the poem itself would be overcome, at once revealed and dissipated.

Hollander begins with the notion that different quests, like the different kinds of poems that enact or depict these quests, produce images of one another. In a tricky mirroring, these "six songs, no, seven," the sections of *Spectral Emanations*, respond to one another (like the *sephirot* or lights of wisdom that kabbalah describes). Hollander summarizes the seven songs, and in doing so recounts the progress of his own poem, in the prose section of his penultimate color, the one recently excluded from the spectrum, "Departed Indigo" (the poem for each of the seven colors is followed, or shadowed, by a prose commentary):

The Battle on the Plains, where heroes stood and fell; the Finding of the Treasure, where it was hard to get to; the Founding of the Fields, where all expanded in peace; the Dancing on the Lawns, where there was nothing wrong; the Visit to the Sky, which was no wearying journey; the Farewell to the Guide, when the next stage was reached; the Darkening of It All, when it had become too late. (150–51)

These seven quests describe the stages of a journey, but they also reflect one another. Such reflection may dazzle, obstructing the quester's forward movement. In Hollander's prose introduction to Red, which alludes to the Jewish sages who studied *merkabah* (chariot) mysticism, he meditates on the interference that may occur between reflection (in both this word's senses) and progress. According to Gershom Scholem, *merkabah* mysticism, based on the study of passages from Ezekiel 1 and Enoch 13, aimed at producing ecstatic meditational states in the service of an end, a forward movement. The goal was to enter a contemplative *pardes* (paradise), a heaven of thought, culminating in a vision of the chariot, or *merkabah*, with "a likeness as the appearance of a man on it above" (Ezekiel 1:26). Each sage, so kabbalistic lore reports, gets stopped at a particular stage of the quest, unable to achieve the final step: all except for Rabbi Akiva. In its description of the passage through "the seven palaces in the firmament of *aravot* (the uppermost of the seven firmaments)," Scholem writes, *merkabah* tradition relates the various deceptive visions that will face the "ascending soul." At the entrance to the sixth palace it will seem as if "one hundred million waves pour down, and yet there is not one drop of water there, only the splendor of the pure marble stones which pave the palace." Rabbi Akiva, who successfully passes through this danger, warns the devotee, "when you come to the place of pure marble stones, do not say 'water, water.'"[7]

Hollander, less heroic than Akiva, depicts himself being stopped "on the way to the seventh chamber," just before completing the seven colors of the spectrum. At this penultimate point, the poet, like the *merkabah* mystic, mistakes hard stone for water: "There were glimmering marble slabs. They dazzled mine eyes, and it was not at mine own tears that I cried out *O water! Water!* Thus was I never to enter" (121).

Blinded by his own sight, then, the quester fails: no Rabbi Akiva, though he comes close, nearly achieving the seventh, or last, chamber. (A famous piece of advice about reading the Talmud warns the student not to find merely his own image mirrored in the text.) Hollander's poem itself corrects this failure, by completing the promised seven colors. But the situation that Hollander takes up from the kabbalistic parable (being dazzled, seeing water instead of bright rock) provides a fitting introduction to his first color, Red. The dazzle seems to be the distortion enacted by the political and temporal. Red is the color of war: under the aegis of red, to cry out, "*O water! Water!*" is to see salvation in a famous military, pagan moment, Xenophon's troops reaching the sea and shouting out, "*Thalassa!*"

Hollander has remarked that Red, which he wrote shortly after the Yom Kippur war, in September 1973, "was the *first* poem, the heroic, the epical, the violent, the poem about simplicities."[8] Red's subject is military or national questing. It depicts a scene from the Six-Day War (whose name sadly reminds us of the creation): an Israeli soldier, here named J, slumps in a shade that protects him from the harsh, reflected

7 Gershom Scholem, *Kabbalah* (New York: Quadrangle, 1974), pp. 17–18.
8 In a letter written to Richard Poirier.

light of the desert sun. It is this secular-Zionist figure, J, who
begins Hollander's poem (a contrast to the J writer, or Yahwist,
responsible for Genesis).

> Along the wide canal
> Vehement, high flashings
> Of sunlight reflect up
> From rock, from bunker, from
> Metal plate. In the mild
> Shade of his waiting place—
> Shade a gourd might afford—
> J sits embracing his
> Automatic weapon,
> Crowned by a sloppy cap ...   (121)

In this tense landscape, Jerusalem the golden has become
Jerusalem the red. The holy city, surrounded by powerful enemies, bristles with warlike defense, though the soldier, J, nevertheless courts a pastoral "mild / Shade," "embracing" the
tool of his trade, an Uzi. What is he readying himself for in this
"waiting place"; what is he waiting out? Death, it turns out. As
J is suddenly killed by a bullet, the tight internal rhymes of
Hollander's curt stanzas unfold, letting us see the history, "the
film of / The ages," whose legendary bustle will culminate in
the dying man's forgetting:

> Slow, greaved legs clang along
> Parasangs of gray road;
> Brave and fair embrace the
> Bad and dark; arrows snap
> Against square parapets;
> Sons of the desert rise;
> Gray, wreathed heads lock crowns on
> Blond curls; the bright tower
> Is truly taken; there
> Are kingdoms, there are songs
> Along the wall——but his
> Films melt into jelly:
> Now at his red moment
> He forgets his city
> As his tongue is made to
> Fuck the roof of his mouth ...   (122–23)

In the final seconds of his life, J sees an obliterating, or dazzling, vision. "He forgets his city," receiving not a future kingdom, a messiah to be "crowned" here, but a secular history of
past kingdoms, whose rigid, dumb spiral responds to the
"automatic" character of the weapon the soldier holds. "Fire at
his right hand, / The fierce ghost of his sire" (122): J is captive
to the past, wound as tightly as Hollander's line, which wraps
"fire" around "fierce" and "sire."

Red shows that war's chivalric brightness is in fact brutal,
sudden destruction. (No revelation this.) By soldering opposites together, the shining battle makes us see the mutual contamination their struggle requires. "Brave and fair embrace
the / Bad and dark" suggests not only a glorious chivalric aura,
a crusade in which "the bright tower / Is truly taken," but also
the crusaders' disastrous interlocking of pastoral ideals and
greedy militancy. The stiff vowel resonances of "lock crowns
on / Blond curls" hint that the fulfillment of the knightly
Christian quest for Jerusalem remains captive to a marauding,
plundering banditry, the real truth about Christian dominion.
The bright, youthful son that these lines picture is really a slave
to the gray, wreathed ghost of the past, his fierce sire. Finally, at
the end of the Crusader-era film strip that occupies J's last
moments, Jerusalem's walls turn into a blank, a loud hiss—the
dash that marks J's death, his "red moment" (———).

Red is, of course, about a Zionist soldier, not a Christian one,
a contemporary figure superimposed on a crusading past. Does
the same burden of imperial violence that characterizes crusading Christianity also apply to the Jewish state? Israel has always
been defensive in its militancy, intent only on its own survival,
unlike the expansionist forces of Christianity. But here, in a rep
etition of the Constantinian IHSV, the Crusades overshadow
Zionist ideals, causing the menorah once again to be lost.

At the moment of J's death, the Jewish past seems as forgotten as the Crusaders, collapsed into an original time in which
the fruit of the earth goes back into that earth. "The pulp / Of
him slips to the ground," we are told of J's body:

> Blood, rooted in earth, makes
> Adam's kingdom, Adom,
> Fruit brought forth of iron,
> The wide realm of the red.   (123)

These lines, with their coiled assonance, bring us back to the determining roots of the name, and of the word: blood is "rooted in earth" because the Hebrew *adom* means both "earth" and "red." Hollander reminds us that Adam, God's creation, is made from *adom*, the red clay of the ground. But then he varies the legend, making humanity's real ground an iron one: we are born from the fact of war, as if Cain and Abel had actually preceded Adam. That's the way it looks in Red, which sees human origins in violence; later sections of *Spectral Emanations* find happier sources for us. The basis for this revision is the redness of blood, a color it shares with earth and with the rusting iron of old weapons. The making of kingdoms makes Adom, earth, not free of dominion (A-dom), as pastoral dreams suggest, but rather suffused with a violent fate.

In the prose section at the end of Red, Hollander rereads redness as the rust of disused weapons, the apparatus of, "Not the Warrior, but the bloodied Saturn, suffused with lateness" (123). As Jean Seznec points out in *The Survival of the Pagan Gods*, Saturn in the Middle Ages is often seen as a warrior god, his sickle the tool of deadly harvesting.[9] But, properly speaking, Saturn remains an antiquated, outdated god of time, doomed to die at the hands of Jove (a deity who will be crucial to Hollander's next section, Orange). So Hollander consigns Saturn to the decaying past, writing in the prose gloss at the end of Red, "By day, the iron sickle leans against the wall; ringing around a pot, its blade reddens with rust" (123).

Western Radiance: America the Golden

> America, America,
> May God thy gold refine,
> Till all success be nobleness,
> And every gain divine.
>
> KATHARINE LEE BATES, "America the Beautiful"

In the second and third sections of *Spectral Emanations*, Orange and Yellow, Hollander meditates on the double image of America: the place of crude material splendor, of cash and gleaming commodities, is also the place of a different substance

9 Jean Seznec, *The Survival of the Pagan Gods* (Princeton: Princeton University Press, 1995), pp. 156–58.

of vision, what Emerson in "Experience" called "this new yet unapproachable America I have found in the West." After Red, in Orange and Yellow we move, as many Jews themselves did, from the Old World to the New. But what remains from Red's scene of an embattled Jerusalem, taken first by Crusaders and then by Zionists, is an argument between the fact of a secular regime and the truth of a place and a people. In the case of Israel as in that of America, it can be hard to disentangle the crude from the refined, what is most material from what most matters.

Explicating the division between, and the strange combination of, America the gold and America the golden requires a brief excursion into one of Hollander's main sources for Orange and Yellow, Hawthorne's account of King Midas. Hawthorne's *A Wonder Book* (1851) is a retelling of tales from Greek mythology that takes place one autumn day in Tanglewood. The storyteller is one Eustace Bright, a Williams College undergraduate; his audience a group of evocatively named children (Primrose, Periwinkle, Sweet Fern, and so on). The second story of *A Wonder Book*, "The Golden Touch," concerns King Midas, who epitomizes the royal eagerness for magnificence in its most literal form: in a "joyful frenzy," Midas runs "grasping at everything that happened to be in his way," and turning it, of course, to gold.[10] But this kingly alchemy, in its literal-mindedness, renders the book of nature unreadable. When Midas takes up "a book from the table," "on running his fingers through the leaves, behold! it was a bundle of thin golden plates, in which all the wisdom of the book had grown illegible."[11] After Midas learns his lesson, Eustace Bright, observing the autumnal afternoon, comments to the children,

Were I Midas, I would make nothing else but just such golden days as these over and over again, all the year throughout. My best thoughts always come a little too late. Why did not I tell you how old King Midas came to America, and changed the dusky autumn, such as it is in other countries, into the burnished beauty which it here puts on? He gilded the leaves of the great volume of Nature.[12]

10 Nathaniel Hawthorne, *A Wonder Book* (New York: Lancer Books, 1968), p. 62.
11 Ibid., p. 63.
12 Ibid., p. 80.

The King Midas that Eustace pictures here is not literal-minded but instead highly imaginative, a genius of the weather who "gilded the leaves of the great volume of Nature." The American Midas that Hawthorne conjures up creates a world of golden days, instead of turning the world, as the original Midas did, into the clotted, unmeaning splendor of actual gold. The result is that our "western radiance," spilling "like golden wine out of a bowl," makes "such a day that you could not help saying of it, 'There never was such a day before!' although yesterday was just such a day, and tomorrow will be just such another."[13] The lateness of October, which stands for the belatedness of America itself, here becomes an image of the perpetually new, a light illusory but satisfying in the way it steals the aura of creation, making after resemble before. America, the *Abendland*, somehow remains the newest nation, the one most promising.

But this promise has its corrupted shadow. Hawthorne's afterthought to Midas' royal crassness, his parable of an American Midas whose touch would burnish the world rather than vulgarizing it, is appropriately meant for children. Our adult world, soiled in the workings of capital, cannot be so easily separated out from the pure sap of youthful hopes—certainly not by the "Jupiter Home Juice Extractor" that Hollander imagines in Orange. (With the Home Juice Extractor, Hollander hints that America's do-it-yourself homemadeness is ineluctably bound to its dependence on gadgetry.) After the bloody fall of Saturn that ends Red, Orange begins with the rising sun, a new god. But "the age of awakening" is cold and solid, hard cash rather than flowing. Jove showers down on Danae: and "the god of gold / . . . comes like coins thumbed into her / Slot: squish, chunk" (125). The eyes of the quester are here temporarily stunned by the turning of the divine into that supremely graspable matter, money. Here is Jove descending to his mortal beloved, or victim:

> Not with the juice of sunlight
> Streaming with magnificence does
> The crude chrysomorph enter her,
> But like light interred in the hard
> Shining that dazzles poor eyes with
> Mere models of the immortal.   (125)

13 Ibid., p. 81.

In these lines, "enter her" modulates to "interred": the erotically incarnated Jove shines with a glory that proves a "mere
model of the immortal." Hollander adroitly sums up a paganism proud of its endless, and endlessly enjoyable, comings of
the divine to earth, an ease of incarnation that generates a plu-
rality of myths, all of them current (like money). The pagan
transformation of god into gold, which is nothing if not
American, mocks the search for the menorah, the one true lost
object, true in its being lost. To refind it requires the following
of a Jewish piety, a resisting of graven images. The question of
Yellow, the poem's next section, is: Can this piety be sustained
in America? Can the search for the menorah be an American,
as well as a Jewish, project?

Yellow tries to locate the promised land, America the
golden, by subliming or refining the images of Orange. It proposes, not a rejection of America, but the meeting of America's
solid (and therefore vulgar) prosperity, history's fulfillment,
with the momentary cresting of imagination:

> To have been kept, to have reached this season,
> Is to have eternized, for a moment,
> The time when promise and fulfillment feed
> Upon each other, when the living gold
> Of sunlight struck from the amazing corn
> Seems one with its cold, unending token. . . .   (128)

Hollander images this sudden illumination, this seeming one-
ness of the corn (the gleaming wheat of Ruth, or of "America
the Beautiful") and the alien coin, as "Brightness rising and
getting on with things" (128): a kind of *echt* American practi-
cality and bustle.

As Yellow continues, Hollander replaces Orange's fable of
Jove and Danae with the story of a "man of earth" (Hollander's
Stevensian and Quixotelike quester, who will return in Blue as
"Pancho Manza, *homme de terre*") and "a girl of air":

> The man of earth exhales a girl of air,
> Of her light who lies beside him, gentle
> And bare, under the living shawl of all
> Her long hair, while her short below softly
> Touches his tired thigh with welcoming.
> It is that she is there. It is the pure

Return of everlastingness in her
Hands and the readiness of the sweet pear
In the touch of her mouth that fill the air
—Even the air within the circle of
His emptied arms—with light beyond seeming.   (128–29)

By this point, the poem's third section, we seem to have come far from the crucial project of *Spectral Emanations*, the search for the menorah. But this was less a straying than an exhaling, an emanating, the breath of a homecoming to America, which is now a place conceived as Stevens's "bare earth" (from "Evening Without Angels") and his pure air of imagination. Here we taste, not the blood fruit of a violent earth, the apple of Red, but the "sweet pear" that combines the ripe and ready with the purity of what one has dreamed up for oneself (rather than what has been supplied by the dazzling, glozing tempter). This is no fall into banality, no capitulation. Not solid gold but air, emptiness, the sight of disappearance, is the best evocation of a desire like that for the return of the menorah, as I will suggest in my conclusion. The return home, the palpable thereness of the wife one has exhaled, created for oneself, compensates for the lost sacred object. Hollander here reminds us that home, familial life, is the place of Jewish continuation, finding life in the honoring of the dead (thus the "living shawl" of the girl's hair). In this respect, "Even the air within the circle of / His emptied arms" suggests a squaring off against pagan disappointment: Aeneas' empty, futile hugging of his father Anchises in the underworld, reaching back for the ancestral source that will never be as substantive or authoritative as he wants. For a Jewish American poet like Hollander, though, missing the object (Jewish tradition, symbolized in the menorah) seems, at least for the moment, the same as finding it. This emptiness *is* substance, "fill[ing] the air . . . with light beyond seeming."

White Light: Divinity and Absence

L. Yarden's *The Tree of Light*, his study of menorah legends, reports that when the First Temple fell to Nebuchadnezzar's armies in the sixth century B.C.E., Nebuchadnezzar was fooled, given a mere replica of the sacred candlestick. Josephus writes that, after the fall of the Second Temple, the Jewish priests cleverly handed over to Titus several copies of the menorah, rather than the real thing. Finally, there are shadowy rumors that the menorah may have been hidden from the Romans in Constantinople.[14]

The more we learn from Yarden and others about the menorah, the more the object itself fades into a haunted series of facsimiles. The closest we can get to an original, in fact, is the image in relief on the Arch of Titus.

The absence of the original menorah seems to prove its authority: its very inaccessibility becomes a sign of its divine character. In the Zohar, the menorah is the infinite light of God, the *Ein-Sof*, that necessarily surpasses our ability to perceive it.

This presumption of divine inaccessibility divides Judaic tradition from its Near Eastern precursors. Yarden notes that the menorah seems to be derived from the Tree of Life, associated in Mesopotamian myth with the earthly paradise. But whereas a Mesopotamian divinity like Ishtar was palpably present in the Tree of Life, in Judaic tradition the lights of the menorah, offering an analogue to God's light, point to a divinity far beyond, rather than immanent to, our world.[15]

A fitting image for the Judaic idea that divine authority, though it has been inscribed throughout creation, is present only as an absence, an elsewhere (what the kabbalists call God's *zimzum*, or withdrawal), is Josephus' description of the inner sanctum of the Temple in Jerusalem. According to Josephus, the "innermost recess" of the Temple, the Holy of Holies, was guarded by a menorah and concealed by a veil from the outer portion of the sanctuary. "In this," Josephus writes, in the very center of the Temple, "stood nothing whatever: unapproachable, inviolable, invisible to all, it was called the Holy of Holy."[16]

The menorah, then, may be simply a decoy or protective sign, a shield before an emptiness, hiding the white light of truth at the center. So Hollander's colorful poem, too, stands in front of two nothings: the divine presence-as-absence at the heart of Judaism, as well as the resourceful bareness that forms the center of American poetic imagination. In Green, the

---

14 Yarden, *Tree*, pp. 4–7, and Bloom, "Hollander's," pp. 304–05.
15 Yarden, *Tree*, p. 39.
16 Cited in Ibid., p. 46.

color that follows Yellow, Hollander reaches the apex of his art, the inmost chamber. In this Stevensian pastoral "the birds and the bugs"

> chanted of nothing that was to be,
> Of nothing. In the unlost green they chanted on.   (131)

This stasis, the white noise or blank canvas of imagination, carries the reader into the light. And Hollander, in his amazing final section, Violet, brings this nothingness back home, offering the idea of a Jewish tradition that persists as sheer self-containment, a chanting that rises each morning, knowing its beginning and its end, and whose quest gives mere continuity the weight of Mosaic revelation:

> Like a star reflected
> In a cup of water,
>
> It will light up no path:
> Neither will it go out.
> .   .   .   .
> —A tree of light. A bush
> Unconsumed by its fire.   (153)

All page references in the text are to John Hollander's *Spectral Emanations*, in his *Selected Poetry* (New York: Knopf, 1993).

16

John Hollander's Game of Patience*

KENNETH GROSS

L'éternité n'est guerè plus longue que la vie.
                    RENÉ CHAR, *Feuillets d'Hypnos*

John Hollander's book-length poem *Reflections on Espionage* collects the deciphered texts of secret transmissions sent out over eight months of an unknown year by an agent code-named Cupcake. He worked, the volume's unnamed spy-editor tells us, "for an altogether inconvenient little republic that ceased to exist a good time ago." This agent sits at his transmitter, alone, mostly at night, sending news to other agents in his network, evaluating reports from spies in the field, ciphering and deciphering messages in known codes, even as he strains to discern hidden meanings in apparently random sounds or noise, in an idle glance or an idiosyncratic news item. There are various pressing but commonplace matters to keep track of: long-term surveillances, the luring of a double agent into a trap set by his ex-lover, or keeping tabs on a spy whose activities threaten operations as a whole. One watches how a lie floated in the world comes back to reveal a truth. Drops are proposed and missed, equipment breaks down, agents disappear. Cupcake at one point wonders about terminating another agent with a secret virus, but in general there is in this fiction little violence, no terrorism, no desperate flights, no secret and vicious interrogations. What we feel most strongly is rather the diurnal labor of spying, its peculiar tediums, its necessary patience. (Its patience is also a *passio*, something suffered, both a passion and, if we are to believe the etymologists, a penury.) The poem catches at the mixture of claustrophobia and delight that seem inseparable from the spy's business of attention, his disciplines of ear and eye; it studies the crafts and costs of secrecy, and

---

* This is a revised version of an article that first appeared in *Raritan: A Quarterly Review* 20.2 (Fall 2000), and is reprinted by permission of the editors.

the uses of what Keats called "negative capability." These compose what this poem calls "the work," something touched by a doubt whose sources are impossible to identify for certain.

Reflections on Espionage was first published as the entire contents of the November 1974 issue of *Poetry*. It came out as a book, somewhat enlarged, in 1976, and was reissued in 1999 by Yale University Press with some additional notes and a new introduction by the author. The poem offers, both plainly and not so plainly, what Edmund Spenser called "a continued Allegory, or darke conceit," a mirror game in which the work of the spy translates the work of the poet and the espionage network itself becomes a trope of poetic community. The quiet, almost breathless immediacy of the fiction—its open treatment of obliquity—and its eerie divagations break through in the second transmission, which reports the death of a fellow agent. Cupcake here addresses, as he does in much of the poem, an unnamed control officer, who himself reports to a spymaster named Lyrebird (a figure called upon directly at intervals in the poem, but who speaks only once):

> Steampump is gone. He died quietly in his
> Hotel room and his sleep. His cover people
> Attended to everything. What had to
> Be burned was burned. He taught me, as you surely
> Know, all that I know; yet I had to pass him
> By in the Square at evening—in the soft
> Light of wrought-iron lamps and the rich, cheerful
> Shadows which rose up from the stones to meet it—
> Without even our eyes having touched, without
> Acknowledgement. And thereby, of course, we were
> Working together. What kind of work is this
> For which if we were to touch in the darkness
> It would be without feeling the other there?
> It might help to know whether Steampump's dying
> Was part of the work or not. I shall not be
> Told, I know.

Part of the fascination here comes from a curious sense of what doesn't quite belong in a spy's official report: oblique questions; a bristling protest; a startling, almost cinematic image of animated shadows; a slight, curious quibble on "in" ("... in his / Hotel room and his sleep"); an unsettling surmise about the relation of death and work. The spy's private thoughts spill over into his reports here, which thus take the form of reports to himself; they suggest a kind of self-overhearing, where the poet's language slips the mooring of the framing fiction, yielding itself to other currents. The balancing act is by turns haunting and delicately comic. (Cupcake in his earnest stumbling can remind one of a clown such as Chaplin or Keaton.) We do not know how out of step the thoughts of this spy really are. Yet one may feel that his devotion to thinking thus about the work is also a kind of systematic undoing of what the work should be, especially in its conversational ease, its pressing intimacy. Cupcake's is a work that often troubles the work, even as it tries to keep faith with a certain way of coding and decoding the world, ciphering and deciphering experience. The turns of this book show us what we might call spy's dreamwork, the spy's pastoral, a sometimes occult repossession of the ordinary world under the guise of espionage. (What secrets are coded, this spy asks, in a change of evening light? in the patchwork patterns of the earth seen from a plane? in the words of a neon shop sign?) We see how the world is changed and vexed by such attentions. The wild inhabitation of the tropes of espionage and encipherment give us back the world more strangely. For one thing, such tropes acclimatize the poet to the weather of the world's lies. They also pry open the world's gifts, its odder voices, its eerier affections. At moments, the powers secreted in common objects and gestures flash forth; they are granted an intentionality at once invented by the perceiver and come upon by accident, as in this brief transmission to an agent codenamed Image:

> Your crocus has reported, its cups aflame.
> The two cats, if you take my meaning, are quite
> Perplexed—there are none of the usual leaves
> To nibble: one can almost believe they feel
> The dark power of all that early burning,
> The promises, albeit indoors, of earth.
> Fancy—the outcry of earth in a small pot
> Enciphered, in an apartment. *Il Grido*
> *Della Terra*—terrible return of spring—
> This will be the password for the coming weeks.

With delicate wit the tropes of espionage turn a domestic tableau into a more haunted, mythic, or interiorized encounter: a pot of flowers shows itself as a coded vehicle for archaic cries, sounds translated further under the guise of the title of an Italian newspaper—not the actual *Corriere della Sera*, the evening courier, but the fictive *Il Grido della Terra*, the cry of the earth.

What kind of work is this? A number of passages in the poem catch up a preoccupation we find in spy novels by Graham Greene, John Le Carré, or John Banville, a fascination with the spy's "dark secret love" of a work that contaminates him, betrays him. We glimpse what George Steiner calls "the cobweb, incessantly torn, incessantly repaired, that knits in a common intimacy of mistrust all agents." (A piece of prophetic luck is that Cupcake's cover life is that of an art historian and museum curator; the poem's composition predates by some years the public revelations of Anthony Blunt's espionage work for the Soviet Union.) Yet this is, overall, a different sort of fiction, one that appropriates the conventions of spy novels for its own uses.[1] What one feels in this poem is not so much the spy gone bad as the spy gone slightly mad. It is a spy almost too drawn to the work, finding in it an eros, a vehicle of revelation, a space of play and question, that might to any conventional spy seem something of a mystery, even an embarassment or betrayal, since it strains at the syntax and tradecraft of secrecy in such strange ways, draws out frights and lights beyond the ends of spying. Cupcake is in his own way, for all his knowing, a kind of innocent, a mystery to himself as well as to others. The spy-editor comments in his notes: "Cupcake's

1 William Flesch, "Playing Patience: John Hollander's *Reflections on Espionage*," *Southwest Review* 86. 2 & 3 (2001): 228–45, subtly investigates the poet's way of extending the self-referential literarity built into more explicit spy stories, such as those of Le Carré. That the poem speaks truths about the actual world of spies seems to have been the judgement of the scholar Norman Holmes Pearson, a man deeply involved in OSS during World War II, and Hollander's colleague at Yale in 1976, who sent the poem to a number of his former colleagues in the intelligence community. (See Robin Winks, *Cloak and Gown: Scholars in the Secret War, 1939–61* [New York: Morrow, 1987], 248–50.) Hollander in his introduction recalls an appreciative message from James Jesus Angleton, to whom the poet sent his book on Angleton's retirement as director of the CIA. Angleton himself was famous for insisting that agents-in-training study William Empson's *Seven Types of Ambiguity*—though this master-spy's own obsessive and paranoid certainties got the better of him in the end.

obsessions with encipherment, and, later on, with night surveillance, seem to emanate from a common source in the
agent's perplexing psyche."

What sort of fiction is this? The various sections of the
poem, each headed by indications of the day and month of
transmission, compose an epistolary novel of sorts. They also
constitute a fictive diary, in which even those messages sent to
other agents are tacitly addressed to the writer himself (with
shadows of a Gogolian "diary of a madman.") Cupcake's story-
telling has elements of Wordsworthian poetic autobiography as
well; it suggests that this is "a poem about the growth of the
spy's mind," weaving together various memories and "spots of
time" in order to identify the nature of a peculiar gift, a way of
seeing the world, considering how this endowment may be
tested, lost, or recovered. So (for example) we hear about how
as a child Cupcake devised wildly impossible geometries to
explain the shrinking of the moon at its zenith; about the startling moment when he received his codename, "invisibly wres-
tling / With my recruiter by the river on an / April evening";
or about a time when he mistook the garden of an insane asy-
lum for an ordinary city park. In another way, the poem recalls
the mythologizing of vocation we find in Milton's "Il Penseroso," where the speaker imagines himself as a brooding seer or
magus who sits alone at night in his watchtower (*specula*),
studying the stars and calling down spirits from another sphere,
or who walks unseen in the shadowy woods, listening to the
sounds of world, spelling the hidden secrets of earth, water,
and air, asking for a mysterious dream to fall upon his eyes as
he sleeps.

The association of the business of codes and encipherment
with divination and forbidden magic is an ancient one. In
Hollander's poem, however, such a romance of the self as Milton sketches has become sparer, more disenchanted, less certain
as well as at times more grimly humoristic. This *penseroso*'s work
entails a less secure solitude, a secrecy that exposes as much as it
protects him; it conjures a darker fear of loss, an unraveling of
self that tracks the unraveling of its messages. Cupcake's situation is closer to that of the baffled, anxious storytellers in Kafka
or Borges. The work, we find, inhabits a discipline whose rules
seem more and more elusive, whose relation to ordinary life is
always in question. Thus, for example, though Cupcake desires

urgently to ask Lyrebird about his contribution to the larger business of espionage, and about how he is trusted by those above him, he yet knows that "heading the list of / Forbidden Questions is 'What are the contents / of the list itself?'" The work catches Cupcake up in a relentless self-consciousness about the work: "Surveillance continues, and surveillance of / The surveillance." The uncanny quality of this attachment (in which the work is always an instance of itself) comes through in a saying of Rabbi Tarphon about the burden of Biblical and Talmudic interpretation (from the *Pirke Aboth*) that Cupcake echoes twice in the poem: It is not required that you complete the work, neither are you free to abandon it.

The solitude of the work is inescapable. Yet one gift of this allegory is its picture of the hidden ties that link poets together. As the lines about Steampump indicate, the fiction of a spy network provides a way of describing certain urgent but tacit bonds, modes of silent collaboration, also certain forms of praise and blame, such as no ordinary literary history or manifesto, no gossip of schools or movements, could provide; it offers a stranger, more labile trope for whatever we call a poetic tradition, a creative community, or visionary company, illuminating the complex webs of love, need, memory, and work that create these things and the subtle betrayals that threaten them. Part of the fascination lies in the names Hollander has given his agents, variously like those of familiar spirits, Spenserian personifications, and characters from a story by Charles Dickens or Edward Gorey: Riddle, Steampump, Gland, Image, Ember, Prettyboy, Tallman, Lac, Lake, Puritan, Grusha, Felucca, The Foot.[2] Some of these agents are purely ideal or fictive. The agent called The Foot, for instance, on whom Cupcake maintains a frustrating, inconclusive surveillance, is a lovely joke about the meter of *Reflections*: the poem employs as its regular

2 Hollander notes that he was spurred most sharply by the strange and playful codenames of real British agents mentioned in John Masterman's *The Double-Cross System in the War of 1939 to 1945* (New Haven: Yale University Press, 1972), an account of the turning of German agents during WWII by members of the British counter-intelligence. The list of codenames includes Snow, Biscuit, Tricycle, Rainbow, Freak, Father, Gelatine, Artist, Lipstick, Careless, Treasure, Shepherd, Meteor, Garbo, Dragonfly, Beetle, Cobweb, Nettle, Zigzag, Hamlet, and Puppet.

measure, or "cipher," a line of eleven syllables with no fixed pattern of stress, in which ghosts of more traditional metrical feet, especially the iambic, come and go in irregular fashion. But other codenames apply to actual poets, living and dead, the labels being generated by often homely puns, anagrams, or allusions: Steampump is W. H. Auden, in honor of his child hood love of mining machinery; Ember is John Ashbery, Kilo Ezra Pound; Image is James, or Jimmy, Merrill; Lac is Robert, or Cal (short for Caligula), Lowell, his name linking him implicitly to Lake, Elizabeth Bishop, whose codename plays on alter-egos the poet assumed in her own fiction.

One does not, however, find a systematic roman à clef here. In his new notes to the 1999 reissue of the poem, in fact, Hollander blunts any too literalistic a hunger to solve the mystery of the agents's names by making plain identities left undisclosed in the poem's first edition. There are, clearly, occasions when Cupcake's reports do frame a pointedly topical commentary; the fictive language of spying indeed makes possible some very nuanced critical discriminations. Cupcake broods over the dark case of Moroz (Robert Frost), for example, considering "the terrors that felled all his / Family, the nearly saintly ruthlessness / He lived his cover with," but also his strange strategy of "putting it out that he was low-grade / Personnel for the other side," a comment on Frost's way of concealing his darker authorial face behind the popular mask of the good, grey poet. The spy also tracks Lac's growing betrayal of the custom and craft of secrecy, an expression of the poet's doubts about the claims of confessional poetry. (Lac seems eventually to join the company of other literalists, including the avatars of "Project White"—the chief representatives of a "them" as opposed to an "us" in Hollander's fiction.) Cupcake praises Ember's recent work as "an illumination of the ordinary," and marvels at Image's "unfinished report" on Project Alphabet, a covert reference to "The Book of Ephraim" (also published in 1976), the first part of Merrill's *The Changing Light at Sandover*, whose twenty-six sections each begin with letters from *a* to *z*. But such adjudications serve mostly to set up a more strictly parabolic account of the work. Some sections speculate on the moral etiquette of spying, as when Cupcake broods on the perennial trials of balancing the demands of one's espionage work and one's cover life, the ways they rhyme or fall apart, how they can infect or betray one another. Other passages use the trope of the espionage network to frame more urgently private fears, as when Cupcake reports a dream in which he feels placed under accusation by fellow agents, including Gland (Adrienne Rich), Prettyboy (W. S. Merwin), and Pike (Anthony Hecht), not knowing when he wakes if, in the dream, it was he or they who had belonged to the realm of the dead.

The messages to Image do an especially remarkable kind of work. These most affectionate of transmissions confront the spy as a creature by turns specular, spectral, skeptical, and despicable. They dwell with particular emphasis on the pleasures and trials of ciphering itself, the part it plays in the world, how it knows the world, what it discovers. Cupcake recalls the curious delight that, as a child, he found even in simple codes, and his discovery that particular codes themselves seem to dictate the secrets they encipher. He meditates on what names, common or coded, dissimulate and reveal. He broods over the difficulty of encoding truth rather than mere fact, even as he fantasizes about the possibility of a code which, by nature, would be unable to conceal lies, errors, or merely official truths. With increasingly speculative verve, Cupcake speaks to Image of the dream of a cipher "beyond the range of / All our contingent codings," a code without any plain text embedded in it, a cipher in which the "letter itself was all the spirit that / Was, where there was no need for withdrawals / Into the dark of trope." What would it mean, he wonders, to come upon a Final Cipher, a code almost invisible, effortless to handle yet "impossible To misuse," a cipher that yielded "a poem whose form was of the world itself"? These transmissions to Image are, Cupcake acknowledges, unauthorized by Lyrebird (he hopes unknown), as if such thoughts about ciphering belonged to a domain of questions that is taboo, questions too secretive, too volatile perhaps, even for those in charge of Cupcake's own network to consider seriously. It is almost as if he belonged simultaneously to two or more different networks, though he never seems to feel himself a double agent. In their parabolic scope, the transmissions to Image are peculiarly important among the many luminous discussions of the ethical demands and creative force of poetic form that Hollander has given us over many years. For they show us with real immediacy how the poet's preoccupation with form catches up an Emersonian and Stevensian inheritance, a fascination with supreme fictions, with visions of a self's transparency to itself and the world, all the more powerful for the fragility of the surmises which undergird them. (Prosody as a secret war of the mind against the sky!) A more oblique gift of these sections is that the texts addressed to Image, framed by the more drily mysterious trope of coded messages from spy to spy, invite us to reimagine in different terms the fiction of occult communication that Merrill himself explores in *The Changing Light at Sandover*, with its vast gathering of Ouija-board transmissions from the ancient dead, from deceased friends and fellow-poets, and from an increasingly complex cosmos of demonic messengers, angels, gods, and elemental spirits. For Merrill's fiction too seeks to decipher hidden orders of knowledge and ignorance, to expose the otherwise unrevealed controls, protocols, and powers that shape our lives or our poems; it likewise seeks to present alternative measures of failure and success, absorbing our life to something larger than itself, a mirror world that is yet our own world. The spirit Ephraim says, as Cupcake might, "WE ARE IN A SYSTEM OF SUCH SILENT BUT URGENT MOTIVES   U & I WITH OUR QUICK FIRELIT MESSAGES STEALING THE GAME ARE SMUGGLERS & SO IN A SENSE UNLAWFUL."

Paired with the messages to Image are a group of transmissions addressed to Grusha (Richard Poirier). These show us, in the poem's terms, not so much Cupcake's poetics as his hermeneutics, a discourse on the work of reading and how it changes one's relation both to the object of study and to oneself. He again speaks of the strange pleasures of the mere surveillance: the sitting still, the habitation of darkness and silence, the discriminations of surprise. He also catalogs its sources of error, for example, concentrating too much on one's object, taking the shadow or glint of a lens for the thing one observes, or misconstruing its meaning by an unguarded hypothesis. To Grusha Cupcake recounts a wonderful representative anecdote about a minor agent who, overhearing madly various music from a piano in an apartment above his place of watching, hypothesizes a monster of virtuosity inhabiting what turns out to be just a place where many different people rehearse. (Breaking into the room to test his surmise costs the agent his job.) The sense that Cupcake himself often stumbles into such errors, indeed that they can constitute a strange sort of gift, only makes his wisdom the more pressing.

The mystery of the text remains what happens to Cupcake. There is no single intrigue structuring this poem, no McGuffin, as may be evident; rather it unfolds as a loose fabric of reports, responses, and reveries. Toward the end of the book, however, one feels a deeper sense of anxiety, even of menace, gathering upon the spy. This agent's sad, reflective doubts acquire a sharper edge; they convey a fear that he is not trusted, that plots are perhaps set against him, that he is being felt out by the other side as a possible double agent, even that he is being tracked and taunted by members of his own network. An undecipherable transmission caught from the air late at night, "ET GLPKX ET VDI VXNT," thickens the atmosphere of blank uncertainty. Even the news that Lyrebird is sending him a gift carries an abusive edge: the work, if it is being done properly, should go on without acknowledgement. The gift turns out to be a jigsaw puzzle. Fitted together incompletely and quickly abandoned, it pictures a "great / Bland frog" sitting "upon a violet / Lilypad" in a swamp, "his bulging plain text a rebuke to all my / Daily twilight messages." (This section, Hollander tells us in his introduction, was the very first part of the poem to emerge, almost a year before the rest; it here becomes the poem's dark telos.) Cupcake's very last transmission changes suddenly from an eleven- to a thirteen-syllable cipher, "sent out on all frequencies," in which his own voice dissolves into unindividuated noise, noise coded—if that is the right way to put it—by a shrinking series of letters, like the opaque cry of Philomel:

> ... Breath
> Enwraps no messages, but of its aeromancy
> There are no end of forms which, enciphered in twilight,
> Are decoded in the blue morning air. The outside
> Wind is an agency of breath. The low fire inside
> Is an agency of rhyming death. Where is my breath?
> *Eeeee* wheezes the respiring wind despairingly, *Eeee!*

The last message of the poem, sent by "Lyrebird, on all frequencies," reads "XXXXXXXXXXXXXXXXXX." What might seem a further coding of meaninglessness—if not a row of epistolary kisses—turns out to be a cipher key for decoding the Greek-or Latin-sounding nonsense quoted above. Using a standard Vigenère table supplied in the notes, the reader can decipher a general order to agents in the network: "Terminate Cupcake."

The death of poets haunts this poem. There are, to begin with, the actual deaths of Auden, Frost, and Pound. Cupcake himself sees the work as inevitably involved with death, hemmed around by dark decorums, by necessary absences and terrible solitudes, by the betrayals of other agents and pseudo-agents, by doubts about the work itself. Describing a plane flight when he sat playing solitaire, the spy remarks with sudden certainty: "Playing patience is always playing patience / With death, opponent and partner both" (Hollander's version of the chess game in *The Seventh Seal*). For the writing poet, one form of death may be the desolation of the literal, the croaking of that puzzled frog, a blank noise, a shape of desire or experience untranslatable by any cipher. Or it may be that Cupcake finally understands himself as simply one of the many forms "enciphered in twilight" and "decoded" at morning, a vanishing dream, a Borgesian author who suddenly knows himself as a fiction. But that the order to terminate so wan and affecting a mask arises from within the spy network, from a control whose name evokes an Orphic or Miltonic muse, raises stranger questions, pointing to a darker fear at the heart of the work. If the work fails Cupcake, one gets a sense that, in some way, Cupcake fails the work. There is a death in that, a sense that there is a certain part of the work of which Cupcake himself is not capable, and that moreoever his termination is necessary if the work itself is to go on, is not to die.

Hollander tells us that he began the poem in order to write at a time when he did not know how to go on writing, thinking that if Cupcake could send off daily messages "on pain of death or disclosure," something might come of it. What comes of this gamble is an ever more exquisite sense of Cupcake's own malaise, a way of discovering (and inventing) the forms of death and disclosure that encroach on the fictive agent. I have no single answer to what is at stake here, what is most mortally in question in Hollander's parable. But I am struck in thinking about this matter by a particular topical reference in the allegory. One of Cupcake's sharpest occasions for sadness lies in the knowledge that he has failed to complete a major espionage project, codenamed Lamplight, mentioned early in the book but never described in any detail. If he cannot abandon this work, Cupcake writes with sad deference, nevertheless "project Lamplight must abandon me," must be left for other agents to complete. The poet's new notes confirm what was, for many readers, clear enough in 1978, when Hollander published *Spectral Emanations: New and Selected Poems.* Project Lamplight is *Spectral Emanations*, a long sequence of seven lyrics followed by seven prose sections, each devoted to a color of the spectrum—red, orange, yellow, green, blue, indigo, violet— each in turn representing a branch of the lost golden menorah from the Second Temple in Jerusalem. The sequence even contains an extended narrative, "Leaves from a Roman Journal," which sketches out a secret plot to recover the vanished lamp from the waters of the Tiber. (In some ancient histories, the menorah was carried to Rome as spoil when the imperial armies conquered Jerusalem; placed on the Milvian bridge, it was said to have fallen into the river during a battle in the time of Constantine.) These two long poems were in fact evolving at the same time (from 1973 to 1976, though the earliest fragment of *Reflections* was written in 1972), and I would suggest that *Reflections on Espionage* speaks obliquely about a crisis in the evolution of *Spectral Emanations*, not so much a literal blockage as a growing sense that some part of this poet other than Cupcake must write the poem.

If the failure to get on with *Spectral Emanations* is so dark a thing, it is because the poem represents so crucial a threshold in the poet's career. One can see a decidedly visionary or mythopoetic strain in Hollander's earlier work, otherwise so celebrated for its wit and formal mastery. The poems are dense with flickering aspects and absences, in which eye and ear are surprised by the gifts of phenomena, gifts which also reflect the mind remembering and turning on itself (also words, sound, and syntax turning on themselves, wresting a subtly surrealistic idiom even from the minute particulars of grammar). The poetry often stands at a genuinely mysterious threshold beween the emblematic and the phenomenological. It is a poetry in which the objects of perception suddenly emerge as volatile, half-allegorical signs, creatures of fable. Just as strikingly, things seen or heard become pictures of attention, as if they provided new eyes and ears, new forms from within which we might see and hear and desire. This poetry finds its radiances acutest at their vanishing, its most precious lusters recovered from fading light and infolded shadow; these apprehensions—often tropes of losses more harrowing—spark a dream of presences below the surface of what is seen or heard, nightmarish at moments, but sustaining. I am thinking of those three elusive, recollected pools in Central Park that are the subject of the final poem of *Visions from the Ramble* (1965); of the strange transformations of outline, word, and figure in *Types of Shape* (1969); and especially of the erotically-charged parables of sleep and awakening that compose the wonderful dream-quest of *The Head of the Bed,* a sequence published first as a chapbook in 1973:

> Half his days he had passed in the shadow
> Of the earth: not the cold, grassy shade cast
> By a pale of cypresses, by pines spread
>
> More softly across stony hilltops; not
> Warm, gray veiling of sunlight that blotted
> Up his own moving shadow on the ground;
>
> But the dark cloak of substance beyond mass,
> Though heavy, flung with diurnal panache
> Over his heavier head, weighed it down.
>
> Way down at the bottom of a shaft sunk
> Through the grass of sleep to deep stone he lay,
> Draped in the shade cast inward by the place
>
> All outward shadows fall upon, and on
> His tongue an emerald glittered, unseen,
> A green stone colder in the mouth than glass.

Even given this body of prior work, however, the vast structurings of *Spectral Emanations* speak of a commitment to visionary and a mythopoetic mode of a different order. No previous work of the poet so directly claims a place in a tradition of visionary quest romance in English that runs from Spenser to Hart Crane. None shows the poet making so extreme, so unsettling a commitment to his own virtuosity. Also, more decidedly than earlier work, this poem claims a place for the poet within the tradition of Jewish poetry in America, reinvents that tradition itself (succeeding, as Harold

Bloom writes, "in being American by being Judaistic, and vice versa"). This is palpable in its explorations of the nostalgia for prophecy, the bent and failure of prophecy, and in its complex, often darkly ironic refigurings of Jewish scripture, rabbinic commentary, and liturgical symbolism, playing in particular on the tradition of mystical interpretations of the lamp itself.[3] The poem confronts and gives voice to the dead more urgently than is possible within the fictive frame of *Reflections.*

If this long sequence fulfills certain ancient impulses in the poet, however, it also entails a relinquishment, even a sacrifice. Here I can only offer a conjecture of my own, at best a half-truth, about the crisis of vocation I spoke of earlier. *Reflections on Espionage* opens with an elegy for the death of the master-spy Steampump, W. H. Auden. This is itself a way of making the death of Steampump a part of the work, as Cupcake surmises it may be (though it is not clear that he *wants* it to be). Yet the poem as a whole is a farewell to Auden. Not only the elegy for Steampump but the termination of Cupcake negotiates the poet's relinquishment of a form of the work that he might associate with Auden's own poetics, and that had been, in part, his own. In moving from reflections to emanations, so to speak, the poet of moral wit and decorum and riddle must be transfigured. The philosophical humor and fluency of craft remain, yet it is as if, in *Spectral Emanations*, the poet stripped himself of his covers, assuming a voice at once more occult and more naked than that available to Cupcake, who is distinctly uneasy with bardic postures. I find myself wondering, in fact, if it was the complex, unresolved nature of the conflict of vocation mapped out in *Reflections* that kept the poet from including any excerpts of this poem within the larger volume of *Spectral Emanations*, the first published selection of his earlier work, gathering texts from *A Crackling of Thorns* (1953) through *Tales Told of the Fathers* (1975), tracing a poetic career of which "Spectral Emanations" becomes the climax and new beginning. One further hint at how the poems are connected might be found in a curious fact that the poet notes in his introduc-

3 Harold Bloom discusses the poem's dense network of allusions to Jewish mystical tradition in "John Hollander's *Spectral Emanations*: The Menorah as the White Light of Trope," in *Agon: Towards a Theory of Revisionism* (New York: Oxford University Press, 1982), 289–317.

tion to the reissue of *Reflections*: that Auden's death coincided closely with the start of the Yom Kippur war in 1973. It is this war which is commemorated in the very first poem of *Spectral Emanations*, "Red," a more violent sort of elegy than that which marks the death of Steampump.

Spectral Emanations makes of each color of the spectrum an ad hoc but necessary myth of seeing, a way of taking in experience, a way of listening to, questioning, inscribing, enciphering, and remembering the world; blue, green, red—each becomes a gift, a type of weather, a form of relation, a mode of temporality, a dream. In the poem's spectroscope, each color becomes not so much a natural thing as a creature or golem the poet himself must make. Each is, in its own way, a small apocalypse; each is also a habitation, a region of questing whose true and false identities, whose purities and impurities, are probed with marvellous complexity—examining, for example, the orange or false gold of commerce; the fragile first light of yellow; a green which is neither of envy, nor hope, nor untried youth, but merely of earth; a blue of sea and sky and desire. The allusive architecture of the poem—at once temple and labyrinth, in Angus Fletcher's terms—is astonishing. Just as important is a Jamesian perfume of discernment, a subtle anatomy not just of individual colors but of the stories that inhere in the imaginary thresholds (passes and impasses, bridges and abysses) between colors. We are always at the edge of things. The poem studies what occurs as the quester must shift from dead yellow gold to golden yellow, the places where yellow ripens directly into blue, or regresses to red; it considers how an earthly green may hedge about or "enisle" blue wisdom; it fictionalizes what happens when "indigo," which once marked the way from blue to violet and held the two colors in dense relation, becomes a vanished presence, a name we scarcely know. Figurations of black and white, muddiness and transparency, attend them all, including "the patience of the deep that black has when green ends."

There are passages of heartbreaking candor and dreamlike play in *Reflections on Espionage*. Cupcake is himself one of Hollander's subtlest and most moving figures of poetic vocation, of its complex patience. But nothing in this poem matches the moral ferocity of "Red," with its picture of an Israeli soldier called "J" like a strange recollection of the frustrated prophet

Jonah under the shadow of his gourd tree, "inhaling the fire of /
White air," dreaming of a heroic and sacred past, even as he
becomes the victim of a blood-red present, assaulted by a
worm of fire and false prophecy that devours its own children.
Haunting as the nocturnal listenings of Cupcake can be, they
do not have the delicate authority and incandescence one feels
in these stanzas from "Violet":

> Here in the pale tan of
> The yet ungathered grain
> There may be time to chant
>
> The epic of whispers
> In the light of a last
> Candle that may be made
>
> To outlast its waning
> Wax, a frail flame shaking
> In a simulachrum
>
> Of respiration. Oh,
> We shall carry it set
> Down inside a pitcher
>
> Out into the field, late
> Wonderers errant in
> Among the rich flowers.
>
> Like a star reflected
> In a cup of water,
> It will light up no path:
>
> Neither will it go out.

This is the poet's answer to the myth of return which spurs the
war in "Red," offering in its place a more fragile, less murder-
ously delusional undoing of the diaspora. Here "late wanderers"
in history and tradition find no promised Zion but become, in
uncertain compensation, "late wonderers"—a characteristic
Hollanderian play on words. A note explains that the image of
the candle in a pitcher derives from a story of Cecil Roth's
about villagers in northern Portugal, obviously descendents of
Marranos, who "were still lighting candles in pitchers on Friday nights, a mere half-century ago, without knowing why
they did so save that it was an old family custom"—an image
of secret survival, and of the survival *of* secrecy, in which a

devotion to form is as crucial as any explicit knowledge of its meaning.

There is throughout this sequence a stark, candid embrace of the unseen that goes beyond what is comprehended by the fictions of espionage, however subtly elaborated. The spy named Cupake can instruct and surprise and touch and haunt; he does not seek, in his terrible dischantment, to hallow, as Hollander does in the closing lines of *Spectral Emanations*:

He remembers this, and thinks not to quest among the regions of black for what lies beyond violet,

But would stay to hum his hymn of the hedges, where truth is one letter away from death, and will ever so be emended.

Blessed be he who has crushed the olive for oil.

Blessed be he who has cracked the oil for light.

Blessed be he who has buried the light for the three tones beyond.

In which, when we have been stamped out and burned not to lie in the ashes of our dust, it will be to grow.

The poem makes, or tries to become, a golem such as that which in one Kabbalistic legend mars the very Hebrew inscription that brings it to life, cutting out the letter *aleph* from the word *emet*, truth, making it into *met*, death. The poet converts such an emending into an occasion for a stranger ongoing song. (Hollander is one of our chief poets of the startling springs of song.)

The ambition and risk, the trust in the work, the daemonic virtuosity visible in *Spectral Emanations*, all these open up much in the poetry that follows. One feels this, for example, in *Powers of Thirteen* (1983)—a sequence of thirteen times thirteen sonnets of thirteen lines with thirteen syllables each—especially in the preternatural intimacy with which the "I" of these poems evokes its fictive "you," a more capacious and more trustworthy muse than Lyrebird. In this sequence, being in the world and being on the page each become a modality of the other. The allusive density of *Spectral Emanations*, as well as its myths of sound and light (of "a light in sound, a sound-like power in light," in Coleridge's words), also emerge startlingly in "Kinneret" (1986). The title of this poem is the Hebrew name for the sea of Galilee and means, etymologically, "harp" (whence the title of the larger volume in which the poem appears, *Harp Lake* [1988]). "Kinneret" gives us a vision of this inland sea as itself an instrument, a site of song, song struck from water, from spaces of reflection and doubleness—something figured most directly in the poem's use of a Malaysian stanza form called the *pantun*, a cross-rhymed iambic pentameter quatrain in which the first two lines must speak to the second two only indirectly, by echo or allusion, negotiating always an abyss of reference. Like Thoreau's pond, this lake becomes the image of a self, a mind, an eye, a gathering place of loss and possibility; it is a trope that keeps marking and testing the thresholds between sea and land, surface and depth, figure and ground, rest and motion, seen and unseen, dream and waking, now and then, showing us how each calls to the other, and transforms its partner:

> A kingfisher flashed by them on their lee
> To lead their thoughts toward a blue yet once more.
> My tears blur world and water and I see
> Each seed of flickering lake, each drop of shore.
> . . . .
> Down in undreaming deeps the heavy carp
> Fed, while above the shining surface trembled.
> Was it my voice that spoke for the bright harp?
> Or was it a heart the singing lake resembled?

"Kinneret" indeed risks appropriating for its disenchanted, private tropes of poetic work the Gospel miracles of walking on water, giving sight to the blind, and resurrecting the dead.

I do not want to oversimplify or literalize the breach in Hollander's developing oeuvre. The poet himself suggests that Cupcake's voice opened up the playful narrative twists of "Leaves from a Roman Journal," and also lent its cadences to the lyric diary unfolded in *Powers of Thirteen*. Most crucial, perhaps, is what *Reflections on Espionage* tells us about Hollander's longstanding, unsettling preoccupation with fictions of poetic failure, fictions of loss and belatedness, visions of the vanishing of vision. This preoccupation—so central to poets after Coleridge and Wordsworth—involves him throughout his career in probing ever more equivocal continuities in the tradition of poetic work and the forms of poetic memory, how texts hide or come to light in our minds. It also involves an ever more ruthless anatomizing of the ways in which once vivid tropic gestures can freeze or waste or collapse into the domain of the literal, the falsely "general," the realm of common rumor and lie. He studies how we inhabit such literalisms, how we take them upon ourselves or impose them on others. This means probing what the poet once spoke of as the vicious parody of adulthood in contemporary America, the result of our "putting away the wrong childish things." Hollander studies the impasses of vision, yet also what those impasses reveal, what they make possible. We thus sense in *Reflections on Espionage*, as always in Hollander's work, how it is that things which might appear epiphenomenal or secondary—our echoes and murmurs, our wavering shadows, the fading ripples we make in air and water— promise a restitution of our selves and our neglected or abandoned powers.

Still, even in thinking about what Cupcake's story contributes to a poetics or mythopoesis of failure, it is telling to put his transmissions beside, say, the 144 *Rubaiyat* stanzas composing "The Tesserae," a work very much about the poetry and wisdom of final things, the shapes of our doubt, about what it means to contemplate the moment of our death and our absence from the world, and with it the collapse of any wisdom we acquire in that contemplation. One task of the poem is to subject the consolations of memory, nature, sex, eloquence, speculation, and skepticism to strange and relentless mockery; here even the beloved forms of moonlight are troped as poison poured into the ear. This is a poem which, as my friend Herbert Marks wrote to me after its publication in 1993, "continues stanza by stanza to fall flat with ever greater virtuosity, intelligence, irony, accuracy of tone, with a kind of masochistic Schadenfreude that by dint of extension becomes something solemn and almost archaic." Falling flat is, as it were, the work of poetry in "The Tesserae," even the sign of a secret community (a *tessera* being, among other things, a broken tile by which members of an hermetic sect could recognize each other). The poem translates Edward Fitzgerald's wanly skeptical, strangely reassuring cadences into a *Totentanz*, as if the very stanza form, with its *aaba* rhyme scheme, served best as tool to flatten the ways of irony itself, its reassuring falls, its deadly mordancy, its clippings, closures, clicks, clunks, catches, cracks, and quips, its can'ts and canting, even as the poem commits itself to ever finer articulations (or cantillations) of doubt and knowledge: "The dark point of this nocturne's both what I / Believe I see and what I know I know." The work here tests itself against the stony disenchantments and knowing solitudes of Ludwig Wittgenstein and Paul Celan. The mastery in this fiction of failure again seems of a different order from Cupcake's—not higher, that's not the right word, rather, more unconcealed, more naked, more present to its own pain, compulsion, delusion, and sense of loss. It inhabits a darker game of patience:

> The Word that now I've come to die: Made clear
> To light eye or to heavy, darker ear?
>   Lying at night in terror of it I
> Defy deaf eye. And yet if ear, I fear.
>   . . . .
>
> The reaping whirlwind sows its rows of night
> Thoughts yet, archaic, innocent and trite
>   Fears of the age of human all too human
> Nature, twisting, capricious in its might.
>
> Mild wind in late, light blossoms cannot stem
> That fevered pulse of this offbeat mayhem,
>   Hard crows in caucus here, as if mid-spring
> Had never come to soften even them.
>   . . . .
>
> Thought brings me to the barely-wakened brink
> Of this still pool. My eyes will only drink
>   Of mirroring, my fear not being that
> I think I dream, but that I dream I think.

The lessons of *Reflections on Espionage* remain powerful, animating. They are all the more available to us now given the fading of merely topical interest in the poem's nameplay. No doubt after the end of the cold war the poem's more private appropriations of the fictions of espionage can take on greater resonance. Cupcake is, if mortal, then hard to forget, and the work he inhabits continues and is ever more necessary. The poem is a treasure. One treasures it for Cupcake's wisdom about the work, and for the window it gives us into the unfolding story of Hollander's body of poetry, in which it constitutes, if not a major poem, then a major minor poem, a text one cannot do without. One treasures it for its reinvention of the idea of secrecy. And one treasures it for its haunting, all-but-unique way of fictionalizing a poetic community—an altogether inconvenient little republic with an alarming memory—of whose civil conversations the poem is a metaphysical courtesy manual, an elegy and song of praise.

17

Self-Knowledge and Self-Deception

DAVID BROMWICH

John Hollander said once in praise of W. H. Auden that he had an ear that was like a moral sense. Of course, nothing could ever *be* a moral sense, not even moral judgment is, but if you have to pick a bodily organ to make the metaphor, the ear is a provocative choice. All the more so in view of Lord Shaftesbury's original epigram, which specifies a different location: "Shou'd One, who had the Countenance of a Gentleman, ask me, 'Why I wou'd avoid being *nasty*, when nobody was present.' In the first place I shou'd be fully satisfy'd that he himself was a very nasty Gentleman who cou'd ask this Question; and that it wou'd be a hard matter for me to make him ever conceive what *true Cleanliness* was. However, I might, notwithstanding this, be contented to give him a slight Answer, and say, ''Twas because I had a Nose.'" Compared to such simplicity of command, the moral ear is subtle, almost secretive—a double agent in the field of aesthetic experience. It has been said that poets in their elegies are often mourning for themselves. We don't notice as easily how poets in their compliments are often describing themselves—or themselves under ideal conditions. Nor is this an instance merely of wishful projection. To declare to others and even, much of the time, to ourselves what we would be known as, is so difficult a task that all but the best and worst eventually have to resort to code.

Hollander seems to me a poet whose ear is sometimes like a moral sense. But to catch the way this works, one has to understand "moral" in close relation to mores and in relation to manners or "small morals." These ideas are affiliated with morale—the poise by which a character seems unexchangeably to accept a style that suits it. Morale is the portrait painter's greatest subject; and the poems I will speak of all have an element of portrait-painting.

One of Hollander's most generous and fully realized earlier poems is "Helicon"—but first a word about its title. Helicon was the mountain in Boetia from which sprang the fountains of the muses, and the characters in the poem are the young Hollander and Allen Ginsberg, "in their unguessing days," when they were students at Columbia, both aspiring poets but neither of them yet known for the work that would make them imaginatively distinct. The action of the poem is a fraternal adventure, a trip to Saint Luke's Hospital to donate blood; and an allegorical conceit is lightly hung on this journey—the unasked giving of blood seeming the analogue and inverse of the gift by the muses of an inspiration that can't be taken on board in number, weight, and measure. Just above the surface of the plot is the poet's memory (sketched in some lines I omit) of a practical joke he once played at the university's public fountains: filling them with powdered detergent and concentrated essence of grape, to counterfeit a scene of religious miracle-making—the only thing in nature as strange, if it *is* in nature, as the inspiration given by the muses.

A last bit of context is relevant to the tone and shading of the poem, which together make such an exuberant and delicate achievement. Hollander and Ginsberg had been close friends. It wouldn't be true to say that either was the ascendant mind, but Ginsberg was a very different figure then from the celebrity who emerged in the late fifties and sixties; and of the two he seems to have been the more consciously advanced: the poems he was writing around that time have been published under the title *The Gates of Wrath*—their style is a blend of Marvell, Blake, and Hart Crane. "Helicon" looks back a decade and a half to an early moment of this friendship. In the years that intervened Ginsberg had published *Howl*, and Hollander had reviewed it with dismissive confidence and scorn, the abrupt and unqualified manner of one making sure not to sound as if he ever could have been the author's friend. I've heard John Hollander speak of Allen Ginsberg, critically and affectionately, but he never mentioned that review and has never chosen to reprint it; and I suspect in some part of himself, looking back, he thought the review misjudged. We find our way to a semblance of self-knowledge "having been steered there only by the heart's mistakes / In the treasonable night," as we are told in "West End Blues," the poem that follows "Helicon" in *Visions from the Ramble*. The double portrait of "Helicon" then is a penance for a small treason of the affections. It offers the revival of a memory, one of the rare gifts friendship alone can give.

> Allen said, *I am searching for the true cadence.* Gray
> Stony light had flashed over Morningside Drive since noon,
> Mixing high in the east with a gray smoky darkness,
> Blackened steel trusses of Hell-Gate faintly etched into it,
> Gray visionary gleam, revealing the clarity of
> Harlem's grid, like a glimpse of a future city below:
> When the fat of the land shall have fallen into the dripping pan,
> The grill will still be stuck with brown crusts, clinging to
> Its bars, and neither in the fire nor out of it.
> So is it coming about. But in my unguessing days
> Allen said, *They still give you five dollars a pint at St. Luke's,*
> *No kickback to the intern, either.*

Voices of proverb and prophecy mingle in these opening lines, with a colloquial speech in possession of worldly wisdom and in search of a way of truth. The Dantesque evocations that follow, in the poem's central scene, are insistent enough to give the poem a traditional continuity, but without the mood music of epic allusion as one comes to know it in a poem like *Four Quartets*. If anything, the gravity of the diction is faithful to a nearer model, the American realist prose of the forties; and that is part of its enchantment.

> Inquiries and directions. Many dim rooms, and the shades
> Of patient ghosts in the wards, caught in the privileged
> Glimpses that the hurrying visitor always gets;
> Turnings; errors; wanderings; while Allen chattered on:
> *I mean someday to cry out against the cities, but first*
> *I must find the true cadence.* We finally emerged
> Into a dismal chamber, bare and dusty, where, suddenly,
> Sunlight broke over a brown prospect of whirling clouds
> And deepening smoke to plummet down, down to the depths
> Of the darkness, where, recessed in a tiny glory of light
> A barely visible man made his way in a boat
> Along an amber chasm closing in smoke above him—
> Two huge paintings by Thomas Cole opened, like airshaft
> Windows, on darkening hearts, there by the blood bank.

Cole's paintings of the voyage of life make an appropriate (ponderous, earnest, impressive) frame for the mock-epic journcy the poem itself recounts with an unmocking dignity. The meter is a touch of craft that completes the effect—a meter shared by other poems in *Visions from the Ramble*, yet it exhibits a special propriety here: loosely accentual, six or seven beats to the line, it has a look and feel close to Blake's fourteener, an invention that certainly belonged to Ginsberg's idea of the "true cadence."

The poem comes to its ending easily, anecdotally, when the plasma bottle is full.

> Then rest; then five dollars. Then Allen
> Urged us out onto the street. The wind sang around the corner,
> Blowing in from the sound and a siren screeched away
> Up Amsterdam Avenue. *Now you have a chocolate malted*
> *And then you're fine*, he said, and the wind blew his hair like feathers,
> And we both dissolved into nineteen forty-eight, to be whirled
> Away into the wildwood of time, I to leave the city
> For the disorganized plain, spectre of the long drink
> Taken of me that afternoon. *Turning a guy*
> *On*, said Allen last year to the hip psychiatrists
> Down in Atlantic City, *that's the most intimate thing*
> *You can ever do to him*. Perhaps. I have bled since
> To many cadences, if not to the constant tune
> Of the heart's yielding and now I know how hard it is
> To turn the drops that leaky faucets make in unquiet
> Nights, the discrete tugs of love in its final scene,
> Into a stream, whether thicker or thinner than blood, and
> I know
> That opening up at all is harder than meeting a measure:
> With night coming on like a death, a ruby of blood is at treasure.

Turning a guy on—to drugs that is—another medical procedure but with a pomp of put-on solemnity: the phrase and the version of community that it sells are an unconscious parody of the companionship the poem has recalled. A guy by definition is anyone, the sort of anyone you can benefit without having much feeling about. And the falseness of that promise is here quietly signaled: "Perhaps." Opening up in poetry or friendship does not mean turning the drip of the faucet into a steady stream. Intimacy, like imagination, happens by accident and oddly. The poem's last couplet draws together the allegory with a metaphysical compactness— blood and wine, spontaneous expression and gush, true cadence and the talking and listening of friends, all gathered into "a ruby of blood," a memory caught in one of those privileged glimpses the unhurrying visitor to his own life may sometimes get.

There are further inspired glimpses of self-knowledge in *Reflections on Espionage*, whose contents are the message of a spy operating under the code name "Cupcake." This seemed to me when I first read it and still does seem one of Hollander's most characteristic poems and at the same time his most unusual. The self of the artist and operative Cupcake is looked at closely as it vanishes into a sense of fellowship with all who share "the work"—the work of poetry and spying that throughout the book turn out to be metaphors for each other. The termination and disappearance of this worker are a consequence of madness and incapacity, but they are also a necessary effect of full-scale effort in an enterprise that dwarfs individuals, as Shelley in the *Defence of Poetry* and Eliot in "Tradition and the Individual Talent" in different ways suggested that poetry must do. By contrast, the peculiar ideal cherished by Cupcake— that one might so submerge oneself as to be lost with a purpose in a collective and impersonal and redemptive project— this is a delusion that gains strength from the vivid idea of a corps or guild or game or circus greater than any of its participants. The hero of *Reflections on Espionage* contrives from his partial wisdom the delirious hope being freed from self-consciousness, as if "the work" could offer a foolproof way to achieve two goals at once: a truth one has pieced together oneself and a truth one can stand and know from outside. This is the dream of every decipherer. But maybe one has to be afflicted with such enthusiasm in order to maintain a generous disposition toward non-utilitarian work of any kind. This seems to be Cupcake's drift when he speaks of a poet or spy named Ember.

> He has grown astonishingly beautiful
> In the past few years as the high quality
> Of the work he does for us has become more
> Apparent. Is it something in his cover—
> Something that builds character where only a
> Personality is called for? Or has he

Secretly revealed himself to take drink of
A sweet and demanding source. That would be bad:
He would be found out all too quickly. But he
Looks too well—it is as if the work itself
Were nourishing him now. How he has risen
From the old ashes of himself! I recall
His former crabbed privacies, his sad, fussy
Insistence on obscure French restaurants at
Noon for passing messages, the bizarre keys
For ciphers he would invent. Now he seems an
Illumination of the ordinary.

Here what might be envy is sublimated into a feeling more akin to wonder: "as if the work itself/ Were nourishing him now." Cupcake for his part, having coded and organized himself to a perfect opacity, is finally consumed by the work. A happier fate is given to the hero of "The Mad Potter"—a touching lyric that belongs distantly to the group of poems I have been describing. This artist pours himself into all his works and finds nothing but himself. It is not clear how madness in such a setting differs from sheer dedication to a calling. Perhaps the only difference is the mad potter's loss of awareness of a world from which he was called.

A work of art that is genuinely interested in (to borrow a favorite phrase of Hollander's) "the matter of art" will be interested in self-deception. This is the part of self-knowledge that stands receptive to construal by the eye and ear—the visible shadow of a recessive object that can never sculpt itself into legible form. I conclude with another autobiographical poem, "Early Birds," from Hollander's most recent book, *Figurehead*. This fragmentary anecdote of a vaudeville performer, George Moran, in his after-years in Los Angeles, makes a natural pair with "Helicon," though I don't know that the poet conceived of it that way. The title refers to an old comedian once known for a bit about the early bird and the worm, and to the boy John age seventeen, in California alone that summer, in flight from a fear he still doesn't fully understand.

I see
The 17 year old boy I was
Adrift one languid summer in
L.A., working from time to time

As an incompetent soda-jerk,
Or pearl-diver, equally
Bumbling, at the Pig 'n Whistle
Downtown (residues of morning
Oatmeal and of barley soup—
Those were the messiest to clean)
Or not working, the while living at
The Hotel Barbara at Sixth
And Alvarado—then a shabby,
Peaceful, not unrighteous spot.

These solitaries old and young idle away the evening hours in talk and in listening: that is the heart of the poem. The rest is a mission entrusted by the old man to the young—to get in touch with his daughter in New York, whom he hasn't heard from in years—a mission that the poet tells us, on his return to a gregarious life, he found plausible reasons disguised as obstacles to prevent his carrying out. Two years later Moran died, at sixty-seven; and writing the poem Hollander is sixty-seven.

And for the unproselytizing
Sect of the Rememberers—
I, the boy then, some of you—
All our various vaudevilles are
Giving way to faster brighter
Dumber slower stuff, and even
Stories told of them perform their
Dimming time-steps as they slowly
Shuffle off to Buffalo.

Faster, brighter, dumber, slower stuff—a totally characteristic phrase, and is it not marvelous how we know what he means? Dumber and slower because of the way it is faster and brighter. What has gone out of American popular culture is much of the wit, much of the humor, much of the sentiment. What has come in is cleverness and knowingness—understood not as the obnoxious traits of an elite but as universally desirable and deployable. Billy Crystal and Eddie Murphy, and Burns and Allen: what to say of the difference of style when it is a difference also of morale? The newer pair are so much faster, brighter, dumber, slower; they are so because they don't have to listen. I think of George Burns (let him stand for any resilient poet, spy, or comedian) pausing as he admires in the last words Gracie said a most peculiar inference or non sequitur or circuitous but irrefutable QED. It leaves Burns only pleasantly stunned, and where a normal man would sputter and bluster he keeps his cool and holds his cigar. But this is a way of listening—a suspended and ever-resumable relation with the world and the mayhem of its attempt to recruit one for its ends. In reading some of John Hollander's poems, we feel we are on the scene as a gifted contemporary performs the work of listening that is another name for self-knowledge and for sanity.

18

"Dallying Nicely with Words": Auguries of Electronic Poetry in a Handful of Essays by "Cupcake"

STEVEN MEYER

Much as one might characterize an especially rambunctious child as a *handful*, so, of John Hollander's essays, one can asseverate: *quite a handful.* These essays are challenging. (Think knights-of-olde, think *aenigma.*) They're not encyclopedia entries, yet they are encyclopedic. Invariably, they are exercises in historical poetics. Like the man himself, they display little patience with dullness but much where a trace of sharpness is evinced. This semester—I am writing these remarks in early March 2002—I have been teaching a course on the very latest thing, electronic poetry, *e-poetry*, so much a creature of the present that most of my colleagues, glancing obliquely my way, aren't even skeptical yet. Whatever it is, it doesn't compute. Now, don't expect me to tell you what it is; perhaps you can figure that out by spending more time online. Instead, I am going to describe how one might go about preparing oneself to think about *whatever.* Washington University is currently on spring break—conveniently so, since in the second half (more exactly, the final 37%) of the course, we will turn to actual poems, and poetic effects, on the net, actual virtual poems, instead of the virtual virtual poems that have hitherto concerned us and the actual nonvirtual poems we've been reading alongside texts like Neal Stephenson's *In the Beginning . . . Was the Command Line*, Loss Glazier's *Digital Poetics: The Making of E-Poetries*, and Charles Petzold's *Code: The Hidden Language of Computer Hardware and Software.*

We've been spending so much time with "traditional" poetry because it occurred to me that most of my students, however much poetry they've read and studied (and half of them are enrolled in the Washington University art school), wouldn't have spent much time thinking about what it is that makes these works poems rather than more or less confused, more and less confusing, discursive statements—what makes them tick, not to mention what makes them good. And how in the world are you going to be able to determine whether e-poetry is poetry or screen art (or both) unless you've got a pretty good sense of what poetry has been? That's where John's essays come in; for I can't imagine a better overview of poetry than that supplied by the essays I assigned, at least if you have only four classes in which to get that view across. Here are the essays: "The Poem in the Ear" and "The Poem in the Eye," from his 1975 volume *Vision and Resonance: Two Senses of Poetic Form*, and "Turnings and Fashionings" and "Dallying Nicely with Words: Poetic Linguistics," from *Melodious Guile: Fictive Pattern in Poetic Language* (1988). I also assigned fifteen poems, three each by five quite distinctive authors: "Often I am Permitted to Return to a Meadow," "Achilles' Song" (along with "Some Notes on Notation"), and "Everything Speaks to Me," by Robert Duncan; "The End of March," "The Map," and "Crusoe in England," by Elizabeth Bishop; "Annunciations," "The Mystery of the Charity of Charles Péguy," and "Cycle," by Geoffrey Hill; "Hot Cross Bum," "Love Songs to Joannes," and "Parturition," by Mina Loy; "The Anatomy of Resonance," "Desire's Persistence," and "The Cradle Logic of Autumn," by Jay Wright.

The first class made it abundantly clear that we wouldn't be able to discuss essays *and* poems—remember what I said above about these essays being a handful—so we spent the full two weeks on the essays, then carved out a week for seven of the poems, and, for four more weeks, juxtaposed one poem each class with the texts by Stephenson, Glazier, and Petzold. Reading John's essays turned out to be a matter of reading the poems in the terms supplied by the essays . . . and of reading the texts concerned with links between writing and computing, and by extension poetry and computing, in the context afforded by both poems and essays. What follows, then, is a journal of the first three weeks the class spent gleaning auguries of e-poetry, of poetry that may or may not exist but which, in any case, is yet to come, whether in the frame of the class ("wait till next week") or the century ("it's a twenty-first century thing") or the millennium ("don't even try to imagine it"). Welcome to the future, Percy Bysshe Shelley!

1 / 15

Cupcake hear

JH argues in "The Poem in the Ear" that it is "the aspects of poetic language that are most like the resources of speech, rather than those of song, which come to the aid of poetic resonance." The Renaissance may have sought to recreate "the original union of music and poetry" of the ancient Greeks (for whom "proper music was almost exclusively vocal" and whose prosody was correspondingly based on "purely musical principles"), yet even as this "nostalgic hope" faded in seventeenth-century England, "poetry's own music"—the music of *speech being watched*, of "the sounds of speech, instrumentalized within the framework of metrical convention"—became "dominant in the organization of verse." This is the principal claim of "The Poem in the Ear," which demonstrates how the "various analogical couplings of music and poetry" have operated as more or less, and increasingly less and less, productive fictions for understanding poetic practice. "If 'the music of poetry' half embarrasses now," JH observes at the opening of the third and final section, "'the sound of poetry' still does not, nor does 'the look of poetry.'"

Poetic power, in other words, remains a function of the "efficacy" of sound, not of music—and it is in large part thanks to the English Romantics and their investigations of what JH terms "visionary sound" that we owe our present outlook. On the one hand, "'the imaginative regions of eye and ear in Romantic poetry are much more responsive to the phenomenology of the senses than were the musical and visual concerns of Renaissance and Augustan literatures." (Here JH alludes to "such matters as those of sweep and discontinuity— the ability of each sense to locate respectively point sources of light and sound in space; what it means that one can shut, or avert, the eyes but not the ears; how hearing outlasts vision as one falls through layers of sleep; and how sound can pierce the dark globe of sleeping consciousness.") On the other hand, even Blake, with his "continuous mistrust of optical vision," created "such fantastic synesthesias as in the London poem from *Songs of Experience*, where all of the apprehended phenomena are spoken of as 'heard,' and yet where sound turns into visual concretion:

How the chimney-sweeper's cry
Every blackening church appalls;
And the hapless Soldier's sigh
Runs in blood down Palace walls."

("Here," JH explains, "the particular audibles condense, out of the waves they make in the air and the motions their impingings make on the consciousness, into a cinematic animation, becoming the blackening that is more than soot, and the reddening that bursts into blood on its contact with the surfaces of blame.")

1/17

[Steam][pump] is gone. He died quietly in his
Hotel [room] and his [sleep]

From "The Poem in the Ear": "It was with the adaptation of Greek meters to Latin that poetry, originally inseparable from music, began to grow away from it. And it was then that poetry began to develop, in its meter, a seeming music of its own." From "The Poem in the Eye": "It was only when Latin poetry adapted this Greek meter for its own uses, when conflict arose between the penultimate stress of the Latin language and the Greek meter's canonical ictus patterns (having nothing to do with speech stress, but with applied downbeat), that anything like an abstract, like a visual meter, developed." (The *ictus* is the upbeat-downbeat contrast so characteristic of Greek prosody.) More generally, "a metrical loan from the poetry of another language always tends to show up, in the borrowing tongue, as an inscriptional coding."

Whereas "the ear responds to the dimension of natural experience," the eye responds "to that of convention"; among other things, this means that "abstract schemata, metrical *and* grammatical," are situated along poetry's visual dimension. In "The Poem in the Eye," JH is less concerned with meter, however, than with shape—except to the extent that meter shapes grammar and may be used, as he puts it, "to diagram syntax, like a set of stage directions, working through the eye, rather than on it." Shaped poems may look like something, as in the axe or wings or egg or panpipe of famous Alexandrian exemplars, but, as JH remarks, "most poems are in the shape of poems, not of pictures." (He furthermore distinguishes shaped poetry from concrete poetry on the grounds that "concrete poetry is a purely graphic art; since a true concrete poem cannot be read aloud, it has no full linguistic dimension, no existence in the ear's kingdom. A concrete poem remains, in the often-quoted terms which Plutarch ascribed to Simonides, 'mute poetry,' and therefore, picture." The distinction may well prove helpful in evaluating works of e-poetry.) Poems in the shape of poems are always in some sense about *themselves* just as George Herbert's altar poem is about an altar and his "Easter-wings" transforms Simmias' wings of Eros.

Near the end of the essay JH discusses how in some works the poet "invents visionary possibilities for which a technology did not then exist, but for which there is now a trivial technical simulation." Among the "greatest developments in nineteenth-century poetry," for example, is "the sophisticated kind of transition between stanzas, sections, parts of poems, transitions that need not be glossed or explained"—a "cinematographic vision" corresponding to "the kinds of transitions which two generations now [three or four *now*], having grown up with moving pictures, can take for granted." Not only might a poet invent possibilities for a nonexistent technology, but the visionary experience might precede the invention of an appropriate poetic format. This, JH suggests, is the case for the "startling cinematic transformation of still picture into motion, of sound and physical sensation into rushing image," which occurs in a mid-nineteenth-century notebook entry composed by Dante Gabriel Rossetti, recording a journey by train from Antwerp to Ghent. "The format is block, blank-verse paragraph":

> We are upon the Scheldt. We know we move
> Because there is a floating at our eyes
> Whatso they seek; and because all the things
> Which on our outset were distinct and large
> Are smaller and much weaker and quite gray,
> And at last gone from us. No motion else. . . .
> The darkness is in a tumult. We tear on,
> The roll behind us and the cry before,
> Constantly, in a lull of intense speed
> And thunder. Any other sound is known
> Merely by sight. The shrubs, the trees your eye
> Scans for their growth, are far along in haze. . . .

How might one go about scanning these lines? Try this on for size: "The world whizzing by outside a train window can find no appropriate genre in Victorian poetry, and there is no expansion of format capable of containing this kind of vision. As it stands, this long poem is without results, and remains an amazing experiment. It will not be until such a poem as [Wallace Stevens's] 'An Ordinary Evening in New Haven' that this kind of vision will be overlaid . . . with a similar kind of vision about the world of the poem itself; that the look of poems, square and framelike as they may invariably remain, open and unendingly page-like as their iambic blocks may be, will serve as lenses for the look of things." Here "The Poem in the Eye" takes up the central concern of the third of the four essays, so I will now turn to that. [For more on the text of "Antwerp to Ghent," see the online Rossetti Archive (http://jefferson. village.virginia.edu/rossetti).]

1/22

No new movements of gods or men

"Cleaving to the literal," JH insists in "Turnings and Fashionings," "can be a terrible entrapment." William Carlos Williams's admiring remark about Nathanael West's novel *Miss Lonelyhearts*, that "the letters in it *must* be authentic," thus had things exactly backward. For "what the imagination might observe about actual letters written to authentic newspaper columns is that they *must* have been written by a cheap satirist. . . . Poetry knows all too well how, the more sincere a literal expression of self (of feelings, beliefs, etc.) or a telling of one's own story, the more conventionalized and the more copied from a tattered paradigm it will be." By *turnings* JH means tropes, "the twistings or turnings of sense and reference of words and utterances"; by *fashionings*, the figures or "patterns made by curious and ordinarily irrelevant arrangements—of words, sublexical and suprasegmental linguistic sounds, syntactic schemes, and graphic elements"—which carry no meanings in themselves; and although he locates "the matter of poetry" in the former rather than the latter ("schemes alienate poetic language from other more frequent modes of discourse, but they are not inherently poetic"), he is particularly interested in the ways these two "kinds of disturbance in the flow of more usual discourse" may act in tandem, generating poetic fictions, fables, stories, parables, allegories by the troping of given schemes.

The "instant when a bit of scheme becomes opaque, calling attention to itself and asking, like a person, to be understood," provides the immediate occasion for mere self-description—of this or that level of linguistic patterning—to turn, and be turned, into a fleeting "allegory of what lies beyond it." In this way poems may be said to "talk to, and of, themselves, not to evade discourse about the rest of the world . . . but to enable it." Take, for instance, the *Book of Common Prayer*'s "In the midst of life we are in death," which, as JH observes, "depends on both the 'in's' being problematic, not literally spatial in either case but particularly figurative at 'in death,' which means 'mortal, doomed, surely to die.'" Even so, "by the very strength of its tropes of location," the statement attests to "our constant suppression of its truth: 'While living we're always going to die and act as if we weren't.'" The scheme here is that of oxymoron, which possesses the "general form [*a* + *non-a*] (or [*a* + *anti-a*])." How, then, is the scheme troped? "Contrary to one's first puzzled feeling that [*a* + *non-a*] is merely self-contradictory and can't make sense," as would be the case with logical paradox in ordinary philosophical discourse, "the understanding arises that [*a*] or [*non-a*] or both," as here, "must indeed be figurative." This means that we are confronted with an instance of *poetic* paradox, and crucial to its effect is the additional twist phrased by JH as "While living we're always going to die *and act as if we weren't*." Though the sentence from the *Book of Common Prayer* is proverbial, it still packs a punch, thanks to the way the scheme is troped.

1/24

I sat in my room
Past the appointed time . . . wondering what would be
Asked of me today

The fourth essay, "Dallying Nicely with Words," concerns just one such genre of troped scheme, namely, poetry's visionary linguistics—the "fictive theories of language that seem to lie implicit in certain local instances of pattern and trope." [For a broad spectrum of such theories, see the 1998 anthology *Imagining Language*, edited by Jed Rasula and Steve McCaffery. The week following spring break, the class will be reading selections from this work. "An eventual site of reception of *Imagining Language*," Rasula and McCaffery propose, "is the 'interactive' environment of multimedia communications systems. Hypertext and the World Wide Web are symptomatic of how literacy is being reconfigured."] The "complex romance" of language ranges from such *synchronic* phenomena as the wordplay about wordplay in *Twelfth Night* from which the essay derives its title (and from which this journal derives *its*), the fictional morphology of names (the way that in Spenser's *Faerie Queene* "Artegall's name reacts erotically with that of his own lover, Britomart," for example), and the troping of rhyme (with rhyming words "so deployed in a poem that they imply any one of a number of nonce theories of the effects of rhyme: for example, a_2 is the echo of a_1; or a_1 and a_2 are in some kind of cause and effect relation; or a_1 is the soul, or the body, of a_2"), to *diachronic* effects involving the troping of rhyme-like schemes ("fictions about sound-change"), of semantic change ("morphophonemic fictions"), and of word order.

Consider the following instances of this assortment of diachronic effects. First, from Geoffrey Hill's "The Mystery of the Charity of Charles Péguy," the lines "Patience hardens to a pittance, courage / unflinchingly declines into sour rage." JH comments: " 'Patience' hardening to 'a pittance' entails a parable about a sound-change." In this "fabulous linguistics," ablaut— the patterned change in the root vowels of verb forms—is "not morphological but moral, the soft fruit of forebearance shriveling into its own pit." (Yet even as "both instances denote a degenerative change occurring over time, the second has an overtone of the synchronic analysis of the 'patience'/'pittance' ablaut, for the process exemplified is both declension and declination.") Second, from *Paradise Lost*, the parenthetical line, "For eloquence the soul, song charms the sense," which Milton's eighteenth-century editor, Richard Bentley, disastrously rewrote as "Song charmes the Sense, but Eloquence the Soul." JH: For Milton, "syntactic order, as Donald Davie and Stanley Fish and others have demonstrated, is always to be read for its parabolic narrative, epistemological, historical, and teleological. / What is the story of this line, then? The ellipsis of the verb 'charms' from the first clause is filled by the extension of its most direct normative position in the second one. But that position, immediately following its subject, 'song,' awakens the Latin etymon lurking in 'charms' (<*carmen*, 'song') and patent still in the modern senses of 'incantation' and 'spell.' Poetry, song, sings directly to sense, whereas eloquence, philosophy, charms the soul in another, higher way, in which the music of poetry [!] is not literally there, just as the verb 'charms'—even in its extended senses of delighting, alluring, bewitching—is not literally 'there' in the clause describing the action of philosophizing on the soul, and, finally, as soul is less literally present than sense. The charm of philosophy is less literally 'charm' in the prior sense of 'song,' then, and the usual parable of linguistic diachrony in *Paradise Lost* is at work here as well. The primary sense of things is present (in both meanings of the adjective); the prior sense is absent, and must be secondarily derived. But presence somehow gets it all wrong, and it is this dialectic that the fictional linguistics of the poem is always assisting the rest of its system of figuration to undo."

Third, from Andrew Marvell's prefatory poem to *Paradise Lost*, when Marvell "expresses his original doubts, before reading Milton, about the success of so ambitious and problematic a task," that "In that wide Field how he his way should find / Through which lame Faith leads Understanding blind." JH: The first line, "all monosyllables, involves Marvell's acknowledgment of Milton's trope of a scheme of monosyllabism. The survey of Hell in the second book of *Paradise Lost* yields a famous prospect in a celebrated line: 'Rocks, caves, lakes, fens, bogs, dens and shades of death.' The reader's progress through the metrical construction of the syntax of listing, even though aided by the final phrase-stress and the internal rhymes and assonance, is itself a figure for contemplating this 'universe of death.' Pope thought of the syllabic paradigm of this line in his self-descriptive 'And ten low words oft creep in one dull line,' and John Dyer, in *The Fleece* (1757), simply alludes to it: 'Woods, tow'rs, vales, caves, dells, cliffs, and torrent floods,' borrowing at most a tincture of sublimity at the end. But Marvell's 'In that wide Field how he his way should find' is immediately applicable to the question of a reader's finding his way through Milton's syntax, blank-verse paragraphs, and complex similies." ("And [the] closing [of] the rhymed couplet that *Paradise Lost* itself disdained to use" is "beautifully handled" with the chiasmus, or crisscrossing, of [*lame Faith: Understanding blind*], which, in suggesting that "the 'blind' might modify—adjectively and adverbially—either 'Faith' or 'leads' or both[,] provides an effective countercurrent to the old figure of the paired incapacities.") "Minor verse," JH concludes, and if *Paradise Lost* is in no way minor a prefatory poem to it would seem doomed to eternal minority status, "will seldom exhibit much of this fictive linguistic thought, seeking to attain a style without raising any disturbing questions about it."

1/29

A bit of transmission has been coming through

"Often I am Permitted to Return to a Meadow": *permitted* because meadows are cultivated, hence liable to trespassing. *A meadow*: "an eternal pasture folded . . . a field folded." Pressing *folded* against *pasture* elicits *sheepfold*, suggesting the etymological fiction *field* < *fold*; actually, the former derives from OE *feld* and the latter from OE *fald*. Turning and returning: "a children's game / of ring a round of roses": the title also functions as the first line and returns in the penultimate stanza, "Often I am permitted to return to a meadow / as if it were a given property of the mind / that certain bounds hold against chaos": of the poem's nine stanzas, the number of lines per stanza follows the pattern: first stanza = last stanza, second = second to last, and so on: 2 3 2 3   3   3 2 3 2. Here is the middle stanza: "She it is Queen Under The Hill / whose hosts are a disturbance of words within words / that is a field folded." *A disturbance of words within words*: *a field folded*: *field* folded into *fold* and *fold* in the field of *field*. This *field* may well be wider than *fold*, but *folded* takes the cake.

"Hot Cross Bum": a much more playful poem than Duncan's, indeed so playful ("prophet of Babble-on") and at the same time so brutally satiric ("the human . . . race / altered to irrhythmic stagger // along the alcoholic's / exit to Ecstasia") that the titular pun that generates the poem ("Some passing church / or social worker // confides to a brother / how he has managed to commandeer / a certain provision / of hot-cross buns // his earnestness / hushed by the hiccough holocaust / of otiose / hoboes hob-nobbing") also provokes the sense that there is something profoundly untoward in this sort of scheme. "Hot-cross-buns," one reads in an example of the phrase cited in the

OED, "are consecrated loaves, bestowed in the church as alms, and to those who could not receive the host made from the dough from whence the host is taken," or as Loy has it, "way-laying for branding / indirigible bums / with the hot-cross / of ovenly buns."

"The End of March": an elemental poem, starting with expo-sure to the elements ("It was cold and windy, scarcely the day / to take a walk on that long beach") . . . pairing realistic detail work in the first two stanzas ("Along the wet sand, in rubber boots, we followed / a track of big dog-prints (so big they were more like lion-prints). Then we came on / lengths and lengths, endless, of wet white string, / looping up to the tide-line, down to the water") with a fantasy of retirement in the third ("my proto-dream-house, / my crypto-dream-house") . . . conjoining reality and fantasy in the final stanza ("The sun came out for just a minute. / For just a minute, set in their bezels of sand, / the drab, damp, scattered stones / were multi-colored, / and all those high enough threw out long shadows, / individ-ual shadows, then pulled them in again. / They could have been teasing the lion sun, / except that now he was behind them / —a sun who'd walked the beach the last low tide, / making those big, majestic paw-prints, / who perhaps had bat-ted a kite out of the sky to play with"). The thing about winter is that it's so damn literal; if it's cold, it's just cold. Yet there's an unmistakable touch of spring in the title, and if less blatantly than Loy's, it also contains traces of a pun: March and march-ing. From the bare, wintry scheme of looping wet white string—the shape of the poem—and the unsentimental figure of the lion-like paw-prints, Bishop draws out the fantastic trope of the lion sun. "For just a minute." *A momentary trope*, as JH puts it, *arising from a local scheme*.

"Achilles' Song": another ocean poem. Recalling the Greek equation of music and poetry, Duncan substitutes the resources of speech for those of music ("I have workt with silences— with caesuras as definite parts of the articulation of the line, with turnings at the end of the verse, with intervals of silence in the measures between stanzas"). The opening line of "Achilles' Song," Duncan writes in "Some Notes on Nota-tion," "could be force-measured as an iambic pentameter":

I do not know more than the Sea tells me,

—"But the reader who seeks to render the line will mistake the verse or turning of the line." "All 'typographical' features," he adds, "are notations for the performance of the reading. Margins signify. Thus, verse 2 of 'Achilles' Song'"—

> told me long ago,   or I overheard Her
>   telling distant roar upon the sands,

 "returns to an inner margin, and in the linear sequence this is like the return of a wave to a systolic margin in the flux; in the 'vertical' sequence of lines returning to the same margin"—

> waves of meaning in the cradle of whose
>   sounding and resounding power I
>   slept.

—"an inner coding of the content emerges."

1/31

> *For instance, this eleven by eleven*
> *Grid I am using seems to dictate to me*
> *Messages it might most lovingly encode . . .*

"The Map": two octets, rhyming *abbacddc*, between which an unrhymed eleven-line stanza swims—or is it floats? Is it sea, or land? And are they really rhymes if a_1 and a_2, d_1 and d_2, are identical terms, framing the couplets between them? Take the poem's opening: "Land lies in water; it is shadowed green. / Shadows, or are they shallows, at its edges / showing the line of long sea-weeded ledges / where weeds hang to the simple blue from green?" Even the shadows have shadows, or maybe they don't (*and* maybe they don't [*a* and *not-a*]) . . . even as the weeds link one line with the next, land to water. This is an early poem—when Bishop wrote it, she was barely older than the students in this class—and she is letting the grid take her where it will, even as *she* tropes the scheme: "Are they assigned," the poem concludes, "or can the countries pick their colors? / —What suits the character or the native waters best. / Topography displays no favorites; North's as near as West. / More delicate than the historians' are the map-makers' colors."

"Annunciations": just one line longer than Bishop's poem—a pair of unrhymed sonnets. What story is being told here about the traditional sonnet sequence, "not merely with, but out of," it? (That last, by JH.) All the unrhyming repetition: "O Love, subject of the mere diurnal grind . . . 'O Love, / You know what pains succeed; be vigilant; strive / To recognize the damned among your friends.'" "Touchable, overt, clean to the touch." "The loathly neckings and fat shook spawn / (Each specimen-jar fed with delicate spawn)" Here is Hill on the doubleness, the duplicity—likely as not, *this* doubling's duplicitous, too near to hand—of "Our God scatters corruption": "'Our God scatters corruption' = 'Our God puts corruption to flight' or 'Our God disseminates corruption.' I may have been thinking of Mr. Dulles's idea of God as Head of Strategic Air Command."

"Desire's Persistence": the persistence of the quest, the quester, the questing—"polychromatic story I will now tell / in the weaving, power's form in motion, / a devotion to the unstressed." In the long middle section of the poem Wright takes a sentence from the *Poesìa Náhuatl*, an important collection of poetry composed in the language spoken in the Valley of Mexico when the Spaniards arrived, and, first supplying an English translation of the Spanish translation of the Classic Aztec original as an epigraph ("I lift the red flower of winter into the wind"), he then retranslates each term the better to convey something of desire's persistence in the line. What each word *means*, concretely. "Down Hidalgo," the translation of "Lift" begins,

> past Alvarado and Basurto,
> I walk a straight line
> to the snailed Paseo Los Berros.
> Here, at noon, the sun,
>   a silver bead,
> veils what **the dawn** has displayed.
> Even so,
>   I have **taken up** the morning's bond again
>   —the lake with its pendulum leg
>   shining in the distance,
>   the boy in white
>   **hauling** his bottle of chalky milk home.
> I know I sit in the deep of a city
> with its **brocade of hills,**

where a thin rain is an evening's fire.
I have heard the women sing
near their gas lamps,
when the rose end of day **lights a hunger**
for the garlanded soups and meat they prepare.
Often, I have taken **the high ground**
by the pond, **over a frog's voice**
        dampened by lilies,
and been **exalted** by the soothsayer
who knows I'm not at home.
I am the arcane body,
raised at the ninth hour,
to be welcomed by the moonlight
        of such **spirited air.**
I am the Dane of degrees
who realizes **how the spirit glows**
        even as it descends.

(The emphasis is not in the original, of course.) One might think of Duncan's "disturbance of words within words" here. One might also think of hypertext links.

Cupcake is JH's alter ego in *Reflections on Espionage: The Question of Cupcake*, his 1976 verse investigation of "the metaphor of code," reprinted in 1999 with a new introduction and additional notes. Between 1976 and 1999 many things happened, but two had a particular bearing on "the question of Cupcake": the end of the Cold War and the advent of the World Wide Web. These may or may not be related; but if the former inevitably "dates" *Reflections on Espionage*, the latter renders it avant-garde, containing layers of significance perhaps only realizable after the fact. Did the poet "invent visionary possibilities for which a technology did not then exist, but for which there is now a trivial technical simulation"? Or is the technology, in this respect, not so trivial?

I have taken the headings for each journal entry from the corresponding entries in *Reflections on Espionage*, which starts with 1/14. (I begin with 1/15.) In his introduction, JH confesses to having always desired, and always been unable, to keep a journal. I must confess to the same conundrum, if it is one. Until now.

A few additional confessions.

First, I had planned to continue the journal for seven weeks. Time constraints reduced it to the present three.

Second, I felt that it was too much to ask the students to read *Reflections on Espionage* given the quantity of material already assigned; hence the frame both was and was not, is and is not, part of the course.

Third, as best I can make out, we actually spent only a week and a half reading the four essays; but I don't know how to make four go into three evenly.

Finally, I have also made subtle, if heavy-handed, changes in the headings; for example, Cupcake actually wrote, "No new movements of goods or men." Cupcake <u>here</u>.

19

A Well-Tuned Life:
Reflections on an Academic Career

ELISE BICKFORD JORGENS

A few years ago I interviewed for a new position. The search committee asked me to describe something I had done, in my academic career, that I had enjoyed and that I could look back on with pride and a sense of accomplishment. After only a brief moment's hesitation, I launched into a description of the long and consuming process of preparing a facsimile edition, with transcription of the texts, of a group of twenty-two solo song manuscripts from late sixteenth- and early seventeenth-century England.[1] Warming to my subject, I talked about my early introduction to these manuscripts as a graduate student in musicology working with John Hollander, telling the committee how I had had an enormous amount to learn from him about the poetry in these wonderful songs as well as about the wealth of conjunction between music and literature in that period. I told them of my visits to a number of small, out of the-way libraries in England (Saint Michael's College in Tenbury Wells was my favorite; I was the only person working there that day in July, and the librarian brought me two electric heaters to take the chill off the air); I had to go there to see the manuscripts since only a small fraction of the fifteen hundred or so songs contained in them was available in modern edition. These songs were the subject of my dissertation and subsequent book, and I told the committee of my struggles to learn to sing them well enough to write with firsthand knowledge of performance practices and interpretive nuances. I described how later, as I began to prepare the edition, I had not only put to use some of what I had studied in Renaissance musical notation as a musicology student, but had then taken a summer seminar in Renaissance paleography in order to tran-

---

1 Elise Bickford Jorgens, ed., *English Song: 1600–1675*, 12 vols. (New York: Garland Publishing, Inc., 1986–89).

scribe the poetry from these songs, many inscribed in the period's "secret" secretary hand. My personal and professional growth as a scholar clearly matured through the various stages of this project. I came to a deeper understanding of the songs as music, as poems, and as ineffable combination of the two; I explored their social, political, and cultural place; *and* I mastered tools of the scholar's trade in order to bring them out of their relative obscurity. Although I had completed the immediate project a decade or more before this interview, I still looked back upon it as a milestone in my academic career.

The only problem with the conversation I have recounted was that the position for which I was interviewing on that occasion was not scholarly but administrative. As I heard myself becoming downright rhapsodic about the joys of immersing myself in the scholarship of music and poetry, I began to suspect that the search committee might well wonder whether I was interviewing for the wrong position! Fortunately, it was a committee primarily of faculty members; they loved it that I was still sufficiently impassioned about music and poetry and the processes of scholarship that I allowed myself that excursion. I didn't get that job, but it was not because of my indulgence in scholarly reflection.

I confess, though, that I am an administrator: dean of arts and sciences at a large midwestern university. Most deans don't know quite what led them to abandon the real work of the scholar/teacher to take on the endless succession of problems that hit them every day. I am no different, but the invitation to contribute a personal essay to this volume of work dedicated to John Hollander prompted me to ponder that question afresh and to think specifically about how my love of music and poetry shaped the path of my career as a scholar and teacher and ultimately an administrator. I considered several titles: "How I Failed to Follow in John Hollander's Footsteps"; "Reflections on a Life Apparently Devoid of Music and Poetry." But the more important truth is that those experiences—studying with John Hollander; working in the various ways that I have with music and poetry—have been among the critical factors in making me the person I am today, doing the job I do today.

Unlike many of John Hollander's students, I came to my work with him largely through music rather than through literature. That I spent most of my teaching career—fourteen years—in an English department owes no small amount to his influence. Indeed, much of what I describe in this essay has come directly or indirectly from his guidance or from the example he set. The work I did both as a graduate student under his tutelage and later as a scholar/teacher was much more deeply integrative than I could have anticipated when I began, leading me to probe what I might call the "process" of song in ways that most music students do not. I came to look on song as a critical genre in its own right and truly *inter*disciplinary rather than multidisciplinary. Joining a relatively small group of people not just working across disciplinary boundaries but creating new dimensions for this kind of scholarship, I began to shape my own career in music and literature.[2] It was the case twenty-five years ago, and I believe it remains largely the case today, that while musicologists are interested in this kind of work, most music departments have little room for it in curricula that sometimes strain to find space for a thorough grounding in music history; hence my move to a teaching career in English, which I was fortunate to find, given a tight job market and my lack of an advanced degree in English.

In my teaching of literature, I sought every opportunity I could to bring music to the discussion. My undergraduate degree in English, as well as my work with John Hollander and the further self-instruction I did during the preparation of my doctoral dissertation, prepared me to teach Renaissance literature, undergraduate Shakespeare, and a fairly rudimentary course in poetics as well as a number of "readings" courses and basic introduction to literary studies. In all of these, and in a course I developed and taught regularly called "Literature and

---

2 Of course I am by no means the only person from either side of the musico-literary equation to devote attention to these interactions. Even considering only English literature, I could not begin to provide an exhaustive list, but among those literary scholars who influenced my thinking were Walter Davis, Edward Doughtie, and, of course, John Hollander; musicologists who have been drawn to these questions include Ian Spink and Joseph Kerman. Many younger scholars now keep these dialogues alive, including some of those whose essays and articles appear in this volume. A number of years ago, a group of interested scholars formed the Lyrica Society to further such discussions. All the same, we are still a relatively small group out of the many thousands of more traditionally focused literary scholars or musicologists.

Other Arts," I routinely used my musical background to shape my presentation of literary subjects. As the years went on, I continued to enhance my ability (and credibility) as an English professor through external seminars and workshops as well as constant reading, and I took on more advanced courses, always seeking to infuse music where I could, and, of course, I continued my interdisciplinary work as a scholar.

Both in the classroom and in my scholarship, I learned early on that there is not a good vocabulary for talking about how the arts—and specifically music and literature—interact. Writing or talking about *song* as an independent art form, one is immediately presented with a cumbersome descriptor: "the musico-poetic relationship" almost belies in its own phraseology the beauty of the thing created by that relationship, and at every turn there seems to be at best an awkward and imprecise way to express the deep and true fusion as the two art forms have come together to produce something new. Further, there is often confusion in what would appear to be the most basic of terms. "Lyric," for example, means something like "verbal text of a song" to a musicologist, but something much more focused on literary affect to discussions of poetry. "Song," as I have been using it to describe an art form comprised of both poem and musical setting, hardly exists; perhaps the closest one can come to that meaning is the Elizabethan term "dittie," but that too is frequently used in other ways. Indeed, even in areas where one might expect correspondence, the vocabularies of the two disciplines do not agree, and a good integrating language does not easily emerge. Metrical terms, for example, are not synonymous; in fact, what is most commonly called "meter" in poetry is more closely related to "rhythm" in music.

And yet this composite art is a part of our everyday lives, from elevator music to pop culture and Broadway musical to art song or opera. The impulse to sing is very strong, in virtually every culture, making the lack of a descriptive language both puzzling and frustrating. Of course, a significant reason why this combination holds the fascination it does is music's very resistance to verbal expression. Music says something different from what the words alone can say, something by definition not expressible in words, yet as scholars who write and teachers who talk, we keep trying. As I am *not* a poet, I found it a constant challenge to write or talk about music and literature in ways that were infor-

mative and evocative and did not simply complicate a relationship that was natural and, at its best, beautiful.

If the lack of a descriptive language is an impediment to
scholarship in this area, it is even more critical in trying to teach,
and the difficulty is compounded by the fact that many students
have very little experience with music, either in making music
themselves or in contact with the conventions of musical notation. Nevertheless, in my experience, the inclusion of music in
teaching about literature was always beneficial to students'
understanding. Let me cite just a few examples. Many undergraduate students I have encountered have had very little grasp
of what we mean when we speak of interpretation. Either they
are persuaded that there is only one meaning, put there by an
author and ours to discover if we can, or they have been led to
believe that a poem, for instance, is available for any meaning
they might happen to choose, whether it grows accurately from
the language or not, let alone from any consideration of external
circumstances such as period or biography or history. Music can
be a significant aid in helping students to refine and shape their
ability to work in what is admittedly a difficult part of coming to
terms with the role of interpretation in reading literature.

Multiple settings of a single poem, for instance, may demonstrate substantially variant readings through such musical devices
as rhythm, meter, tempo, and melodic shape. There are two well-
known Elizabethan or Jacobean songs that I used frequently to
talk about interpretation, not only in a Renaissance Literature
class but even in a freshman-level "Introduction to Literary Interpretation." A poem by Thomas Campion, "I must complain, yet
do enjoy my love," was set both by Campion himself and by his
great contemporary, John Dowland—as well as by at least two
other composers that we know of from roughly the same period.

> I must complain, yet doe enjoy my Love;
> She is too faire, too rich in lovely parts:
> Thence is my grief, for Nature, while she strove
> With all her graces and divinest Arts
>   To form her too too beautifull of hue,
>   She had no leasure left to make her true.
>
> Should I, agriev'd, then wish shee were lesse fayre?
> That were repugnant to mine owne desires:
> Shee is admir'd, new lovers still repayre;

That kindles daily loves forgetfull fires.
Rest, jealous thoughts, and thus resolve at last:
Shee hath more beauty then becomes the chaste.[3]

If one's introduction to the poem is through one of these settings, as was the case for my students, its first impression will be considerably shaped by the music. Dowland's setting is romantic, even voluptuous, emphasizing playful enjoyment of love. A sustained, relatively high note on "doe" suggests the precedence of immediate pleasure over the complaint of the first phrase; quick, dance-like repetitions of "enjoy" promote the playfulness that Dowland seems to find in this line; emphasis through both rhythm and harmony on "faire," "rich," and "lovely" enhance the romantic stance; and so on. By contrast, the last line of the strophe is straightforward, without interpretive nuance of specific words; in context, it passes quickly and with relatively little attention. Dowland's is a delightful song, a fine example of the exquisite blending of music with the poem to create a new and altogether convincing whole; the student who hears that one first is very likely to think that's the way the poem was intended to be read.

Campion's own setting is rather plain, as many of Campion's musical settings were, refusing to use rhythm or any other means of creating the word-painting loved by many of the period's composers. This setting keeps us uncommitted to an interpretive tone, thus setting the stage for full appreciation of the ironic twist at the end. One of Campion's editors has noted that "Campion's contemporaries perhaps found the cynicism of the second strophe hard to accept, and so composed many substitutes for it"[4] (including an added strophe in one of the other musical settings). Dowland's setting seems to be a compromise, allowing that difficult strophe but minimizing its ironic impact.

That Campion provided his own musical setting might lead the student to a conclusion that his was the "correct" interpretation. But if she has *first* become persuaded of the "rightness" of another, such as the Dowland reading, there has been at least a seed of understanding planted. Furthermore, the fact that there are so

3   Walter Davis, ed., *The Works of Thomas Campion* (New York: Doubleday and Co., Inc., 1967), p. 184.
4   Ibid.

many different musical settings—and all quite different in style and interpretive stance, although I have only cited two—suggests that such reinterpretation was common in the period. It is doubtful that even Campion thought of his as the only viable reading.

In the other example, we do not have a setting by the poet, so a "correct" interpretation is not an option. "Sweet, stay awhile, why do you rise?" was long thought to be by John Donne, probably because of its superficial similarity to his "'Tis true, 'tis day, what though it be?" They even appeared together as one poem in some sources, although they are very clearly two separate poems and probably our song text is by someone else. The interpretive possibilities of this conventional lyric again become clear through music. No less than six English Renaissance composers found this *aubade* an appealing vehicle: A madrigal by Orlando Gibbons and a lute song by John Dowland appeared in 1612; anonymous settings occur in two manuscripts included in *English Song, 1600–1675*, as does a highly dramatic setting by Henry Lawes dating from the 1620s; and a very *un*dramatic setting with keyboard accompaniment is in *Elizabeth Rogers hir Virginal booke* (also reproduced in *English Song, 1600–1675*). Among them, these six settings demonstrate a broad range of interpretive stances and make an excellent vehicle for asking students to consider what might lead a composer to hear and understand the poem as he did.

Multiple performances of a single setting can also be useful. I remember one class in which I asked that students read and ponder this poem:

> Sorrow, stay, lend true repentant tears,
>   To a woeful, wretched wight.
> Hence, Despair with thy tormenting fears:
>   O do not my poor heart affright.
> Pity, help now or never,
>   Mark me not to endless pain,
> Alas I am condemned ever,
>   No hope, no help there doth remain,
>   But down, down, down, down I fall,
>   And arise I never shall.[5]

5 Quoted from *John Dowland, Second Book of Songs (1600)*, The English Lute-Songs, Series 1, vol. 5–6, ed. Edmund H. Fellows (London: Stainer and Bell, Ltd., 1921), p. 10.

Not, perhaps, a great work of literature, the poem occurs in musical setting by John Dowland, printed in 1600, and provides opportunities to discuss a number of poetic devices common in Elizabethan poetry. Apart from the unfamiliarity of the term "wight," the poem is relatively accessible to unsophisticated students, and they were appropriately moved by the dolorous tone and ponderous pace wrought by its language. I played a recording of Dowland's setting, which reinforced the generally positive assessment I had been leading them to find in the poem's ability to evoke a solemn mood. Then I put on another recording of the same song; I knew, as they did not, that it would create a rather different effect! My students listened respectfully until the singer and lutanist got to "woeful, woeful, wretched wight." At that point I began to hear some muffled snickers, and when he got to the song's reiterated "Pi-ty, pi-ty, pi-ty," with one accord they burst out laughing. Why? It was much too slow, the singer lingering heavily on the alliterations and repetitions, to the point that the poem's effect turned from pathos to bathos. The singer's interpretation, in other words, had failed to negotiate the poem's treacherous boundary between touching sadness and maudlin overstatement of grief. His interpretation, as the students could *hear*, was legitimate given the words of the poem but inappropriate to a desired result of fidelity to the poem's subject and to lack of any evidence that poet or composer intended to make a joke of sorrow. No doubt I could have found a way to talk to the students about the poem's potential for such over-interpretation and the need for sensitivity to context in finding a good reading, but the musical illustration did all that for me—and much more powerfully than I could have done with more words.

Above I mentioned teaching a course called "Literature and Other Arts." This was a wonderful course for students who were willing to explore the cognitive and expressive possibilities of the arts, separately and in combination. I used a lot of art songs, of course. The twentieth century has produced a wealth of musical settings of serious poetry from composers such as Gerald Finzi, Ralph Vaughan Williams, Benjamin Britten, Ned Rorem, and many others, setting such disparate poets as John Donne, Emily Dickinson, Walt Whitman, Thomas Hardy, W. H. Auden, Theodore Roethke, and more.[6] Using examples like these, I could interest students in the poetry by helping them focus on what the composer was trying to say through and about each poem. We *had* to read the poetry well to talk about the song, but conversely, the song led students back to the poem. I was able, for instance, to help them see how Donne's "Holy Sonnets" were alive and well in the twentieth century through the powerful musical settings of them by Benjamin Britten.[7] These dramatic settings, produced at the conclusion of World War II, are not only a tour de force for vocalist and pianist alike (and yes, I even tried to sing these myself, at least in the privacy of my own home), they evoke a poignant recognition of the emotional bond that a work of art can create between and across periods and cultures. An example like this is also illustrative of why the interdisciplinary perspective became so fundamental not only to my scholarship but to my teaching. Britten's songs are strong statements that need no explanation, just as Donne's poems can stand on their own. But the inquiring mind—the kind my best teachers sought to engender in me as I did in my students—wants to know more than that. Hence, with songs like these as my texts, I asked my students to consider history, religion, and war as well as literature and music, and together we began to piece together a sense of the *role* of the arts, even as they learned specific examples of the music and especially the poetry and interpretive skills that they could carry out of that class.

In a similar example, I recall teaching, in that same course, John Gay's *Beggar's Opera* and the Brecht/Weill *Three-Penny Opera*, using them as occasions to consider not only how music interprets a text but how the same story can lead to such divergent expressions in differing social and political context. It was near the start of the semester and this group of students was not yet accustomed to my exploratory method. One student in the back of the room, a little testy because I had asked what was going on in Germany in the 1920s that might have led to the creation of *Three-Penny Opera*—a question he obviously could not answer—asked me what business I had asking a

---

6 I have not even mentioned settings of the songs from Shakespeare's plays that have elicited literally thousands of musical settings.
7 Benjamin Britten, "The Holy Sonnets of John Donne" (London: Boosey and Hawkes, Ltd., 1946).

question about history in an English class. *His* question was wonderful for me; it gave me the perfect occasion to talk about the power of a work like this to demonstrate why knowledge of one facet—the music, for instance, or the dramatic text—in isolation from all others, does not create an education. As an enthusiast for musico-literary arts, and a lover of that work in particular, I wanted him to come to an appreciation of it. More importantly, though, as an educator, I wanted him to learn to keep asking "Why?" and to keep piecing together for himself an understanding of the arts as a critical function of any society.

No doubt some will criticize me for my willingness to swing through political and social as well as literary history, performance practices, and divergent musical styles as well as notes on the page, as I try to assemble as full a picture of a work of musico-literary art as I can. I did not begin to do that for myself until I was a graduate student, but once I did, what had been isolated phenomena—perhaps a song or poem or play I particularly liked—began to have much greater depth and meaning. So I do not apologize for encouraging under-graduate students to explore broadly, to create for themselves a picture of a work of art in a context.

Going back to that interview I described at the start of this essay, when I recognized the extent to which I had become carried away in a direction that was not very much relevant to administrative work, I made a quick turn to the development of organizational skills and the ability to supervise others (a research assistant; several computer techies), which were also parts of my growth through this project. I talked about its role in forcing me to learn computer skills. I suspect that the devel-opment of such skills is a factor in the movement of more than one scholar/teacher toward the administrative side of our endeavor. One does have to have some basis for confidence that he or she can keep a large operation functioning and even guide it toward some productive ends. Rescuing my interview, I talked about these things and was even persuaded myself that I had learned valuable administrative skills through my scholar-ship. On reflection, however, I think that the more important role of that project and of my scholarship and teaching career prior to my becoming an administrator comes from the pen-chant they developed in me for liking to ferret out how a sys-tem emerges from its component parts, taking on a life of its own that is more than, and different from, those component parts. I have a genuinely interdisciplinary perspective on academia. As an arts and sciences dean and passionate advocate for its broadly conceived mission, I have loved learning enough about all twenty-six departments and interdisciplinary programs in the college so that I can see and speak for the intellectual whole that grows from them. I actually *like* being an academic administrator, and I believe that my prior years as a scholar and teacher, in literature and in music, developed not only the so-called administrative skills I have needed, and the compassion, the patience, the respect for the often arcane processes of academia that can come only from working within it, but most importantly the ability to reflect on and envision a whole that is richer by far than any one of its parts could be.

I also still love literature, and music, and their coincident appearance in so many exquisite moments. I am known among my colleagues for incorporating into most presentations, no matter how far afield they seem to be, a poem or a passage from a play, often involving music somehow. I can do no better here than to end with the lines from Thomas Campion's "Now winter nights enlarge the number of their hours" that gave voice to my early explorations, with John Hollander, into the precise ways in which musical setting might interpret poetry. These lines seem equally apt to describe a satisfying stage in an academic life, when its separate strands have come together into a well-tuned, amazing whole.

> Now winter nights enlarge
>   The number of their houres,
> And clouds their stormes discharge
>   Upon the ayrie towres;
> Let now the chimneys blaze
>   And cups o'erflow with wine,
> Let well-tun'd words amaze
>   With harmonie divine.[8]

8 Davis, *Thomas Campion*, p. 147.

In Translation

STEPHEN CUSHMAN

Forty-five years old and a smiling, mostly
private man, I'm visiting Latin class and
schoolboys reading Horace's little poem
    written in Sapphics:

Persicos odi, puer, apparatus.
"I hate Persian showiness, boy." Or something
close to that. But they haven't heard of Sappho
    pining on Lesbos,

so I tell them, wondering whether Horace—
no, *the speaker*—fancies this fellow serving
wine to him, and some of the guys discover
    possible inklings,

what he may have had on his mind; yet mine turns
elsewhere, frightened, drawn to their teacher, writhing
in a chair, his Parkinson's symptoms awful,
    much worse than yours, Dad,

arms convulsed with hideous, constant spasms
twisting hands and neck that keeps torquing sideways,
downwards. Damn. No wonder the gospels would have
    called it a demon.

Much worse now. But this will be you soon, won't it?
How I want to turn to the blackboard, blubber
like a kindergartener badly bullied,
    forfeit on being

stoic, uncomplainingly cheerful, steadfast.
And I would, if not for the boys who never
smirk or shudder, learning instead the lesson
    always before them

in his bothered body and love of Latin,
slowly learning languages no one speaks now
do not have to dwindle and die, whatever
    happens to fathers.

Telling Tales Out of School:
John Hollander's Faith of Profession

AIDAN WASLEY

John Hollander's poems tell us, in the title of one that gave its name to the eighth (of the current sixteen and counting) of his books of poetry, "Tales Told of the Fathers." In that poem— which meditates on its own contingency and lateness by ring- ing changes on tropes of reflection and shadow, water and earth, surface and depth, son and father—the ambiguous "of" in the title is *telling*, in every sense. The semantic uncertainty it inhabits and illuminates is both characteristic and revealing of this poet's habit of obsessive attention to the potential rewards of what Emily Dickinson named, as a definition of poetry, "dwelling in possibility." It *tells* us that it is a Hollander poem. And, reflective of the title for which it serves as a kind of signi- fying fulcrum, it tells a tale. That tale, recounted in the mul- tiple meanings that "of" allows, is about *telling* itself and about poetry and about teaching, all of which, for Hollander, as we will see, are reflective tropes for the same thing: what he calls (following Richard Poirier, and again employing that provoca- tive preposition) "the work of knowing."[1]

Hollander, as is his wont, has himself already addressed in his prose criticism the intricate evasions of "of" encountered in his poetic practice, outlining a few of the more noteworthy of the sixty-three definitions of "of" offered in the OED and sin-

---

1 I'd like to gratefully acknowledge the assistance of Jennifer Lewin, Sarah Spence, and Anne Mallory in the writing of this essay. I've also found Willard Spiegelman's excellent book, *The Didactic Muse: Scenes of Instruction in Contemporary Poetry* (Princeton: Princeton University Press, 1989) to be extremely helpful in thinking about Hollander's place in the late twentieth-century tradition of poetic didacticism. On "the work of knowing," see John Hollander, "The Philosopher's Cat," *Melodious Guile: Fictive Pattern in Poetic Language* (New Haven: Yale University Press, 1988), p. 228.

gling out for special consideration the poetic implications of the preposition's sense as "concerning" or "about."[2] This is an obvious primary meaning for Hollander's poem's title, suggesting a reading of the phrase along the lines of "tales told on the subject of the fathers," and implying that it is the wisdom, deeds, or traditions of the "fathers" that the poem is concerned to transmit to their putative heirs and posterity. As we will see in a moment, this is an understanding of poetry's role and function that Hollander's own poetry everywhere manifests, in implicit and explicit terms. Hollander, more than almost any American poet since Pound (with whom he has a vexed poetic relation), sees his poetry as an act of what he terms "restitution," the preservation and restoration of an inherited tradition in danger of being lost to the ignorance, apathy, or ideology of an unreflective present oblivious to the danger of faith in a past-less future.[3] He is a scribe, an exegete, a curator (the "cover life" of the poet-spy hero of *Reflections on Espionage*) of a storied cultural and poetic past, recording, interpreting, and telling those stories to and for the future, and the figures of Hollander's own poetic "fathers" occupy prominent clearings in the groves of his own verse.

This aspect of Hollander's poetic project is echoed in a number of the subsidiary interpretive readings of the "of" of his title. Those readings would include the genitives of possession and of origin, yielding "tales told that belong to the fathers" and "tales told by, or issuing from, the fathers." The notion that the poet is either the mere custodian of inherited tales, with which he has been entrusted but of which he can claim no personal ownership, or the willing and empty vessel inspirited by the tales of the father-muses, accords further with Hollander's understanding of his filial place in what he elsewhere calls the "father's house of our speculative life,"[4] though, in a revision and reversal of the trope, in the latter figure of tradition-as-house it is now the son—the Poet *fils*—who fills the vacant rooms and stories (such turnings of trope are, Hollander would say, where poetry resides). This conception of the poet

2 Hollander, "Of *of*: The Poetics of a Preposition," *The Work of Poetry* (New York: Columbia University Press, 1997), pp. 96–110.
3 Hollander, "A Poetry of Restitution," *The Work of Poetry*, pp. 39–63.
4 Hollander, "The Philosopher's Cat," *Melodious Guile*, p. 231.

surrendering himself to be filled by the voices of his fathers (bottles and pots are two more favorite Hollanderian poetic tropes) also paradoxically marks the tradition-minded Hollander as a child of modernity, schooled in an idea of poetic impersonality inherited from two of his younger poetic parents, Eliot and Auden. It also corresponds with yet another related reading of the "of," which posits a similar trope of containment, but instead of the son being possessed of and by the tales of the father, in this case it is the tales themselves that contain the fathers. Interpreting it as "tales told in the form of, or consisting of, the fathers," we approach the somewhat startling conceit in which tale and father become synonymous: the tales *are* the fathers. Hollander explores this idea in his poem "Others Who Have Lived in This Room," in which the "rooms" are, as poets and Italians know, another name for "stanza," and in the poems' rhyme scheme is found lurking the figure of the father: "The daughters' measures may surprise, / The Mother Memory can amuse, / But *Abba*'s spirit must infuse / The form which will memorialize." This concept of the poem both memorializing and being inhabited by the Miltonic spirit of the poetic fathers is one shared by Hollander's friend James Merrill, who builds an epic poem out of the voices of his dead poetic fathers (and mothers), including Auden (a mentor, in life, of both Hollander and Merrill), whom he affectionately terms, "the father of forms."

Two more readings of Hollander's telling title may be apposite here. One follows closely on those already mentioned but emphasizes the transitive possibilities implicit in the verb, suggesting a sense of audience that implies both contestation and homage: "tales told to, or for the fathers." Hollander's sense of his responsibilities to his poetic precursors, his anxieties at measuring his meters against theirs, and his ambitions to honor and satisfy the gallery of listening dead, all contribute to our understanding of his work as being written, as he titles one of the sections of *A Crackling of Thorns* (his first book), "For Tellers of Tales" (my italics). In one last reading, we can also see the phrase, if we choose to, as "tales told on the fathers," in the sense of telling rude, irreverent stories about one's elders, or spilling family secrets. This, too, is apt for the poet who delights in unearthing and bringing to vivid contemporary life a series of pornographic maledictions from Catullus in *Town & Country*

Matters, or the one who reveals a subtext of youthful erotic yearning behind the primal Platonic scene of instruction in "Songs for Glaucon" from his first book. The student who willfully "muddles the lesson," as he puts it in that early song-sequence, or the smart-alecky class clown, making impolite jokes and throwing spitballs at the teacher, are roles that Hollander enjoys playing throughout his books, even as he turns the joke on himself in the double-dactyls of *Rhyme's Reason*, where "Schoolteacher Hollander" starts to "mutter and grumble and / cavil and curse," turning grumpy over the labor of his lesson in verse. And while humor, both erudite and earthy, is one of the hallmarks of Hollander's poetry, this frivolity can be serious business, too; after all, as Hollander the tale-telling student knows, the words "play," "child," and "teach" all had the same etymological root in Plato's schoolroom. And the notion of the poet as informant, as the tattletale of the tradition, is one that Hollander also takes seriously, troping this concern with the tale of Cupcake, the spy in *Reflections on Espionage* who is "terminated" (and note the complex pun on "term" here: the textual avatar is killed with words—or, more precisely, with silence) for telling too much.

Hollander's poetics, then, is fundamentally concerned with the notion of *telling*. Hollander's poems are poems that tell, and tell about their own telling. But, characteristically, in order to fully understand Hollander's understanding of the idea of poetic telling, we need first to read him reading his own poetic "fathers" (and for Hollander, student of Sappho, Dickinson, and Moore, "fathers" is, obviously, a trope for all his poetic forebears, regardless of gender). And since Hollander has, by common consensus, read everything, a truly diligent student of the poetic tradition who has listened to its lessons with sufficient depth of attention, imagination, and insight would want here to trace a thorough history and taxonomy (a favorite Hollander word) of the trope of poetic *telling*, beginning with that first "father," who kicked off the proceedings by asking, "Sing in me, Muse, and through me tell the story / of that man skilled in all ways of contending" (translation of Robert Fitzgerald). Or limiting himself to English poetry, he might choose to start where that story begins, with the "tales tweye" of Chaucer's pilgrims, and follow the thread of the tale up through, among countless examples, Shakespeare's sonnets "still telling what is told," Wordsworth's "Simon Lee," and Coleridge's Ancient Mariner, Lewis Carroll's "Tale of the Mouse" (another Hollander favorite), Dickinson's "Tell all the truth but tell it slant," and ending, perhaps, with Wallace Stevens, looking for an idea of order and entreating the notional Ramon Fernandez to "Tell me, if you know." But as such a student is hard to come by—indeed, it's a job-description perhaps best filled by Hollander himself—we'll content ourselves with a more informal and episodic study of some of the ways Hollander relates to the tales told by a few particular presences in his poetic house, and suggest that in relating to them he relates them to us, in the double sense of connecting us with them as well as in the sense of *telling* them to us. And it's in this multiple sense of relation, and in the many tales of telling that he tells, that we can begin to see how Hollander's double vocation of poet and teacher amount, in the end, to the same thing: he is one who, in every sense, tells.

For Hollander, the story truly begins with Spenser, the most beloved of all his poetic fathers. And, in particular, it's in "The Shepheardes Calender" that we first hear many of the tales of telling that Hollander will echo. In fact, from the perspective of those many readers and students who have learned the tale of the tradition from listening to Hollander's telling of it, one might even hear the echoes calling in reverse, in a phenomenon that his friend Harold Bloom would call *apophrades*, but which Hollander himself more suggestively describes as hearing "the earlier poem . . . send[ing] back echoes to the voice of the later one, echoes that resound from the cave of memory and remembered poetry."[5] Everywhere we look in "The Shepheardes Calender," we see Hollander, from the schematic arrangement of poems by month, each with its own thematic, figurative, and autobiographical agenda, reminding us of Hollander poems like "Spectral Emanations," which takes its poetic scheme from the colors of the spectrum, to the copious explanatory footnotes—offering "a certain Glosse or scholion for thexposition of old wordes & harder phrases"—well-known to any reader of Hollander's own books. The allegorical emblems woven into each of Spenser's poems similarly suggest Hollander's interest in emblematic shaped poems in which the

5 Hollander, "Poetic Answers," *Melodious Guile*, p. 58.

incorporation of the picture into the text, as Hollander puts it in his introduction to *Types of Shape*, "allows the poem to talk to and of itself, in modern allegorical fashion, and thereby talk even more about its 'subject.'"[6] And within those emblematic woodcuts themselves, with their attention to the allegorical meanings of the various zodiacal constellations, we see a reflection of Hollander's own recurring obsession with messages hidden in the stars, both actual and figural, in poems like "The Observatory," "The Great Bear," "Movie-Going" ("Never ignore the stars, of course"), "Seeing Stars" (a love lyric to "Asteria Stern"), "Under Cancer," "Under Capricorn," and "Under Aquarius" (the latter three, especially the last, which takes Auden as its elegiac subject, echoing the elder poet's "Under Sirius"). For Hollander, as for Spenser, "The stars are lessons for my learning," as his ephebic representative Glaucon puts it in *Crackling of Thorns* ("Glaucon Returns to School").

The three classes of poetry in which "The Shepheardes Calender" announces its interest—"Plaintive," "Recreative," and "Moral"—also serve usefully to classify Hollander's own distinct poetic genres, which range discretely between poems of longing and loss, poems of play and restitution, and poems of high cultural and moral sentence. And there are other echoes, too, in terms of both poetic theme and form. For instance, Spenser's fictive poetic agent, the shepherd Colin Clout, fades into silence, death, and blankness (Colin's emblem at the end of the poem is, famously, an empty space) at the conclusion of the poem's year, just as Hollander's pastoral-spy Cupcake (an alliterative echo of "Colin Clout") is silenced with a final, fatal transmission of "XXXXXXXXXXXXXXXX" in *Reflections on Espionage*. And the perfect formal square of Spenser's epilogue of twelve lines of twelve syllables, mirroring the poem's monthly theme, finds its reflection—enhanced, as if by the student's good-natured attempts to outdo his teacher, with an extra syllable and line—in Hollander's triskaideka-sonnets, thirteen lines of thirteen syllables, in *Powers of Thirteen*, whose collection of diaristic poems further relates it, along with the book of daily espionage dispatches from Cupcake, to Spenser's calendrical poem. And, as we learn in the envoy to Spenser's poem,

---

6 Hollander, "Introduction," *Types of Shape* (New Haven: Yale University Press, 1991), p. xi.

"To His Booke," in which the poet instructs his text, "A shep-heards swaine saye did thee sing, / All as his straying flocke he fedd," even the career path of the shepherds themselves echoes Hollander's own since they, like him, have two jobs—poets and tenders of a flock.

Importantly, it's also in that envoy, which begins with a famous act of echoic telling, "Goe little booke, thy self present, / As child whose parent is unkent," that we hear Hollander's own tale-troping ringing most tellingly in our ear. Here, the book (another trope for the poem itself) is the child who is also simultaneously the tale told by the poetic father, about the father, belonging to the father, and standing in for the absent father. And, in constructing this poetic self-representation, Spenser tells his own tale of the father, self-consciously echo-ing Chaucer's opening to *Troilus and Criseyde*, "Go litel bok, go litel myn tragedye." In yet another layer of reflective fiction-making, Spenser has his notional critical envoy, "E.K." (in the initials of whom we might read, among other things, the Greek "ek," for "out," thus reinscribing the poem's mission out in the world; a joke on the notion of an "ekename"—spelled "ekname" as recently as the late fifteenth century—meaning an alternative- or nickname; or a phonemic echo of "echo"), explain in the poem's "Epistle" both the putatively anonymous poet's imitation of Chaucer and his decision to mask himself in the poem in the "base" figure of Colin Clout (still another level of taletelling) as the necessary effect of his ambition to succeed his poetic predecessors through "following the example of the best and most auncient Poetes, which devised this kind of wryting." Spenser tries to equal his poetic fathers by surren-dering to their example, and gives their old tales a new life by retelling them. He submerges his identity within layers of tale-telling: tales told of the fathers and tales that, following their example, he tells of himself.

Another word for "envoy" is "agent" and Spenser's multiple poetic envoys—the "To His Booke" poem, "E.K.," Colin Clout, and "The Shepheardes Calender" itself—are all, in fictive terms, working undercover. The poet commands his poem to go out into the world under a cloak of strict anonymity (a demand considerably belied by the many coy allusions to the author's true identity throughout the poem), and report back on what it finds:

But if that any aske thy name,
Say thou wert base begot with blame:
For thy thereof thou takest shame.
And when thou art past jeopardee,
Come tell me, what was sayd of mee:
And I will send more after thee.

The poet, "E.K." tells us, "chose rather to unfold great matter of argument covertly, then professing it," and here Spenser announces his covert method even as he insists on the necessity of secrecy. In the process of establishing the terms of his own fiction, he conspicuously blows his own cover as orchestrating fiction-master. With every successive layer of fiction of anonymity, he points ever more obviously to himself as author. The poem *tells* of the poet precisely through its claim to tell nothing of its origins, with Spenser setting up a complex series of tropes on the notion of telling. The poem is an old tale that he is retelling and to which he is surrendering his own poetic identity, yet in articulating this surrender, he both tells a new tale and asserts, or "professes," his own poetic authority. He is, as "E.K." puts it, "applying an olde name to a new worke"; a work that bears the "names" of his predecessors—full, as the poem is, of poetic retellings of Chaucer, Theocritus, and Plutarch—yet is manifestly Spenser's own. The poem tells the world about the poet and then, in a reversal of the trope in the envoy's final lines, the poem itself tells the poet about the world and about himself: "Come tell me, what was sayd of me." The poem is both ambassador and spy, and the tale it tells of its own reception and place in the world serves to illuminate that world to both the poet and the reader. The word "calendar" carries with it, along with its chronological meaning, an implication of guide, model, or example, along with a sense of report or announcement. Spenser is using his "Calender" to quintuply tell: to count off the months, to retail old tales, to inform the world of his existence, to glean news of that world that will be helpful for his future work, and to announce himself as a model—a new "father"—for future poems and poets (a secondary meaning of "calender"—Spenser spells it with an "e"—as a machine for papermaking may be further suggestive of Spenser's notion of himself as a page others will write on and of). It's a model that Hollander himself clearly follows, down to the distinctive verse form of Spenser's envoy—eight-syllable rhyming triplets—which he will use to praise the "origi-nality" of, and assert his own connections to, one of his contem-porary poetic elders in "To Elizabeth Bishop."

Spenser pursues the trope of telling throughout "The Shep-heardes Calender," which consists almost entirely of shepherds vying with one another in "telling tales." There's a pastoral pun here (which Milton, as the OED helpfully alerts us, later picks up in *L'Allegro*'s "every shepherd tells his tale / under the haw-thorn in the dale") in that the shepherds are simultaneously recounting stories to one another, while counting the number of their sheep—"telling tails." We can see an example of Spenser's concern with the resonances of telling in the February eclogue, in which the aged Thenot and the irreverent younger shep-herd, Cuddie, contend over the old shepherd's offer to "tel thee a tale of truth, / Which I cond of Tityrus in my youth," after which Cuddie impudently responds: "Now I pray thee shep-heard, tel it not forth: / Here is a long tale, and little worth." In Thenot's retelling of the old tale of Tityrus, whom "E.K." glosses as the figure of Chaucer, Spenser enacts his principle of following the example of the "best and most auncient Poetes," while Cuddie's mockery allows him to playfully tweak his pre-decessor for excessive didacticism, even as his poem ironically rehearses Chaucer's famous admonition that those who "shall telle a tale after a man" must "reherce" it as exactly as he can, "Or ellis he must telle his tale untrewe, / Or feyne thing, or fynde wordes newe." The fact that Thenot's tale turns out not to be from Chaucer after all, but from Aesop, may be a self-conscious reflection on, or evasion of, the burden of "telling a tale after a man." This trope of telling, and its relation to the parental influence of Chaucer, returns most forcefully in the June eclogue, in which Colin Clout, amid a love lament, elegizes Tityrus, the original shepherd poet:

> The God of shepheards *Tityrus* is dead,
> Who taught me homely, as I can, to make.
> He, whilst he lived, was the soveraigne head
> Of shepheards all, that bene with love ytake:
> Well couth he wayle hys Woes, and lightly slake
> The flames, which love within his heart had bredd,
> And tell us mery tales, to keep us wake,
> The while our sheepe about us safely fedde.

Nowe dead he is, and lyeth wrapt in lead,
(O why should death on him such outrage show?)
And all hys passing skil with him is fledde,
The fame whereof doth dayly greater growe.
But if on me some little drops would flowe,
Of that spring was in his learned hedde,
I soone would learne these woods, to wayle my woe,
And teache the trees, their trickling teares to shedde.

Colin Clout credits Tityrus, Spenser's stand-in for Chaucer
(and, elsewhere, Virgil, the father of the eclogue form Spenser
employs), with teaching him, "as I can, to make." This instruction, Colin recalls, came in the "mery tales" the elder poet told
"to keep us wake," suggesting that those tales had a double
ambition to entertain and to educate. And with the death of
"the pure well head of Poesie," as Spenser calls Chaucer in *The
Faerie Queene*, Colin here proposes himself as Tityrus' heir and
next in the line of taletelling poet-teachers, with such powers
that he can even "learne these woods" and "teache the trees."
The pedagogical aspirations of Spenser's poetic tales will be
sounded again in the "Calender's" epilogue, which asserts his
aim "To teach the ruder shepheard how to feed his sheepe, /
And from the falsers fraud his folded flocke to keepe." One
young shepherd who took careful notes on Colin's lectures was
Hollander, whose very name, which translates (via Dutch) as
"woodlander," seems to nominate him as one of Colin's pastoral heirs.

Listen to Cupcake's second dispatch from *Reflections on
Espionage*:

> Steampump is gone. He died quietly in his
> Hotel room and his sleep. His cover people
> Attended to everything. What had to
> Be burned was burned. He taught me, as you surely
> Know, all that I know: yet I had to pass him
> By in the Square at evening—in the soft
> Light of wrought-iron lamps and the rich, cheerful
> Shadows which rose up from the stones to meet it—
> Without even our eyes having touched, without
> Acknowledgment. And thereby, of course, we were
> Working together. What kind of work is this
> For which if we were to touch in the darkness

It would be without feeling the other there?
It might help to know whether Steampump's dying
Was part of the work or not. I shall not be
Told, I know Until next time, this is Cupcake.

In an explicit echo of Colin's lament for the elder shepherd
Tityrus, Cupcake mourns the passing of Steampump, the
elder spy who "taught me, as you surely / Know, all that I
know." Steampump, as readers of Hollander's spy-pastoral
learn (helped along by his own glossing in the recent edition), is Auden, who earns his codename through his well-
known love of industrial machinery, and whose own figuration of the poet as a spy in poems like "The Secret Agent"
serves as source for Hollander's poem. Auden's "The Orators," in fact, unmistakably anticipates the enigmatic milieu,
portentous atmosphere, and didactic ethos of Hollander's
poetic fable in its conflation of the worlds of the spy and the
public school: "They speak of things done on the frontier we
were never told, / The hidden path to the Pictish tower /
They will never reveal though kept without sleep, for their
code is / 'Death to the squealer.'"

Hollander has often acknowledged Auden's formative influence on his own career and work, and in elegizing the twentieth century's chief poetic elegist in the figure of Steampump
he follows Spenser's figuration of poetic inheritance in terms
of retelling tales told of the fathers. In "The Sheapheardes Calender" "E.K." invokes a Ciceronian metaphor in his justification of Spenser's echoes of "the most excellent Authors and
most famous Poetes," suggesting that since "our Poet hath
been much traveiled and thoroughly redd" in the words of
those poets, "how could it be, (as that worthy Oratour sayde)
but that walking in the sonne although for other cause he walked,
of those auncient Poetes still ringing in his eares, he mought
needes in singing hit out some of theyr tunes." Spenser's pun
on "sun" and "son" will be retold in the title poem of "Tales
Told of the Fathers" ("The father is light's general, / The son is
but a morning star"), and his idea, that the younger poet walking in the sun of the elder can't help but get a little sunburnt, is
one that Hollander himself has both recognized and wrestled
with in terms of his poetic relation with Auden, observing in
an essay his own struggles as a young poet in "trying to emerge

from a region of ventriloquism" of Auden.[7] This ambivalence on the part of the older Hollander is figured in the impossibility of Cupcake acknowledging Steampump in his elegy, even as that lack of acknowledgment itself constitutes a recognition of the debt: "And thereby, of course, we were / Working together." In asking whether Steampump's death shadows his own work, Cupcake poses the problem of poetic influence—anxiety versus acknowledgment—and leaves it as a mystery befitting a spy story: he, and we, "shall not be told."

Evidence of Hollander's "working together" with Auden is everywhere in his poetry: Clearly, the younger poet has the words of the older one "still ringing in his eares." Indeed, the first poem of Hollander's first book—chosen by Auden for the Yale Younger Poets series—opens with a retelling of the Icarus myth, including a rewriting of Icarus' encounter with the ploughman made famous in Auden's poem on Brueghel's painting (Auden, unsurprisingly, chose not to comment upon this self-conscious echo—which is simultaneously an homage and a challenge—from his poetic child in his introduction to the book). A poem like the young Hollander's villanelle on capability, "A Theory of Measure," with its refrains, "We draw our own dimensions after all / Our shadows at evening tell us that we're tall," calls back to Auden's own mid-career villanelle on failure, "If I Could Tell You:" "Time will say nothing but I told you so / If I could tell you I would let you know." Here, Hollander takes Auden's trope of "telling," in the sense of "saying," and turns it toward a different sense, meaning "to inform," while revising Auden's use of one of his trademark words, "tall." In poems like "Taller Today" and "O, Where Are You Going," Auden liked to use the word in its Anglo-Saxon sense, meaning quick, active, strong, capable or brave, and often employed its contrastive qualities to suggest the inevitable fate awaiting such self-possession: "The gap is the grave where the tall return." Hollander hears this lesson but, fittingly for a poet just beginning an ambitious career, optimistically amends it to tell a story of growth and achievement rather than unsuccess. By "drawing our own dimensions," says Hollander, we learn our own capabilities: the

---

7 Hollander, "A Poem for Music: Remarks on the Composition of *Philomel," Vision and Resonance: Two Senses of Poetic Form* (New Haven: Yale University Press, 1985), p. 293.

"shadows" of the work we do "tell us that we're tall." Just as the word "tall" echoes but phonemically revises the word "tell," Hollander echoes Auden but revises him, in an assertion of the student's mastery of the teacher's lesson. He "measures" his measures against those of his master and finds himself measuring up, following Colin Clout in his assertion of his place as Tityrus' next in line: Steampump is gone, but, "Until next time, this is Cupcake." Hollander stands tall in his inheritance of Spenser and Auden's tradition of telling.

Indeed, we can say that Hollander's principal poetic subject— he would say *poetry's* principal subject— is precisely the tale it tells about its own telling. The recurrence of this theme and its figuration in his poems is so continual and pervasive that we might even be tempted to say it constitutes his "tell," the repeated gesture in poker that gives the game away, in a meaning of the word that does not show up among the OED's twenty-eight definitions but of which we can be sure Hollander is aware. Hollander's poems speak of "tell's" other meaning too, including the telling of time (clocks and calendars are frequent motifs), as well as its related sense of "counting," not just of hours and days (and of Colin Clout's sheep-tails) but also of metrical units in poetry. "Times of counting are times of remembering," Hollander says in "At the New Year," speaking of both the calendar's and poetry's capacity to order time and memory. But it's in the opening poem of *Powers of Thirteen,* titled "Refusing to Tell Tales," that Hollander addresses the question most explicitly of how poetry tells:

> This is neither the time nor the place for singing of
> Great persons, wide places, noble things—high times, in short;
> Of knights and of days' errands to the supermarket;
> Of spectres, appearances and disappearances;
> Of quests for the nature of the quest, let alone for
> Where or when the quest would start. You are the wrong person
> To ask me for a circus of incident, to play
> Old out-of-tunes on a puffing new calliope,
> Or to be the unamused client of history.
> But tell me of the world your word has kept between us;
> I do what I am told, and tell what is done to me,
> Making but one promise safely hedged in the Poets'
> Paradox: *I shall say "what was never said before."*

Rewriting the sixteenth-century modesty *topos* of Spenser's envoy in terms of a late modernist's anxiety about how in singing not to sing, Hollander begins his own envoy to his sequence of diminished, thirteen-line sonnets with an assertion of its diminished ambition. With a list of poetic options—inherited tales—that his poem will *not* rehearse, Hollander's poem claims to define itself through its negation of previous poetic models even as it confesses its knowledge that this negation is itself an inherited tale. As in Spenser's envoy, Hollander addresses his poetic fiction directly, but rather than telling it "go, little book," he engages it in debate, disputing the demands of poetic convention it brings. Spenser's poem is sent on its way; Hollander's seems to have arrived from somewhere else and started an argument. Where it has come from is Spenser himself—poet of *The Faerie Queene*'s "knights" and *The Shepheardes Calender*'s "days"—and Auden—author of a sonnet sequence called "The Quest" on "the nature of the quest"[8]— and the poetic tradition they stand in for; the argument Hollander is having with himself, and that tradition, is how to say something new when everything has already been said. But that argument, the poet knows, is the oldest poetic argument of all; indeed, every poem by every poet is an effort to resolve that argument, each poet's answer to that first of all questions. Hollander finds his solution by "refusing to tell" the inherited tales themselves, and instead telling about poetic *telling* itself. "I shall say 'what was never said before,'" he concludes, with the quotation marks around the final phrase telling the story: "What was never said before" is what every poem claims to tell. But it's the poem's knowledge of, and capacity to communicate, that paradox of telling that gives it what Spenser might call its "clout," and gives the poet something new to say, in the same old way.

8 One sonnet from Auden's "The Quest," entitled "The Pilgrim" (or "The Traveller"), in *Collected Poems* (New York: Vintage, 1991), seems especially apropos here:

> Could he forget a child's ambition to be old
> And institutions where it learned to wash and lie,
> He'd tell the truth for which he thinks himself too young,
> That everywhere on the horizon of his sigh
> Is now, as always, only waiting to be told
> To be his father's house and speak his mother tongue.

Hollander's envoy riffs on various tropes of telling, finding poetry's power and purpose simply in its multiple capacities to *tell*. First, poetry "tells" in that it *gives voice to* something. Here the poem itself speaks: *in propria persona*, for the poet, and for all of poetry. This is a theme to which Hollander returns repeatedly, in poems like "A Fragment Twice Repaired," in which a scrap of an incomplete poem by Sappho finally "gets to / speak her piece," or in "Tesserae 109," where, "These lines, these bits and pieces, each a token / Of ruined method, of 'a knowledge broken,' / Inaudible, leave traces when they pass / As if fragments of our speech had spoken." He has also written numerous poems on Philomel and Arachne, figures of art and poetry's power to give voice to the silent. Hollander also sees poetry, as all poets must, as a means to stave off our final silence, even if those efforts, as in the case of Cupcake, are doomed inevitably to fail. His vocation (a word, after all, in which we hear the call of the voice) is to give a voice, both to his own retold tales and to those who might lack the power to tell their own.

Poetry also tells the poet "of the world your word has kept between us"; it *informs* him, and us, about the world through its efforts to embody that world. As Hollander puts it in an interview with the critic and scholar (and one of Hollander's old students, now carrying on the tale) Langdon Hammer, "Poems get to be about the world by being about how to talk about it."[9] For Hollander, poems are what Wallace Stevens calls "parts of a world": they "talk to, and of themselves, not to evade discourse about the world but to enable it."[10] Poetry does this by telling us what it knows about itself: that it, like us, is part of a story that was begun and will be continued by others, but to which we, like every new poem, can constructively contribute and add a new chapter. The vast history of poetic taletelling in which every poem is implicated stands itself as a trope for our own connectedness to a world larger than ourselves, and, by encouraging us to see our inescapable place within that world, invites us to engage in it. The raw

9 Hollander, "Working Through Poems: An Interview with Langdon Hammer," *The Poetry of Everyday Life* (Ann Arbor: University of Michigan Press, 1998), p. 161.
10 Hollander, "Turnings and Fashionings," *Melodious Guile*, p. 15.

material of poetry, language itself, imparts the same lesson, as the etymology and placement within a sentence of a word both reveal its dependence on wider systems of signification: without knowing where a word comes from, or how it works in relation to other grammatical units, we can't know what it means. The moral fable that poetry and language tells is that in order to know who we are and where we, like Spenser's "little book," might go, we need to know where we come from— the history written by others but of which we are a part. It's a fable whose lesson is a notion of community, an idea of citizenship in what Auden liked to call the "civitas" created by the voices of the dead still speaking in and through the living. To read a poem is to affirm one's place in a world of relations— intellectual and moral, historical and contemporary, civic and familial. It is this tale, says Hollander, which poetry has told from the start and, as long as poetry continues to be read, will always tell.

In Hollander's line, "I do what I am told, and tell what is done to me," we get two more related notions of telling. In the poet's earlier request that the poem tell him about the world, and in the grammatical ambiguity of the latter half of this line, we get a sense of poetry's power to tell in terms of its capacity *to reveal* hidden truths or unknown information. The final clause of that line can be read in two ways, either as the poet saying that his poetic job is to "tell what is done to me," in the sense of revealing the influences acting upon him, or as the poet asking the "you" of the previous line, the poem itself (as Spenser does of his own envoy) to tell the poet "what is done to me," suggesting that the poet learns about himself in the act of writing the poem. This dual idea of poetic revelation is closely allied with another important meaning of "tell," which is *to instruct*. Poetry tells us things we didn't know, sometimes things we didn't know we didn't know. Readers—and especially critics—of Hollander's poetry are familiar with a certain aspect of this idea that poetry is, and should be, didactic. Every reader of a Hollander poem learns something, whether it's about the taxonomy of movie-theaters that used to line Broadway in the 1950s, or that "*Vin albastru* is blue wine in Rumanian," to pluck two exemplary nuggets at random. Hollander can't resist passing on some share of the enormous store of information he's gathered over the years, and the reader is the beneficiary of that impulse to disclose. But it's not in its dispersal of useful facts, or even in its retelling of forgotten narratives of history, art, and language, that Hollander's poetic pedagogy truly happens. Rather, it's in places like that grammatically ambiguous poetic line, where, as he puts it in another poem, "Meaning is up for grabs, but not for sale" ("Edward Hopper's 7 A.M."). Here, what we don't know is what we think. We are forced to decide for ourselves the answer to the questions of meaning the poem provides. In the process, we learn not about some specific piece of information or course of action, but about knowing, and how we know. "I do what I am told," says the poet, but the irony is that the poem doesn't tell the poet to *do* anything, except *tell*. The poet retells the old tales, but not in the service of any idea other than an idea of idea itself. It's like the sound of the enigmatic Trumpeter of Hollander's visionary poem "The Head of the Bed": a melody that clearly tells something, but what it heralds or mourns depends on the hearer. "Poetry makes nothing happen," says Auden, but for Hollander, who has written a poem in praise of "Making Nothing Happen," that "nothing" is everything. The "nothing" a poem makes is the open space of Dickinson's "possibility," a place of pure questioning where the old tales become windows into new self-understandings. The way we answer the questions the poem poses tells us who we are. In this way, "telling" becomes synonymous for Hollander with "asking," rather than its antonym.

This is where John Hollander's careers as both poet and teacher reveal themselves to have been "working together" all along, and are, in fact, merely reflections of a single central project: teaching us to *tell*, in its final sense, meaning "to perceive" or "to discern." Hollander's poems are like seminars: stanza builds upon stanza in the equivalent of a poetic semester, at the end of which we, as his students, understand a little more about how we go about understanding the world. A poet is one who tells, who professes: a professor. And the lesson is less in what to do and say than in how to look and think, and think about thinking, informed but unfettered by the old tales. The poems teach us to perceive the old world, draw our own new conclusions, and then go, like Spenser's book, out in the world to tell what we've learned and keep the tale going (which may account for the large number of Hollander's stu-

dents who have gone on to become teachers and poets themselves). Auden famously ends his elegy for Yeats with a statement of ambition that is also a prayer for poetry's power to
console: "In the deserts of the heart / Let the healing fountain
start, / In the prison of his days / Teach the free man how to
praise." Hollander has revised the tale of his old teacher, expressing his faith not in consolation but in perception: He works,
and has been working for half a century now, to teach the free
man and woman, not how to praise, but to tell.

Bibliography of John Hollander

BOOKS

Poetry

A Crackling of Thorns (New Haven:Yale University Press, 1958)
Movie-Going and Other Poems (New York: Atheneum, 1962)
Visions from the Ramble (New York: Atheneum, 1965)
Types of Shape (New York: Atheneum, 1968)
The Night Mirror (New York: Atheneum, 1971)
Town and Country Matters (Boston: David R. Godine, 1972)
Selected Poems (London: Secker and Warburg, 1972)
Selected Poems, translated by Yorifumi Yaguchi (Tokyo: Bunri, 1972)
Tales Told of the Fathers (New York: Atheneum, 1975)
Reflections on Espionage (New York: Atheneum, 1976)
Spectral Emanations (New York: Atheneum, 1978)
Blue Wine (Baltimore: Johns Hopkins University Press, 1979)
Powers of Thirteen (New York: Atheneum, 1983)
In Time and Place (Baltimore: Johns Hopkins University Press, 1986)
Harp Lake (New York: Alfred A Knopf, 1988)
Types of Shape [second edition, with ten new poems, notes, and introduction] (New Haven:Yale University Press, 1991)
The Death of Moses [libretto for oratorio by Alexander Goehr] (London: Schott and Co., Ltd., 1992)
Selected Poetry (New York: Alfred A. Knopf, 1993)
Tesserae and Other Poems (New York: Alfred A. Knopf, 1993)
Figurehead and Other Poems (New York: Alfred A. Knopf, 1999)
Reflections on Espionage [second edition, with an introduction and additional notes] (New Haven:Yale University Press, 1999)

Chapbooks and Limited Editions

Philomel (London: Turret Books, 1968)
An Entertainment for Elizabeth, with an introduction by Irving Cummings (Storrs, Conn., *English Literary Renaissance Monographs* 1.1, 1972)
The Head of the Bed (Boston: David R. Godine, 1974)
In Place (Omaha, Neb.: Abbatoir Editions, 1978)
Looking Ahead (New York: Nadja, 1982)

Dal Vero [with Saul Steinberg] (New York: Whitney Museum
of American Art, Library Fellows, 1983)
A Hollander Garland (Newton, Iowa: Tamazunchale Press,
1985)
Kinneret (New Haven: Eighty Seven, 1987)
Some Fugitives Take Cover (New York: Sea Cliff Press-Jordan
Davies, 1988)

Criticism

The Untuning of the Sky (Princeton: Princeton University Press,
1961)
Images of Voice (Cambridge: Churchill College and W. H. Heffer,
1970)
Vision and Resonance (New York: Oxford University Press, 1975)
The Figure of Echo (Berkeley and Los Angeles: University of
California Press, 1981)
Rhyme's Reason (New Haven: Yale University Press, 1981);
[expanded and revised edition, 1989]; [further expanded
2000]
Melodious Guile (New Haven: Yale University Press, 1988)
William Bailey (New York: Rizzoli and Milan: Fabbri, 1990)
The Gazer's Spirit (Chicago: University of Chicago Press, 1995)
The Work of Poetry (New York: Columbia University Press,
1997)
The Poetry of Everyday Life (Ann Arbor: University of Michigan
Press, 1998)

Edited

The Wind and the Rain [with Harold Bloom] (New York:
Doubleday and Co., 1961)
Jiggery-Pokery: a Compendium of Double-Dactyls [with Anthony
Hecht] (New York: Atheneum, 1966)
Poems of Our Moment (New York: Pegasus, 1968)
Modern Poetry: Modern Essays in Criticism (New York: Oxford
University Press, 1968)
American Short Stories Since 1945 (New York: Harper and Row,
1968)
The Oxford Anthology of English Literature [with Frank Kermode,
Harold Bloom, J. B. Trapp, Martin Price, and Lionel Trilling]
(New York: Oxford University Press, 1973)
I. A. Richards: Essays in His Honor [with R. A. Brower and Helen
Vendler] (New York: Oxford University Press, 1973)

Literature as Experience [with Irving Howe and David Bromwich] (New York: Harcourt Brace Jovanovich, 1979)

The Poetics of Influence (New Haven: Henry R. Schwab, 1988)

The Essential Rossetti (New York: Ecco Press, 1990)

Spoon River Anthology by Edgar Lee Masters (New York: Signet Classics, 1992)

American Poetry: The Nineteenth Century, 2 volumes (New York: Library of America, 1993)

Animal Poems (New York: Alfred A. Knopf, 1996)

Garden Poems (New York: Alfred A. Knopf, 1996)

Marriage Poems (New York: Alfred A. Knopf, 1997)

Nineteenth Century American Poetry, one volume edition (New York: Library of America, 1996)

Committed to Memory: 100 Best Poems to Memorize (New York: Books & Company and Turtle Point, 1996)

Poems of Robert Frost (New York: Alfred A. Knopf, 1997)

War Poems (New York: Alfred A. Knopf, 1999)

Christmas Poems [with J. D. McClatchy] (New York: Alfred A. Knopf, 1999)

Sonnets (New York: Alfred A. Knopf, 2000)

A Gallery of Poems [with Joanna Weber] (New Haven: Yale Art Gallery, 2001)

For Children

Various Owls (New York: Norton, 1963)

The Quest of the Gole (New York: Atheneum, 1966)

The Immense Parade on Supererogation Day (New York: Atheneum, 1972)

FICTION

"In the Year of the Comet," *The Noble Savage* 2(1961): 161–64.

"In the Creep Block," *Partisan Review* 36.2 (1969)

"Tales of the Supernatural," *Canto* 4.11 (1981): 103–18

"From the Memoirs of an Administrator," *Commentary* (September 1981): 64–65

"In Ancient Days," *Moment* I (1982)

"Terah's Idols," *A Jewish Journal at Yale* (1984): 6–7

"The Twin's Story," *Partisan Review* 51 (1984–85): 530–34

"From an Old Notebook," *Raritan* 4.1 (Summer 1984): 48–63

"The Treasure Hunt," *Conjunctions* 2 (1985): 119–21

"In Bed Together," *Southwest Review* 86 (2001): 254–61

TEXTS FOR COMPOSERS

with dates of first performance

Philomel for Milton Babbitt (1964)

An Entertainment for Elizabeth masque for New York Pro Musica (1970)

"In Eius Memoriam" for George Perle, *Songs of Praise and Lamentation* (1975)

A Song of Celebration cantata by Hugo Weisgall (1977)

The Hundred Nights opera in one act by Hugo Weisgall (1977)

Lyrical Interval song cycle by Hugo Weisgall (1985)

The Death of Moses oratorio by Alexander Goehr (1992)

OTHER POETRY SET OR ADAPTED

"The Head of the Bed," Milton Babbitt (1984)

"Blue Wine," Rodney Lister (1989)

"The Virginal Book" (from *In Time and Place*), Milton Babbitt

"Inglorious Fourth" (from *Powers of Thirteen*), Rodney Lister

"The Shape of Time," Rodney Lister

"The Mad Potter," Rodney Lister

Various poems set as "Of Challenge and of Love," Elliott Carter (1995)

Poem from "Lyrical Interval" set by Ned Rorem

Biographical Notes

DAVID BROMWICH is Housum Professor of English at Yale University and author most recently of *Skeptical Music: Essays on Modern Poetry*.

JOHN BURT is Professor of English at Brandeis University and is the editor of Robert Penn Warren's poems and author of two volumes of poetry.

STEPHEN CUSHMAN teaches at the University of Virginia and has books on William Carlos Williams and of some of his own poetry.

JEFF DOLVEN teaches English at Princeton University. He has published his own poetry and essays on Spenser in several journals.

LEE EDELMAN is Professor of English at Tufts University and author of works on gay literary and cultural theory and a book on Hart Crane.

MATTHEW GREENFIELD teaches at the College of Staten Island and is co-editor of essays on Spenser and has published poems and essays.

DAVID GREETHAM is Distinguished Professor at the City University of New York Graduate Center and has books on textual scholarship.

KENNETH GROSS teaches English at the University of Rochester and has books on Spenser, Pygmalion myth, and Shakespeare.

HANNIBAL HAMLIN teaches at Ohio State University, Mansfield, and is currently working on a study of the Bible in Shakespeare.

ELISE BICKFORD JORGENS is a dean at Western Michigan University and is author of a study on musical interpretations of English poetry.

JENNIFER LEWIN teaches at the University of Kentucky and has written on representations of sleep and dreams in early modern literature.

J. D. MCCLATCHY has taught at Yale and Princeton and is editor of *The Yale Review* and has had many books of his poetry published.

STEVEN MEYER teaches at Washington University in St. Louis and has published on Gertrude Stein and radical empiricism.

DAVID MIKICS teaches at the University of Houston and his books are on Spenser and Milton and Emerson and Nietzsche and others.

CORNELIA PEARSALL teaches at Smith College and is presently at work on a book on Victorian mourning and memorialization.

JOAN RICHARDSON teaches at the Graduate Center of City University of New York and has works on Wallace Stevens and pragmatism.

JOHN ROGERS is Professor of English and Master of Berkeley College at Yale and working on a book on Milton.

AIDAN WASLEY teaches at the University of Georgia and writes on modern British and American poetry including work on James Merrill.

JOHN WATKINS teaches at the University of Minnesota and has written on Spenser and Virgilian epic and a study on Elizabeth I.

Index

Abuses Stript, and Whipt (Wither),
68
"Achilles' Song" (Duncan), 277,
286–87
Ackerman, Bruce, 184, 186, 187
Adorno, Theodor, 161
Aeneid (Virgil), 18, 22, 32
"Alastor" (Shelley), 177
Allegorical Temper, The (Berger),
37–38
allegory: lapses into ordinariness,
37, 45–52; linguistic materiality
and, 230–31; reading strategies
for, 52–54; rifts in, 36, 37–45
Allegro, L' (Milton), 311
Allen, Steve, 274
Alpers, Paul, 44n19
Alter, Robert, 128–29
America: inalienable rights as
insight, 182–86; Jewish poetic
tradition in, 259–60; in *Spectral
Emanations*, 240–44
Analogy of The Faerie Queene
(Nohrnberg), 35
"Anatomy of Resonance, The"
(Wright), 277
Anderson, Benedict, 156
Andrews, William L., 190
Angleton, James Jesus, 250n1
"Annunciations" (Hill), 277, 287–
88
"Antwerp to Ghent" (Rossetti),
280–81
Archbishop of Canterbury, 64, 72
Arendt, Hannah, 182, 184–85; *Life
of the Mind, The*, 171; *Between
Past and Future*, 170–71; *On Revolu-
tion*, 177, 182
Aristotle, 89–90; *Politics*, 75–76,
76n10; *Rhetoric*, 41

"As I Ebb'd with the Ocean of
Life" (Whitman), 173
Ashbery, John, 253
Astrophel (Spenser), 69
"At a Solemn Musick" (Milton),
97–99
"At the New Year" (Hollander),
315
Auden, W. H., 319; Hollander on,
268; influence on Hollander,
305, 313–14, 318; in *Reflections
on Espionage*, 253, 257, 260–61;
song categories of, 122–24;
works: "If I Could Tell You," 315;
"In Memory of W. B. Yeats," 320;
"Music in Shakespeare,"
122–23; "The Orators," 313;
"O, Where Are You Going,"
314–15; "The Pilgrim," 316n8;
"The Quest," 316, 316n8;
"Secret Agent," 313; "Taller
Today," 314; "Under Sirius,"
308;
audible ecphrasis, 122–46
Augustine, Saint, 170–71, 172
Austen, Jane, *Sense and Sensibility*,
124–26
authenticity theories, 176–77

Badius Ascensius, Jodocus, 17
"Ballad of the Red Harlaw,"
141n35
ballads, 127–35, 138–46
Banville, John, 250
Bateson, F. W., 193
"Batter my heart, Three-personed
God" (Donne), 171
Beaumont, Francis, *Salmacis and
Hermaphroditus*, 66n18, 69
Bee, 132

Production Editor
JAMES MOONEY

Designer
GREER ALLEN

Typesetter
ASTERISK

Printer
PHOENIX PRESS

Binder
NEW HAMPSHIRE BINDERY